AN EPOCH IN IRISH HISTORY

TRINITY COLLEGE, DUBLIN
ITS FOUNDATION AND EARLY FORTUNES

1591–1660

KENNIKAT PRESS SCHOLARLY REPRINTS
Ralph Adams Brown, Senior Editor

Series In
IRISH HISTORY AND CULTURE
Under the General Editorial Supervision of
Gilbert A. Cahill
Professor of History, State University of New York

AN EPOCH
IN
IRISH HISTORY

TRINITY COLLEGE, DUBLIN
ITS FOUNDATION AND EARLY FORTUNES,

1591–1660:

BY
JOHN PENTLAND MAHAFFY, D.D.,
KNIGHT COMMANDER OF THE ORDER OF THE REDEEMER;
MUS.DOC., DUBLIN; HON. D.C.L., OXON;
SOMETIME PROFESSOR OF ANCIENT HISTORY
IN THE UNIVERSITY OF DUBLIN

KENNIKAT PRESS
Port Washington, N. Y./London

AN EPOCH IN IRISH HISTORY

First published in 1903
Reissued in 1970 by Kennikat Press
Library of Congress Catalog Card No: 77-102617
SBN 8046-0794-X

Manufactured by Taylor Publishing Company   Dallas, Texas

KENNIKAT SERIES IN IRISH HISTORY AND CULTURE

Præhonorabili

GEORGIO COMITI CADOGAN DE GART. EQ.

apud nos utrusque legis honoris causa Doctori

Quem per septennium pro Rege

in Hibernia

præsentem coluimus

nunc

absentem desideramus

D D D

amicus auctor.

Contents

		PAGE
INTRODUCTION	. . . . .	ix

CHAPTER		
I.	IRELAND IN THE CLOSING YEARS OF THE 16TH CENTURY	1
II.	THE FOUNDING OF THE COLLEGE . .	60
III.	ALVEY (1601–9)	112
IV.	TEMPLE (1609–26)	145
V.	BEDELL—ROBERT USSHER (1626–34) .	192
VI.	CHAPPELL AND THE CAROLINE STATUTES (1634–40)	228
VII.	THE GREAT REBELLION AND THE CIVIL WAR IN IRELAND . . .	264
VIII.	THE PROTECTORATE—WINTER (1652–60)	293
APPENDIX.	BEDELL'S STATUTES . . .	327
INDEX	. . . . . .	377

Introduction

THE title of this book is intended to inform the reader that though the history of a particular Foundation fills most of its pages, the general history of the country, and its social and intellectual conditions, have been always before the author's mind. The great struggle for the education and creed of the people between the reformed Church of England and the Jesuits has been viewed from a special point of view. But the author claims to have made a contribution to the Elizabethan and Jacobean history of Ireland, as well as to the knowledge of the early fortunes of the great Irish University and College. He also claims, while in no way concealing his Protestant convictions, to have represented the merits and the faults of all the conflicting parties in this struggle without fear or favour.

The history of Trinity College, Dublin, which up to the present includes that of the University of Dublin, has been many times written, and these essays have been at least in five cases published. It might therefore fairly be expected that each succeeding work would utilise its predecessors, and thus gradually attain to an adequate account of the origin and development of " the only English foundation that ever succeeded in Ireland." But this is not the case. The earliest systematic (though unfinished) history is that of

Provost Hely Hutchinson, composed about 1790-2. It was never printed, but was utilised by the late Dr. Todd in his historical Introduction to the first College Calendar (1833), and again by Dr. Stubbs in his History, though very inadequately.[1] The many papers left by Vice-Provost Barrett, and now in the Library, show that he was accumulating materials, and making special studies, for the same purpose, but he never carried out his intention. His transcripts of many early documents were, however, very serviceable to those of his successors who were unable to read the originals. There is yet another MS. history, hitherto lying in the Bursar's office. This very neat MS., evidently a careful copy from a rougher original, especially from the Barrett papers, is probably the most valuable of all the attempted histories. It is anonymous, the only clues to its date and author being that it copies and cites Dr. Barrett, and was in the possession of Provost MacDonnell. As the writer had complete access to all the documents in the Muniment Room, or else to Barrett's copies of them, he must have been one of the authorities of the College; the most likely author is, I think, Charles Elrington (the editor of the life and works of Ussher), who was Professor of Divinity 1829.

Many original documents, some of which are now mislaid or lost, are cited in this history, and it is far less tinged with subjectivity than the work of Hely Hutchinson, whose lifelong quarrels with his Fellows colour the accounts he gives of similar dissensions in earlier times. Unfortunately this anonymous author has not carried his work beyond the life of Winter, the Cromwellian Provost; but he has added, in somewhat random order, transcripts (Barrett's) of many of the old documents in the Muniment Room.

The first published history is Taylor's (1845), a rhetorical

[1] The original MS. has only recently been recovered by the College, and is now in the Muniment Room—a typewritten copy being deposited in the Library.

book, provincial in tone and full of bigotry, and unhandy to consult, as it has no index. Taylor must have known and used Todd's first Calendar, though he does not cite it. The mediæval attempts at founding an Irish University are evidently described from this source; and the false estimate of Archbishop Loftus's importance as a founder of Trinity College appears here, as it does in the subsequent History of Stubbs. Taylor's book is nevertheless useful, in that he searched the annals of the Irish House of Commons, and transcribes for us many important documents, down to the Report of the Wide Street Commission of 1800 on College Street, from these records. But of the documents in the Muniment Room, or the earlier MS. histories, he seems to have known nothing. His judgments are often partial and wrong. His estimates, *e.g.*, of Provost Chappell, are entirely from the charges brought against him by his enemies in the Parliament of 1640, and ignore Chappell's personal defence, as well as the evidence in Laud's and Strafford's letters. Taylor also brought into fashion the practice of evading the more troublesome task of writing a systematic and orderly history by giving mere biographical sketches of eminent men, and the annals of special schools in the University. These digressions and supplements are often interesting, but often irrelevant to the task of the historian.

The late Dr. Stubbs, when Bursar, undertook the work afresh, though untrained for it by any general historical studies. He knew Hely Hutchinson's MS. and had full access to the Muniment Room, as well as of course to the Anon. history in his own office. Here again the documents printed in his Appendix—many of them hitherto inaccessible—are of great value to the student. There was not one of them, indeed, unknown to Hely Hutchinson or Barrett, and they were apparently all given by Stubbs from Barrett's transcripts. But here many official documents relating to the founding of the College are to be found, though many still remain to be printed. The narrative brings us up to the year 1800. As regards the characters of the early rulers of the College, who lived in perpetual controversies, and who are described to us either by warm friends or bitter enemies among their contemporaries, Stubbs offers us no independent judgments. He seems hardly to have looked into the Calendars of State Papers, or the documents in the Record Office, still less into the Records of the Corporation of Dublin.

It was indeed unfortunate that he did not begin, instead of concluding, his work with the year 1800. For many of us remember how full he was of the traditions and the gossip of the early and middle nineteenth century in Dublin. If he had set down all the facts and stories repeated to him in his youth by garrulous seniors, he would have left us a picture of Trinity College in the days of its greatest wealth (and its greatest sloth) which is now lost for ever.

At the moment of the Tercentenary Celebration (1892) two new documents concerning this history appeared, of which the smaller and less pretentious had a real and independent value. This was Urwick's *Early History of Trinity College, Dublin* (1591–1660), a little shilling book in a bright green cover. It was written to support a definite thesis. The author, a representative Non-Conformist, found that the services of the Puritan party and their importance at the founding of the College and during the Commonwealth had been ignored by Episcopalian historians. Even the characters of men like Travers and Winter had suffered from the unpopularity of their views among the Church party. In this short but most valuable tract Mr. Urwick sought to set things right. He knew where to find the proper sources, and he knew how to use them when found. His book is therefore a notable contribution to the history of the University, the more so as it gives us general views of religious politics in Ireland, and not mere controversies about petty internal affairs. The *Book of Trinity College*, published for a gift to the guests at the feast, was compiled by various hands, and in a great hurry, owing to the jealousies and oppositions then brought to bear upon it. It therefore does not represent a tithe of what could have been done with a little more generosity and sympathy on the part of the Bursar.

But even in this hurried volume documents were cited and views set forth which were fresh to the public. The College plate, for example, was hardly known or appreciated till it was described, and some of it pictured, in the volume. The old seal of April, 1612, was unknown till the parchment appointing the first Duke of Ormond to be Chancellor was found, and the appended wax seal photographed in Kilkenny Castle. The importance of the Jesuit Crusade against the College was then for the first time, though very inadequately, stated.

Since 1892 the two men who still felt a keen interest in the records of the College—Dr. Carson and Dr. Stubbs—are gone, and there is at present a great dearth of antiquaries among the staff. There are even some among them to whom a name so recent and so great as that of Hincks conveys no meaning.

It is therefore very encouraging that Professor MacNeile Dixon should have undertaken a brief but very interesting account in the first of the "College Histories" published by Robinson (London). The limits of his space precluded anything like a complete or detailed treatment, nor was it within the scope of a popular work to quote original deeds and documents. But it might perhaps have been expected from him to do what none of his predecessors (except Mr. Urwick) has attempted either in MS. or in print—to treat the College as a mirror of the public state around it, and to bring its internal affairs into closer relation with the general history of Ireland. This is of course the only permanent interest in such a history. The perpetual squabbles of the fellows regarding the interpretation of their statutes and the petitions of tenants for remission of rent which fill endless letters and pleadings, are of little moment compared with the general policy of various Provosts and Vice-Chancellors towards the *natives*, and the very interpretations they put upon this name; their attitude towards the Irish language, and towards the Roman Catholics who sought for education in their House.

Such and such like are the questions which are discussed in the following history with only so much of the petty internal details as give us an insight into the life of students in those early days. There are, moreover, many difficulties in interpreting the meaning of an account or of a statement which was obvious in its day; and to this task far more space must have been accorded, had not the Board of Trinity College liberally consented to have the principal original document printed as a companion volume to this history. In the Introduction and Notes to that volume such questions of interpretation will have their proper place.

It is due to future students to set down in this Introduction the catalogue of the contemporary or original sources known to me, for the period to which this volume is confined—from the foundation of the College to the Restoration. There may be some which have escaped me. (1) *The Particular Book*, printed as the companion to this volume. (2) The early Registry, reaching from 1637 to 1660. These two volumes to some extent overlap in time and in subjects; the latter has no detail of the accounts, and is a more meagre record than the former. (3) Boxes of loose papers in the Muniment Room, dated and undated, covering this period, and of very varied character—accounts, bonds, petitions of tenants, petitions to the State, &c. &c. Of these, many valuable specimens are printed in Stubbs' Appendix. I have sorted and catalogued them in their various boxes (A to G) so far as they belonged to my period, and my MS. Catalogue can be consulted in the Muniment Room. Some of them are printed as Appendices to the following chapters. (4) The Carew Papers at Lambeth Library, and the Calendar of Irish State Papers in the London Record Office, in which the whole period of the present book is now covered by recent volumes, except that for October 1600 to 1603, which is in preparation, and contains the all-important crisis of Lord Mountjoy's government. (5) The State Papers in the Irish Record Office, which are not yet accessible in printed Calendars, though the individual volumes are briefly indexed. This is so vast a storehouse that it would require many years to search it for any special purpose. On the Commonwealth period alone (1649–60) there are at least forty volumes which Mr. Urwick has consulted. And yet, until some one has examined and sorted the whole collection, important facts may lie hid which would solve the problems and puzzles so frequent in the following pages. (6) The Thurloe Papers contain a few stray allusions to the College, and these are not without interest. Such are also Henry Cromwell's Letters in the British Museum. Strafford's, Laud's, Ussher's, and Bedell's correspondence, were all known and used by previous historians of the College. (7) The Journals of the Irish House of Commons. It is obvious that to search this enormous mass of materials requires not the leisure of a busy man, but the whole labour of a man of leisure. Pending the advent of such a specialist, the present volume contributes what new matter the work of a few years among the College archives has brought to light.

I have to thank my friends Mr. Richard Bagwell and Mr. J. R. Gautin, both high authorities on Irish history, for many valuable suggestions and corrections.

TRINITY COLLEGE, DUBLIN.
September, 1903.

NOTE.

H. H. means Hely Hutchinson MS.

Anon. the other document above described.

S. P., unless further specified, the Calendar of State Papers (Ireland) published by the Record Office, London.

C. P. the Carew Papers from Lambeth Palace Library, published in the same manner.

M. R. is the Muniment Room of the College.

Mullinger is Mr. Bass Mullinger's "History of the University of Cambridge."

An Epoch in Irish History

CHAPTER I

IRELAND IN THE CLOSING YEARS OF THE 16TH CENTURY

THE reasons why Queen Elizabeth was induced to sanction the foundation of her College in Dublin are plain enough, and are stated in the preamble of her Charter and her Letters Patent[1]; but the contributing influences both in England and in Ireland which made her policy a success, and again only a partial success, have been either ignored or misunderstood. Moreover, none of the historians has ever undertaken to consider what the Ireland of that day was in its private life; in its culture, or in its want of culture; in its society, or its absence of society. What was the population from which the College could hope to draw students; what were the classes that either desired, or could be persuaded, to educate their children under its influence?

---

[1] "A College for learning, whereby knowledge and civility might be increased by the instruction of our people there, whereof many have usually heretofore used to travaile into ffrance, Italy, and Spaine to gett learning in such forreigne Universities, whereby they have been infected with Popery and other ill qualities" (Letter of Elizabeth in Stubbs' Appendix iii, p. 354).

When we examine the great mass of contemporary documents to seek the answer to these important questions, we find ourselves minutely informed about official Ireland and about the wars in Ireland; also about the jealousies, calumnies, quarrels, and intrigues of Elizabeth's governors and officers; about the violences and exactions of British soldiers and Irish kerne; but concerning the private life of the people our sources are almost silent. Letters from people of the middle classes; letters from ladies, except those of the highest degree; letters from citizens of the outlying towns, or the civilised counties, about their daily life and private affairs are very rare. The observations set down by the few travellers whose works are still extant, though highly interesting, are but partial, and frequently inconsistent with each other. Thus, for example, Stanihurst's very favourable description of Dublin with its civic splendours and hospitalities is flatly contradicted by Barnabe Rich (*New Description of Ireland*) who says (in 1610) that he has known Dublin for forty years, and that it is no such place as Stanihurst describes, but a mere nest of Papists and alehouses.[1] But the fact is that there were then, as there are now, the most extraordinary contrasts in the life of Ireland, and partial or occasional spectators were likely to receive wholly different impressions, according to the spot, or the moment, or the temper, of their observations. Thus the Four Masters, themselves contemporary, or copying from contemporary documents, describe the year 1595 as one of war and tumult in Connaught. We have among the College documents irrefragable evidence that as far as Tuam and the neighbouring country were concerned, things were as quiet and safe as they are at present. In the spring of that year the College sent down James Hamilton, one of its

[1] The Editor of the *Records of the City of Dublin* prints the former account in the appendix to his second volume, but not the latter. This is an instance of the omission of evidence unfavourable to his creed. Yet Rich is so violent a Protestant, that any advocate of the other side would have been wise to exhibit his strongly biassed statements.

fellows, to collect the temporalities of the archbishopric of Tuam, granted by the Queen to the College during a vacancy in the See. He travels about the district, sues the tenants, distrains their cattle and "garaunes" (ponies), and yet he meets with no other obstacles than a new agent would encounter to-day on a similar errand. The tenants broke their promises to meet him at Tuam market, they denied that they had ever paid rent; they would not buy the distrained cattle when put up for sale. So it resulted that Hamilton realised no more than £16 by the whole transaction; but he was in no danger, and neither he nor his bailiffs ever express any apprehension. This condition of the country is only to be explained by its condition ever since and even now. The mass of the population—called churls by the old observers—were peaceable and easily controlled. But this control could be exercised not only by the law, but by the enemies of the law. The peasant could be coerced not only by the judge at assizes, but by the raider in politics or in arms, who often drove him into disastrous rebellion, sore against his will. In the case of Hamilton's dealings with the Mayo and Galway natives, we know that there were near him two strong men, who ruled with a rod of iron—Clanrickard, whom they now revered as a native lord, and Bingham, who from the fortress of Athlone watched the interests of British law and order in Connaught with bloody severity. Yet not three years elapsed when his tyranny proved powerless against the revolt of the whole province.

These sudden alternations of order and disorder were not only promoted by the revolt of a chieftain or the caprice of a band of robbers; they were often caused by the reversal of a policy and by bitter dissensions among the officials entrusted by the Queen with the government of the country. For, in the first place, there were two policies among the governors. The one was that of keeping the Irish totally distinct from the English and in absolute subjection. They were not to be legally persons who could sue a British subject; they were to have no rights, even of property, no recognition of their native law and native customs. Any revolt was to be crushed by martial law and wholesale executions; any constitutional complaint of their leaders by their imprisonment during the Lord Deputy's pleasure. Such a policy must, of course, fail in the long run, even if it had been successful for a time, even if the two races had been, or could be, kept wholly distinct. The Irish would have found their Toussaint L'Ouverture or their O'Connell in the seventeenth century, even had all the Anglo-Irish been kept apart from them. But since the original conquest in 1172 a great fusion had taken place, not only in the coast cities, but throughout the country, of settlers and natives. However constantly forbidden by the law, marriages of Englishmen with Irish women were frequent, and unlicensed connections an occurrence of every day. The old settlers, abandoned by England during the long wars of the Roses, save when their lords were recruited to fight in England and lose their lives in the great English quarrel, were forced to fall in with native customs. The English gentlemen in Mayo, who came to see Sir H. Sydney on his official tour (1575) through the West of Ireland, had not only learned to speak Irish, but had adopted Irish names.[1] He mentions what we think very Irish names—Lynch, Cusack—as English. Of these people, once important, he adds "that now they have not three hackneys to take them and their train home"; also "that Galway had almost forgotten they had received any Corporation charter from the Crown." And if the old English settlers had amalgamated with the native population of the country, there was likewise an infiltration of Irish into the Danish and British settlements on the coast. The names in the old records of Dublin, Waterford, and Cork show

---

[1] Cf. *Carew Papers*, ii. 49. Barrett was now McPhatten (McFadden); Stanton, McIvilye (McEvilly); Dexter, McJordan; Nangle, McCoshtelo; Prendergast, McMaurice, &c.

unmistakable Celts among the Danes and Saxons; for in these cities there was no reason for assuming an Irish name—nay, on the contrary, many an Irishman must have called himself by an English name in the hope of attaining to British privileges. It was this mixed population, both within and without the Pale, which made the policy of treating the Irish as aliens and slaves not only absurd, but impossible.

It also afforded the strongest argument to the advocates of the rival policy—that of conciliation, of gradually leavening the natives by the introduction of the English language, the English law, and the English morality. If these innovations, gradually and wisely tempered, had not been associated with a change of creed; if they had been honestly carried out by humane and unselfish officials; if they had not been accompanied by confiscations of land to help the poverty of the English Exchequer, Ireland might readily have been converted into another Wales.

But *might have been* is no word for the historian; what *has been* is his province. There were sporadic and unwilling concessions made, which were not unfairly interpreted by the natives as weakness. The *Jus quinque sanguinum* whereby five great clans obtained from the Crown *denization*, or the right of pleading in court like English subjects,[1] must have been more galling to the rest than the exclusion of all. The formal recognition by Henry II. of O'Conor as a king in the West of Ireland must have exasperated other chieftains of far greater importance, though it obtained him unusual respect from English officials.

Quite apart from the influence of the Church, which we shall discuss presently, the Anglo-Irish lawyers in the days of Elizabeth were a very important factor in emancipating the people. Though some of them did attend the Inns of Court in London, the majority seem to have qualified by foreign

[1] Cf. Sir John Davis's famous tract, *A Discovery of the true Causes why Ireland was never entirely subdued*, &c., p. 104 (Orig. Ed.).

studies. Though they were well able to plead in English, they knew the Irish tongue perfectly. They were masters of the art of training disloyalty to keep within the law. They were adepts at finding flaws in Acts of Parliament and letters patent from the Crown. Above all, they explained to the gentry of the Pale and the burghers of the cities their rights and the frequent violation of these rights. Constant are the complaints and the warnings of English officials against promoting these native lawyers to high judicial positions. They were very apt to censure English violence and to acquit the Irish victims of false accusations. Native juries only wanted a hint from such a judge to disagree or find a verdict of *not guilty*. Yet to employ them was necessary, because English lawyers, when sent over, regarded Ireland as a land of exile and were always urging their own recall. Many would not even accept their appointment, except on the condition of serving a short term, in a country which they described as "little better than hell."

Nothing has been more misunderstood and misstated than the position and power of the Roman Catholic Church as regards the civilisation of Ireland in Elizabeth's times. We must go back, of course, to Henry VIII.'s disestablishment and disendowment of the wealthy orders and houses of that Church to understand its position in the early part of the sixteenth century. In his day the religious houses seem to have possessed almost all the wealth and all the patronage of the Church of Ireland. There were, according to Allemand,[1] four hundred of these houses in the country. They possessed, besides their estates and chantry lands, the tithes of many parishes, for which they were supposed to provide curates. But so badly was this done that a vast number of churches was in ruins; in many of the remainder no mass was said. Such parochial duties as were performed were in the hands of

[1] *Histoire Monastique d'Irlande*, Paris, 1690.

very poor and ignorant priests. Where these men had received their education and under what conditions they were ordained by the bishops it is not easy to discover. Thus I find as late as 1619, among the Patent Rolls of James I. (year 17, No. lxxv.) a list of witnesses to a document, among whom Sir Pat. Nevell, curate of Connall (in Kildare), signs with his mark X. Here then was an ecclesiastic who could not write English nearly a century later.[1] The preaching and most of the pastoral duties seem to have been performed by the various orders of friars, who at this time kept alive the spark of religion by their zealous and unselfish labours.

It has commonly been stated and believed that in the religious houses education, both for clergy and laity, was provided, and that the lamentable state of the secular clergy was due to the abolition of these houses by Henry VIII. The evidence we have does not bear out this current opinion. In the first place many of the monasteries in the north and west were beyond the reach of the English king.[2] Several notable houses

---

[1] See an excellent summary concerning the state of the Roman Catholic Church in Ireland before Elizabeth's reign in Mr. Brewer's Introduction to vol. ii. of the *Carew Papers*, pp. xiv. sq.

[2] Cf. Davis' tract, p. 255: "For the abbeys and religious houses in Tirone, Tirconnell, and Fermanagh, though they were dissolved in the 33 of Henry VIII., were never surveyed nor reduced into charge, but were continually possessed by the religious persons, untill his Majesty that now is (James I.) came to the crown." This can be proved by contemporary evidence. The conference of Spanish officers with O'Neill and his confederates in 1596 took place in the monastery of Donegal, as the most suitable place, and Captain Alonzo de Cobos, in the course of his despatch (S. P., Spanish, 1587–1603, p. 640), says: "The guardian of the monastery of Donegal, a Franciscan friar, gave me a memorial for your Majesty. It is to the effect that the enemy was there last year for seven days, and ruined the place. He asks your Majesty to give something to repair the monastery, some chalices and ornaments, &c. The friars there are very religious; there are 25 or 30 of them." It is perfectly notorious that the North-West was among the most uneducated, and therefore barbarous, parts of all Ireland. The conclusion that the religious houses were no educators may thus be established by the Method of Difference.

escaped, such as that of Moyne, in which, Allemand says, philosophy and theology were taught, not pillaged by the English till 1578, and of which the buildings were still standing in 1690. The Franciscans were not driven out of the north till the rule of Chichester in 1602. Several of the houses which had escaped ruin under Henry VIII. and Edward VI. were again filled with monks and nuns by Queen Mary. If, therefore, the Church of Rome had possessed even a fraction of the zeal shown after 1590, there was ample opportunity for much earnest teaching. But there is no evidence that any such zeal existed, and Edmund Spenser speaks [1] of the creed of the natives as no religion, but merely the superstitious worship of the sacraments, and the blind reverence for the clergy who celebrated these sacraments in an unknown tongue. The nobles of the Pale were quite satisfied to see the monasteries abolished because they received a large share of the spoil ; the wilder chieftains, such as Shan O'Neill, had not scrupled to harry and even burn monasteries in the course of their incessant raids for plunder. The former did indeed, by the mouth of Lord Deputy Gray and his Council, petition that six houses should escape confiscation, viz., S. Mary's Abbey, a house of White monks, and Christ Church, in Dublin ; the nunneries of Gracedieu at Swords ; Conall (near Newbridge) in the Co. Kildare ; Kenlis and Jerpoint in Co. Kilkenny. They give as their last reason, that "in them young men and childer, both gentlemen's childer and other, both of mankind and of womankind, be brought up in virtue, learning, *and in the English tongue and behaviour*, to the great charges of the said houses : that is to say, the womankind of the whole Englishry of the land, for the more part, in the said nunneries, and the mankind in the other said houses." But their main reason for the petition is that which Allemand says caused an universal murmur, when they were abolished, throughout the land. "For in these houses, and others such-like, in default of

[1] Cf. below, p. 24 (note).

common inns, which are not in this land, the King's Deputy and Council and officers, also Irishmen, and others resorting to the King's Deputy, is and hath been most commonly lodged at the costes of the said houses." This hospitality was also extended, we gladly believe, to the poorer classes, and alms distributed to the needy. But we can find no outcry about the loss of any national education owing to the king's act. The monastery at Donegal is the only one mentioned as possessing a good library, and here the Four Masters were able to study and write in peace a century after the suppression. But we hear nothing of a school of history or of theology at this place.

We are, of course, far better informed about Dublin than about the rest of Ireland. We can find no trace of any monastic schools here beyond the definite statement that the youth of the Pale were sent to the schools above mentioned.

The Dominican Friary of S. Saviour, on the site of the present Four Courts, is reported [1] to have kept a school of theology and philosophy opposite their house, on Usher's Island, to which they built the so-called Old Bridge.

The ancient "College" of Maynooth, founded by Gerald, Earl of Kildare (ob. 1513), with a provost, vice-provost, five fellows, two clerks, and three boys, was to pray for his soul and that of his wife, not to teach anybody anything.[2]

I will add that in the speech of Archbishop Loftus to the citizens of Dublin, urging the establishment of an University,[3] the advantages to trade of the religious houses, and the consequent damage done by their disestablishment, are specially mentioned. It would have been an obvious point to compare their false education (had they given any) with the pure education of the proposed Protestant Academy, but of this there is not a word.

---

[1] *Monasticon Hibernicum*, ii. 72.
[2] ibid., ii. 282.
[3] Stubbs, *Hist. of Univ. of Dublin*, App. ii.

The city of Dublin had a grammar school as early as 1560; there were grammar schools even earlier at Waterford, Kilkenny, Cork, and Limerick. We do not hear that they were set up to replace monastic education, but this may have been the case, so far as the six houses were concerned.

If these things were so, we can well imagine respectable citizens of Dublin, whether Catholic or Anglican, regarding not without satisfaction the abolition of religious corporations which had absorbed most of the wealth of the city. We know of at least four great houses with a host of smaller ones,[1] round Dublin: those of S. Thomas (à Becket), S. Mary, All Hallowes, and S. John of Jerusalem.[2] English monasteries at Bristol owned property in the city, and as late as 1610 Luke Challoner was able to trace fifty lots of houses and lands in and by the city which were chantry lands bequeathed for masses by private individuals. Queen Mary, in spite of her reactionary policy and her persecutions of the Reformers, did not restore any of the confiscated lands that had been granted away from the monks, though she did restore monks to buildings, and perhaps even to property still derelict. Though the Mass was re-established, the reformed service was not put down by her with any thoroughness in Ireland; and when Elizabeth succeeded, the civilised people of the country were not yet divided into two hostile camps, guarded and disciplined by hostile priests. The desire and the need of establishing an University to educate the youth of the Pale and the cities, at all events, was felt both by Roman Catholics and Protestants; and in promoting the earnest and enlightened attempts of Sir Henry Sidney to meet this want no one was more prominent than James Stanihurst, a Roman Catholic, Recorder of Dublin, and Speaker of the House of Commons. He was the grandfather of Primate James Ussher, the staunchest of Protestants.

[1] Cf. *Mon. Hib.* i.
[2] Cf. on their value Hogan's *Ibernia Ignatiana*, i. p. 68, quoted hereafter.

CLOSING YEARS OF THE 16TH CENTURY 11

But the very desire to found an University implies the feeling that it is a public need, and therefore implies some education diffused throughout the public that desires it. What means had the people of Ireland, in default of a learned or zealous clergy, of obtaining education? There were in some of the walled cities schools under lay schoolmasters. Of these we know that Waterford, Cork, Limerick, Kilkenny, and Cashel received the sons of what were then the local gentry. The sons of chieftains as important as the O'Sullivan Bere were thus educated. It is remarkable that every one of these schools, when we get any insight into them towards the close of the century, are hotbeds of opposition to English interests.

Here is some fragmentary evidence of education, or the lack of it, in Elizabethan Ireland. In the Calendar of State Papers, Ireland (1587, p. 342) Donald O'Sullivan says that the heirs of that house were habitually brought up in Latin and English and civility, but that Sir Owen was not. Their own master, then but a child, was at school in the city of Waterford. Sir Morogh ne Doe O'Flaherty, the Lord of Iar Connaught, signs with his mark (ib. 471). The same vol., p. 390, mentions a young Scot, Davies Omey, who is secretary to Sir T. Lynagh O'Neill, writes for him and keeps his seal. Letters were dictated in Irish, and then done into Latin by translators. In 1588 many Irish gentlemen (who are named) have withdrawn their sons from school in Limerick, lest the Spaniards (of the Armada) should take them as pledges.[1] Young O'Rorke, a great personage, had been sent by his mother, sister of Lord Clanrickard, to Limerick (p. 464) and then to Oxford (p. 188). We have in the same vol. (p. 275) a petition of Brian McGeoghan to the Queen, stating that he has been compelled from poverty " to draw home two children he was bringing up in England in good civility and literature." We hear also [2] that McMahon's children know English and

[1] *State Papers* (S. P.), 1588, p. 340.   [2] ibid., 1593, p. 70.

are civilly educated. O'Donnell knows English, but hardly speaks it, but can sign and date in English.[1]

It is plain from these stray allusions that many Irish chieftains, living in rude fashion at home and among their clansmen, had felt the necessity of better education and culture for their children. I am in doubt how far the confessions of Bern. O'Donnell, a priest arrested with letters to the King of Spain,[2] are to be trusted. He says he was educated mostly by his father in Ireland (Mayo) and did not leave it till he was twenty-six years old, in 1588. But for Jesuit interference, as will be shown presently, these youths would all have been sent to Trinity College. The description of John FitzEdmund Fitzgerald, of Clone (co. Cork) is that of a highly educated gentleman (ib. p. 47), but we are not told where he was educated. All these people used Irish as their habitual language. Sorley Boy McDonnell writes and signs himself in Irish, which was then hardly different from the language of his home in Argyllshire. But there were many learned men of good condition—Sir Henry Duke, Sir Nich. White, &c.—able to interpret. Several of the bishops—*i.e.*, Nich. Walshe, of Ossory, who married an English wife[3]; Garvey, Bishop of Kilmore[4]; Thos. Burke, Bishop of Kilmacduagh (of the McWilliam clan); and Owen O'Connor (Sligo), Bishop of Killala, must have used Irish as their native tongue. In 1596[5] there is a petition of David Bourke, son of McWilliam Eughter, educated at Oxford, made J.P. for Co. Mayo, student in the Inns of London. The chief McWilliam, he complains, is endeavouring to exile him.

Nehemiah Donnellan is recommended by Ormond in 1594[6] to succeed to the Archbishopric of Tuam, as he is translating the Bible into Irish, the New Testament being then in the press.

---

[1] S. P., 1594, pp. 224, 289. [2] ibid., 1597, p. 351.
[3] ibid., 1585, p. 8. [4] ibid., 1588, p. 118.
[5] ibid., p. 155. [6] ibid., pp. 264, 307-8.

There are several autograph letters from the Earl of Tyrone in the S. P.[1] showing that he wrote English as well as any English statesman. He had been educated for years in England.

But the great lords either kept a resident tutor for their children, or sent them to England, whether to the Court or the Universities. We know also that the higher-class citizens of Dublin sent their sons to Cambridge, Oxford, and even abroad for higher education. Of the Irish chieftains many that knew no English could converse in Latin. When Shan O'Neill appeared before the queen he could speak no English, and signed his submission in Irish characters, yet he negotiates with the Queen of England on almost equal terms. O'Conor Sligo, at Hampton Court (November 8, 1568), speaks to the queen through an interpreter. A strange picture of the barbarism and civilisation existing side by side in great Irish houses is the interview of a foreign nobleman who visited Mountjoy's secretary, Fynes Moryson, as late as 1600. The traveller landed from Scotland in O'Cahan's country, where he was politely received by the ladies of the chieftain's household. They brought him into a thatched cabin, which was their residence, and having thrown off their mantles, sat down stark naked round the hearth, inviting him to do likewise. Nevertheless, the chief, who comes on the scene presently, addresses him fluently in Latin.[2] As there were as yet no towns in Ulster, which was far the most barbarous part of the island, this Latin was probably learned from a resident tutor, such as those we find at the same time educating the Earl of Tyrone's sons. Old Sir Turlough O'Neill, who contributed liberally to the foundation of Trinity College, seems to have been very little educated, and probably spoke English imperfectly. But his wife is noted for her speaking of three languages.[3]

---

[1] 1590, p. 321 ; 1593, pp. 170–2.
[2] Cf. Sidney in *Carew Papers* (C. P.), ii. 49, on his tour in 1575 in the west : "I found McWilliam Eughter very sensible, though wanting the English tongue, understanding the Latin."
[3] C. P., ii. 349.

The castles of Ormond, Kildare, Desmond, Thomond, Clanrickard, and even of the Mayo Burkes, were modelled after English ideas. The owners were great lords even in England, and they imported English refinements into their homes. Tyrone, who was a polished courtier on the surface, with a barbarous core, set up the same refinements at his house at Dungannon. These few great establishments must have taught the ruder gentry the meaning and value of civilisation. We soon find it sporadically among obscure people far from the towns. Thus the Earl of Sussex, making a progress through the west as early as 1558, encamps "beyond O'Sheneshon's (O'Shaughnessy's) called the Gorth [Gort in Co. Galway], and at the said house dined so worshipfully, as divers wondered at it, for the like was not seen at no Irishman's house."[1] Here is another item. William Cantwell (*temp.* Henry VIII., about 1541, S. P., iii. 526) complains that he had property in Co. Kilkenny which was seized, with the connivance of Ormond and the Bishop of Ossory, while he was absent at Oxford for his education. He adds that unless he can obtain justice "very few of the Irishry will put their children to learn English, or be brought up as he was."

We may therefore picture to ourselves the country parts of Ireland, mostly savage and uncultivated, but containing a good many oases in the desert, and many men who desired further enlightenment. Even in the cities, including the capital, I take these contrasts to be the real cause of the conflicting accounts we hear of their condition. Both Stanihurst's and Rich's descriptions had their counterparts in reality. There were many rich burghers, living in comfort and even luxury, not without the refinement of that day, able to entertain Edmund Spenser as well with hospitality as with good conversation. But there were also squalor, filth, and vice unconcealed in the streets. The very existence of an officer under the Corporation of Dublin, called "Warden of the beggars and

[1] C. P., i. 277.

custos of the swine"; the constant orders against allowing either the former and the latter to roam about the streets without control; the apparently vain regulations against throwing out "filthred" into the public ways—all this points to the conclusion that even in Dublin civilisation was not yet in the ascendant throughout the mass of the population. How far the same was true of provincial English towns I leave an open question. The enormous number of alehouses has been mentioned, and we may be sure that at most of them *aqua vitæ*, "which sets the Irishman a-madding,"[1] was to be had in spite of severe prohibitions.

Still worse was the state of sexual relations. If there be one point on which all observers at this period agree, it is that Irishwomen were then as notorious for their looseness as they now are famed for their strictness in this respect.[2] Strafford, in the next century, gave the College authorities the same right of entry into public houses in Dublin as the proctors have at Oxford and Cambridge. The first fruits of this privilege were the conviction of a student who passed the night in one of them, instead of having the city gate opened and going home

[1] *Carew Papers*, ii. 398.
[2] It is unnecessary to quote details upon this subject. All English observers agree upon it. But if their evidence should be doubted, as that of tourists, who (for obvious reasons) have this side of a country's morals obtruded upon them, it is enough to cite the fact that every chieftain at this period, without exception, is surrounded by "base brothers," who are his rivals or open enemies, for bastardy in the first step of descent was no bar to any inheritance; *i.e.*, a bastard son ranked with the legitimate son in estimation, though a bastard's son did not. This is clear evidence of the sexual looseness of Irish society at this time. When therefore a man's origin was to be blackened, it was not enough to call him a bastard; something more unusual must be alleged. Thus it is said of Patrick Condon, a great personage in East Cork, that "he was a foul great lubber, whose mother was but eleven years old when he was born!" S. P., 1598–9, 499.

As a further indirect piece of evidence we may note what I may call the Ptolemaic treatment of Irish princesses, who were handed about from one husband to another for mere political convenience. Cf. C. P., ii. 172, 185, 198, 201 for instances.

to his father's house. In this case the penalties to which the student and the woman who harboured him are subjected show the character which these alehouses bore in public estimation.[1]

As for material comforts, we hear that in a respectable house in Galway there were still wooden shutters instead of glass windows, as is the case in the Arcadia of our day, or in any Greek villages far from the sea and from high-roads. On the other hand William Daniell (1596), who preached the gospel in the same town, had all his windows broken.[2] Sir H. Sidney, visiting Limerick officially in 1575, found it progressing well in civilisation since his last visit ten years earlier.[3] Indeed, his whole impression of the country[4] is favourable, and he writes in a hopeful spirit of the future, provided more opportunities of education were given to the people.

But all these hopeful appearances, such as they were, in the early part of Queen Elizabeth's reign, were blighted by three baneful influences. The first was the outbreak of rebellion, the consequent cruelties, and the devastation of the country. These might have been thought untoward accidents, and might possibly have been adjourned for a few years; but they arose, and must have presently arisen, from the other two, which were world causes, almost impossible to neutralise. One was the absolute *want of sympathy* between the great mass of the English officials, new settlers and soldiers, and the Irish natives; the other the organised and *vigorous crusade* of the Church of Rome, now represented by the Jesuits, against Protestant England. As these causes are active even to the present day, they are worthy of careful consideration.

Nothing is more remarkable in all this history, from the days of the English conquest down to the present day, than the assimilating power of the Irish. The dominant English that live among them are without fail absorbed into the nation, and

---

[1] Cf. below, Chap. VI.   [2] below, p. 35.   [3] C. P., ii. 30.
[4] C. P., ii. 30, 38, 47, 21 (Waterford), and 479-80.

presently bring their influence to aid the Irish side which they were commissioned to suppress. The evidence of this fact in the State Papers is overwhelming. Thus, in 1588,[1] concerning the state of Connaught, the Lord Deputy and Council proclaim that "weighing and considering the cause how those of the English race, as well within that province, as universally throughout the land, are grown to such barbarous disordered manner and trade of life, as heretofore hath been, and at this day is used among the very Irish, in speech, habit, feeding, trade of housekeeping, manners, conditions and conversations in trade of life," they are fully resolved to enforce the old Kilkenny Statutes against Irish habits, "the brief of which laws they shall receive in a book lately put in print." There follows (p. 565) an order "that all persons at all Sessions of law, &c., do use and wear English attire and apparel, the judges punishing all such as appear before them attired in mantles and rolls, by fines and imprisonment, and to expel all glibbs."

There are large modern instances to corroborate these arguments. The city of Dublin has been for many centuries dominated by Northmen and then by Englishmen. The officials, the professional men, the University men, the leading traders were all at first, and for a long time, Englishmen. The English language has been commonly, and for the last 150 years universally, spoken in Dublin. Yet to the present day Dublin is a thoroughly Irish city. Galway, founded by English families settled for the mere purpose of commerce in Connaught, secured by walls and forts against the wild O'Flahertys and their followers, has nevertheless become so Irish that the "tribes of Galway" are now cited by the public as specimens of what wild Irishmen say or do. The result of this quality in the Irish race was that the original settlers, and all their successors, down to the time of the plantation of Ulster, being small bodies of men, and still smaller of women, became, in spite of themselves, absorbed into

[1] S. P., p. 563.

the native population, adopted their dress and customs, and adding their Anglo-Saxon sturdiness to the vivid national sentiment of the mere natives, formed that remarkable blend which has given Ireland all its great political leaders, literary men, and soldiers, and made the real conquest of the country a problem unsolved to the present day. It is easy to say, nowadays, with all the long history of English failures before us, that the obvious policy of England, when the Tudors took in hand the Irish problem, was to encourage this remarkable blending of races. No effort should have been spared to find out how much of the Brehon law, how much of the traditional customs, was compatible with peace and order. The Irish language should not have been proscribed, but utilised to teach the natives to understand English law, justice and religion, with the prospect that these would gradually make their way among a people living under arbitrary and often capricious rulers.

Let me cite a parallel instance from a civilisation ancient in date, but far more advanced than were the England and Ireland of Henry VIII. When the Ptolemies undertook the control of Egypt, and proceeded to weld it into a Hellenistic monarchy, they found a large population of natives, directed by an old established priesthood, with a hereditary nobility, primeval land laws, traditions of ancient sanctity. To face these obstacles they had a superior military force, a capital city settled with a population of Hellenistic immigrants, two or three city settlements of the same kind in the inner country, and the complete control of imports and exports on the frontiers. But the immigrant population was as nothing in numbers compared to the millions of natives. Ptolemaic procedure under these circumstances, so far as we know it, would, indeed, have been a useful lesson for the English to learn. They began by persuading the priesthood and the nobility, if this latter was a distinct force, to acquiesce in legitimising the new dynasty, as the only remedy against internal anarchy and foreign invasion. That was done by Henry VIII. for Ireland. In return they secured and enlarged the endowments of the priesthood, until their own power was consolidated. They took care to honour and worship, at least outwardly, the national gods. The Tudors boasted of burning the idols and sacred rites worshipped or venerated in Ireland. As successors to the native dynasty the Ptolemies found themselves possessed of extensive crown lands, which they increased by escheating the estates of such as had resisted their intrusion, or otherwise forfeited their rights by law. On these crown lands they made plantations of Hellenistic soldiers and traders, who spoke Greek, lived under Greek law, and observed Greek customs. For these settlements, and for the inland "Greek" towns they held assizes, to which Greek judges made circuits. They had also Greek benches of magistrates holding petty sessions. These courts were open to native and settler alike. But they took care not to wound Egyptian sensibilities by abolishing Egyptian law. They permitted native courts, side by side with the Greek, and native judges to settle disputes among the people in the native language. Any dissatisfied litigant might appeal from the native to the Greek courts. By this toleration they hoped to wean the conquered population from what seemed to them barbarous and obsolete, but hallowed by tradition and custom (like the Brehon law in Ireland), to modern and enlightened procedure. They permitted natives to own land ; they did not object to intermarriage of races ; they adopted the fiscal system of their predecessors in most of its details. By this policy they ultimately made Egypt a homogeneous and united people, ardently loyal to the imported dynasty. But it was not accomplished for several generations, during which the Ptolemies had to contend with repeated native insurrections, fomented by the native clergy, and carried on with cruelty and treachery. Nor did they at last overcome these manifold obstacles without ceding a great deal to the national sentiment. Natives were promoted to the highest offices ; the ceremonial of the court adopted many native practices, so much so that the latest members of the dynasty pose as national sovrans leading a united people to resist Syrian or Roman aggression.

It is indeed true that the Egyptian creed and civilisation stood in a far higher relation to the Macedonian than did the Irish to the English. But the general conditions are, nevertheless, very analogous. The country was too large and too wanting in thoroughfares to be held by any garrison England could command, or to have English judges distributing justice in every district. Even a complete conquest would produce little permanent result without a military occupation of a size and cost wholly out of the question. It was therefore quite obvious that the advice tendered by M'William Eughter, of Mayo[1] and by Tyrone, was sound. The Queen must in the wild districts have native chieftains as her lieutenants, with Palatinate powers, keeping such order as they could by native law among a population willing to obey them. Native law should have been tolerated and recognised wherever the Queen's writ did not run. Above all the mere Irish should have been taught both law and religion through the medium of the Irish language.[2] If the native customs in war or in peace were cruel or barbarous, the conduct of the more civilised English should have afforded a contrast of humanity and forbearance. But wherever an ancient custom was harmless, such as the admission to the title of M'Carthy More by the white wand handed him by O'Sullivan Bere, or to that of

---

[1] S. P., 1589, p. 300 for the arguments in favour of a M'William over Mayo. "It is not possible to rule so many bad people without a chief man to command the rest. No peace will hold unless some one of them carry authority of the country by some title"—of course a native title.

[2] There is sporadic evidence that speaking Irish *was* thought a qualification for promotion among the clergy. Thus Henry Ussher, one of the founders of Trinity College, is recommended for the See of Armagh, because he was very perfect in the Irish language (S. P., 1594, p. 311). There is no evidence that his nephew, James, knew it. Cranmer had ideas about the Irish language, cf. Bagwell's *Ireland under the Tudors*, i. 369, also ii. 362, for the case of Robt. Dale, Bishop of Kildare.

O'Neill by the O'Cahan throwing a shoe over his head,[1] it should have been respected, and made a concomitant condition of these chieftains' English earldoms.

Every one of these precautions was disregarded by the English politicians who undertook to conquer and pacify Ireland. The initial steps taken by Henry VIII. were easy enough, and produced a "fear of him throughout the land." But to be recognised king by the chiefs was only a preamble, while to get rid of the Kildare chieftains, most of them by judicial murders, was to undo the work of pacification. Nor did either he or his statesmen, except in one solitary Act,[2] think of undoing the mischief worked by the statute of Kilkenny and other such enactments, proscribing Irish dress, language, customs, and law, and asserting a complete separation between the races as essential to English interests. The fact brought out so strongly, and proved from actual trials cited by Sir John Davis, that up to the time of James I. the natives were not persons in the eye of the British law, and that, therefore, no Irishman (unless he belonged to the *quinque sanguines*, or five privileged clans) could obtain redress against an Englishman for any outrage, was in itself enough to make the pacification of the country impossible. The English were taught by the law to despise the Irish as an inferior race, so that even to use them as soldiers against civilised men was an outrage. Nothing infuriated the mob of London so much against Strafford, and made his reprieve impossible, as the belief that he had prepared an army of Irish savages to invade England in the interests of

---

[1] "Given him with the brutish ceremonies incident to the same" is the contemporary English estimate (C. P., ii. 339).

[2] This is the Act 33 Henry VIII., in the Council Book of Ireland, beginning with the remarkable preamble: *Quia nondum sic sapiunt leges et jura, ut secundum ea jam immediate vivere et regi possint.* Then follow ordinances quite inconsistent with English law, such as paying fines for manslaughter in the Irish countries, and the appointment of orderers or arbitrators, to act instead of the Brehons. If this solitary attempt at a compromise was the suggestion of Sir Anth. St. Leger, then Deputy, he was a statesman of rare insight.

Charles I. Nothing in the same war set the Parliamentarians so bitterly against Prince Rupert as his employment of Irish kerne among his troops. The pious Puritans executed them at once, when made prisoners of war, until Rupert retaliated by hanging an equal number of his English prisoners, to the horror and astonishment of his foes.

We have, then, two great counteracting forces tending to keep up disorder in Ireland. The first was the strong hand of nature, producing intermarriage, assimilation, adoption of native customs, wherever the English settlers had really made a home in the country. The second was the persistent policy of the English Government and new officials to keep the natives distinct, if possible in blood, if not so at least in privileges, customs, and language, from the English intruders.

We turn now to the most momentous and the most disputed of all the factors in the condition of Ireland at the moment when Trinity College was founded—the policy and influence of the Roman Church. It is quite plain from the evidence we have of the state of this Church in Ireland during the earlier part of the century—the absence of any religious education, the neglect and ruin of the parish churches, the irreverence with which ecclesiastical property was raided by the native chieftains—that it was not likely to resist with any vigour a determined Reformation, carried out with patience and persistency. At the command of Henry VIII. several of the bishops had abjured the Papal supremacy, and were ready to continue in their Sees under the new conditions. During the oscillations of Church policy which followed the king's death there was never a bold or steady claim set up for the re-endowment of the religious houses. The titular bishops and archbishops whom the Pope appointed in opposition to the Crown were mostly absentees,[1] and had shown no fervour in maintaining the Roman supremacy. Typical

---

[1] As Dr. Groves has shown in his interesting essay, *The Titular Archbishops of Ireland in Queen Elizabeth's Reign* (Dublin, 1897).

examples of the selfish and time-serving episcopate of that day are Miler Magrath, Archbishop of Cashel, the friend of both sides, the adviser both of Queen Elizabeth and of the rebels, the plunderer of the property of his See; and William Lally, Archbishop of Tuam, whom we find accused in the correspondence of the day by each side as belonging to the other. Both were married men, both were engaged in enriching their families; neither of them would have faced the smallest danger to support either Roman or Reformed principles. There were, indeed, exceptions, such as Dr. Creagh, titular Archbishop of Armagh, and the Pope's legate, whose activity and ubiquity is the subject of many letters and inquiries; but in general the machinery of the Church of Rome in Ireland was far too rusty and out of repair to save the country from conversion to Protestantism.

Yet there were old and still active causes of antagonism between England and Ireland, old wounds caused by violence and oppression, which were cicatrised in the short intervals of peace, such as in the days of Sidney or of Perrot, but recrudescent and inflamed with every outbreak of disorder. Sir John Davis, when rehearsing all the causes which had impeded the complete conquest of Ireland, wholly ignores the influence of the Roman Church, which he nevertheless had seen the promoter of the fiercest rebellion that had ever arisen against the English power. Nor do his many extant letters show any want of appreciation of this new and powerful cause. But though he does not write it explicitly, he plainly felt that the opposition of Rome was not one of the old historic causes producing separation, and that difference of race and habits, together with blunders of policy, were ample causes to explain all the earlier phenomena. He omits altogether from his historical review the recent causes aiding and abetting Irish rebellion, and he accordingly thought this mischief had been finally removed by Mountjoy's campaigns, and by King James's enlightened policy of peace.

For a long time back the friars, especially the Dominicans and Franciscans, had laboured to keep alive the sparks of religion, the respect for the sacraments, among a neglected and barbarous people; but, as we have already learned from Spenser, this veneration for the forms of the Roman ritual was, at least among the country folk, a mere superstition without rational foundation,[1] and the sacrificing priest was little more than a "medicine man" among savages. The adventures of Captain Cuellar, wrecked from the Armada on the coast of Sligo, show us the real condition of the "mere Irish" as late as 1588. He describes them as Christians indeed, but as ignorant and reckless savages. Nor had they any local priesthood to teach them that the Spaniards were their best friends, and likely to save them from English tyranny, which they had felt and already hated. The barbarous population thought of nothing but wrecking and plundering the strangers, and of murdering them in case of resistance. They thus played directly into the hands of Fitzwilliam and his very small force, which might easily have been checked, and terms made, had the natives or their advisers possessed one spark of political sense or the smallest rudiments of political education. So utterly useless and powerless were the local clergy in a province not yet seriously affected by the Reformation, or peopled with reformed ministers. It is a lamentable truth that the English clergy appointed to cures of souls by the bishops or ministers of Elizabeth were hardly of better mould.[2] There is myriad

[1] "The fault I find in Religion is but one, but the same is universal throughout all that country; that is that they be all Papists by their profession, but in the same so blindly and brutishly informed (for the most part) that not one amongst one hundred knoweth any ground of Religion, or any article of his faith; but can perhaps say his *Pater-noster*, or his *Ave-Maria*, without any knowledge or understanding what one word thereof meaneth."—Ed. 1763, p. 129.

[2] In many cases, however, the old curate must have been continued in his charge. Thus in a tract on the state of Munster in 1587 (S. P., p. 463) the writer recommends to repress the kerne and exalt the churl, to have

evidence that the newly-established clergy was as slothful, as idle, as selfish as their predecessors had been. No care had been taken to rebuild the ruined parish churches,[1] or to insist on a resident parochial clergy, or to prevent shameful accumulation of pluralities in greedy and godless hands. The unfortunate natives, long neglected or plundered by their idle and selfish shepherds, were now being invaded and plundered by a pack of wolves under the guise of a reformed clergy.

But the whole aspect of things changed during the last thirty years of the century, and more especially during the last ten. A great revival of the Roman faith occurred, which has not yet been perceived or described by any historian of Ireland. Yet the main facts are still easy of access, and speak for themselves.

It is now a matter of common knowledge that it was the influence of the Jesuits which educated a few Roman Catholic princes to stay the rapid progress of Protestantism in Germany in the next century. The Jesuits were the real promoters of the Thirty Years' War, and it was that terrible war, while it threw back Germany at least a century in civilisation and in progress, which saved for the Roman Church what still remains to it in the German and Austrian Empires.

As early as 1540 the great Ignatius himself had turned his attention to an Irish mission, and in 1552 he suggests to Cardinal Pole the expediency of training clever Irish youths in foreign colleges in order that they might return and teach the natives in their own language. Accordingly single Jesuits, such as David Woulfe, were sent to Ireland, and, in agreement

the Lord's Prayer and the Belief [*i.e.*, *Credo*] taught in English where the incumbent can, and in Irish, where he may not have so much learning ; to erect free schools, &c. These incumbents who knew no English must have been men that kept their places by conforming, really or nominally, to the Anglican doctrines. Moreover, they must have been "massing priests" ordained in Ireland without any foreign education.

[1] C. P., ii. 458. In 1587 there were one hundred ruined churches in the diocese of Leighlin. In 1600 (S. P., 273) similar complaints are made of Dublin and Meath.

with the general policy of the Order, at once attacked the subject of education. With their exceptional abilities and training they easily obtained influence over the schools existing or founded in the cities, and so began to train the youth of the better classes to understand and maintain the creed of their fathers. This they did in Cork, Kilkenny, Limerick, Youghal, possibly even in Dublin, where the watchfulness of educated Puritans made the task more difficult and dangerous.

In 1564 Pope Pius IV. issued a bull authorising his Archbishop Creaghe and David Woulfe the Jesuit to found and endow from ecclesiastical property Universities in Ireland on the model of Paris and Louvain.[1] This Woulfe, harried by the Irish Government, and escaping with difficulty from Tarbert to Spain, could nevertheless boast that he had converted the Anglican Bishop of Limerick (William Cahessy or Casey), who wrote his recantation and resignation to "the Rev. Lord David Woulfe, appointed the apostolic messenger for all Ireland from the most holy Lord the Pope."[2]

Notwithstanding these symptoms of success, we learn from a letter of the general of the Order to James FitzMaurice in Paris (June, 1578) that he thought the moment for a larger mission to Ireland not yet come[3]. He says he is waiting for the fulness of time, which lies in God's hand. We may interpret that he was waiting for the results of the Spanish Armada, which was in preparation for many years before it really set out.

This delay is all the more remarkable because the Pope had thrown down the glove and challenged the contest by his bull of 1570, declaring the queen illegitimate, a heretic, and not the lawful sovran of England. In this document he acquitted all her Roman Catholic subjects of their allegiance. But this action of the Pope was evidently thought premature by the Jesuits. So it was, strange to say, by Philip II. of Spain, whose letter shows how slowly and badly these docu-

[1] Hogan's *Ibernia Ignatiana*, pp. 14-15.   [2] ibid., p. 18.   [3] ibid., p. 24.

ments, even Papal bulls, were then published. Here are his words to Don Guerau de Spes, his ambassador in England.[1]

"What I have now to say is that the copies I received from you of the two bulls despatched by his Holiness, one declaring the queen schismatic and depriving her of the throne, and the other written to the Earls of Westmoreland and Northumberland [in support of Mary Queen of Scots] were the first information I had received on the subject. His Holiness has taken this step without communicating with me in any way, which certainly has surprised me, because my knowledge of English affairs is such that I believe I could give a better opinion on them, and the course that ought to have been adopted under the circumstances, than any one else. Since, however, His Holiness allowed himself to be carried away by his zeal, he no doubt thought that what he did was the only thing requisite for all to turn out as he wished, and if such were the case I, of all the faithful sons of the Holy See, would rejoice the most. But I fear that not only will this not be the case, but that this sudden and unexpected step will exacerbate things there, and drive the queen and her friends the more to oppress and persecute the few good Catholics still remaining in England."

This very curious letter expresses what I suppose to have been the Jesuit policy at this moment, which speaks of waiting for *the fulness of time*. It also offers a curious commentary upon Philip's orthodoxy, and his acceptance of the infallibility of the Pope, speaking officially the voice of the Church.

Indeed the general character and attitude of Philip II. are sufficient to give us the key to the long delays in the prosecution of the Jesuit campaign. The king was very slow, cautious, hesitating; he was being constantly urged to take up the cause of the Pope against the English queen. We now know from the Spanish correspondence published that he was indeed a sincere Catholic, but mainly from State reasons, because he saw in Protestantism the rise of private judgment in politics, and so the gravest danger to that monarchical despotism which he cherished beyond all other objects. It is now equally well known that Elizabeth was a Protestant, not

[1] S. P., Spanish, 1569–78, p. 254.

from religious fervour and conviction, but from its political significance in opposing foreign enemies. Hence the Jesuits might well hope for either a Spanish conquest, or such an accommodation to avoid it as would give them a free hand not only in Ireland, but in England. If Philip and the Jesuits had acted twenty years sooner, who can say that they would not have been victorious? But the king's stupid caution lost the opportunity. Protestantism made giant strides in England; the queen became popular even among Recusant Englishmen, and so the whole nation was welded together to oppose the invasion of 1588, which ended in disastrous failure.

But in Ireland the effect of the Jesuits was already manifest. They had so far reconquered the towns, that even in Dublin the lawyers, aldermen, and other important citizens regarded the defeat of Spain as an Irish disaster, and absented themselves from the thanksgiving service in Christ Church Cathedral.[1]

The failure of the Armada seems to have shown the Jesuits that a Spanish conquest of England was now very improbable. They did not, indeed, cease to stimulate Philip to renew his efforts, and in the second Armada, wrecked off Cape Finisterre in January, 1597, a large number of Irish ecclesiastics was drowned. Of Jesuits alone, twenty-three were on board, of whom several were lost. But they had begun to fight with different weapons. They preached an assiduous propaganda in the Irish towns. The scholars they had influenced were growing or grown up. And now for the first time the national quarrel of Ireland with England, a quarrel of race, is identified with a religious quarrel, that of the Anglican with the Roman Church. As in Germany in the next generation, the Jesuits were not content to convert the schools, they made themselves indispensable to the Irish chieftains. This was notorious in the case of Tyrone. Even in the case of Shan O'Neill, whose revolt was in no way a religious revolt,

[1] S. P., pp. 365, 397. Cf. also pp. 109, 120 of same volume.

they had so influenced him that he poses in London as a zealous Catholic, attends mass secretly in the Spanish ambassador's house, and is reported by him to Philip as "being so good a Christian that he cuts off the head of any man who dares to enter his dominion, if he be not a Catholic." Almost all the letters sent by Tyrone to Lords Deputies are manifestly composed and probably written by Jesuit hands—most eminently the demand for an University "endowed from the Crown lands, wherein all the sciences shall be taught after the Roman Catholic manner."

This brings us to the question of higher education for both laity and clergy. The conviction that Ireland needed free schools (which had been nominally established by a statute 11 Eliz.), and an University wherein the better youth might be educated, had for a generation forced itself upon thinking people of every creed. The project of making an University out of the buildings and endowments of S. Patrick's, an old collegiate church regarded as a sort of second cathedral, close to Christ Church, was in Elizabeth's mind since 1563,[1] and was an instruction not only to Perrot, but already to Sidney. So, too, the Plantation of Ulster was in her mind, and attempted more than once, but as a bulwark against the invading Scots, not against the rebellious Irish. There can be no doubt that the mistake in policy of seizing an existing endowment, and violating vested interests, delayed the execution of Elizabeth's project for twenty-five years, during which the Jesuits were re-converting the generation which should have filled Trinity College. The quarrel about S. Patrick's became very violent between the imperious Perrot and the wily and tenacious Loftus, who, together with his archbishopric, had managed to secure a dozen of the appointments in S. Patrick's for himself and his friends. This quarrel therefore became so absorbing that it stopped all progress in the real and important object of which all approved. These considerations show that

[1] C. P., i. 359.

Loftus, far from being the founder of Trinity College, as he is represented in Taylor's and Stubbs' histories, was rather the chief obstacle that delayed its foundation till the golden opportunity had been lost. He promoted its foundation on the site of All Hallowes because this scheme saved S. Patrick's and its revenues from further danger of being alienated to a great national purpose.

Meanwhile the necessity for an Irish University had become more and more pressing, on account of the re-adoption of an old policy, laid aside since the reigns of Richard II. and of Queen Mary. The former had planted English settlers in the wilder parts of Wexford and on the coast of Wicklow. The latter had built Maryborough and Philipstown in the O'Moore's and O'Connor's countries (Leix and Offaly), and settled round these fortified towns a similar plantation. Elizabeth, upon the defeat and attainder of the Earl of Desmond, determined to utilise his vast estates, or rather the territories over which he claimed suzerainty—more than 550,000 acres stretching across the south of Ireland from Youghal to Tralee—in settling there (1588) English gentlemen and yeomen for the civilisation of the country and its defence against future rebellions. It was obvious that these people's children, if sent back to England for education, would never make permanent settlements. They must therefore be provided for in Ireland, and it was by these and other such planters that Trinity College was supplied, in its earliest years, with pupils. But on the other hand, this plantation, which was all but ruined by the bloody outburst of popular fury, under Tyrone's instigation, in 1598, must have afforded the Jesuits a new and potent argument with the Irish to join in resisting every English influence. It was now plain that what England coveted was Irish land. If a chieftain rose in arms, and was conquered in open war, not only was he attainted, exiled, and ruined, but all his dependants, all the lesser men who were members of his clan, and had lesser rights to portions of land under his suzerainty, were dispossessed, and their property given to strangers. Ancient freeholds, ancestral traditions, the rights of land property so dear to the Irish nature [1]—all were rudely violated.

Yet for the moment England triumphed, and by the zeal and persistence of Henry Ussher, Luke Challoner, and the Protestant party among the citizens of Dublin, the site of All Hallowes, a suppressed Augustinian house which had been granted sixty years before to the Corporation of Dublin, at their eager petition, by Henry VIII., was allotted for the new College and University.

The Jesuits were keenly alive to the danger. In a supplication addressed to the Pope for aid in Ireland, they speak as follows [2]:—

"Sixthly, though Ireland was once such a school of religion and learning that many came from neighbouring nations to learn, and from it went out many to special knowledge and faith abroad, this glory had gradually decayed, whether by frequent and fierce invasions of foreign nations (*i.e.*, Northmen) or because of the constant civil wars among the chiefs,[3] or by other concurrent causes. At all events the English [who] became masters of Ireland, though at first they corrected there some things inconsistent with the Christian religion, yet afterwards deliberately contrived to keep the natives in the gloom of barbarous ignorance, so as thus to retain them like slaves in abject obedience.[4] Whence it happened that the Irish, though full of genuine love of the Catholic faith, were not educated enough

---

[1] This love of land is often spoken of as something curious and unreasonable in the Irish. In Elizabeth's days it was merely the desire to protect the only property they possessed. Their only wealth was cattle, in which they actually paid almost all their accounts. They had hardly any agriculture, no commerce, no houses worth selling, no industries to occupy their energies. Hence the lesser chieftain or country gentleman, if dispossessed, had no resource left except to adopt the profession of arms abroad, or cattle-lifting at home.

[2] *Ib. Ig.*, p. 36.   [3] In this Spenser and Davis agree.

[4] Observe how the 400 religious houses are absolutely ignored as educators. It is worth remarking that this is the very argument used nowadays by violent Protestants against the Roman Catholic hierarchy in Ireland.

to detect and repel that corruption of religion which for some decades of years the English have sought by fraud and force to introduce into Ireland. This policy of keeping the Irish in ignorance dates from the days when the Catholic faith flourished both in England and Ireland, but now, a year or two since, a new policy has been adopted, whereby England, devoted to heresy, may draw Ireland into the same snare, and bind it closer to itself. This is the building of a certain ample and splendid College beside Dublin, in which the Irish youth shall be taught heresy by English teachers. From this College a great danger threatens the Irish."

The Roman Catholic counterblast was very significant. While the new College near Dublin was in course of building, Irish Colleges—that is to say, Colleges for the reception and education of the higher class Irish students, both lay and clerical—were founded at Lisbon (by Peter Houling, S.J.), Valladolid, Salamanca (by Peter White, S.J.), not to speak of special inducements for Irish students to go to Louvain and Douay for their training in theology and Irish politics. In support of this the Jesuits kept urging O'Neill, O'Donnell, and other chiefs to rebel; they kept urging Philip and the Pope to send them aid, and they began to convert the people of the towns from sullen acquiescence and secret opposition to the Anglican Church into declared adherence to the Pope, and to his secular arm, the King of Spain. For many years of her imprisonment Mary Queen of Scotland was upheld as the legitimate Queen of England, and so long as James VI., her son, gave promise that he would be a Roman Catholic his claims were also supported by Spain and the Vatican. But when he turned heretic there are many statements in the Spanish correspondence of Bernardino de Mendoza, the Spanish ambassador in England, that Philip was the next heir after Mary to the throne of England, and the king takes special credit that he does not propose to add England formally to his dominions. The soul of the Jesuit movement was at this time Archer, a Kilkenny man, who reminds us of the mission of Gylippus to Syracuse, to put life and spirit into the defence against the dilatory and unsteady attack of Nicias and the far superior armament under his command.

There were never many Jesuits sent to Ireland. But those that came were generals or organisers[1] of the Roman Catholic revival, who claimed from the Pope control and direction over the ignorant secular clergy, and maintained their pre-eminence, though not without internal disputes. Two such ambitious and dominant spirits as FitzSimon and Archer were not likely to assume control of the secular clergy or even to co-operate without friction. But this does not now concern us. There is another class of ecclesiastic constantly mentioned in the State correspondence of the time, which is never, so far as I know, clearly defined. I allude to *seminarists* and *seminaries*, which seem to mean deacons or priests educated at the foreign schools, in contrast to the home clergy, ordained in Ireland by the Popish bishops. The relative danger of these three classes to the English control of Ireland is very clearly expressed in a document issued by Sir H. Brouncker, President of Munster, at the opening of King James's reign (1604).[2] In this he orders all Roman ecclesiastics to depart from the country before the following September, and for any of them found after that date and produced he offers as a reward for a Jesuit £40, for a Seminary £6 3s. 4d., for a massing priest £5. These figures would be fairly represented by £300, £50, and £40 at the present value of money. The relative estimates, made by a man who knew the country well, speak for themselves.

The Jesuit crusade had by that time already borne its dangerous harvest. But we must quote in detail some of the evidences for this sudden spiritual revolution in the Ireland of Queen Elizabeth's closing years. Loftus, writing to Burghley,[3] and complaining of the increase of recusancy,

---

[1] "Ex hac schola, velut ex equo Trojano, meri principes exierunt," as Cicero says.
[2] S. P., 1603–6, p. 190.   [3] ibid., 1590, p. 365.

dates its origin six years back, when Lord Deputy Perrot, following the advice of Nich. Whyte and Nugent (eminent native lawyers), declared for liberty of conscience. Since then there is a general refusal to go to church, because the statutory fine of 12d. for each absence is not enforced. How superficial and false was the view of Loftus, whose main object was to damage Perrot, appears from a letter of the very Nich. Whyte just mentioned to Burghley,[1] wherein he notes that " the sting of rebellion, which in times past remained among the Irishry, is transferred and removed into the hearts of the civil gentlemen, aldermen and burgesses and rich merchants of Ireland, papistry being the original cause and ground thereof." This account agrees perfectly with what Sir J. Davis says some years later about Ulster,[2] that the population before the Plantation, and even after the defeat of Tyrone, was quite ready to conform to the Anglican Church. There were at that time no towns, no merchants, no trade in all Ulster.[3] Here is the evidence of William Lyon, Bishop of Cork, in July, 1597,[4] when the war with Tyrone was in progress. Having stated that the muster of troops to serve in the north, from Carbery to Bantry, had been a complete failure, owing to the power of the priests, who were Tyrone's partisans, he proceeds: "But the cities and towns are very well furnished with weapons, and show themselves very perverse and obstinate, the young merchants among them going to their masses with daggers and pistols ready prepared." None of these would serve in Ulster against Tyrone. Even magistrates now refuse the oath of allegiance. Hence, "*Within the last two years* where I had 1,000 or more in church at sermon, I have now not five, and whereas I had 500 communicants and more, I

---

[1] S. P., p. 341.   [2] ibid., 1606, p. 468.
[3] Knockfergus (*i.e.*, Carrickfergus) had a charter, but only fifteen or twenty burgesses. Newry was a mere fort. Armagh was so barbarous a place, despite its cathedral and religious houses, that the Primate resided at Drogheda. The cathedral was burnt by Shan O'Neill.
[4] S. P., 1597, p. 13 *sq.*

have now not three, *and not one woman at either.*" This was in Cork; he thinks Waterford even worse. There was now not one Irish preacher in Munster to teach the country people, but that mattered little, for the towns led the country. "In them," says Sir J. Norreys,[1] "where the most of the inhabitants are of English race, yet they are more Spanish in heart than the country people." Carew and his Council write, two years later, "Besides, the priests have in their devilish doctrine so much prevailed among the people in general in the province, as for fear of excommunication very few dare serve against the rebels, and this infection has so far crept into the cities and corporate towns, as the chief magistrates and mayors thereof do now refuse to come to the church, *which at no time heretofore hath been seen.*"[2] Thomond writes from Limerick, a few years later, "I never saw them obstinater or unsweeter than they are now."

The suddenness of the change described by Lyon is fully corroborated by William Daniell, one of the earliest products of Trinity College, who in writing to Burghley[3] as a "preacher of the Word," says he was chosen by the Lord Deputy and Council to preach the Word of God in Galway, at the suit of the magistrates of that town, and all the bishops of the province. He came readily, though "he was very necessarily employed as a reader in Her Majesty's new College in Dublin. He has now spent three quarters of a year most painfully (*i.e.*, diligently) in instructing the people both in the English and Irish tongues, with great hope of prospering, having already rooted out their famous idol, which they served. But through the suggestion of these traitorous seminaries, the smoking firebrands of all these troubles, they have been of late persuaded to stone him, and have attempted this, as his chamber windows can testify. Now the people dare not hear sermons, baptize or marry, except according to Roman superstition."

[1] S. P., p. 53. [2] Quoted in F. M'Carthy's *Life and Letters*, p. 260.
[3] S. P., September, 1596, p. 121.

Bishop Lyon discloses to us one active cause of this disloyalty, which we have already noticed. The bishop examines the schoolmasters in Cork, and makes search quarterly for the books taught in their schools. He finds Her Majesty's titles torn out of the grammars all through the diocese, "though the books came new from the merchants' shops." He forthwith commits the schoolmasters to prison, and asks what further punishment he shall inflict. He also suggests an order "that no scholar shall depart the realm to go beyoud the seas to any University, save those of England."[1] Reform the cities and towns, he adds, and you reform all the countries round about them. He repeats that all this mischief *is only two years old*.[2]

The sole remedy which these worthy men can suggest is greater stringency of the law. But severity had often been tried and failed. However a single governor of absolute heartlessness may keep up for his time a rule of oppression, no succession of rulers can do it. Most men have within them instincts of humanity; most men prefer, if possible, to govern by persuading rather than by terrifying their subjects.

If we come to consider how the Jesuits obtained their sudden and enormous influence over the whole of Ireland within a very few years, we can answer it at once as regards the inhabitants of the wild country. Since the Munster plantation of 1588 it was easy to persuade the

---

[1] This seems to prove that the schoolmasters had foreign education.

[2] Yet we find that in Waterford, an old hotbed of Recusancy, a Protestant schoolmaster was refused by the town as early as 1583 (S. P., 1583, p. 573); and in 1582 Sir N. Malbie in his valuable notes on Ireland (C. P. ii. 310) says that the new phase of the quarrel is the introduction of religion into it. There is an interesting general account of the country in a letter from Sir J. Dowdall to Burghley in 1595 (pp. 485-8). He also attributes the whole rebellious spirit to the towns, and there to the schools. "Every town is established with Sunday schools, where the noblemen and gentlemen's sons of the country do repair. These schools have an idolatrous or superstitious schoolmaster, *and each school overseen by a Jesuit*, whereby, &c. Hence they go to Spain, Italy, Rheims—young men both of the English and Irish nation." He also says that Waterford led the way.

CLOSING YEARS OF THE 16TH CENTURY

local chiefs not actually dispossessed that *their* turn would come next, and that the rule of the English queen meant not only coercion of conscience, and change of old laws and customs, but the confiscation of land, and the abolition of the privileges of chieftaincy, which were very great, and to which many members of each clan might aspire. For the Irish Brehon law knew no entail on the eldest son, such as the new law imposed.

Every chieftain, from Tyrone downwards, was attended and watched by a Jesuit, or a friar, who instructed him in this policy. As regards the poorer people, there was ample evidence that English rule was a rule of cruelty, and of cruelty on the part of strangers, which has a different effect on men's minds from those cruelties to which they have been used from their hereditary chiefs. The progress of a Lord Deputy, not only in war, but in pretended peace, was frequently a progress in blood. Thus Sir William Drury in 1578 reports his doings at Kilkenny.[1]

Lord Gray of Wilton likewise reports that during his deputyship (September, 1581, to November, 1583) " 1,485 chief men and gentlemen have been slain, not counting those of meaner sort, nor yet executions by law, and killing of churls innumerable." And yet these poor churls were the only natives who made any attempt at cultivating the country. Such statements remind us of the Germany of the Thirty Years' War.

Nevertheless it was not a time of dangerous war, and we have at this very date a widely expressed desire for higher education with various proposals.[2] The students of Trinity College, for years after its first foundation, could not pass the Castle on

---

[1] C. P., ii. 144.
[2] S. P., 1583. Proposal of Rev. Robert Draper to found an University at Trim, p. 513 ; Nich. Taaffe's plan for schools in Ulster, p. 562, and Mr. Attorney Calthorpe's letter to Walsingham, p. 519 ; also the proposal of Archbishop Lancaster of Armagh to erect a free school with scholarships to be held at S. Edmund's Hall, Oxford (S. P., 1581, p. 302).

their way into Dublin without seeing the heads of great natives rotting over the battlements. One deputy (Russell) even complains [1] that the air is corrupted with the number of them. The four quarters of a Wicklow outlaw [2] are carried to Dublin to be so exposed, while his head is sent over to Queen Elizabeth, to her just dissatisfaction.

St. Leger in his province of Munster orders (January, 1579) that all rhymers, bodrags, coursers of horses, makers of *aqua vitæ* (among others) are to be executed by martial law.[3]

But there were worse things than these. It was the custom of both Irish chieftains and English deputies when accepting surrenders of their foes to demand as pledges of their sincerity children or near relatives of their subdued enemy, who were kept in ward, and whose lives were the first to be sacrificed if that enemy renewed his revolt. There were constantly a number of these unfortunate prisoners, mostly children, in Dublin Castle whose life hung upon a thread, and whose support was often neglected and sometimes repudiated by the parsimonious queen and her grasping officials, so that they were living on scant charity, or the very irregular assistance sent them from their homes.[4] In 1589 the constant reports of Bingham's cruelties in Connaught, whereby the inhabitants were being scared from their homes and the province desolated, produced a Commission of high officials from Dublin, to report upon his conduct. Among other details they tell us that they found in camp three children—Burkes of Mayo—as pledges, the eldest 14, all of whom had learned English, and could read and write, being scholars. These Bingham was about to execute, owing to some recrudescence of rebellion

---

[1] S. P., 1597, p. 315.
[2] Feagh McHugh (S. P., 1597, pp. 286, 300).
[3] C. P., ii. 197.
[4] S. P., 1588, p. 155 and 163: "They lie in the grate to beg and starve whatever is their quality, they (their relations ?) so use them." I suppose the grate is the grille, through which prisoners received charity from their friends, as was the case in our day at the gaol in Athens.

in Mayo, but the Commission objected. Bingham, however, took the opportunity of their being at supper to carry out his purpose "most devilishly and Turkishly," for the children begged to see a priest and confess themselves, and died with the most pathetic heroism. The result of this brutality was that the whole province joined O'Donnell and Tyrone, and all the English settlers were driven out in a few days (in 1596), as they were in Munster in 1598.[1] Sir William Drury [2] goes even further, and threatens to kill two little children, sons of Rory Oge, at Leighlin, whom he has in pledge, *with tortures*, and in sight of their relations in the opposing force, by way of intimidation. Carew also [3] threatens to execute an infant son of the Knight of Glyn, but spares him at the last moment. These horrors we hear not from adversaries, but from official reports and letters, or from the complaints of humane men like Sir William Herbert, who speaks frequently of Sir Henry Denny's "fury, rigour and outrageousness towards the Irish" (Kerry), whom Herbert is seeking to civilise with gentleness and to instruct through the medium of their native language.[4] In 1598 [5] we hear that Captain Thomas Lee, an adventurer of doubtful loyalty, meeting a pardoned rebel, Art O'Toole, in the Co. Wicklow, who was under English protection and had his licence upon him, "pulled out his eyes," and so left him upon the road; apparently Lee had

[1] In 1596 Sir J. Norreys reports (S. P., p. 21) that Bingham has lost forty-six strong castles, besides forts in Roscommon, and seated in Mayo six or seven score English gentlemen in good castles and houses, all driven out without resistance. Of the 35,000 sent over from England (when and where?) only 1,000 remain; the rest are dead, or *converted into Irish*. Both he and Fenton ascribe this failure directly to Bingham's cruelty (p. 108), "without forming the people first to love Her Majesty and her Government, it is vain to expect that they will remain in duty and subjection" (Norreys), and Fenton accordingly calls Bingham *Improvido*.
[2] C. P., ii. 141.   [3] ibid., iii. 333, 411.
[4] Cf. also the Bishop of Ross's letter on the cruelties used towards the Irish in Hamilton's Pref. to S. P., 1574-85, pp. civ-vi.
[5] S. P., pp. 75, 101.

been dispossessed, by Lord Burgh's authority, of some O'Toole land given him by Fitzwilliam. Worse than this hideous crime is the difficulty of inflicting punishment for it, and the cool way in which it is discussed by the Government officials.

These facts—a few selected from a very long catalogue of what we know, and this but a fraction of what really happened—explain to us how easily the Jesuits persuaded the mass of the Irish poor throughout the wild country that English domination would afford them no escape from cruel oppression.

There was another side to English tyranny, cloaked under legal procedures, which weighed upon that most obscure but most important class, the small Irish or Anglo-Irish landholders, scattered through the country. When great lords were attainted and their fortunes escheated, their lands were ascertained by survey and distributed to new owners, except in such cases as when titles from the Crown could be produced by the smaller proprietors. Of such titles there were many, especially among the older Anglo-Irish settlers, who had been obliged, from stress of circumstances and want of support from England, to submit to the suzerainty and the exactions of a Desmond or a MacCarthy More. When the great acts of confiscation had been carried out, these people, if then unmolested or recognised as owners, should have been safe. But no; there were two engines of torture still brought to bear upon them—the search after "concealed lands" and the Inquisition into defective Titles. It was alleged, no doubt truly, that the survey of the great escheated estates had been inaccurate, that many corners and outlying townlands had been overlooked, and that in this way the Crown had been defrauded of its rights. These scattered bits of land must frequently have been small freeholds, deliberately omitted from the escheat either by the benevolence, or negligence, or ignorance, innocent or interested, of the surveyors. The grasping queen, and her more grasping Exchequer, permitted or encouraged individual adventurers to scour the country, collect evidence, and inform the Crown of these *Concealments*. The reward was a grant of such lands to the discoverer at a small head-rent, which he far more than recovered by letting them to the occupier, hitherto a freeholder, now made a tenant, with the possibility of being ejected. It was an everyday petition of men seeking a pension or income for their services from the Crown to ask it from the profits of "concealed lands now unjustly detained from the queen." The petitioner undertook the search at his own cost, and his pension would not diminish the present income of the State. Worse, if possible, was the informer against some old title, hitherto unsuspected, and apparently given by the Crown of England as the security against disturbance, but now questioned as defective in form, or as void owing to the non-fulfilment of some of its forgotten clauses. The people of Waterford, we are told,[1] are satisfied to see the lands of recently attainted rebels divided, "but it goeth hard with them, and not without murmur, to see the Commission stretched to inquire of old concealments, such as have lien in their possession many years."

Among the individuals notorious for prosecuting such inquiries for their own profit was Richard Boyle—afterwards first Earl of Cork, and ultimately a great benefactor to the South of Ireland—and Patrick Crosbie of Maryborough. The latter was employed by the new College to find for them concealed lands from which they could derive £100 per annum, the allowance given them by the queen out of this doubtful and unpopular source. They petition the Lord Deputy that ample evidence for the lands they require will be found in "Mr. Boyle's trunk," then seized by his adversaries in Dublin, upon suspicion of unjust practices. The maps of the College estates in the south show to this day, together with large estates, the escheated property of the Earl of Desmond, Brian O'Connor,

---

[1] S. P., 1586, p. 194.

and others—small patches here and there, selected upon no apparent principle and scattered over various counties. These are the "concealed lands" from which they derived the pittance allowed them by the queen, and which they let to the old occupiers[1] at very low rents. But in the plantation of Munster the original undertakers had been forbidden to let to natives, and required to bring over English settlers to their lands. It was by evasion of this law, and for the sake of higher rents offered by the old possessors, that many of the escheated lands remained in the hands of the original population, which, of course, rose with Tyrone when he appeared in Munster in 1598, and expelled the intruders with fire and sword, just as the northern planters were afterwards cleared out in 1641.

We now approach the more difficult question: How did the Jesuits in these few years conquer not only the country parts of Ireland, but the cities and the Pale? Why did the merchants, the burgesses, the lawyers—in fact the great majority of the educated Anglo-Irish classes—pass over either openly or secretly to the Pope's side in this great quarrel?

We shall not find a satisfactory answer to this question without insisting upon the distinction between the English by birth and the English by descent, as they are commonly described in the State Correspondence of the day. Perhaps it would be clearer to distribute the whole population of the island not into two, but into three kinds—English, Anglo-Irish, and Irish. For the Pale and the walled cities had been peopled long ago by either Northmen, Dutch, or English, with special privileges over the natives. Yet these people had been so long either neglected or oppressed by England, that they were prompted by proximity, by intermarriage, by community in grievances, to identify themselves with the interests of Ireland and the Irish against those of England. None had fared worse than

---

[1] This was a licence allowed to the bishops and to the College formally by James, practically, as we see from the tenants' names, by Elizabeth.

the settlers of the old Pale. They were constantly being raided and plundered by the wild Irish on its inland frontier, and sometimes up to the very walls of Dublin. Either they must wield the sword with one hand, and the plough with the other, like Nehemiah's workmen, or the Greeks of the Crimea, described by Dio Chrysostom, or they must appeal for help to the Lord Deputy. If they did, an English army of occupation, including the hired light troops known as Her Majesty's kerne, was quartered upon them, and the exactions of this army were worse than the raids of the savage natives. Even for wars far beyond the Pale, such as those against Tyrone, the provisions of the troops were all exacted from the Pale at the Queen's price paid in bills, which, being difficult to realise in cash, were usually of no value at all.[1]

The result was that the Elizabethan wars in Ireland completely ruined the yeomen of the Pale. Many returned to England; the others were reduced to beggary.[2] Hugh Tudor, servant to the late Kyffin, writes an account of the ruffianly conduct of the soldiery, and hence the poverty of the people. He says that in the days of Fitzwilliam, Perrot, and Russell he had known wealthy and charitable farmers who gave meat to every traveller gratis. "I have seen very ancient men, truly affirmed to have been rich farmers of the Pale, sufficiently able in their time to have entertained the Lord Deputy for a night or two, go a-begging, not spoiled by rebels but soldiers." When Ormond[3] complains of the scandalous conduct of large landholders with castles in Leix (we hear the same from Munster and from the Pale) who give them up without a fight, we must remember that the alternative was to support these terrible bands of mercenary soldiers who ate them out of house and home.

---

[1] Thus the garrison of Carrickfergus were fed by cess upon the Pale, the supplies being sent to them on horses or in ships. Meanwhile the country round that town, once well tilled, lay desolate because of the garrison. C. P., Introd. to vol. iii. p. xciii. On the exactions of the soldiers, ibid. 175, 187, 264.

[2] S. P., 1598, p. 208.   [3] ibid., p. 212.

This lamentable condition of things, of which there are many bitter complaints in the State Papers, of course impoverished not only the yeomen, but the gentlemen and lords of the Pale. The old Irish exactions of coyne and livery, so cried out against by many witnesses, seemed less odious than this maltreatment by strangers under the pretence of protection ; and it may have been an honest reply of the gentry of Pale, when asked to contribute to the building of Trinity College, that they were too poor to give anything. But behind their refusal was another potent reason. The Jesuits had taught them that this College was a new scheme for spreading English influence by means of English religion, and bringing upon them an alien clergy with an alien ritual.

I have so far endeavoured to look at the matter from the material point of view, for men's interests must surely be enlisted in any such quarrel to ensure a victory. But these considerations were enforced by sentimental reasons also, and to the Irish blood in the gentry of the Pale such reasons were very exciting. The main preachers of the New Gospel were Puritans, harsh inconoclasts whose first anxiety was to insult and destroy the venerable relics or high places held in superstitious reverence by all the old inhabitants.[1] Such a form of controversy is needlessly and stupidly irritating ; we may see it even in our own day in the Protestant hatred or suspicion shown towards the sign of Cross, the great emblem of all Christianity.

The general result was, that the Jesuits were able to retain even the lords of the Pale and their families in the old faith. Not a few of the sons of these great and ancient houses joined the Order ; some of them remain to the present day staunch Roman Catholics. The English had for centuries seen the danger, and tried by many oppressive enactments to retain the

---

[1] Cf. the public burning of the image of S. Sunday in Cork by the bishop, at the High Cross, openly, with great lamentation (of the people), C. P., ii. 137, 143, and Daniell's action in Galway, above, p. 35.

Anglo-Irish as an English settlement in Ireland. The Jesuits succeeded in bringing them over completely to the Irish side by the bond of the old creed.

It was indeed round these Anglo-Irish that the great battle between the English and the Pope raged. Let us look at it in the towns. Here again there were the sentimental reasons —*e.g.*, Daniell in Galway, Lyon in Cork burning sacred images in the market-place amid the horror and lamentations of the population. But there were also practical reasons. The richer classes in the towns consisted of merchants and of professional men—these latter either officials or lawyers, for we do not find other professions, such as the medical, as yet of any importance. The alternative set before the merchants by sea was that the many English restrictions upon exports and imports would be replaced by the control of some more distant and careless power, probably Spain, with whom the shipping trade would enormously increase, while smuggling would proably be uncontrolled, and hence the source of great profits. Turning inland, the traders must have regarded the native chiefs with their continual raids, and need of the provisions for war, a source of immediate wealth, which English conquest was gradually drying up. The supplies for British forces were undertaken by English contractors, who bought in England the requisitions for the English soldiery; any ordered from Irish houses were scantily and irregularly paid, if paid at all. These arguments were no doubt bad, and could have been answered by any one who looked far ahead, but they were sufficient to set ignorant men, and their more ignorant wives, against the English side, and therefore against the English religion. For the great hope of emancipation lay in Spain and the Pope, and to secure these it was essential to maintain the old religion.

In the case of the lawyers and officials it is even more necessary, but also easier, to show how their material interests were involved. The policy of sending over strangers from England to fill all the important posts—judgeships, treasurer-ships, bishoprics, governorships [1]—was one resented by the educated Anglo-Irish from that day to this. It was alleged regarding the judges that if of Anglo-Irish descent they treated the natives with too much favour, and could not be trusted to secure the rights of undertakers and adventurers. We can well imagine the answer of the Walshes, Whites, and Dillons. With them, and with them alone, had the natives any chance of justice. The imported judge was certain to favour the imported criminal.[1] For with him the *English interest* was the first thing to support at every cost.[2]

In fact the Irish lawyers at this moment are the great champions of the Anglo-Irish against the English. We find the towns electing them constantly as their mayors, in order that they may defend them against inroads upon the Charters.[3] We find them the spokesmen of the lords of the Pale, when prosecuted for recusancy. They had therefore a great *rôle* to play on the Roman Catholic side,[4] whereas on the Protestant or English side they saw the rewards of their toil snatched from before their eyes by some English place-hunter.

Of course this statement only aims at generalities, and does not seek to deny that eminent English lawyers did sometimes adorn the Irish bench. But to persuade good men to come

---

[1] Of this notable examples may be found in Primate Boulter's correspondence far into the eighteenth century.

[2] S. P., 1597, 222. Cf. the complaints against Irish lawyers as judges (S. P., 1585, pp. 14, 324), and Sir Owen O'Toole, O'Donnell's chief councillor, p. 63. Wadding, mayor of Waterford (1597, p. 19) "is a great lawyer and a bold Recusant," never in Church, and as State adviser misleading Perrot (ib., 210, 222)."

[3] S. P., 1597, p. 19; C. P., iii. 492. Carew cites the cases of Cork (John Meade), Limerick (Geoffrey Gallway), Waterford (Edward Gough), Clonmell (J. Whyte), besides the portreve of Cashell, the profoundest lawyer in the kingdom, and the sovran of Kinsale—all were trained in the Inns of Court. This shows a systematic policy, probably suggested by the Jesuits. In Flor. McCarthy's Life, p. 108, there is a list of Irish gentlemen students at Gray's Inn, London.

[4] S. P., 1597, p. 20.

over was difficult, and I have already said that they were always demanding their own recall from a very unpleasant position. This is urged by the Privy Council in answer to a demand for some good English lawyers. They say [1] "the sending thither of lawyers is most requisite, but such opinion is conceived of the barbarism there, as at all times when any have been chosen to be sent thither, they do ever make some means to Her Majesty whereby they may be stayed."

These were the materials with which the Jesuits effected the reconquest of a well-nigh lost province of the Roman Church. Their consummate ability, energy, zeal, and devotion command the admiration of any fair-minded historian. Whatever force or fraud they used, they could defend as justified not only by the excommunication of the queen, which relieved all her subjects of their allegiance, but also by the far better plea, that they were carrying on war for the King of Spain against the English in Ireland, and that the conquest of the island, and through it of England, was the declared policy of the Most Catholic King. But this cautious person was very difficult to urge into decided action. He hesitated and temporised, while they were preparing the ground, collecting munitions of war, educating the Irish chiefs to submit to their dictation. Having made a disciple of O'Neill, they urged him to take up arms. If his long and dangerous insurrection which spread over the whole country had been promptly and liberally supported by Spain, the conquest of Ireland was inevitable. In the earlier stages of the war (1596–9) Tyrone was steadily gaining ground. In 1598 his appearance in Munster caused a rising of the natives against the English of the plantation, which cleared the whole country of settlers in a week. The horrors of 1641 in the north found their prototype in the horrors of 1598 in the south. For this latter was the first Irish insurrection in which creed was put forward as a concurrent cause with nationality.

[1] C. P., ii. 53.

Any one who examines the public documents of O'Neill in the Calender of State Papers can see at once that they were dictated by Jesuits, and that of the two concurrent forces, creed was rapidly becoming the leading factor. Here is an example. Tyrone writes to Ormond :[1] "From henceforth, if you write to me, I wish you command your secretary to be more discreet, and to use the word *traitor* as seldom as he may. By chiding there is little gotten at my hands, and they that are joined with me fight for the Catholic religion and the liberties of our country, the which I protest before God is my whole intention." Presently[2] we have a note from Richard M'Geoghegan, who had seized Herbert's house at Castleisland (Kerry) in the revolt of 1598. The house cannot be restored to Herbert, " because Tyrone hath chiefly entered into action for matters of religion, and this house being (*i.e.,* having been) a religious house, must be restored to the Church." Meanwhile he retains Herbert's son and daughter as pledges. There is a formal Papist declaration in Tyrone's articles to which Ormond replies.[3]

At the opening of 1600 the Jesuits evidently thought their cause victorious. Even without military aid, and with small subsidies from Spain, Tyrone was practically master of the island. He set forth terms to be accepted by the queen, and addressed her as a sovran on equal terms, signing his name as such at the head of his missive, " contrary to all duty." He claimed not only freedom of conscience for all Romanists, but even a Roman Catholic University to secure the training of the young under Jesuit influence. How high the hopes of his party had risen will best appear from the Jesuit correspondence published in Father Hogan's *Ibernia Ignatiana*.[4] I translate from his text a letter written to the General of his order by Field and dated July 20, 1600 : " And since a great hope has arisen of restoring the Catholic faith from the happy success

---

[1] In 1599, p. 209.
[2] p. 217.
[3] ibid., pp. 279-81 ; p. 293.
[4] pp. 44, 68.

of the war, seeing that in almost all the engagements the Catholic[1] army has the advantage, and new forces are expected from Spain (would that His Holiness would join in aiding this object!), I think it worth while to mention to your Reverence some ecclesiastical benefices which would be very suitable to our Society for building colleges, if His Holiness would grant them to us. There is beside Dublin a monastery of S. Thomas the martyr,[2] which is commonly valued at £550 yearly, Irish currency. 2. The monastery of the Blessed Virgin beside Dublin, yearly value £463.[3] 3. The Hospital of S. John Baptist outside the new gate of the city, worth £156.[4] 4. The Monastery of All Saints' near Dublin, where the heretics have built a splendid college, worth £84 (per annum). 5. There is also a priory or monastery of Holmpatrick in the County of Dublin by the sea, a very suitable place for relaxation, worth £69. Many others less known to me, situated in divers parts of the kingdom, written down from the books of the Queen's Exchequer, I have given the bearer of this letter."

The "newly founded illustrious College" was to the Jesuits a special object of alarm. For here the English queen was adopting their policy, and seeking to complete her conquest by educating the better classes. Hence they not only founded simultaneously their Spanish Colleges for Irish students, but strained every nerve to prevent young gentlemen from going to Trinity College. Here is the story told by the Jesuits concerning the founding of the College at Lisbon. Father

---

[1] Not the *Irish*, nota bene.

[2] *I.e.*, Thomas à Becket, granted by Henry VIII. to Sir H. Brabazon, th ancestor of the Earl of Meath, who still owns this property, now the Earl of Meath's Liberty, in Dublin.

[3] Granted by Henry VIII. to the Dublin Corporation, and reaching from the present Mary's Abbey to Sackville Street, and across the river on the east side of Westland Row.

[4] Now marked by a handsome Augustinian Chapel. Cf. *Monast. Hibern.*, ii. 56, 59.

Houling, S.J., had been carrying on a successful mission at that port among the Irish skippers and sailors who frequented it, also among the kidnapped Irish, brought there by pirates.

"But nothing stirred his grief and his zeal so much as the sight of a crowd of youths, who in tender age, having deserted parents, country, means, had escaped from the Dublin University. This University, formerly instituted by Roman Pontiffs [?], then collapsed by the troubles of the times, Queen Elizabeth had lately renewed, with the design that it might be in Ireland a defence as well as an armoury of error. She had also invited Catholic parents to send their children thither to be taught and maintained free. This offer had allured a good many orthodox people, whose love was cold and whose means narrow; but the children, wiser than their parents, hating the wolves their masters, with one consent deserted the school of error, and borne to a foreign shore, there landed in utter destitution."

These were provided for by Houling in his new College of S. Patrick in Lisbon, founded in 1594.

It is indeed first of all to be noted that none of the State Papers, or the documents in the Muniment Room of Trinity College, or in its Library, make the smallest allusion to this picturesque piece of history. There was no crowd of youths of any kind, least of all Roman Catholic youths, at the College in 1594, the year after the completion of the buildings. The first impression, therefore, made by the story is that of deliberate invention. But a more careful study of the text will show that though the narrator implies it, he does not state that these *aliquot juvenes* appeared at Lisbon at the same moment, which is the form the story takes in more recent transcripts. It is not only probable, but almost certain, that owing to the Jesuit mission in Ireland there were frequent cases of individual children rescued from the influence of their parents, and sent abroad to avoid the dangers of Protestant education. These isolated occurrences have been brought together upon one canvas by the Jesuit artist, in order to make an effective picture. The general account of the policy and

CLOSING YEARS OF THE 16TH CENTURY

of its results is true, in the same deeper sense that dramatic poetry, as Aristotle remarks, is truer than history.

The foregoing inquiry has been indispensable, if we would seek to understand the Ireland of 1590–1600, for which Trinity College was founded. I have stopped at the year 1600, because in that year the whole course of events was changed, and the most ambitious of the Jesuit hopes dashed to the ground, by the appointment of Lord Mountjoy as Lord Deputy. It is not within the scope of this work to enter into a detailed estimate of this very great man. A few words, however, must here be added in order to justify so strong a statement, and to show the complete revolution of affairs produced in Ireland by one master mind. Elizabeth, herself growing old, had hitherto employed in her Irish Government and command nothing but old men, to whom she had been long accustomed as her servants. It is the usual fate of senescence. Men and women fail to realise that those who have been once vigorous are no longer fit for arduous and exacting labour. Nothing is more melancholy in reading the Irish State Papers of the time than the constant complaints of the queen's trusty servants that their powers are failing, and that they long for retirement and rest.[1] At last the queen appointed a young man, because he was her favourite, who was the second Lord Essex she had sent to Ireland with an army, but he too proved a failure. For she showed the weakness of her sex by allowing all manner of unofficial and unauthorised scandal to be transmitted (behind the Lord Deputy's back) by his enemies, and this secret campaign at Court not only sowed distrust in the queen's mind, but filled every Lord Deputy with uncertainty

---

[1] As specimens, cf. Russell, C. P., iii. 184; Sir R. Lane, S. P., 1596, p. 113; Sir R. Bingham, ib., p. 128; Sir H. Wallop, ib., p. 136; Loftus and Gardner, S. P., 1597, p. 459; Ormond, 1598, p. 12; Chief Justice Saxey, 1598, p. 396, and Fenton—all complaining of their age and infirmities. Norreys and Burgh died in harness.

and alarm. Each one of them is in constant dread that he will be undermined at Court, if he is not there to defend himself. But though Essex failed, his appointment was a wholesome break in the series of elderly and worn-out Governors. For Elizabeth next appointed Charles Blount, Lord Mountjoy, a man of under forty years, but of many accomplishments. The first sign of reform in the government of Ireland is the complaint of the old gentlemen of the Privy Council that their advice is neglected and younger men consulted in their stead. Mountjoy answers that he had taken the advice of no man who was not older than Alexander when he conquered the world. Of course the new Deputy had found out at once that their counsels were as infirm as their limbs. He next reformed the abuses of the army, stopped the plunder of the Pale by requisitions, and gained such confidence from the Anglo-Irish that with a small but most efficient and devoted army, mostly gathered in Ireland, he overthrew both Tyrone and the Spanish invaders in a desperate campaign, and then pacified the country by the coercion of famine. It was a cruel measure, though Mountjoy was not a cruel man. Of this we have ample evidence. But there have been moments even in our own experience when trenchant measures would have been far more merciful than that sentimental generosity which prolongs indefinitely the horrors and the losses of war.

When the Jesuits raised their heads in the Irish cities upon the accession of James, who had doubtless "practised" with them during Elizabeth's reign, Mountjoy not only coerced them by displaying a prompt and efficient army at their gates, but by confuting their arguments from St. Augustine, whose works he carried with him in his tent. When he retired from his command to England he still remained Lord Lieutenant, and his influence was paramount in the English Privy Council as regards Irish affairs. We can trace in every advice he gave moderation and toleration towards the Irish. Most unfortunately he died of a fever in 1607. Had he been permitted to guide the Irish policy of the next twenty years, the whole history of the country might have been different. I do not know whether he would have sanctioned the plantation of Ulster. I think he would. But I am quite sure that he would have made very different provision for the natives in the six counties, and if a great number of them had been restored to a portion of the lands they claimed by Irish custom, it is probable that the massacre and expulsion of the settlers in 1641 would never have taken place.

Seeing then that the Jesuits, by their vigorous and able action during the closing years of the sixteenth century, saved Ireland for the Papacy, and consolidated both Irish and Anglo-Irish under the banners of the King of Spain (so long as the war lasted), and then under that of the Pope, now the hereditary enemy of heretic England, we are in a position to answer the questions so often put, and so seldom adequately answered by historians : Is the great antagonism between England and Ireland, which has lasted so many centuries, a struggle of race or of creed? Are the differences between them ineradicable, or are they merely due to the blunders and hesitations in English management?

Sir John Davis, in his book, attributes the whole difficulty to the contrast of the races in their habits and laws, coupled with the constant alternations and hesitations of British management. But he speaks (in 1616) of all the difficulties as now overcome, and confidently looks forward to an age of harmony and prosperity. Barnabe Rich, his contemporary, not looking back so far, and weighing the evidence of his own experience, attributes the whole difficulty to Popery, which deliberately sets the Irish people, not disinclined to peace and loyalty, to keep up war and hatred against the English. So in our own day Prendergast, a man who under the guise of learned and impartial research betrays the animus of a bitter and prejudiced controversialist, ignores the influence of Popery in creating and stimulating these hatreds, and writes as if English brutality and tyranny towards the Irish as such were the only causes of Ireland's just discontent. On the other hand, Froude, a man of singular power in grasping a historic situation, though impatient of research, and inaccurate in the use of his materials, has made the whole quarrel one of religion. He regards the Papal system as the permanent and irreconcilable foe of the English in Ireland. But Froude's researches, like those of Mr. Lecky, are mainly in later centuries than those with which we are here concerned. Mr. Lecky's view, much influenced by Prendergast, is strongly adverse to Froude. But Mr. Lecky again has been subjected to severe criticism from Dr. Thomas Ingram, whose remarkable but one-sided work marshals all the evidence in favour of the English, and exposes the partisan treatment of the facts by some of his predecessors.

The present inquiry points to the following solution of the problem. Up to the time of Henry VIII.'s quarrel with the Pope, there can be no question that the causes of hostility between the English and Irish were simply the contrast of language, law, and customs arising from contrast of race. These feelings, quite apart from the conflict of creeds, were kept up by that class constantly persecuted in English enactments—bards, harpers, and rimers, who make songs in favour of rebellion, and who were frequently executed by martial law.[1] It was, as often stated down to Perrot's time, the question of England and Wales over again. Even as the Lords Marchers had extended English influence, and held the Welsh population under control partly by alliances with Welsh princes, partly by arms, so the lords of the Pale or indeed the English lords all through the country, were to leaven and civilise the mere Irish.[2] Had any strong king come over and completed the conquest, as Edward did of Wales, similar results might have been attained. Even as late as Henry

---

[1] Cf. Bishop Lyon in S. P., 1597, p. 19.
[2] Perrot states this in one of his letters.

VIII.'s time the ready acceptance of his sovranty in Ireland shows clearly that an expedition to Ireland, a residence of some duration, and a proper settlement of the country under Presidents of the provinces, might have been rewarded with lasting success.

We cannot find in any of the contemporary documents that there was great lamentation in Ireland over the suppression of the monasteries. Many Recusants (if we may so term them proleptically) were glad to accept gifts of the sequestrated estates from the king,[1] nor was there any attempt at restitution made by or under Queen Mary. The practical duties which the religious houses should have performed, viz., the parochial duties of the parishes of which they were rectors, and the education of the youth, had been grossly neglected, and it is likely that something better was expected from the new parochial clergy. For as yet the differences in creed were not considered vital. Henry himself was anything but a Protestant in the modern sense. He believed in transubstantiation, and was horrified at the marriage of a priest. It was only with Elizabeth that the profound cleavage of Popery and Protestantism came to be understood in Ireland. Shan O'Neill set up his standard in Ulster on the ground of hereditary rights; he foresaw and endeavoured to forestall the subjugation and plantation of the province with English officers and English customs, but though he professed himself to the Spaniards a devout Catholic, that was not his real ground of quarrel. Had Elizabeth conceded to him his independence, she might have made his altered creed a condition which he would not have considered impious. But along with the hopes of help from Spain grew the alarm of the native clergy, and the prosecution of Recusants by Sunday fines. They began to identify their creed with the native cause, and to preach the doctrine that the crusade against the

---

[1] *E.g.*, the nunnery of Grace Dieu to Patrick Barnewall, Esq., who was noted as an opponent of the reformed religion.

old faith was part and parcel of a crusade against Irish rights of property.

That this idea was alive in Ireland as early as Sidney's time seems certain ; it never acquired strength and missionary enthusiasm till taken up by the Jesuits. It was they who translated the quarrel of race into one of creed, and gradually made the latter so predominant that in the present day, when the distinction of Irish and Anglo-Irish is well nigh obliterated as to race, the distinction of Catholic and Protestant has so completely replaced it that a Kavanagh or an O'Brien, because he is a Protestant, is regarded by the common people as an Englishman,[1] and even as a stranger, while a Martin or a Domvile, nay even a settler of the last generation, is taken to be an Irishman, if he be a Catholic. The difference of race has not really disappeared, far from it. The blend of Anglo-Irish and Irish has produced a population with intellectual and social qualities very different from those of the present English, and these qualities are now often cited by men who desire to keep open the gulf which past history has made between Great Britain and Ireland. But these contrasts are only auxiliary arguments ; they are as nothing compared to the contrast of creed. If this were abolished we may say confidently that the "Irish Question" would presently be laid at rest. Thus the old conflict between the tribal, pastoral, semi-nomadic Irishman and the civic, agricultural, settled Englishman, which was at the root of all the earlier troubles, was replaced by a spiritual conflict in which reverence for the Pope and the clergy with their sacraments and relics was adopted as the one fixed point of his life by the Irish Esau, while the English Jacob allowed himself the mental disturbance of exercising his private judgment, and insisted upon the necessity of rational persuasion by preaching the Gospel, which preaching he might dispute if he chose.

[1] Thus Prendergast, in an incautious moment (*Cromwellian Settlement*, p. 202), calls Ormond an Englishman !

What then was the population, and what the conditions, of Ireland which could afford to the pious founders of Trinity College a good hope for its success?

The first unavoidable observation is that, like all the attempted benefits of England to Ireland, it came too late. If the lavish Cardinal who founded Christ Church, Oxford, had expended this zeal upon Ireland under Henry VIII., and at the moment of the king's assumption, under the most pacific and favourable auspices, of the royalty of the country, there can be little doubt that the success of Trinity College would have been immediate and great. The miserable and sporadic attempts at education by a very few religious houses would have been at once replaced by a proper system, and at that time it would have been gratefully accepted. Had Edward VI. carried out such a plan, there was no zeal and vigour in the adherents of the Pope to resist it. Nor were there wanting definite proposals to realise the policy. The great letter of Browne, the first Protestant Archbishop of Dublin, expounds in full detail the transformation of the suppressed Collegiate Church of S. Patrick into "Christ's College of the foundation of Edward VI.," thus giving definite shape to the pious aspirations of his enlightened contemporaries.[1] Had even Sidney, in the earlier years of Elizabeth, not been thwarted by Loftus and the office-holders of S. Patrick's, from founding the University on Browne's plan, the religious Reformation of the country might yet have been achieved.[2] For it was just

---

[1] This document is so important that I reprint it in an appendix from Shirley's *Original Letters*, No. ii., together with Loftus' letter (lxxix.), before he had obtained the Archbishopric of Dublin, which gave him the patronage of the prebendaries.

[2] The Archbishop's plan was taken up vigorously about 1563-5, and recommended by many learned and pious men, such as Hugh Brady, Bishop of Meath, whose letters Shirley has printed (*op. cit.*, Nos. lxii., lxvi.). The then office-holders, Archbishop Curwin and his party, resisted the plan with ridiculous objections (lviii.). But when Brady heard that Loftus (then Primate) had got the deanery of S. Patrick's *in commendum*, he evidently saw that the prospect of an University was ruined, and bursts out into a pathetic

between Sidney's Government and FitzWilliam's that the Jesuit mission in Ireland did its mighty and effectual work. During those years the country people had been taught to regard the Reformed faith as a part of English tyranny. The townspeople, who had acquiesced in its preaching, and gone in thousands to church, now scowled at the minister as sullen Recusants, or pelted him in the street. Young men of ambition were told that in Spain there were Royal Colleges specially founded for both lay and clerical students. Clever lawyers with foreign training were appointed mayors of the cities, and devised legal subtleties to make the old charters a cloak for liberties other than municipal. Trinity College was, therefore, at its untimely foundation regarded as a bulwark of English and Protestant influence, and, unless it could bribe or seduce, or the English Government could compel, was not likely to draw its students from the sons of the chieftains and their followers, who had been sent to Recusant schoolmasters in Cork or Waterford, or had seminary priests with them as resident tutors, such as the educators of the O'Donnells and O'Neills. There was plainly in Dublin a strong and earnest body of Reformers—most of them educated at Puritan Cambridge—who were the prime movers and supporters of the work.[1] Of these, Luke Challoner, Henry Ussher, and other men of old city families, are prominent. But how little stir the foundation of the College made throughout Ireland, except in the minds

---

lamentation, though Loftus had got the deanery under a bond of £1,000 to resign it when wanted for a College, and though he had himself thereupon written to Cecil (October, 1565, April and June, 1566), (lxxix., lxxxv., xci.,) strongly advocating the plan. The first letter, condemning explicitly the very policy which he afterwards pursued to save his own profits, puts the dishonesty of Loftus beyond all question ; cf. Appendix to this volume. The plan was revived by Perrot ; cf. his correspondence (S. P., 1574, and Pref., pp. cxvi-xxx, and C. P., i. 359).

[1] See the *Book of Trinity College*, p. 3, for further evidence of this movement, especially Case's *Speculum Moralium Quæstionum* (1585), who in his Preface appeals to the Chancellors of Oxford and Cambridge to help in the work.

of the watchful Jesuits, is plain from the complete ignoring of it by Miler Magrath in 1592,[1] in the very year of its foundation, and of the collecting of funds for it in Munster. In the same year[2] William Lally, another Archbishop (of Tuam), writing about the religious state of Connaught, and proposing, as Magrath had done, Irish preaching, also recommends that the schools be watched, priests arrested, and the sons of the gentry sent to *Oxford and Cambridge*. These silences are very significant. The failure and retirement of Travers, the first acting Provost, point in the same direction. He was an eminent preacher, and strong advocate of Puritan views, such as are now called Presbyterian. But he evidently found that there was no scope, no platform for his talents, in Dublin. He had paid special attention to reforms in Oxford and Cambridge as well as in the English Church, but his controversy was mainly directed against Episcopacy and against Ritualism, not against Popery. His quarrelsome temper at the Temple, where he preached, was already notorious, and an extant letter from him to Burghley, his patron[3], shows that he had not been appointed without careful instructions to pursue a quiet course towards the bishops in Ireland. This outlet for his activity being foreclosed, he seems to have been quite unable to find any scope for missionary labours among the Roman Catholics. Either they understood not his English, or they would not come to his preaching.

How the College gradually outlived these initial difficulties, how it attracted not only the sons of the English plantation, but those of the Irish gentlemen left as tenants upon their estates, will be narrated in the following chapters.

[1] Cf. the evidence in 1603-6 in the S. P. *esp.* 169 *sq.*, and 1591, pp. 489-502, for Miler Magrath's Essay.
[2] S. P., 1591, p. 449.　　　　　　　　[3] ibid., 1591, No. 50.

CHAPTER II

THE FOUNDING OF THE COLLEGE

THE long conflict concerning the transformation of S. Patrick's Cathedral into an Irish University came to a conclusion with the retirement and disgrace of Perrot, its hottest advocate. Loftus and his party had the satisfaction of discrediting all the proposals of their adversary, and this solution of the question, which had for forty years seemed the most practical and probable, and had old traditions to support it, was finally abandoned. But if the ecclesiastics of S. Patrick's saved their incomes, what was to be done for the endowment of the new University, which all desired? To expect any liberal grant from the queen was out of the question; fair words and a charter, which cost nothing, might be obtained. Under these circumstances it seems to have occurred to a group of earnest citizens, of whom the clerics had been educated at Cambridge and abroad, that they would make a beginning by any means, and trust to the future for larger support. Of these men, Archdeacon Henry Ussher (afterwards Primate) and the Rev. Luke Challoner are to us the most prominent, the former in being the agent sent to Court to persuade the queen; the latter, by his constant labour and care of the growing College, and by subsequent missions to England, so much so, that he was justly considered the real founder by the men of his day. Archbishop Loftus helped by making speeches, and gave the dignity of his name to the College by posing as its first Provost; but he neither

THE FOUNDING OF THE COLLEGE

actually governed the society nor contributed more than a decent thankoffering (£100) for the profits he had retained in S. Patrick's. No sooner was the building inhabited, and its academic life begun, than he retired with the queen's licence in favour of the first acting Provost—Travers.

The real founders worked upon three distinct lines. In the first place they procured a Charter from the queen, upon the political plea that the youth of the country were now going in numbers to be educated abroad, in Spain, France, and Flanders, and coming home imbued with Popery and disloyalty. Moreover, they satisfied the queen on a second point. They had persuaded the city of Dublin to grant them a convenient site—the disused and ruinous monastery of All Hallowes, of which the lands were let to citizens on short leases as orchards or gardens. Thirdly, they moved the Irish Lord Deputy and Council to promote a public subscription throughout Ireland for the erection of the new buildings. Recent historians have put in the forefront the influence of Archbishop Loftus as another efficient cause. The reader will already have learned that the contemporary documents do not justify that opinion. His influence was very strong negatively, in resisting another scheme; he deserves no further credit in the matter. What he had to say may be read in the report of one of his speeches given in Stubbs' Appendix II. It was addressed to people more zealous than himself in the cause. His argument is a mixture of Puritan piety and worldliness such as his portraits, and his voluminous correspondence in the State Papers of the day, would lead us to expect.

The three real moments in the foundation are worthy of detailed attention.

We have four documents bearing directly upon the subject. The earliest seems to be the speech of the Archbishop, urging, under many religious ornaments, the material benefit to the city of such a foundation, and how all the trades would profit by it, and asking them to call a Common Council to give practical effect to his views. This the city did not do; for the speech is dated soon after the Quarter Sessions of St. John Baptist (June 24th), and therefore at least six months before the Corporation took any action, except that they sent over Archdeacon Henry Ussher to Court, to ascertain the wishes of the queen. Most historians say he was "employed by Loftus" to do so; the facts that the Charter mentions the petition as Ussher's, and that the Corporation absolutely ignore Loftus, are sufficient to disprove that assumption. On December 29, 1591, the Queen issued a letter[1] to the Lord Deputy and Council, authorising them to erect and make the Corporation of a College, similar to those at Oxford and Cambridge, and with licence to receive and hold such property as might be bestowed by pious persons, up to £400 per annum.

The preamble is what concerns us now.

"Whereas by your Letters we perceive that the Mayor and Citizens of Dublin are very well disposed to grant the scite of Allhallows, &c., of the yearly value of £20, whereby knowledge and civility might be increased by the instruction of our people there, whereof many have usually heretofore used to travel into France, Italy, and Spain to get learning in such foreign Universities, whereby they have been infected with poperie and other ill qualities, &c., and also we perceive that the said Mayor and citizens and divers others there are well inclined to give some maintenance of livelihood—to readers and scholars in the said College."

Such is the substance of the letter. There follows, "on the 4th Friday after 25th December," 1591, Edmund Devenish being mayor, this modest but momentous resolution of the Corporation :—

"Forasmuch as there is in this Assembly by certayne well-disposed persons peticõn preferred, declaring many good and effectual per-suacions to move our furtherance for setting upp and erecting a Colledge for the bringinge upp of yeouth in lerning, whereof we,

---

[1] Stubbs, Appendix III.

THE FOUNDING OF THE COLLEGE 63

having a good lyking do, as farr as in us lyeth, herby agree and order that the scite of All Hallowes and the parkes thereof shalbe wholly gyven for the erecōn of a Colledge there ; and withall we require that we may have conference with the preferrers of the said peticōn to conclude how the same shalbe fynished." [1]

The ignoring of Archbishop Loftus and his speeches seems to me something like a deliberate slap in the face to this dignitary. The old book of Benefactions in the College Library is equally explicit in ignoring Loftus. "In the 34th year of Queen Eliz. *by the motion and procurement of Luke Challoner, D.D.,* there was a free grant made by the city of Dublin of the precincts, &c., of All Hallowes."

The next item is the actual Charter of Elizabeth, now in the College archives, dated March 3rd, 34 Eliz. (1591, old style). It is printed at the opening of the College Statutes, and is therefore accessible to any reader.[2] In the preamble Henry Ussher's petition is mentioned, but there is no allusion to foreign and Papist colleges.

The most interesting and peculiar feature in this Charter is undoubtedly the description of the College as *the Mother of an University*, with the provisions which depend upon this notion. It has been a matter of recent controversy [3] whether the University of Dublin is distinct from Trinity College—indeed, whether it exists at all. For while some hold that it is the primary body, ranking above its only College, others hold that

---

[1] Gilbert's *Records of Dublin City*, ii. 240. The editor having added in a note that this text is partly obliterated, I examined the parchment roll among the muniments of the city, and found on it, not without emotion, the MS. of the resolution, not partly obliterated, but faint, and difficult to read on account of a deep brown stain on the parchment. Gilbert's great experience of such MSS. had enabled him to decipher it accurately, as any student can now verify.

[2] Also in Morrin's Calendar.

[3] Cf. the pamphlet (1902) of Dr. Walsh, Roman Catholic Archbishop of Dublin, wherein he strongly advocates the distinct nature of the College and the University against an adversary supposed to be inspired by the Jesuits. The view given in the text supersedes the exclusive character of the rival arguments.

the University is merely the creature of Trinity College, called for shortness' sake the University of Dublin. The intention of the original Charter is, however, quite plain. As the first College was to depend upon the charity of pious and liberal men for its endowment, it would have been premature and mischievous to speak of the foundation of other Colleges. So long therefore as Trinity College should remain the only College, it was expedient, nay necessary, that the Charter should confer upon it all the rights and privileges of an University. Not only were the Provost and fellows of the College therefore empowered to elect all College officers from the Provost down, so soon as the first holders named in the Charter vacated their places, but the same body was empowered to perform all University acts; to arrange and carry out all the exercises necessary for obtaining degrees in the various Faculties; and even to appoint a Chancellor, Vice-Chancellor, and Proctors for this purpose. The only body beyond the control of the College was the original Board ot seven Visitors, consisting of the Chancellor (or Vice-Chancellor), the Archbishop of Dublin, the Bishop of Meath, the Vice-Treasurer, the Treasurer at War, the Chief Justice of the Common Pleas, and the Mayor of Dublin. Thus all the ordinary University business was handed over to the Provost and fellows of the College. The College seal was affixed to all University documents. The appointment of a Chancellor (*e.g.* that of the Duke of Ormond in 1645) is done by a decree signed by the Provost and Senior Fellows and with the College seal. All the testimoniums for degrees to this day are similarly signed and sealed. Though the Chancellor and Proctors are the proper University officers who perform the solemn conferring of degrees, their names do not appear on any of these documents, except that the Senior Proctor, almost always a Senior Fellow, puts this title after his signature on the testimonium. But were he not a Senior Fellow, which is quite possible and legal, he would never be

THE FOUNDING OF THE COLLEGE 65

mentioned thereon, any more than the Chancellor. So long, therefore, as the College founded by Elizabeth remains alone, it exercises all the functions of an University, as the preamble of the letters patent of James I. in granting it Parliamentary representation, recites : *Quum sit atque habeatur Universitas.*

On the other hand the obvious example of Oxford and Cambridge must have suggested to the founders that in course of time more Colleges would be added. Several attempts to do so were made[1] at various times, and none of the men that made this proposal for a moment thought that such a thing was unconstitutional or impossible. But they all must have known that no new arrangement could be made without the surrender of the Charter of Queen Elizabeth, and the abolition of the clauses giving all the appointments of University officers to the Provost and fellows of the Mother College.[2]

The other point of interest in this Charter is that it orders all the property of the College to be free for ever from all taxes, tallages, cesses, subsidies, exactions, compositions, or demands whatsoever, either in time of peace or war. The grant of the city, to which we now proceed, concludes with a similar clause freeing the College on their part from all such burdens, with the proviso that this freedom from taxes to the city holds good so long only as the Provost, fellows, and scholars devote their life to letters and study. The last clause guards against the liberality of the city being diverted to objects other than education.

The actual grant of the site and gardens is dated July 21, 1592. The duplicate, which should be among the College archives, has disappeared. The copy belonging to the Corpora-

---

[1] It is to be noted that the new houses actually established were not called Colleges, but *Halls*, inasmuch as they had no independent Charters, and their heads and lecturers were appointed by the Provost and fellows of Trinity College. The College was also liable for debts of these Halls to tradesmen for their supplies.

[2] This appears plainly enough in the controversies of 1612-13, to be noticed hereafter.

tion is still extant among their documents, where I consulted it. This very formal document gives the dimensions of the site, &c., the bounding properties, and appoints an attorney to make over the legal possession to the attorney of the College. The mayor was Thomas Smyth, who also laid the foundation stone on the 13th of March following. It is strange how the historians have insisted on putting this date one year too early, and Stubbs even says that they anticipated the completion of the legal documents. It is even more absurd to say that they should lay their foundation stone, which implies architect's plans and estimates, before the Charter signed March 3rd could have been in their hands more than one or two days, if at all. For the ordinary journey from London to Dublin required, with favourable weather, eight or ten days. Smyth came into office March 25, 1592, the first day of that year, old style; it was therefore at the very end of the year (March 13, 1592), that he must have laid the foundation stone. The fact that the period January 1st to March 25th is counted by some modern writers as the end, by others as the beginning of the year, causes constant confusion. The dates, as I have arranged them, are at all events consistent, and leave from March 13, 1592, to January 9th, near the end of 1593—that is to say, a period of ten months—for the sufficient completion of the building to be occupied by the new society. The legend recorded by Fuller, that during the building it never rained in the day, so that not a moment was lost, shows that the Dublin people were enthusiastic about the enterprise, and possibly Lord Deputy Fitzwilliam set his coat-of-arms over the gate,[1] just as the second Duke of Ormond's (when Lord Lieutenant) was set over the main door of the Royal Hospital, Kilmainham.

[1] This is Fuller's statement (*Church Hist.*, p. 211), I suppose from hearsay, and is in itself unlikely. There is in the Library a handsome stone with the arms of Elizabeth carved upon it in deep relief, and very suitable to set in such a place. A vague but credible tradition asserts that this is the very shield mistaken for FitzWilliam's.

THE FOUNDING OF THE COLLEGE

But with what funds was the College built? This brings us to the third moment of importance in the foundation. The queen had only given a Charter full of fair words, with permission to hold and acquire property. Probably she would never have done so had she thought that the College would eventually cost her public money. The Corporation of Dublin had given a valuable site, estimated at £20 per annum (perhaps worth £150 at our value of money), but which is presently estimated by the College at £40, by the Jesuits at £80 per annum. Whence did the funds come for the first erection of the College?

So far as Dublin was concerned, it was certain that many citizens would subscribe, and there is an entry in the Records,[1] that the mayor and Council desired to confer with the promoters of the College regarding the collection of money for the building. To the counties, or rather to the baronies in each county, the Lord Deputy Fitzwilliam and Council sent a circular letter (printed in Todd's *University Calendar* for 1833, p. 29 *sq.*), to which several of the answers are extant. We have in an early and incomplete copy of the book of Benefactions (now in the Library) a list of the first donors— high officials of the Crown and representatives of the Barony collections. Fitzwilliam, though accused of stinginess and grasping in his administration, gave £200; Loftus, who was appointed the first Provost, £100—Norreys, Bingham, St. Leger, and Gardiner gave liberally, but these are not the interesting features of the list. In the first place two great Irish chieftains who hardly spoke English contributed—Sir Turlough O'Neill, £100, and Sir Hugh McGuinnis, with the gentlemen of his county (Down), £140, besides the gentlemen of the barony of Lecale (also in Down), £59. The latter case is explained from the character of the old chieftain, who was very Anglophil in policy, so much so that he put on English dress, no doubt to his dire inconvenience, on Sundays and

---

[1] Gilbert, ii. p. 253.

holy days. Sir Turlough Luinagh O'Neill was the uncle of Tyrone, and at constant strife with him regarding his claims to be *the O'Neill*. He depended, and with some success, upon the English Government to maintain him in this rivalry, and he had even obtained from it a division of the lands claimed by the O'Neill, paying a small rent to his dangerous nephew. His £100 was therefore clearly a benevolence to the Protestant party, and also to Burghley, the Chancellor of the new University. A remarkable piece of liberality, which I can only explain from the character of the donor, is £100, £20 a year *durante vita*, and £10 a year for ever (for the support of a scholar) from Francis (afterwards Sir Francis) Shane, an Irish gentleman of Connaught, but a sound Protestant and loyalist, often officially commended (S. P., 1600, pp. 75, 293). It shows at all events another instance of what has been stated in the first chapter, that through the wildest parts of Ireland there was sporadic civilisation even among the lesser gentry.

But what shall we all say to the absence from the list of all the bishops except Dublin, Armagh, and Meath, and of the clergy, except those of Meath? Some of them were very poor, but in the case of the Sees of Cashel and Cork this cannot have been the case. It is very significant that in his " Book drawn and delivered to Fitzwilliam " by Barnabe Rich about reforms in Ireland, there is very severe censure of the reformed clergy for great sloth, negligence, &c. He adds, "*If they stana against the erecting of an University* for the good of the nation, they were only acting in their own selfish and ignorant interests, and so far wisely." He evidently believed they were opposed to enlightenment, like their Popish predecessors, but he cites no facts. The gaps in the present collection, and the proposed draft (to be discussed hereafter) about printing the Bible in Irish, are at least in harmony with his view.[1] Drogheda subscribes £40, but Waterford, Cork, Kilkenny,

---

[1] S. P., 1589, p 182. This Book, 19 pp. long, is only indexed in the S. P. The original in the English Record Office is vol. cxliv. No. 35.

THE FOUNDING OF THE COLLEGE

nothing. It has been mentioned already that Miler Magrath, and Donnellan of Tuam, ignore the new College in their correspondence at this time. Very likely the call for subscriptions may have been the real reason of this deliberate ignorance. The Pale, excepting Drogheda and the clergy of Meath, seem to have given nothing. Taaffe, in the barony of Louth (in Co. Louth), says curtly that the gentry are too poor. As this was on the northern boundary of the Pale, and constantly under heavy requisitions for the troops serving in Ulster, the excuse seems a valid one, but we have already seen that Jesuit influences were at work, which dreaded the new College and which were certainly directed to prevent the gentry from helping so Protestant a foundation.

The list of subscriptions we have amounts to £2,047, and is incomplete, as Dr. Stubbs has observed. Even the original list of benefactors set up in the Chapel was defective, for there is a letter extant from Matthew Holmes[1] complaining that the names of the Connaught gentlemen, who had been very liberal, were not there enumerated. Perhaps the most remarkable gap in the list is that of individual subscribers from among the undertakers whom Elizabeth had planted in Munster in 1588, for whose sons the new College must have been particularly important. We should have been glad to see the names of Edmund Spenser and Sir William Herbert, and other such men of known culture, in the list; but so far as we know, except for the item of £100 from the province of Munster, advanced by Norreys, these undertakers show no interest in the matter.

If the City of Dublin only appears for a sum of £27 in the list, we must remember that individual citizens gave liberally, and that many may have contributed to the building in giving materials, and service of their workpeople. Those that rented part of the lands of the old Abbey seem to have surrendered their leases voluntarily, and some of these leases are still in the Muniment Room of the College. One very remarkable item

[1] Cf. Appendix IV. to this chapter.

in these contributions has been wholly ignored by the historians, or else, I believe, falsely described. There is a letter, dated March 14, 1592, from Challoner, Lee, and Money (Launcelot Monie) to Burghley concerning the cashing of bills given by captains serving in Ireland.[1] We learn from a subsequent letter in 1594,[2] that this money was then not yet realised. The gift amounted to £623 in bills. There is no evidence of its being obtained till we come to an entry in the old Book of Benefactions, which states :—

"In the year 1601 there was a contribution made by several persons of quality, and especially souldiers and officers then in H.M. service (the names of whom lie on record in the College books)[3] which being collected *then* by SIR JAMES CAROLL, Knt., receiver of H.M's. money in the Exchequer, came to about £700, and was to be disbursed for books for a Library, which was done accordingly."

This gift has been misrepresented by Dr. Bernard, in his funeral sermon on Ussher (London, 1656) in this way : "Not long after the defeat at Kinsale, the officers and commanders of the army gave at once £1,800 to buy books for a Library for the College at Dublin." The money was laid out by Challoner and Ussher. This again has been modified into the story that the army at Kinsale subscribed from the loot of the conquered Spaniards £1,800 to found a Library in the College. The Rev. Dr. Bernard, for a long time private chaplain to Ussher, ought to be a sound authority, yet he is clearly inaccurate. The sum he names is more than double that given, according to the Book of Benefactions; this is his first clear inaccuracy. In the next place, as the siege of Kinsale was not over till February, 1601 (old style), it is impossible that any such subscription could have been made, and made known within a month. Late in 1602 would therefore have been the earliest possible date for such a gift. But there is besides an argument *ex silentio*, which I think conclusive. We have two most minute histories of the siege of Kinsale, and the sub-

---

[1] S. P., 1592, p. 81.   [2] ibid., p. 248.   [3] Now lost.

sequent events, written by Stafford, the private secretary of Sir G. Carew—his *Hibernia Pacata*—and by Fynes Moryson, the private secretary of Mountjoy. We hear every detail from day to day, we have numerous documents printed, and nothing is omitted which redounds to the credit of either of these heroes in Irish history. In neither book is there one allusion mentioning this curious and interesting munificence. A MS. oration, intended for Mountjoy's reception in the College in 1601, still among its MSS., observes the same silence. Mountjoy especially was a lover of books, and might readily have promoted such a gift among his soldiers, but most certainly not with profound silence on the part of his panegyrist. The story, therefore, is to be rejected. The facts are that officers serving in Ireland in 1591 subscribed from the pay due to them in bills a sum amounting to £623 for the purpose of a Library. The money was difficult to realise, and several attempts failed. At last Sir James Carroll, a man who had money dealings with the College for thirty years, got the money paid when Vice-Treasurer, but not till 1601. The Library-room being ready,[1] it was applied as the donors had intended, to the purchase of books.

With the earlier subvention—about £2,000—and we must remember that the sum represents at least eight times as much in value as it would now—the College was so far completed in January near the end of 1593 (old style) as to be occupied, without any opening ceremony, so far as we know. The nominal Provost, Archbishop Loftus, of course, did not desert his palace at S. Sepulchre's and come into residence. Probably the reason of his appointment was that of economy. He could afford to take the post without salary. But if so, he did no practical work. Provost Hely Hutchinson, in his MS. history, notes particularly that Loftus did not even draw up

---

[1] Travers (1593) speaks of the room as finished, and of course there must have been some books there from the beginning to educate scholars such as James Ussher.

statutes for the management of the new College—a necessary duty, one would think, for the first Provost to undertake. When the Society had been five months in existence, he resigned his post to Walter Travers, the first real Provost. It is from the latter that we have the earliest, alas! too brief, description of the appearance of the College as he found it. But we must first reproduce in imagination the site and its surroundings.

The old Monastery of All Hallowes stood on the sandy, but not swampy, flat bordering the Liffey, nearly half a mile to the sea side (east) of Dublin City. The nearest point of the city was the Castle wall and Dame's Gate, both protected by a fosse, supplied by the River Poddle, which ran round the wall (the present Ship Street) and then to the Liffey near the present Essex or Grattan Bridge, where the old Custom House stood. Between the city gate and the monastery lay one of the commons of the city—Hoggen Green, not so called from the many swine that grazed there, but from the Hogges, or mounds, of ancient date, which were situated on the first hump of higher ground now covered by the houses between College Green and Suffolk Street. This was afterwards a favourite site for a gentleman's residence, and was occupied in turn by several notable people. But as yet there were no buildings between the city and All Hallowes except a ruined S. Andrew's Church, close to, but outside, the Castle, south of the Green, and used as a stable by the Lord Deputy.[1]

I understand the whole condition of this suburb quite differently from Gilbert, if, indeed, he had any definite picture in

---

[1] There had also been the Monastery of the Holy Trinity, the General College for all the friars of S. Augustine throughout Ireland, which the *Monasticon Hibernicum* (ii. p. 77), places on the site of the present Crow Street on the water side of Hoggen Green. I believe that location to be wrong, for there is no trace of the buildings in Speed's map (1610), and Tyrrell's Park, which is often mentioned at this time, was about Grafton Street and Molesworth Street. Now Walter Tyrrell had been granted this monastery by Henry VIII.

his mind.¹ When the citizen came out of Dame's Gate and desired to travel eastward, he found indeed before him the open common of Hoggen Green, but no roadway through it, its east end being barred by the buildings and precincts of All Hallowes. He must therefore choose one of two routes, either along the river, the course of the present Fleet Street, which led to Lazar Hill (the present Townsend Street), and so to the mouth of the Dodder, which he would cross in a boat (as we now do), to reach Ringsend, and in so doing he would leave the steeple and gate of the monastery, facing north, on his right; or he would keep to the south of the Green along the higher ground now marked by Chancery Lane and Suffolk Street, which brought him to the famous S. Patrick's Well (still existing under Nassau Street in the Fellows' Garden). Hither the whole population of Dublin made pilgrimage on the Saint's day, and the bushes about it were bedizened with rags and other votive offerings to thank S. Patrick for some wonderful cure—offerings of small material, but often great sentimental, value, like the widow's two mites, that made a farthing. On their way to this holy place the populace had to cross a marshy place known as "the bog," in front of the south corner of the present façade of the College; for here a stream draining the swamps of S. Stephen's Green, and running down the present Grafton Street, was stayed upon reaching the flat ground, and was crossed by a causey (*chaussée*) of large stones.² This rivulet, which now runs underground, crossed Hoggen Green in front of the present gate, and made its way to the Liffey. It is complained of (in Gilbert's City Records) that the swine feeding on the Green used to lie in this water, known as "the ditches," and interfere with the spawning of the fish which came into it from the Liffey. The steeple of the monastery and the gate faced the river and the road which ran by along its banks. This steeple was preserved as affording a feature in the view from the city, or a landmark for ships

¹ I refer to his *History of the City of Dublin*.   ² M. R., D 49, a and b.

coming up from the sea, and upstairs in it was the porter's lodge of the College beside or over the gate, which likewise faced north. The west front apparently possessed no public entrance, in spite of Speed's map, which seems to give one. This can be proved, I think, from documents to be cited hereafter.[1]

From the porter's lodge there was a varied and beautiful prospect in every direction. Looking due west across the Green, the city rose steep from Dame's Gate, the towers of the Castle and of the Cathedral of Christchurch dominating the lesser buildings. Across the river the tower of S. Michan's Church marked the centre of the old Danish settlement, Oxmantown, on the north side of the river. Nearer on that side were the large buildings of S. Mary's Abbey, still a hostelry, where distinguished visitors were received. Then the eye wandered to the gentle slopes leading north, and round to the woods of Clontarf, and its flat shore, the scene of Brian Boroihme's last battle. Howth was in sight, and on this side of the river Ringsend and Irishtown, with its massive church tower. Then to the south-east came the fair slopes above Merrion, and beyond them Dalkey and the Killiney hills. All was there barren or wild country; for behind them to the south lay the high moors still known as the Dublin mountains, where wild Irish tribes defied the law, and often raided the farms close to Dublin, lifting cattle and burning houses. For

---

[1] The early accounts in the Particular Book, which contain constant items for the mending of locks, specify (34b) "the dore next the sea," which I take to be "the great gate" (28, 30b), the back gate eastward (28), but also "the gate towards the city" (31), which would naturally be interpreted as a west entrance. But this was merely a back-door for carts, the main gate being through or beside the steeple, which was at the western end of the north wall of the enclosure. It is also to be noted in Speed's map that there were surrounding walls at some distance from the actual buildings, and that the entrances through these are distinct from the great doors of the College. "The great door at the stair's foot" (32b) is spoken of—"for mendinge of lockes of ye great gate, hall dore, and mendinge ye great key—24s." (30b). These references are from Provost Alvey's accounts. Cf. also Appendix II. to Chap. V.

THE FOUNDING OF THE COLLEGE

the country behind was as yet no shire, nor had it yet been brought within the pale of the English law as the county of Wicklow. Even now much of this moor district, more fit for a deer forest than anything else, is as lonely and wild as any part of Ireland. The many beauties for which the Bay of Dublin is not sufficiently renowned, were, in the absence of all houses near the new College, visible from any vantage-ground.

But the buildings were by no means equal to their fine surroundings. The monastery had been ruinous, and was all demolished but the tower; there was also a cemetery there, wherein an Earl of Kildare had been buried, which disappears without leaving a trace beyond its mention in the city's gift. Of the new buildings we hear only brief, and not very clear, descriptions. Dr. Stubbs (pp. 11–12) gives an account drawn from sources which he does not specify, and in which some details seem to be wrong. The most trustworthy piece of evidence we possess is the letter written by Walter Travers to Burghley shortly after his arrival in Dublin. As this letter has only been indexed in the State Papers[1] and printed by Mr. Urwick in his little-known pamphlet (p. 19), the reader will be glad to see the text (omitting complimentary jargon), which affords matter for much commentary :—

"Right Hon. It may please your good L^{d}ship to understande that uppon my arrivall here and the deliverie of your favourable l^{rs} on my behalf to my Ld Chancellor [Loftus] it pleased His Lo^p that I should remayne in the new College. Soone after resyninge his place of being Provost [which he did the 5th of June] by his L^p order I was chosen to succeede to that place. By reason whereof beside the common charge of the House I am appointed there to read a latin lecture in Divinity in the tearme tyme. For my mayntenance in dooinge of these duties it is promised that I shall be allowed 40$^{li.}$ yearly, all which comforts as I acknowledge nexte unto God to come unto me by your L^{ps}

---

[1] Ireland, vol. clxxv. No. 50.

honourable l^{rs} and favour, so my care shalbe, God willing, which I hope, to approve myself in all good duties right thankfull to your L^p for the same. In which duties I know your L^p most requireth my chief care shalbe in the maintenence of the godly peace of the Church, to perform with quietness the things that belong to my service, without just cause of offence to any, and with as much fruite to all, especially those whom my labour doe most respecte, as by any means I may be able to perform. Thus much having written . . . I crave pardon, in a few more lines, to certifye the state of this new Colledge. Beinge a quadrant of bricks of 3 storeys, and on every side within the court, it is 120 feet broad, the west side which is of chambers, and the north side wherein are the Chapell, hall, buttery and kitchen, are orderly fynished. The other two sides are only walles, saving some little beginninge of chambers, which for want of further meanes, is yet unperfect.[1] If the whole were fynished, it would conveniently lodge 200 scholars and 20 fellows. Of assured perpetuitie it hath 40^l a yeare, whereof the chiefe parte are 16^l, which is raised of the grounds about the Colledge, given by the citye with the seate thereof, and 10^l is the gift of Mr. Shane, a gentleman of Conaght. Thus farre I presume to satisfy your L^p of our poore and harde beginninges."

He goes on to support the petition of the College, sent by the same messenger, and dated like this August 15, 1594. The petition (printed in Appendix V.) adds only two facts—that "the College was now inhabited and furnished with some number of students these seven months," and that up to this time not £2,000 of the money subscribed had yet been received. We fortunately discover from his further petition for sustenance in 1597 [2] that the number of residents to be supported

---

[1] The description of *Anon.*, p, 67, whose authority Stubbs follows, adds *a library with a gallery*. This writer also assumes from the beginning a second court to the west of the original quadrangle. Neither of these are mentioned by Travers, but may have been in building during his Provostship. I have not yet found the original authority for this description, independent of Traver's letter. Sir E. Trevor, in a letter recommending his brother-in-law, Robert Ussher, for the Provostship (S. P., 1629, p. 218) states that the east block of this quadrangle was built by his father, Henry Ussher, at an expense of £300. This fact appears nowhere among the Benefactions.

[2] Muniment Room, box F. No. 11.

were the Provost, three fellows, ten scholars, and two servants. Such were the modest beginnings of our great House.

But we will adjourn the question of finance, at no time an agreeable subject for the reader, till we have endeavoured to appreciate the actual society at this moment assembled within the walls. For walls there must have been, unless the students were confined to the inside of the quadrangle, and we find frequent items in the accounts showing that the old walls of the monastery were being constantly repaired. Outside lay orchards very tempting to youths who were very poorly and scantily fed. It is to be observed that the list of fellows and scholars named in the Charter had already undergone modifications, and that of the original fellows all did not reside and work within the College. The account of the receipts and disbursements of the College from January 9, 1593, its first inhabitation, to Christmas, 1595, audited by Ware, tells us that neither Henry Ussher (appointed in 1595 Primate) nor L. Monie, who signs a letter to Burghley on March 14, 1592–3, along with Henry Lee and Challoner, as a fellow, had accounts with the College. Daniell, who was named a scholar in the Charter, appears as a fellow, or at least with larger receipts and disbursements than the rest, and senior to Fullerton and Hamilton, to whom at Christmas, 1595, *two whole years of wages* are due ; so these two had been elected fellows at the outset. But, strangest of all, Challoner's name is wholly absent from this account, though the Provost heads it with his, and the butler, Roger Parker, concludes it with his. It seems to me that as Challoner had undertaken to supply the College from his farm with meat, corn, &c., he could not appear in the account before us as dispensing College money. Yet the first Provost, Loftus, being non-resident, the chief man, often called master of the College, was this Luke Challoner, a man of learning and piety, and a " man of special note here in Ireland,"[1] whose character we shall discuss hereafter. We may

[1] As Temple writes, *Anon.*, p. 113.

presume that his books, which he freely lent,[1] were the best means given to James Ussher, then a scholar, to begin his portentous accumulation of learning. The next in importance, though not nominated in the Charter, were the two Scotchmen who had settled in Dublin—James Fullerton as schoolmaster, and Jas. Hamilton as his assistant—elected immediately after the foundation. As Henry Ussher, among the original fellows, had experience of Oxford and of Paris, so these men had Scottish traditions, and introduced into the nascent society that variety of social qualifications for which it is still remarkable. The way in which Bingham, in a letter, speaks of their intimate knowledge of Scotch affairs [2] suggests that they were no mere schoolmasters, and the promotion which both attained under the new king corroborates these hints. Of Fullerton's promotion we shall speak hereafter. Hamilton is far better known to us, being the business man employed by the College in external affairs, and sent to Tuam and to York in their employ. In later years we shall again find him deeply concerned with the College estates.

Neither of these seems to us a learned man or an educator, but both men of the world, and evidently of social condition fit for courts and public affairs. The rest of the original teaching staff and scholars is only known to us by its connection with the Church of Ireland. Not to speak of James Ussher, William Daniell, afterwards Archbishop of Tuam, has already been mentioned in the first chapter as a "painful preacher of the Gospel." Of his lighter moments, and of those of other students who received promotion in the Church, we unfor-

[1] Cf. the article on the College Library (and Challoner) in *Hermathena* for 1902.

[2] S. P., 1599, p. 449; but the information probably dates from 1595, when Hamilton was in Connaught on College business; also in 1598 (S. P., p. 339) Bingham, then in Dublin, assures the queen that the rebels are supplied with men and powder from Scotland, "which by conference had with a couple of Scottish gentlemen, which are of the College here, I could allege good reason for."

tunately know nothing. For these lighter moments were few, and all sports much discouraged in the education of that day. The scheme for a northern University, to be made out of the endowments and buildings of Ripon, which was promoted by the queen of James I. (Anne of Denmark), and, like the similar attempt on S. Patrick's, was defeated, gives us in curious detail the regulations then thought proper to control a student's life. Every quarter of an hour, from 5 a.m. till bedtime, is to be accounted for, and of these only one, that immediately after supper, is to be allowed for the recreation of conversation.[1] At all meals (as is still the case in Roman Catholic Colleges) a chapter from the Vulgate was read. Similar regulations were observed in Trinity College. It was a great crime to keep a hawk, for in that day hawking was a very aristocratic sport, and no country produced better " tassel gentles," " passengers," &c., than Ireland. The State Papers teem with letters accompanying gifts of these birds to Burghley, Walsingham, Robert Cecil, and others from Ireland. Perrot was presented by the Irish chiefs with dozens of them in token of their affection. From all absence of any mention of a day's hawking near Dublin (before FitzWilliam) I conclude that though the birds were plentiful and excellent, and there was no want of game, Irish chiefs did not indulge in the sport, while in England every great person did. But we do hear that Lord Howth came to hunt the fox with de Bathe at Drumcondra, that Lord Deputy Russell and his wife, then at the Hospital of Kilmainham, their summer residence, went down to the river to see fish, presumably salmon, caught, and went to hunt the wolf towards Tallaght; they also went a-hawking.[2]

[1] That these strict notions still survive I learned from a curious experience when I was inspecting Irish schools in 1881. Coming to a large boarding-school in Belfast, I asked the Principal (since a Roman Catholic bishop) where was the playground. He looked at me with some astonishment. "What do they want with a playground?" said he. "Don't they come here to work, and not to play?"

[2] C. P., iii. 245, 249.

Possibly the youth in Trinity College had no antecedent training in these amusements, for Travers, in the earliest petition for money quoted by Hely Hutchinson, says: (August 18, 1594): "As for any maintenance to be hoped for from the better sort of this kingdom, so small is their affection towards that work, by reason of their backwardness in religion, as they will not so much as send their children thither; and for the poorer sort, who might prove good and profitable instruments in this Church and Commonwealth, there is no maintenance." So then there was no great number of aristocratic, and therefore sporting, youths at the College to distract the rest from their diligence.

It would be a matter of interest to know what was the average cost of living in the new College, and what fees were paid by students. But in the early College accounts, preserved in the *Particular Book* of the College, the only fees paid to the College are the so-called *detriments*[1] (which now figure as Decrements), and which amounted to 2s. 6d. per quarter for undergraduates and 5s. for fellow commoners (and graduates). As there are only two of the latter in a list of forty-six students paying in the years 1605 and 1606, this source of income must be regarded as very small. The fees for degrees appear somewhat large in proportion, and they were doubtless, as was the case afterwards, divided between the Vice-Chancellor, Proctors, and Bedell. Moreover, at the earliest Commencements (Commemorations) formally recorded, Dr. Challoner disbursed for the gowns of six masters £17 0s. 3d., and for three gowns or sophisters £3 6s., though we cannot explain why gowns should be required for sophisters at Commencements.

The first intention of the foundation was to support fellows and scholars, and educate the latter free of charge. But it must always have been contemplated that other students should come to the College at their own charges, and so we

[1] Detriments is still the Cambridge term, corresponding to Decrements at Oxford, and means the money paid for the wear and tear of the House, but also, in the *Particular Book*, the same money paid out for necessaries.

THE FOUNDING OF THE COLLEGE

find that the bursar, Hamilton, receives between October 9, 1598, and November 1, 1599, £43 2s. 2d. for the pensioner's commons;[1] and in Temple's time (1620) there were "fourteen fellow commoners and pensioners, and sixteen other students, the sons of settlers in Ireland." It is also to be noted that the detriments due to the College were received not only through the fellows (as tutors), but also through the cook and the manciple. In the first instance it appears that pensioners (or their guardians) gave a bond, varying in amount, to the College (in one instance it amounts to £20) by way of caution money that they would remain in the College, and submit to all lawful conditions, till they took their M.A. degree. Such bonds made to Challoner, as "master of the College," are still in the Muniment Room. The strange fact remains, that there is no formal provision (perhaps prepayment of commons fund was sufficient security) for pensioners dining regularly in the hall. In all old Colleges commons was a sort of parade, and evidence of *bonâ-fide* residence. The very small salaries of the fellows must be explained by their receiving, in addition, tutorial fees, but this was a private matter between tutor and pupil, and does not appear in the College accounts. I imagine that the amount of these fees was only theoretically fixed, and varied according to the student's means.

I find no mention of chamber rent, unless the solitary item paid by Mr. Mullinex, probably a fellow commoner,[2] may be such, and a solitary entry makes such a matter of no value. When we arrive at the end of the next Provostship, at the close of the years of scarceness and the advent of Provost Temple, I shall revert to this subject.

Diligent search has only been rewarded by finding one inchoate tutor's account, that of Ambrose Ussher with five

---

[1] Par. Book, p. 6. In the accounts of 1596-7 [Mun. Room, B4 and B6] I find sums paid for the commons and for the sizings of Dawson, Hamblett, Kinge, and perhaps another, which show that there were pensioners from the beginning.

[2] M. R., B., 7 *verso*, line 6.

pupils, probably his whole chamber, in 1605. The sum received in trust for each of the five is given, but the detailed accounts of expenditure for each, being probably sent to the parents, are missing in four cases. In the fifth the name of the student, beginning with a Mac, was erased in every case, and the very Irish name Gemrean superscribed. This was probably the cause of its preservation, for I assume that the careful and neat tutor could not tolerate to send out such an erasure in a formal document, that he sent out a clean copy of the account, and that this remained as a rough draught in his possession. The account is so curious in many ways, that I print it in an appendix (II.) to this chapter. Here for the first time a tutor's fee of 10s. appears, paid at entrance, but the period it covered is not stated.

We are better informed concerning the theological temper of the place, not only from the well-known characters of the earliest teachers and scholars, but from the controversies carried on by the early Provosts and the causes which led to their appointments. We must remember that the cautious Burghley (Chancellor) was the guiding spirit at this time, and that no appointment to the Provostship was made except by his direction, though the election of their head lay nominally with the fellows. His action towards Trinity College shows clearly that while taking strongly the Protestant side against Popery, which latter he knew to be the great danger to England, he was not afraid of those anti-monarchical tendencies in Puritanism which showed themselves so strongly in the next reign. His first practical appointment was that of Walter Travers.

By the kindness of the Master of Christ's College, Cambridge (Dr. Peile), I am able to give some dates and details of Travers's early life, which are not in the histories. As he matriculated at Christ's College, December 14, 1560, and is set down as *imp(uber)*, he must then have been under fourteen; the earliest age the Master finds noted, and rarely, is ten! He was pro-

THE FOUNDING OF THE COLLEGE

bably therefore twelve or thirteen, born about 1547. He migrated to Trinity, from which he got his A.B. in 1565, his M.A. 1569. He got his B.D. and incorporated at Oxford 1576. He was therefore a man under fifty, but not by many years, when appointed Provost.

The only historian of the College who has said a word concerning the character or Travers worth reading is Mr. Urwick. He, approaching this history from the Nonconformist side, saw at once that a distinct policy had animated the first Chancellor, and that the early Provosts, who had always been noted as Cambridge men, were rather to be noted for being strong Puritans. Lord Burghley must have been very determined in this way of thinking, seeing that he employed Travers as tutor for his son Robert. He did not, so far as I know, enter into the controversy between the extreme Protestants and the Anglican Church party, but his constant efforts to obtain for the former a fair hearing,[1] and his appointments, show plainly where his sympathies lay. Travers had shown himself an obstinate and ungovernable man as a fellow of Trinity College, Cambridge, according to the overbearing Whitgift, then Master. He had left the College and gone to Antwerp, where he was ordained by a synod of twelve ministers and "almost the same number" of elders on May 14, 1578;[2] he had also visited Geneva, the hotbed of Calvinism, and was the author of two remarkable books, intended for the reading of the queen and Council—the one is an elaborate reply (1583) to the plea of a Romanist advocate for toleration of that creed in

---

[1] In Brook's *History of the Puritans* there are numerous cases of appeals to him as Chancellor against the tyranny of the bishops or Vice-Chancellors, and temperate letters from him advising moderation to them.

[2] The document is given by Brook, *Hist. of the Puritans*, ii. 314, and is of importance because the validity of this ordination was afterwards questioned by the High Church bishops. His reply, that as they admitted the Orders of the Church of Rome, with which they were not in communion, they might well admit those of the Reformed Churches on the Continent, was a pertinent answer, but not likely to satisfy Whitgift. Hooker, in his reply to Travers, did not dispute this point.

England ; the other concerning the reform of Anglican Church government. The former takes the side of Protestantism generally against Popery, and not only answers the usual attacks upon the Reformers, as the authors of ecclesiastical novelties, at variance among themselves, but carries the war into the enemy's camp, and argues that no genuine Papist (owing to the Bulls issued by the Pope) can logically be a loyal citizen to the English queen, and must therefore be treated as constructively guilty of treason. But though he is very ready to deplore the influence of that Church upon the ceremonies and discipline of the Church of England, he is himself a striking example how far the early Reformers had breathed in from the atmosphere of the Roman Church that haughty spirit which claims to be the only exponent of the truth of God and insists on imposing its creed upon all dissentients. So long as any creed in that day was in the minority, or on the weaker side, it cries out against the intolerance of its oppressor. No sooner do political circumstances give it power than it persecutes like all the rest. A great part of Travers's tract, if we substitute the word Protestant for Papist, might have been penned by Philip II. of Spain.

Much more interesting and important is his earlier book on the true discipline of the Church (1574), written in very classical (though not impeccable) Latin, with great richness of illustration from Greek and Roman literature, and presently translated by his friend Cartwright and printed (but suppressed) at Cambridge, and afterwards at Rochelle. In the other work he had defended Protestantism as such against the Church of Rome ; he had advocated its doctrines as in spirit, if not in the letter, an uniform and consistent protest ; he had classed Luther, Melanchthon, and Calvin together as of equal importance in proclaiming the reformed faith. But now he directs his arguments against the Anglican Church, and shows that, having adopted the *doctrines* of the Reformation, they had not been bold enough to cast off the *discipline* of the Church of

Rome—the extravagant powers and pretensions of bishops, their claims to the exclusive right of ordination, their assumption of political power, their secular offices, the pluralities of the clergy, not to speak of the laymen holding emoluments and power in every diocese.[1]

If we concede to him that we have in the Bible, Old Testament as well as New, the actual word of God, and that we should revert to it exclusively from the various aberrations of the Mediæval Church, his argument is very logical and convincing. If we further regard the Protestant upheaval not as a Reformation, but as a Revolution, we shall be disposed to agree with most of what he says. He rejects the whole canon law, the whole system of bishops, and of their powers both secular and spiritual, and divides his clergy into Doctors, whose duty it is to explain the Scriptures; Pastors, who are to teach the flock, pray with them and administer the Sacrament; Deacons, who are to watch the property of the Church, and the distribution of alms; a Presbytery, or council of elders, who with the clergy are to have the power of inflicting penalties for offences against the law of God. In an appendix (III.) to this chapter I have given specimens of his Latin style and way of thinking. He concludes by saying that he binds himself, even with a bond, to God and the Church, that no zeal, labour, or diligence of his will be wanting to aid this reformation. If it be granted to him to see it, that will be the happiest moment of his life; if not, he will at least rejoice in having kept its image in his mind, and will console his longing by the example of David and of Ezechiel, whose condition in this matter was not unlike his own.

[1] This book was written four years before his ordination, and printed at Rochelle; an early English translation printed at Cambridge was seized and destroyed by the Vice-Chancellor, with Archbishop Whitgift's strong approval. It was the translation found among Cartwright's papers after his death, which was printed by order of Parliament in 1644, and as the authority for the Discipline substituted for the Prayer Book (cf. Brook, *Hist. Pur.*, ii. 314).

This was the man whom, after being silenced by Archbishop Whitgift in 1586, Burghley recommended to the election of the fellows in 1594. What he had been doing in the interval I have not discovered. He was possibly an old College friend of Loftus,[1] probably of Challoner, perhaps also of Henry Ussher, and these men, all of them of the serious type of Low Churchmen then at Cambridge, may have suggested to Burghley what agreed with his own sentiments. We have many notes for sermons of Challoner still extant; his assiduous and "painful" preaching, and the almost incredible number of his sermons, show clearly that he held the Puritan view of the superior importance of preaching as compared with reading the liturgy.[2]

At all events Travers, this uncompromising and almost turbulent Presbyterian, lives in Trinity College and lectures daily in Divinity, without suffering complaint, or making complaint, of others. We know[3] that he preached before the Lord Deputy Russell on April 4, 1596, and certainly gave no offence. He was a man of zeal and great learning, not only in theology, but in languages, and was James Ussher's master in these things.[4] For the latter was then a

[1] The speech of Loftus commending his election, which is quoted by Mr. Urwick (p. 18), does not sound to me like the speech of an old personal friend. "I am further moved to think well of him, as knowing him to be a person of many solid excellences, and to be much approved of," &c.

[2] There are in the Library notebooks of Challoner containing the abstracts of many of his sermons. They are all on Puritan lines. He had not only Travers, after his appointment, but also Mr. (Humphrey) Fen, a notorious and controversial Puritan, to help him in his preaching. There are notes of Travers' sermons (Coll. Libr. MS.), apparently taken by James Ussher, but exceedingly hard to read. Ussher's persistent defence of Episcopacy in later life was evidently his recoil against the extreme Puritan teaching he received in his youth.

[3] C. P., iii. 244.

[4] The zeal for learning, and the importance attributed to it, are features marking the early Puritans, in contrast to the Puritans of our day. As may be seen in Brook's History, they are always courting open conferences and theological discussions with the most learned prelates, in presence of the great political lords, and in these discussions, and in their many con-

THE FOUNDING OF THE COLLEGE

scholar of the House, and beginning his theological studies. It is no rash inference to say that the complexion of Ussher's theology, the Evangelical character of his teaching, the utter distaste he shows for High Church practices, were all results of the influence of Travers. We may even go further and say that to the group of Puritans, who trained the first generation of the reformed clergy in Ireland, is due the permanent Low Church character of this branch of the Anglican communion. The rule of Lord Strafford and of Provost Chappell was too brief to enforce, and too high-handed to induce, the formation of any opposite school.

The first difficulty, however, that faced Travers on his appointment was not the opposition of tyrannical bishops, but the vulgar demands of the flesh. The College was built, its education inaugurated, but no means had been provided for the daily sustenance of the Society. What were the best means of relieving this distress? At the moment official circles in Ireland were excited by the proceedings of Richard Boyle, who was nominally engaged in hunting out, in Munster, lands concealed from the Crown's possession, and therefore not producing their lawful rent to the queen, really in carving out for himself and his patrons an estate from these lands, which were always made over to the discoverer for a Crown rent far below their value. But Boyle was apparently succeeding too well, and had enemies. Wallop and Gardiner persuaded the Lord Deputy to seize his trunk (with all his papers) and imprison him. Of this his friends Weston, Napper, and St. Leger complain, to which the other side retort that St. Leger is a confederate, and is proving concealed lands in Munster for himself.[1]

---

troversial writings they show themselves accomplished scholars. The great majority of the prominent men among them had been fellows of Colleges at Cambridge, many also at Oxford.

[1] S. P., 1594, pp. 254-5, 264 and 1596, p. 76, in which Wallop and Gardiner recommend to Burghley Sir Francis Shane (the benefactor of the College) for "his services in discovering the great deceits of the

It is obvious that this case, being much discussed in June, 1594, and by Sir Francis Shane, suggested to the College the petition to obtain £100 per annum from such concealed lands.[1]

But it very soon became clear to the College that they had been badly advised in looking for a prompt and secure income from concealments. The first practical result of which we are informed was the granting to them (on April 4, 1595) of the *Custodium* of the temporalities of the archbishopric of Tuam, left vacant by the death of William Lally. In doing this Bingham had regard, no doubt, to the suspicious character of the Archbishop, who, like his co-prelate, Miler Magrath, was a mere Irishman, and a lukewarm Protestant, temporising with the Roman Catholics, though at the same time a married man, and likely to provide for his family out of his See. It was more than likely that during the vacancy much of the episcopal property would be concealed, and not found by his successor. Hence the policy of having this matter at once attended to by a foreign body, whose interest it was to ascertain the full value of the Archbishop's tithes and rents. We have the actual letters patent, and, moreover, a long correspondence

substitute-escheator Boyle, the deputy-surveyor Rupstock, and their confederates." I will add another notice from December, 1597 (S. P., p. 473). Gardiner and Wallop attribute much of the national discontent to the continual searching after, and granting of, concealed lands, which is "not the least motive of so general a rebellion. The great practiser—this word was then always used in a bad sense—in these cases is one Boyle, who is not yet dealt with, because to avoid danger he continues in prison for execution of debts of good value." The agent of St. Leger for this work was one Newman (cf. S. P., 1597, p. 312).

[1] The text will be found in Appendix V. The bearer was to be Henry Lee, one of the fellows. (It is strange that this man's name is omitted from the list of the earliest fellows, in Alvey's hand, in the Partic. Book) To this the favourable answer is the document printed vii. in Stubbs' Appendix (but misdated 1595). The following clause in the document points to the angry discussions upon Boyle's case. "But because it hath lately appeared to H.M. that in passing such concealments in that country many disorders and abuses have been committed by conveying into the books such particulars as were unfit to be passed, &c., &c., so she straightly enjoineth that there be great care and regard had of the par-

THE FOUNDING OF THE COLLEGE 89

with and from Hamilton, who was sent down as the agent of the College to collect the rents due in May. This grant was evidently Bingham's practical response to Burghley's letter. Hamilton found Lally's widow and son in possession; he finds the Dean and the Archdeacon of Tuam, and endeavours, with the help of some local agents, to realise this property. But of course every kind of difficulty was set in his way: no one would buy distrained cattle; no one had ever paid any rent; no one would keep an appointment; in autumn a new archbishop was appointed, and the temporalities restored to him the day after his consecration. Possibly the obtaining of this Custodium had raised great hopes in the College; it may have been on paper a considerable sum, could it have been realised, but this failure showed the College that prompter means must be adopted to escape from positive destitution, and so they address on August 16, 1595, when the failure at Tuam became manifest, a new and different application to the State. They disclose their reasons in a letter to Sir R. Bingham,[1] in which they purpose to change their suit from

---

ticulars to be chosen and passed in the book of the College." It is dated the last of September, 1594. The formal document follows, dated 17th of October in the same year (Stubbs, App. ix.), and a Commission was issued 28th of November to inquire into the concealed lands found by the College (Ibid., App. x.). In order to smooth over difficulties Burghley had written a personal letter, dated 7th of October, to Sir R. Napper (Chief Baron) and Sir R. Bingham (President of Connaught) to assist the College, on account of their having the best knowledge of lands in Connaught, and directing that in cases not yet legally transferred the College should receive provisionally a Custodium of the lands (Stubbs, App. viii.) in order to relieve their distress. The novelty in this document is that Burghley mentions Challoner and Daniell, and not Henry Lee, as having brought the petition to London. It is followed up by the queen's letter of October 17, 1594 (Stubbs, App. ix.) The last document of this year seems to be the petition of the Provost and Fellows, that as they foresee long delays in finding out the concealments, and they are not men of business, they may be satisfied from the documents found in Mr. Boyle's trunk (Stubbs, App. xi.). The copy in the Muniment Room is not dated, but is probably from the end of 1594, or early in 1595.

[1] Stubbs, Appendix v.

one for *concealed* lands into one for *attainted* lands, and pray for his advice and support in so doing.[1]

This new suit is supported by letters from the Lord Deputy and Council both to Burghley and to the English Privy Council,[2] dated August 16, 1595.

The distinction was evidently of great importance from a practical point of view, though of course both classes of land were often confused, for no land was so likely to be concealed as outlying parts of a property attainted. But in the case of attainted property the previous owner was known and his rights abolished by law, whereas in the case of concealments the ownership was doubtful, and even after the grant some lawful possessor might bring an action of ejectment against the College for illegal description and occupation of his land.

There was some delay in the queen's response to this application for attainted lands, and meanwhile the college was so destitute that upon their renewed petition to the Irish Government the Lord Deputy and Council granted them for temporary relief a clear and definite income of "£100 sterling, to be paid unto them quarterly out of such Casualties as either are or shalbe due unto H.M.," and to continue until the one-half of the previous grant shall be realised.[3] This order is dated December 1, 1596, nearly a year after the previous correspondence.

Meanwhile the College had appointed private agents to seek out and report to them attainted or concealed lands—not a pleasant duty or one likely to be undertaken by a humane man. For whatever the legal rights might be—and they were often full of uncertainty—there were in most cases occupiers whom

---

[1] This letter is dated August 7, 1595. Accurately speaking, the suit was changed from one for concealed lands, and failing them attainted lands, into one for attainted lands, and failing them concealments. It is, however, evident that the first-named source is in each case regarded as the real point of the application.

[2] Stubbs, Appendix vi. [3] ibid., xii.

years of possession had led to believe they would be undisturbed. Men of the moral type of Richard Boyle were, however, easily to be found, and we have the legal instrument appointing Patrick Crosbie,[1] gent., of Maryborough, to do this dirty work upon very favourable conditions. But the existing letters patent specified only lands "concealed and unlawfully detained from us," and doubts seem to have arisen whether this phrase would include attainted lands.

This doubt is solved in favour of the College by letters dated May 7, Eliz. xxxix. (1597), and in the same year follows the first real and solid grant of the queen to the College. By it two large estates—the one in Kerry, part of the lands of Gerald, Earl of Desmond, attainted ; the other in Limerick, and in Kerry, the estate of Brian O'Conor, attainted—as well as many small parcels of concealed lands scattered over all the counties of Munster—were granted to the College for ever for a head rent of £24 10s. 9d. Taking this at the ordinary rate of 2d. per acre, we find it about 3,000 acres, and at 1s. per acre profit would produce more than the £100 which the College desired. The queen, however, specially desires that in measurements and estimates the College shall not be exactly but liberally treated, and this was certainly done, for thus the College acquired a property which, with the increasing prosperity of the times and the change in prices, has risen to several thousands per annum. The letter of the 7th of May was supplemented by one on the 17th of May (Stubbs, xiv. B) to the Irish Council, giving facilities for the prompt realising of the grant. But in acknowledgment of a clause in these letters exhorting them "that such careful respect herein shall be had by you for the discerning of the said parcels there, as no inconvenience or offence shall grow thereby to any of H.M.

[1] The other men so employed were Nich. Kenney and Wm. Hussey. Letters from all three to Fullerton, then Bursar, are in *Anon.*, pp. 34 *sq*. That from Kenney gives a very clear view of the situation. Crosbie (or Crossan), a native, who became an important English agent, is severely criticised in S. P., 1600, p. 298. He was put in charge of the young Earl of Desmond on his return ; cf. S. P., 1600, pp. 141, 486.

subjects in that land,"[1] we have a circular sent out on September 21, 1597, by the College to all the former owners or occupiers of the lands now granted by the queen.[2] This very interesting document shows how far the agents of the College had endeavoured to conciliate the occupiers. These are now promised undisturbed possession, provided they will pay the rent due and come to Dublin to make out the necessary legal documents securing the College as owner and themselves as tenants under lease. Strange to say, very few of these occupiers were English settlers arising out of the plantation of Munster in 1588. Probably the speculators had, contrary to the conditions of the plantation, let lands, which they falsely claimed, to Irish tenants, whose tenure was therefore doubly illegal. Such Irish occupiers would find it a direct gain to show the College agents that the lands on which they lived were really concealed from the Crown and claimed by the undertakers under no proper title; for then the grant to the College and a re-grant from it would secure the natives in their possession. The names of the people to whom the College reconveyed the estates, reserving a head rent, and the bonds (of which many are extant) under which these (practically middlemen) were compelled to make leases to the actual occupiers, not only show that the College was almost wholly concerned with the native Irish, but that the grant of these lands must have been a very great boon to the native population. In many cases the rival claims of several cousins, or of brothers, were settled by the recognition of one and the protection as tenants of the rest. It was by such negotiations that we can explain the apparently friendly intercourse between such men as Patrick Crosbie and the country people. We do not hear of any conflicts or of any acts of violence in this whole transaction.[3]

[1] Stubbs, Appendix xiv. C.   [2] ibid., Appendix xv.
[3] There are in the Muniment Rooms letters recommending Crosbie to the Munster authorities, and several letters from him which show that there

These natural conjectures are fully verified by extant correspondence.[1] It is quite plain from these papers that the College had four classes of people to deal with—(1) the English undertakers of 1588, who had of course laid claim to various outlying pieces of land not in their original grants; (2) the smaller Irish proprietors who, though they paid various exactions to Desmond while he enforced a kind of suzerainty over most of Cork and Kerry, were really owners on old and often provable titles, and who should not have been ousted on his attainder; (3) the actual tenants, almost all Irish, who occupied the land and paid rent to the absentee undertakers or to the smaller Irish landlords; (4) rival seekers of concealments, who in their own or other people's interests would offer easier terms, or seek to jostle the College out of its claims by any intrigue. Of these last Boyle was evidently the most active and dangerous.

By this long and perhaps tedious commentary I have brought into historical sequence the very important series of documents printed in confused order, and with inaccurate dates, in Stubbs' Appendix. But there still remain a few which I have kept apart, as they belong to another order of grant. Had the country remained at peace, had the College agents in 1596 and 1597 been able to collect any or large proportion of rents, all might have been well. But Tyrone's rebellion, smouldering for some years, burst into flame and soon began to affect the west and south of Ireland, even before 1598, at which date the Munster undertakers were swept out of the country with fire and sword. This state of war indeed justified the queen in new attainders, and removed any odium

were difficulties and differences, but of an amicable kind. It is remarkable that here Fullerton is the correspondent for the College, and Hamilton takes no part, probably because Fullerton was then Bursar.

[1] Which *Anon.*, pp. 34 *sq.*, has rescued from oblivion, with the addition of one important document remaining in a modern transcript among the papers in the M. R. (and now catalogued Box C, 6 c). Cf. Appendix to the Chapter.

from the College of having participated in the spoils taken from undoubted rebels; but for the collecting of rents it was an impossible condition. There are extant receipts to Challoner for six years' rent, not paid till 1604,[1] when the war was over.

Under these circumstances we do not wonder that the College, in spite of its now considerable but only nominal endowment, applied to the Lords Justices in 1597 (closer date not given) to make some further allowance and to pay in advance some of the Concordatum of £100, otherwise they threaten to leave the house and let others who have private means take up the education of the youth.[2] There follows a statement of their yearly income and outlay, wherein it appears that they had, in addition to the rent of their gardens and sundry benevolences from good citizens, got a lease of some land in Baggotrath (now beside Upper Baggot Street near the canal bridge) for two years, and had bought a part of George Isham's grant. In reply to this petition the Irish Government granted from the money supplied for the army in Ireland a physician's pay, £40 a year, six dead pays, £72 6s., and a canonier's, £104—in all £214 per annum —which the queen not only confirmed, but added £200 from casualties, so that the income of the College from Government salaries now amounted to £524. This was, of course, intended only as a temporary help till the Provost and fellows had tided over their debts and come into receipt of their rents. But seeing that a war was still raging, that there was constant outcry from the generals against the starving of the army in supplies, the concession seems very liberal.

By these means, and with much other private help of which we know no details, the young Society was able to weather

---

[1] *E.g.*, M. R., E 16. Receipt to John Oge Pierce, of Ballymackequem, for 6½ years rent of the land he holds from the College in Kerry, from Michaelmas, 1597, to Easter, 1604 viz., £11 6s. 6d. (Signed) Lucas Challoner, James Ussher, Abell Walsh, John Richardson.

[2] Stubbs, Appendix xiv. A.

out the years of war and famine with which the reign of Elizabeth in Ireland came to its gloomy close.

Long before the College had emerged from this financial crisis Travers had visited his old patron, Burghley, and begged to be relieved of his office. The Chancellor accordingly writes on May 22, 1597, to the Lord Deputy[1] as follows: "And whereas Mr. Travers, the bearer of this my l^r, hath declared unto me that he hath a desire to leave his place in that Colledge and bestow himself here in England as he shall have means to be employed in the Ministry, because he doth find he cannot have his health there in that land, I do pray your lop^s that after his place shall be furnished with a fit and sufficient man, &c., he may be dismissed." And so, without noise or quarrel, and with the formal approval of the College, this once prominent man retires (October 10, 1598) into England and obscurity, wherein he lived on at least twenty-seven years. Ussher kept up his friendship with him and offered him aid, which he declined. His Oriental books, which were valuable, and £50 worth of plate he left, not to his Dublin College, but to Sion College in London. The causes of this eclipse and disappearance of Travers are nowhere stated, beyond the plea of ill-health, which certainly did not prevent longevity. But he and his fellows had often preferred even imprisonment to any deserting of their duty. There is no sign of any theological difference with his fellows—nay rather, the appointment of another strong Puritan to succeed him shows that his doctrine was acceptable to the College.

We cannot but conjecture that he was one of that myriad band of confident English reformers who come to Ireland with the intention of setting everything right, and who find the problems, which they expected promptly to solve, gradually growing in difficulty and ultimately insoluble. Travers had spoken out vigorously (in his book on Church discipline) against the abuses of English Universities and the necessities

[1] Stubbs, xiv. C.

of reform ; he had, so far as we know, no active opposition to his views in Dublin, yet he leaves in less than five years, apparently conscious of his failure. It remains for us to consider what the Irishmen who stuck to the ship had been doing, and what was the condition of things inside the College, during these anxious years of storm and stress in Ireland. But for this purpose we have but the evidence of a few scanty and often enigmatical Bursar's accounts and some stray notices in the *Particular Book*.

The general state of Ireland had been growing worse and worse every year. At the moment when Travers retired the rebels were in possession of most of the country. In December, 1598, the queen writes to her Irish Council that she hears even the suburbs of Dublin are unsafe for her Privy Councillors. The enemy had in November burnt Dunboyne, "within six miles [?] of Dublin," and ravaged the country round about it without hindrance. In the following January they burnt Kilmainham and Crumlin, close by the city. They even broke into the bawn of S. Patrick's and stole the cows of the archbishop's tenants in Patrick Street, yet Captains Stafford and Atherton dare not sally out, for want of sufficient horse and because the townsmen were not to be trusted.[1] And if this was close to Dublin in 1598; it had been so in remoter districts ever since the end of 1595. In June, 1599,[2] things had gone so far that "there is gone out of the Lord Chancellor's house" (*i.e.*, S. Sepulchre's by S. Patrick's) "this last night eight of his servants to the enemy." Well might Captains Stafford and Atherton hesitate to pursue an enemy outside when such was the condition within. Of course, the hindrances to obtaining money which we have already detailed

---

[1] It appears from the Registry that on May 20th in this year the Concordatum of £100 was voted to the Provost to repay the debt due to him ; whether he lent the College money or whether his salary was in arrear is not told us. In S. P., 1598, are letters of commendation of the Provost, sent by Loftus and Fenton, viz., pp. 282-3, 387, 403, 416, 419.

[2] S. P., p. 67.

THE FOUNDING OF THE COLLEGE

must have been accompanied by like hindrances to obtain ng pupils. As Kilmainham and the liberty of S. Patrick's were not safe from the Irish, we begin to wonder how Trinity College itself, further from the city and without defences, escaped. Its poverty was its security. The closes and fields beside it were set as orchards and vegetable gardens and not grazed by cattle. Had the latter been the case it is not likely that they would have escaped a visitation. Most of the students must have been sons of Dublin citizens, and in case of urgency could be withdrawn to their homes within the walls of the city.

In the small list of names in early accounts, there is not a single clearly Irish name, except that of Francis Shane, or M'Shane, the Protestant supporter of the College in Connaught. All the rest seem distinctly Anglo-Irish or English people. We do not hear of any question yet about teaching the Irish language, except that one of the earliest printers, William Kearney, was kept for a time in the College, and that successful attempts were made to have the Book of Common Prayer and the New Testament translated for the benefit of the natives. Two documents, now printed by Mr. Dix,[1] show that a few people were anxious to instruct the Irish people in the Protestant creed intelligently or at least intelligibly, and there were many parsons, once unreformed priests, throughout the country who could not, even if they would, read the service in English. Of the original fellows we know that Henry Ussher could speak Irish, so could the scholar elected in his place, afterwards sent to preach in Irish to the people of Galway, William Daniell (translator of the New Testament). But as for the rest, Challoner and James Ussher, Fullerton and Hamilton—Dublin men or Scotch men —they show no knowledge of Irish; regarding Monie and George Lee we have no information, and they seem not to

[1] Cf. his interesting pamphlet called "The Earliest Dublin Printing," pp. 26, 28.

have been occupied in teaching. Even the monasteries of the Pale had made it their strong point to instruct whomsoever they did instruct in the English tongue and manners; it is therefore almost certain that no mention of Irish was made, and that no part of the original programme recognised it in any way.[1]

There is no reason to suppose that the general rising under Tyrone affected the students in the College, beyond reducing their number, and probably curtailing their fare. The dearth of 1595 was such that the cost of provisions was increased by £40, in an average outlay of £200 in all, on the items of bread and beer alone. The threat that the Society must break up for want of sustenance can hardly have failed to make them all sad and gloomy. From this time on till the end of the war (1602) we have hardly an old paper left. There was no Provost for some years resident, and the whole outlook was extremely dark. Yet it was in those years that James Ussher was building up the great structure of his learning. He had access to plenty of books, either Challoner's or Travers', and those in the incipient College Library.[2] He probably paid as little attention to the turmoil of the outer world as Hegel did, when he was finishing his *Phenomenology* amid the thunder of Napoleon's cannon about Jena. But concerning all these matters, which make history to be alive, we have only conjectures. Private correspondence there seems to

[1] It is worth noting, in the face of recent developments, that the Roman Catholic "Royal College of Maynooth" travelled much further in the same direction. For the first one hundred years of its existence Irish studies were there neglected and despised. That is manifest from the Centenary volume published by Bishop Healy in 1895, *in which Irish studies at the College are hardly mentioned*, and from the evidence of many old Maynooth men to me in private conversation. If that volume had been compiled seven years later, would this silence have been observed?

[2] Cf. the little catalogue of 1600, printed in my article on the Library in *Hermathena* xxviii. The lending of books by Challoner to him is also shown in the same article.

be none. Public letters are of course occupied with public affairs. The most careful search through the State Papers only produces for us an occasional hint, a mere breath, of the feelings and habits of the average citizen of Dublin in these days. The records of the Corporation give us only the Acts of the city as such, and nothing of social interest. The solitary fact, that two students persistently and violently quarrelling were compelled to sit in the stocks all the time of supper, in the hall, and are threatened with expulsion upon another offence, is quoted by all the historians. The Fellows' Garden was then an orchard let to a man who kept it in order, but in the mud wall separating it from the College there was a door, to which the fellows had keys. The constant mendings of locks and keys, and of breaches in the surrounding walls, which appear in the accounts, point to a good deal of license, and to difficulties in keeping order.

APPENDIX I. (A

A Scheme for the Endowment of a University to be erected in Dublin, from the funds of the late suppressed Cathedral Church of St. Patrick, &c., by George [Browne,] Archbishop of Dublin.—[1547.]

(Reprinted from E. P. Shirley's *Original Letters*, No. II.)

A DEVICE or peticion framed by th'archebysshop of Dubliñ for an Uniūsitie to be founded and erected in Irland wth a playne declaration howe the same maye be easilie doōn by the King^s Matie to the great glorie of God, his Ma^{ty} honor^r and immortall remembrance, and the spedier reducem^t of the people there to a due obedience and acknowledging of their duties in that behalf.

ffyrst where the Cathedrall churche of Saint Patricks beside Dublin hathe of late been suppressed and dissolued, That the same Cathedrall Churche may be erected agayne and established for ever, together w^t all the howses appteyneng and lyeng coõmodiously abowte it, and therof a faire and lardge colledge to be made, for the fyrst planting of an uniūsitie there, and there to be placed a certaine nombr̄ of felowes to be contynwall students (in all discipline necessarie) and so in tyme and by degrees convenient to growe to be prechers.

Secondarilie that for the better pceding in all good litterature of the saide students and others that shall repaire to the saide universitie for learneng, there may be found ppetuallie to endure ffowre ordynary lectours to be instytuted & erected, One of the Latten tongue, another of the Greke tongue, the thirde of Cyvīll Lawe, and the iiijth of Dyvinitie, and of theis the fyrst ij to be read euȳ working day^e in terme tyme, The other ij thrise in the wick, that is to saye, Mondaye, Wednisdaie, and frydaye, the Dyvinitie lecto^r, and on Tuisdaie Thursdaie and Saturnday the Cyvīll lawe.

Itm̄ euȳ sondaie and feastefull daie throughowte the yere one sermoñ to be preached in the saide Colledge Churche by the dyvinitie reader or one other of the felowes of the Colledge being a devyne, or by some other godlie mañ to be therunto admitted by the Master and Seniors of the said Colledge, or by th'archebysshop̄ there for the tyme being.

Itm̄ that where as Christechurche standeth w^{t}in the Cittie, that the Dean and Mynistres therof maye be transferred to serve god at the saide Colledg, ffor there is rowme ynoughe for theym all, and where the Kings Matie is nowe charged w^t lxvii^{li} yerely owte of his g^{cs} cofers for mayntennce of certaine prestes and coristors in Christechurche, the same may be releued and resumed w^t an honest portion of the tempalties of the said Christechurche to the Kings Ma^{ts} use, appointing to the Dean and felowes nowe being there sufficient lyvings and salaries to serve in the said Colledge to be erected, during their lyves.

Itm̄, that the Churche nowe called Saint Patricks may be named the Churche of Holy Trynitie and the Colledge to be called Christes Colledge of the fundacioñ of King Edwarde the Sixt &c.

Sixt, that theis benefices folowing may be annexed to the saide Uniūsitie for the fynding of the forsaide Lectours, ffyrst the psonage of Trym̄, the psonage of Armulgh, the psonage of Rathewere, the psonage of Callañ, the wardenship of Yougȟil, the psonage of Dungarvan, and a lector to be kept apon th'archedeaconry of Mythe for ever, and that the M^r of the Colledge do pay to euȳ of the readers xl^{li} yerely.

Itm̄, that towardes the com̄ens of the saide Colledge and studentes maye be applied all and singuler suche portions and allowñncs as ded belonge to foure pety canons and xvi^{ten} vycars afore the suppression of Saint Patrichs aforsaid and the com̄ens of the churche whiche w^t the benefics abouenamed will suffice; wherin is to be noted that of the same benefices the kings Matie is patrone of Rathe-

THE FOUNDING OF THE COLLEGE 101

were, Ardmulghan and Roslare, my lorde of Ormonde patrone of Callane, The Bysshop of Mythe patrone of Trym̄, and the Kinges Maiestie in possession of Dungarvan̄, th'erle of Desmond patrone of the wardenship of Youghill.

Itm̄, the kings Ma^{rs} moste gratious lr̄es tenderlie to be directed to the lordes and bysshoppes of Irland that they will helpe w^t some other more psonages & benefic̄s to be applied and annexed to and for the better indowem^t and mayntenñce of the saide un̄iusitie.

Itm̄, That com̄ission under the kings great seall here maye be directed to suche as to his hieghnis shalbe thoght good, ad audiendas et terminandas causas eccl̄iasticas, to th'intent that thereby the people may be occasioned to leave and omitt the popishe trede, whiche many of them now imbraseth, and also to swere all bysshoppes and preistes to the obedience of the Kings maiestie and his successou^{rs} as their immediate hed and goūno^r under god and for th'executio˜ of other his Ma^{ts} p̄cedings according th'order used in Inglande.

Itm̄, That twoo Archedeacōns of Dublin̄ may be againe restored to ayde and assist th'archebysshop there for the tyme being whiche was taken awaie at the supp˜ssion of Saint Patricks, and this the rather that there is no bysshop in Christendome w^{t}owte an archedeacon, but onely Dublin̄, and so the saide Archebysshop the wors hable to supplie his chardg who had befor the saide supp˜sion ij Archedecons.

In margin [they to finde ij lectours.]

Itm̄, That now immediately may be sent thither iij to be Bysshoppes and to preche, eūy one of theym to have a sufficient lyving to th'intent that neither they throughe default or lyving be bordenous to any pson, and yet may withoute that care most diligently and ernestly travaill in setting forthe to the people by an uniforme doctryne the words of god and the Chry^{tian} p̄ceding^s of the Kinges Matie as it is here in Inglande.

Itm̄ that th'archebysshop of Dublin and certaine others may be incorporated by the kings charto^r to receyve to th'use of the saide uniũsitie as well all the saide landes tents Rectories and hereditam^{ts} to be gyven therto for the maynten̄ñce of the same by the kinges Matie as by all other lordes and bysshopes that woll depte w^t any thing for that p˜pose, the statute of Mortemayn̄ not withstanding.

Itm̄, that the Dean, dignities and p̄bendaries of Christechurche in Dublin upon theire translacion to the saide churche of the trinitie besides Dublin may be incorporated by suche name as shall pleas the king^s Matie w^t honest lyvinges to them apointed having a chapiter and coēnseall to assist th'archebisshop̄ for the tyme being, in comen mattirs as the Kings lawes shall p̣mytt.

Thys may an noble Uniūsitie be founded for an immortall memory of the kings hieghnis, and to his maiesties no great charge, so that his graces com̄ᵃndemᵗ may goo withall unto the lordes and bysshopes of Irlande that eūy of them̄ truelie and faithfully put to their good aide and help for the saide uniūsitie to be erected in Dublin as a place of all other in Irland moste p̣pir for the same.

Itm̄, that a cōmissiō be nowe directed to resume in to the Kings Maᵗˢ handes all colledges fre chapels and chauntries wᵗin that Realme, *and that sondry free scoles may be erected upon the same for educatiō of youthe there,*[1] whiche shalbe a good augmentacion of his hieghnes Revenuez.

ffyrste for th'erecton of an unyversitie to be established wᵗʰin the Realme of Irlande by Dublin to be ther remanent for ever as well for th'encreace of gods divine s̄ʳvice as the Kings Maᵗⁱᵉˢ immortall fame, & the unspeakeable reformacōn of that realme and for edu-cacion of students & youth, whiche may from tyme to tyme growe, aswell in the knowlege of god th'autoʳ of all goodnes, wᵗʰout whom, the knowledge of the kinge, the obedience of his Lawes, shall neū be hade ther, the lacke wherof hathe been only the ruyne & decaye of that realme, and so by p̣ces of tyme the same students beynge repayred to ther natyve shyres shall by ther learnynge and goode educacion be bothe example of goode lyvinge & also a lyvely trompe to call that barbarous nacion from evill to goode, & consequently from goode to bettʳ, & so to be p̣fight & Civill.

It is thought goode that the late churche of Saynt Patricks by Dublin wᵗʰ all the houssis, mansions, orchards & gardyngˢ, whiche the late deane pʳbendaries peticanons & vicars choralls of the said late churche hade, shalbe gyven by the kingˢ Maᵗⁱᵉ to suche as the kingˢ Maᵗⁱᵉ and his mooste honorable Counsaill thinke goode, or others to be named by the deputie & Counsayll ther for & to th'use of the Chauncelorʳ or ruler of the same Unyūsitie, and the felowes therof, and the deane & felowes of the cathedrall churche and colledge there for eū, or suche other as the kinge and his Maᵗⁱᵉˢ Counsaill shall thynke mete & convenyent.

Item, for the establishinge of a Deane & chapiter ther, it may passe well, that the deane and felowes of the Cathedrall Churche of the blessed Trinitie of Dublin be translated to the said late Churche of Saynt patricks, ther to cōtynue wᵗʰ ther lyvingˢ for ever, for the bettʳ mayntennce of gods devyne S̄ʳvyce ther.

---

[1] Erased.

THE FOUNDING OF THE COLLEGE 103

Item, for asmyche as the Chauntries there, ar yett undissolved, & that th'incumbents therof make spoile of the same as in yevinge lesses of them for so many yeris, as in tyme nether the Kinge shall have eny ꝓfate therof, ne yet eny godlynes therby mayntened, for avoyding wherof, & for the mayntennce of the said uniūsitie, it may please his Matie to directe his highnes comyssion for dissolucōn of the same chauntries, and the revenuez therof to be applied to th'use of the saide Unyūsitie in mañ and forme folowyng.

foure lectors to be kept ther cōtynually, that is to saye, viz. the greake lector, the civill lector, phisike, and the divinitie lector, to be reade from tyme to tyme, as they are read in the Unyūsities of Oxford & Cambridge ; & that eūy of the readers of the said lectors shall have yerlie of th'essues & ꝓfits of the said chauntries xl li. and furder that upon the reaste of the yssues & ꝓficts of Chauntries ther shal be meyntened for eū˜ in the said Unyūsitie the nomb^r of ij^c students to learne the said lyball artes, receving of the said yssuyes & ꝓficts ther living^s & sustentacōn, as the thing shall extende sufficientlye for that p^rpose, & so shall his ma^{tie} haue cōtynuall Orators to pray for his highnes moost victorious & immortall fame for eū˜.

and where upon the dissolucōn of the said late cathedrall Churche, it was declared by Sr Anthony Sentleg^r then the King^s deputi^e ther, that the Kinge, his Maties pleasur was, that the said Churche should be cōuerted to a bett˜ use, viz : an unyūsitie, which myche the rather ꝓvoked the deane & felowes ther, to cōdisende to the surrend˜ therof ; therfor <u>yf it</u> mooght please the king^s Matie to graunt the Vnion of the bnfics late appending to the said Churche, to the said Unyūsitie ; thyssuy^s & ꝓficts wherof was wount to be payed in corne, & nowe dimised for mony to be payed to the King^s Maties use. The archbusshope of Dublin und˜ his chapite^r Seale & the Maio^r of Dublin und˜ his comen seale shalbe bounde to pay the K^s˜ highnes yerly according the survey therof taken, & this only because that the masters & students ther shall haue corne at a reasonable pryce for ther bett˜ mayntenaunce, not meanyng herby that eny of the p^rsent fermors of any ꝑcell of the p̄myss˜, other then suche as woll for that godly p^rpose depte wth some cōmoditie ; shalbe dampnyfied therby, but only to haue the corne after the yeris of the nowe fermors shalbe expyred in the p^rmyss.

[endorsed in Sr W. Cecils hand.]

B. of Dubly˜s
  devise for a Uniūsite.

(B) LETTER FROM ADAM LOFTUS TO CECIL.

From Shirley, *op. cit.*, No. LXXIX.

As I certeynly knowe, Right honorable, your towardnes and herty desi[re to] preserve a common place of learninge in this rude and ignorant c[ountry], so will I, (leaving all arguments of perswasion as superfluous,) procede in sheawinge myne opinion the next and readiest waye to bringe the same to perfection; only assuringe your honnor as the want thereof, hathe browght a generall disordre in this land, so the hauinge, will not only bringe godly quieatnes withe good ordre, but also ppetuall fame and praise to her highness, but commendation to your honour as to the cheefe instrument in preferringe the same; As S. Patrykes (lest charginge her highnes and readiest for that porpose) ther-for is the fittest place in the land, and as I am by her gracious liberalyte placed in the deanry, as well willinge to forder this woorke as any man els, so the olde bisshoppe, a man (yf I shall saye my opinion) as un-willinge to this, as to furder anny other our busines, to be provided for at home, and in the bisshopprike one placed as willinge faythfully to ioyne w^t me, as I w^t him, bothe we shall procure the voluntary resignation or just deprivation of all the gansayers, and placinge favorers of the matter, then folowethe the full resignation in to her highenes hands of the bisshope, the deane, and the chapter, to doo w^tall what her gracious will shall be; and as the geuinge of the prebends, w^t other thinges therunto appertayninge, is a speciall ornament of the bisshopprike, so he that shalbe placed, is warely to be delt withe-all, lest, beinge once placed for his privat profitt, this common benefite may be hinderid; for myne owne parte, as inwardly I desire to se an happy ende of this necessary woorke, so I committ my self wholy to her Matie, whos care I knowe will be suche, as I may haue where withe-all to live, more then whiche I looke not for. I have written muche of this effect to my very good lord th'erle of Lecester, and withe my worke fellowe and brother, the bisshope of Methe, haue also written to her highnes, all whos hertes I pray god to moue w^t his speciall grace effectually to take in hand this so necessary a woorke, as by whiche his glory may be fordered, and this poore cuntry relevid. Th'one of us, I meane my lord of Meathe or my selfe (wer it not for uery pouerty) had suerly c^ume our selfe, neuer to leaue, but lyke the widowe in the gospell with importune sute, tary sume ende of this matter; we haue therfor sent this younge man, whom this far I dare commend to be honest, zelous, and, for his tyme, not meanly learnid. Thus w^t my humble sute concerning my broother for the rectory of Dunboyne, that your honour will

THE FOUNDING OF THE COLLEGE

have him in remembrance, I humbly take my leave, withe one speciall request more; your honour will take good care whome you preferre to chirche promotion here. I heere saye ther is one Iohnson suithe for the bisshopprike of Ossery, of whome I beseache you, beware. from Termonfeghone this x of octobre 1565.

Your honoures assured at com̄andment,
Ad Armacħan.

To the right honourable Sir Willā
Cecile, knight, principall secre-
tare to the Quenes most excelent
maiestie.

[endorsed.]

x 8bris, 1565. Tharch b.
of Armaugh to my M^r
for the deanry of St Patricks to be ēployed for
lerḡ.

APPENDIX II.

Ambrose Ussher's Tutorial Account.

From the College Library MS. 287 (or C. 3, 5).

"A note of receipts and disbursements of money receaved and employed to the use of five students, namely: Patrick Birn, Cohonaghe Dowyn, Philip Conin, Daniel Lally, and Henry Gemrean, Dec. 9th, an. 1605:

Receaved for the use of Patrick Birn iii^l—xv^s ⎫ xxv^l—xv^s
„   „   of Cohonaghe Dowyn iii^l—v^s ⎪ current
„   „   of Philip Conin iii^l—xv^s ⎬ money
„   „   of Daniel Lally vii^l—x^s ⎪ in
„   „   of Henrie Gemrean vi^l—x^s ⎭ England

Ambrose Ussher.

Disbursed for Henrie Gemrean.

reserved for a bible ... ... viil^s—0
to his Tutor ... ... x^s—0
ffor his gowne 3½ y. at 11^s the y. bought at Mapasse
  his shoppe ... ... xxxviii^s—6^d
ffor baeyes [baize] to face the gowne 1½ y. bought in
  the same place ... ... v^s—iii^d

ffor cotten to line it	vii^s—vi^d
ffor fustian unto his dublet	xi^s—o
ffor lininge unto it	vi^s—o
ffor silke and buttons	ii^s—o
ffor a yard of cloath unto his hose all being bought in the same place	ix^s—o
ffor lining to the same	v^s—o
unto the tailor for making the apparaile	viii^s—o
ffor two payre of stockings	v^s—vi^d
ffor a payre of shoes	iii^s—o
ffor two bandes	i^s—vi^d
ffor pointg	o—vi^d
ffor a girder	i^s—o
ffor a hatt, being bought in the Castle street...	viii^s—o
ffor paper and inke	i^s—o
ffor his diet before he was admitted into commons	v^s—o
To the butler for his Entrance	i^s—o
ffor three poundes of candels	i^s—o
A table	ii^s—o
remaineth	viii^s—iii^d "

[Outside the figures is] "Summa vii^l—x^s"

The most interesting light we can throw upon this account of Ambrose Ussher is from the Statutes of Bedell printed in the appendix. The supplementary notes facing the front page are dated September, 1628, so that the body of the book must have been composed shortly after his advent as Provost in August, 1627. There is no evidence that in the interval between 1605 and 1627 there was any serious change in the expenses of living or in the fees of the students. Bedell was therefore, in all probability, setting down what had either been accepted from Temple's Statutes, or from the traditions of the College. The salaries of the Provost and officers of the College in his cap. 20 are the same as in Temple's time. Now, in the chapter (9) *de Tutorum ac Pupillorum officio*, we read : "Ac cum Tutoris officium sit multi laboris et curæ, quo alacrius et fidelius munere suo defungatur, placet, ut quivis pupillus, nisi de ipsius inopia plane et liquide constiterit, tutori suo annuum salarium gestæ tutelæ nomine persolvat pensionarius nempe et scholares Collegii sumptibus sustentati 40^s., commensales vero sociorum quatuor libellas [*i.e.*, £4]. Placet insuper ut nemo pro pupillo re et actu admittatur, priusquam tutori partem dimidiam et annui salarii pro tutela, et expensarum pro communiis faciendarum in manu [*sic*] tradiderit, neque admissus re-

THE FOUNDING OF THE COLLEGE

tineatur diutius, nisi tutori caveat tum de recta et expedita solutione debitorum et Collegio debendorum, tum (si sociorum commensalis fuerit) de calice argenteo ad usum Collegii conferendo." This statute was adopted by Laud excepting that the scholars' fee was reduced to 20s., and the clause about *argent* (still a tax on the students of some Oxford Colleges) omitted: the Provost is also distinctly permitted to hold pupils himself, if he chooses.

In the face of this statute we must assume that in Ambrose Ussher's case he was content with a quarter's tutorial pay in advance. The provisos for cases of poverty, and the wording of the Laudian statute that the tutor shall not exact more than these sums, all point to a considerable freedom in fixing the tutorial fees. The 8s. 3d. still left in Ussher's hands was ample to provide for commons for some weeks, and he may probably have accompanied his account to the parent with a demand for further supplies. At all events, five or six pupils at this rate would bring up a Junior Fellow's salary, supplemented by Lectureships at £4 per annum, to a reasonable competence in these days of little coin and modest requirements. The price of the student's clothes seems extravagantly high in proportion to the other expenses.

APPENDIX III.

Specimens of Travers' Style.

[From page 46*a* of his book entitled :

> Eccles. disciplinæ, et anglicanæ Ecclesiæ ab illa
> aberrationis, plena e verbo Dei & dilucida
> explicatio, Rupellæ, Adamus de Monte 1574.

The English translation in my possession is imprinted MDLXXIIII., but without printer or place named. For the bibliography of this famous book cf. Mullinger's *Hist. Univ. Cambridge* vol. ii.]

Quo magis turpissimi errati nostri hac in parte nos pudere debet, qui etiam ad gravissimum munus sacri ministerii indignissimos quosque patimur accedere, et cuivis sordidiori artifici e taberna sua prosilienti, aratori relicta stiva, philosophastris et grammaticastris, nihilo magis divinarum rerum peritis quam artificibus et agricolis, denique tibicinibus, citharœdis, dominorum famulis et asseclis, bubulcis, opilionibus, baiulis, qui etiam aliquando non modo indoctis, sed et contaminatæ vitæ hominibus Ecclesiæ fores aperimus, ac promiscue fere et sine discrimine doctos, indoctos, probos, improbos, dignos, indignos, ad Ecclesiæ gravissimum munus adhibemus.

Ibid., p. 111 : Nunc vero Academias otium pro labore, pro pace et honesto otio contentio bonis studiis inimicissima, pro pietate et timore Domini religionis neglectus ac pæne contemptus, et profusa quædam in omnem luxam et libidinem licentia invaserunt. Ac horreo quidem cogitare ipsas Musarum ædes tam a Musis alienas esse, et hæc spatia a forensi strepitu remota (ut liberiori animo honestis studiis vacaremus) clamoribus a turbulentis ingeniis excitatis perstrepere, et mutuis odiis, injuriis, contumeliis, vindictis perturbari, atque adeo ipsa religionis templa, aras sanctitatis, pietatis sacraria, profana fieri. Quid illos nobilissimos heroas qui amplissimis sumptibus collegia fundarunt, ut cultus Dei, vitæ sanctitas ab his fontibus in universam Ecclesiam manare possent : quid (inquam) si in unum congregati ex illa æterna domo collegia sua despicerent, dicturos esse existimamus ? Annon putamus eos apud se invicem conquesturos, collegia sua tanquam castra quædam inimicitiarum et simultatum facta esse ? et quæ illi divini mellis alvearia esse voluerunt, in iis innumeros fucos jam exortos esse, qui non modo ipsi nihil colligant, sed aliorum sedulitatem improbent, et vexare eos nunquam desinent, donec alvearibus suis pepulerunt. (apparently referring to his own expulsion from Trinity College, Cambridge).

Ibid., p. 116 (in discussing the office of Pastor) : Quod hominum salutem procurandi tam necessarium et præclarum officium atque omnino omnium quæ sub cælo sunt optimum et præstantissimum, Deus bone, quam infinitis pæne modis profanatur ! Adeo ut hodie fere nihil aliud sit pastorem ordinare, quam precum et certæ liturgiæ recitatorem et lectorem constituere. Neque vero hoc tantum fit inter plebem, sed in media Academia, in ipsis scholis et collegiis : unde tanquam a sacris quibusdam fontibus reformatio peti deberet, illinc, illinc, inquam, huic profanationis et ἀταξίας turpissima exempla manant, et in universum regnum derivantur. Si utramque Academiam perlustremus, quid gymnasium, quis doctorum hominum cœtus justum et legitimum pastorem habet ? Sed aut capellanus aliquis (ut appellant) vel etiam plures ad liturgiam certis et statis horis legendam conducuntur, aut ipsi collegiorum socii juramento astricti ad ministerium certo tempore capessendum, eam recitant. Unde etiam fit ut aliquando in eodem collegio decem vel duodecim ejusmodi pastores reperiantur. Pastorem vero qualem ex Dei verbo descripsimus, vix aut ne vix quidem unum invenieris.[1]

---

[1] I have selected these passages as giving the reader Travers' opinions as well as his style. This book must have been well known to Burghley when he appointed him to control the new College.

APPENDIX IV.

M. R., C. i. c.

I HAD noe tyme to superscribe the letters enclosed, doe that part for me.

Mr. Challener, I have receyved three or foure letters from you since I answered, but it was want of messengers. That w^h was materyall in your letters was about mye brother's unnecessarie debtes whereof now I have written to y^r brother Christopher. I sende his letter inclosed in this; reade seale and delyver it. You knowe mye state better than anye in Irelande, yet make it not much knowen, least it hinder mee in England. Touchinge [the] note it was false in Sir George's somme hee gave but 20^{lb}, and Thomonde or Clare, for all is one, gave 70^{lb}, w^h you have put in at 66^{li} 13^s 4^d. J—— Morgan had of mee three pounds for collectinge. I send you his acquittance, w^h if you beleeve not my Ladye doth witnesse ffor it. The other fyve poundes difference twixt you and us, I thinke was given to those that brought the monie, and I am sure so much or more was given. Sir Richard [Bingham] desyred the note, not because hee distrusted you, but because hee would have you amende the table that hangeth in the chappell whereunto our province men take such exception that they thinke some of the money to bee purloyned awaye. I sende you againe your own note, and the acquittance desyringe you to amende that open table afore the next tearme. Touchynge Galwaye, I am sorye you receyved billes they consined you, and yf you will send Sir Richarde the bills, it may bee hee will send them to the Galwaye men, and when hee should paye them monye (for once in a year hee is in their debte) hee will paye it you. And had he not dealt so with them before you had not had so much of them as nowe you have by 50^{li} stg. Touchynge the Comition graunted to Sir Richard about Concealments, I wryte at large to Mr. Travers, and referre you to his letter with this inkelinge that I think you deceave y^r self about benefytinge by that Comition, which he sought for his business, not for you. Anye thing els I remember not to be answered in y^r letters. The Lord blesse you. Athlone, this 18 of Januarye. Commende me to y^r . . . and your father and his. Mr. Traverses letter I also sende you over

       Y^r to his power,
        MATHIAS HOLMES.
      [A Fellow of the College.]

[*Some time in* 1594.]

APPENDIX V.

Petition of the Provost and Fellows of Trinity College, Dublin, August 15, 1594.

R^t Hon. o^r very good, &c., Chancellor,—The experience of y^r special favor whereby we have our beginning and hope of a Colledge and University in this land doth move us in regard of the unsettled and unprovided estate of our poore society to become most humble suytors to y^r L^o for it. The present state of this new Coll. inhabited and furnished with some number of students now this seven months, ryseth not in any yearly certain and perpet^l endowment bestowed upon it, to the sum of £40 per yeare, nor tho we accompted the benefit of the grounds that lye about it, and are as parte of the state thereof. There hath been given neare £2,000 for the building of it, and yet the whole is not finished for want of meanes. But when it may be so fited, it will be fit to receave and lodge 220 students. In maintaining of whom at their studyes, whereas all the hope of the fruite of this endevor consisteth, and our poor and mean condičon of lyfe yieldeth us not any hope otherwise to find means for procuringe of the same. O^r only refuge is herein to y^r good L^o hopinge to find yet some comforte, whence we have re^{cd} so much already. Wherefore as we have been advised, o^r most humble seute to y^r L^o hearing is that of y^r accustomed goodness to this poor country and in Christian compassion for the rude and weake estate thereof, it may please you L^o by y^r honorable mediation to H. excell. Maj. for us to procure to this College a grant of £100 of attainted and concealed lands a year. We have sent humble petition hearof by Mr. Henry Lee one of the Fellows, directed to H.M. that yf y^r good L^o shall see it convenient to be delivered o^r duty might not be wanting.

The rest is only trivial. It is dated the same day and way as Travers' letter.

APPENDIX VI.

M. R., 6, c. (A copy, with gaps. Original lost.) The Circular sent to Munster.

MAY it please you we having experience from the beginning of the foundation of our Colledge that your favorable assistance hath been alwayes readie to further the same, in that humble dewtie that cōcerneth us we earnestlie pray y^t w^{ps} the comfortable folk, in a case which much concerneth us. Her excellent Matie having graunted the feefarme of concealed lands to a good value for advance^t of the Colledge here, we have by advise and direction of some of Her highness counsel for the state of this land, procured one Patrick Crosbie to travel in that bussiness, that this societie may [reape] the benefit of such graunt. Who   as he is to deall in y^r honorable Government of the province of Munster, as in other parts, o^r humble and earnest request is, that it may please y^r wor^{ps} to assist him by y^r favour in Munster as he may nede it, that this bussiness importing (as we take it) the good of all this countrie, may with convenient spede take good effect, for better fulfilment whereof, it may please y^r w^{ps} [by] o^r hands and comon seale we have bound our societie to satisfie the p̄ties whom it may concerne, with making them plate of feefarme of such as shalbe patentented to us from her Matie whereof the said Crosbie shalbe the instrument to show, and where y^r w^{ps} may see the care we have to prove all good cōtentemēt to such as we mighte have to deal withal. In w^h we do the rather hope for, and humblie beseech y^r favor to (be ?) shewed us. So shall both we and the posteritie of this societie stand much bound to y^r w^{ps}, and it shalbe a remembrance of great cōfort in all tymes to your self in all tymes to your self [sic] to have geven a cheerful and strong hand to the furtherance of such a service of Good as this is. Thus commending your w^{ps} to the Almightie God— we humblie take our leave. Dublin, this xiith of April, 1596.

                 Y^r w^s to cōmandment,
                         WALTER TRAVERS.
                         LUCAS CHALLONER.
                         JAMES FULLERTON.

CHAPTER III

ALVEY (1601–9)

THE interregnum between the Provostship of Travers and that of his successor Alvey, and the long delays and absences of the latter, have struck all the historians as extraordinary, but no explanation of them has yet been offered. The first obvious cause of difficulty regarding the appointment was the rapid succession of Chancellors at this time, for we may be certain that without the Chancellor's nomination or approval the Fellows dare not elect. Now Burghley, the old friend of the College and of Travers, died on August 4, 1598, and Travers departed the following October. The second Earl of Essex, then in high favour with the Queen, was then appointed Chancellor of Cambridge, and apparently as a natural consequence (for I find no express act concerning it) of Trinity College, Dublin. But we hear in Ussher's Life (p. 11) that when suddenly appointed Lord-Lieutenant and sent to Ireland, where he arrived in April, 1599, there were "solemn acts" in his honour held by the College, at which James Ussher, then a lad of nineteen, greatly distinguished himself as respondent in a public disputation. The new Lord-Lieutenant in the following month granted afresh the State allowance to the College, and it is well nigh impossible that he and the Fellows should not have discussed the question of the new Provost, and agreed about the nomination. The Puritan party were still dominant, and it seems likely enough that Travers recommended a man related to his old master at the Temple (Richard Alvey), and a man whose principles were unmistakably Puritan. All this happened in May, 1599, and as it was the regular fashion to send over two fellows to invite a Provost, or to swear in a Chancellor, they would naturally delay doing so till the June[1] Vacation, especially as all the country must have been in high excitement over Essex's great expedition to Munster—an expedition much criticised in England, as well as in Ireland, but to my mind obtained by the influence of the undertakers, who had been driven out with violence and cruelty in 1598, and also promoted by the College with whatever influence it possessed; for the recovery of the rents of the new College estates in Munster was impossible till those who had resumed their alleged properties were again dispossessed. The College had indeed, as I have already stated, let very little of its estate to undertakers, such as Browne, or adventurers, such as Boyle. But in every case whether the Fellows had selected a Mac or an O, there were rival claimants—cousins, base brothers, &c.—and these would naturally take the part of Tyrone against the adherents of the Queen. Thus the expedition of Essex, a great failure as regards the subduing of Tyrone, must have been of great value in reasserting, even for the time, the English supremacy in the south, and threatening all that had seized upon lands granted by the queen with attainder, and the loss of all claim to any restitution of what remained to them by any older title. We may assume that the College was so deeply interested in these great military operations that the advent of the new Provost was not held to be a matter of pressing importance. But there came (in September) Essex's sudden flight to England, and his disgrace, followed by his trial and execution. He had been unable to bear, with his high

---

[1] We may assume the terms to have been the same as those defined in Bedell's Statutes (Appendix, cap. xvi.)—viz., Christmas term, January 10th–March 10th; Easter, April 16th–June 8th; John Baptist, July 9th–September 8th; Michaelmas, October 15th–December 8th. It is much to be desired that the College should restore this very practical distribution of the year.

and impatient temper, the worry which drove even the most patient governors of Ireland to desperation; I mean the constant intrigue and backbiting at Court which strove to ruin every man who was not there to defend himself. It is the weakest spot in Queen Elizabeth's administration. Hence even so great and victorious a public servant as Mountjoy was always fretting at the thought of his rivals and enemies occupying the queen's ear, and compassing his disgrace and exile from her favours; much more so her impatient and vainglorious favourite, Essex.[1]

The disgrace and execution of their Chancellor made it impossible, of course, for the fellows of the College to carry out any agreement they had with him regarding a new Provost. They therefore awaited the appointment of a new Chancellor of Cambridge—Sir Robert Cecil (Earl of Salisbury), son of Burghley, and educated by Walter Travers. Nothing could suit the Puritan party in the College more perfectly. They probably approached him privately, and asked him to confirm the nomination upon which they and Essex had agreed. The latter was executed February 25, 1600-1. Two fellows were sent to invite Alvey some time during the following summer. He arrived in Dublin, October 7, 1601, and was appointed by an extant Latin Act stating that he had been invited by public letters of the Privy Council (*senatores Regni*), and approved by the votes of the fellows and lecturers.

With these considerations before us all delays in his appointment are amply accounted for; we may even say that all reasonable despatch was used in filling up the vacancy. The most curious fact in the interval is that the first Commencements (conferring of degrees) was held on Shrove Tuesday (Feb. 6), 1600-1, that is to say, a few days before the execution of the

---

[1] Cf. Mountjoy's indignant letter to Cecil, S. P., 1600, p. 397. It is remarkable that even Henry Cromwell, acting as Lord-Lieutenant for his father the Protector, shows the very same annoyance and agitation in his correspondence, and the perpetual desire to return to England to defend himself against private accusations.

Chancellor of the University! At these Commencements Lucas Challoner apparently became D.D., James Ussher M.A.[1] It has not been noticed by any of the historians that this was the first moment at which, according to the laws that have ever since prevailed, a degree of M.A. could be conferred. It comes three years after the B.A. degree, which comes four years after matriculation, in the normal course. Hence James Ussher, entering in January, 1593, would be qualified for his M.A. degree in 1600. But it seems also necessary to assume that these orderly and experienced educators, accustomed to Cambridge precedents, must have had Commencements for the conferring of B.A. degrees in 1597. Of this we have no record whatever in the sparse notices that survive. Nevertheless we are bound to assume it, and it is stated as a fact by Ware in his account of Ussher (*Anon.*, p. 21). But who could then have presided as Vice-Chancellor? Judging from the device adopted in 1608, we may assume that Travers, though Provost, did so.

After six months' residence, and these during the crisis of the Spanish invasion, the siege of Kinsale, the desperate straits of Mountjoy between Spaniards and Irish, and his great and unexpected victory, Alvey again left for England (March 20, 1600–1), and did not return till October 23, 1603. We can give some good reasons for this renewed absence; we can

[1] Even if the execution had been over there could be a legal Vice-Chancellor, as he was appointed by the Provost and fellows; but as it was impending, only the urgency of having Commencements could excuse the College from the accusation of *impietas* towards its nominal head. In any case it shows how completely the fellows acted upon the conditions of their Charter and performed all University acts on their own responsibility. In September, 1608 (the day is left blank) one of the fellows, Charles Dunn, now a judge and Master of the Prerog. Court, binds himself (having obtained the LL.D. in advance) to perform the exercises belonging to the degree, to H. Alvey, Provost of the College, and Pro-Chancellor of the University, and in the English explanation following, to perform "the exercises prescribed by the aforesaid Vice-Chancellor, Dr. Challoner, Mr. James Ussher, proctor, or the greater part of them." Hence Alvey was clearly Provost and Vice-Chancellor at the same time!

even do so for its long duration—more than 2½ years. During the great crisis of the war it was certain that the College must remain in great poverty. Not only the estates, but the State subsidies, would yield little and that irregularly. If Fullerton had already suggested[1] that the cost of supporting a Provost was too much for the College, and that a man of means should be found (like Loftus at the outset) who could afford to live at his own expense, it was evident that until peace was re-established some such economy was imperative. If Alvey found the College under sound and able management —and to this we shall presently revert—if he found that it had survived without a Provost for a considerable time, he would argue that he ought not to be a burden to it till the war was over. And then came the gradual decay and death of the queen, with all the excitement and suspense about the succession, all the uncertainties of the future, which might well stay an Englishman of the best sort from leaving his home. As soon as the war was over and King James settled on the throne, the Provost returned.

Such were the possible public reasons for his absences. There is also a Collegiate reason of another kind that may be suggested. The money subscribed by officers in Ireland for the benefit of the College had not yet been realised. It is a definite fact in the legend of this gift, already discussed, that it became available about the time of the victory of Kinsale. For James Carroll was then "Receiver of Her Majesty's money," and it was his influence which turned the bills into money. *Anon.* suggests that Alvey's later absence (1608) was connected with the buying of books, then entrusted to Challoner and Ussher. It seems to me more likely that now, at the very time when the money was first available, he went to England in connection with its outlay. It was a bold and splendid policy of the fellows, when in their poverty they at last, and perhaps unexpectedly, realised £700 from an old gift,

[1] *Anon.*, p. 62.

that they should at once determine to apply it not to make good salaries, but to invest it in the peculiar treasure which distinguishes a seat of learning. As their successors in 1709 planned and completed a vast building, for which they had not books to fill more than the fiftieth part, so the men of 1602, though the war was still raging, though the great queen and foundress was dying, though the country was drifting away from their creed, "had the confidence of things hoped for, the evidence of things unseen," when they invested what they had for the benefit not only of their own, but of future generations of students. Their sentiments towards the great Mountjoy are perhaps more concealed than disclosed to us in the Latin oration still preserved among the MSS. of the Library. But if it was ever delivered, it shows that Mountjoy made a formal visit to the College after Kinsale, and before the end of the war—that is to say, in 1602—that he was addressed by an orator, whom we cannot identify (Alvey was absent), and that in the record of his virtues and triumphs not one word is said concerning his army having given a princely gift to found a College Library. Here the argument *ex silentio* becomes almost a demonstration that the current story is false.

We shall choose the time of Alvey's absence to consider the particular men to whom the College owes its preservation during the great straits of Tyrone's rebellion (1596–1603). None of them ever became Provost, and no Provost was there during most of the time, either to support or hinder them.

Foremost among them in Collegiate importance stands Luke Challoner, owing to whose "endeavours and procurement" the site had been given by the city, and who remained in close touch with the struggling Society till it emerged from poverty and danger under the generous rule of King James I. Challoner died in 1613, and even then his death was a very great loss to the College, for he had just procured from the King a grant of fifty-seven lots of chantry lands in and about

Dublin,[1] for a Crown rent of £22 16s. 7d., which the fellows found so difficult to find and prove without his long and minute knowledge of Dublin, that they surrendered the grant to the next king. This pusillanimity, which refused to risk an annual rent of £23 for the future realising of an important estate, has resulted in the loss of a great city property. But without Challoner's procurement they felt themselves helpless. This shows how important he was even when the College was twenty years old and becoming prosperous.

There are still materials enough for an interesting monograph on this man, all the more necessary as the existing accounts of him are inaccurate. He was not a fellow of Trinity College, Cambridge, though educated there. Phœbe, afterwards the wife of James Ussher, was not his only daughter, for he was twice married, and had several sons and daughters, all of whom are said to have been buried with him in the College. His first wife, the mother of Phœbe, was Elinor Ussher. Thus he was closely connected with the other name so prominent at the outset, and, like his own, long and honourably known in the annals of Dublin. In addition to the great act of his life, the founding of the College, we know him, chiefly, from his note-books, still preserved in the Library, as a man of learning and fond of books, so that he was fit (with James Ussher) to choose for the growing library of the College.[2]

In his London residences for this purpose his daughter Phœbe accompanied him, for we find items in his accounts such as " Phœbe's peticote, her hatt and gloves," showing that the metropolis, then as now, demanded special outlays in female dress. In the next place we know of Challoner as a

---

[1] Details are given on p. 156.
[2] In Bodley's correspondence, as edited in Hearn's *Reliquiæ Bodleianæ*, I find several references to Challoner, and to his sister Phœbe (? daughter) as a buyer and exchanger of books. The name of James Ussher, so frequently mentioned by historians in this connection, never appears in the published letters. This suggests to us that Challoner was the leading man in the College deputation to buy books in England.

"very painful preacher of the Gospel," giving minute expositions of the Scripture from Dublin pulpits, and probably, though we are not told so, in Divinity Lectures. The absence of all mention of his lecturing work in College is, however, strange, and requires explanation. Apparently his parochial or clerical duties took up so much of his time that he left the daily teaching of the students to others. We have in his notebooks the heads of many discourses, exegetical and doctrinal, showing his Puritan principles. We must remember that as the Authorised Version did not appear till near the close of his life (1611), the duty of reading and expounding the Scriptures from the pulpit was even more urgent than afterwards, the older versions being both scarce and imperfect.

Such being Challoner's theological qualifications, the wonder is that he was never made a bishop. Equally strange is it that he never was Provost, for he often governed the Society when Provosts were absent; he is known as "chief of the College" in contracts with the outer world, and if not formally, he was practically Vice-Provost for several years.

This brings us to another side of his activity—that of the shrewd and careful business man. He had a large farm near Finglas—Dr. Stubbs says he had leased some of the Archbishop's lands there [1]—and from this he used to supply the College, as his accounts show, with the provisions they required. The catalogue of his private library is in another notebook, and so is the catalogue of the College Library about 1612, the latest date of the publication of any of the books being 1611.[2] It might have been expected that he would be-

---

[1] I read it, "lease held from the Lo. Bishop of All—h," certainly not Dublin, possibly Ardagh.

[2] At the head of it there is a note, but erased, stating that it is the catalogue of the College library in 1610. The main catalogue of Challoner's library is dated 1598, and the prices are marked opposite each book. Why this latter precaution was taken does not appear. If he placed them at the disposal of the College it would be the natural thing to do. The

queath his books to the Society which he so long and generously served. But his will is extant,[1] wherein we see that after bequeathing particular books, or a certain number of volumes to be selected, to individual friends among the fellows, he gave all the rest to his daughter Phœbe, whom he also, on his deathbed, bequeathed to Ussher, if he would marry her. Thus with this lady Challoner's library became Ussher's, and through this channel came ultimately into the College Library.

The impression produced by all these scattered facts is that this excellent person, to whom Ireland owes a permanent debt of gratitude, was somehow wanting in greatness, and left no widespread impression upon his contemporaries. It is likely that the Latin oration to Mountjoy, already alluded to, and the letter to Burghley asking for the realisation of officers' bills, are his composition. If so, his style in both languages was clumsy and unattractive. A handsome monument was set in the old chapel to his memory by his favourite daughter, Ussher's wife. It was a recumbent figure of the man in alabaster. When the older chapel was demolished at the close of the eighteenth century, and the present one built, this monument was stowed away at the back of the new building, close to the vault where Provosts were then laid. But it was left in the open air, and under the drip of the roof, and so neglected or forgotten that in about thirty years the whole surface was worn off, and the figure hopelessly defaced. If this history ever reaches so late a date in the annals of the College, it will be shown that this is but one of a host

collection contains most of the books serviceable to a theologian and a man of letters then attainable. Greek and Hebrew, both texts, grammars, and dictionaries, appear in it. On a page following the catalogue is an interesting list of *books abroad*, showing that he kept account of the books he lent, and scored out each according as it was returned. Each little list is headed with the name of the man who had borrowed. And here we find the names of the existing fellows, Ussher, Richardson, Walsh, Dun, King. The only notable names absent are Provost Travers and Messrs. Fullerton and Hamilton.

[1] Printed in Wright's *Ussher Memorials*.

of vandalisms perpetrated by the Governing Board of that day.

The next man in value, from a Collegiate point of view, was William Daniell, named among the first three scholars in the original Charter.[1] He, after the promotion of Henry Ussher in 1595, was the only Irish scholar we know of among the fellows. I have spoken already of his mission to Galway, though he objected that he was urgently required to teach in his College; he ultimately became Archbishop of Tuam. To him is due the completion [2] of the Irish version of the New Testament (first published 1602), and that of the Common Prayer (1608). It is to him that I would refer the draft of an agreement to bring back into the College, with the appointments of a fellow, William Kerney, the printer, who had gone off with his press owing to some dispute.[3] Daniell's letters from Galway, printed in the S. P., show him to have been a pious, hard-working man, of the same Puritan type as his theological colleagues.

Less successful in life, and eclipsed by his great brother, Ambrose Ussher, the first librarian, has hitherto received no recognition as one of the builders of the reputation of the College near Dublin for learning. We have no entry of his election as a fellow, but in the accounts of 1601 and 1603 he gets "wages" as Sir Ussher, a title never, I think, used of a fellow; in 1605 he is Mr. Ussher, and his salary is £3 per half-year, which shows him to have been then elected. Fellows and lecturers were then not necessarily identical, for Masters of Arts were sometimes employed and paid to lecture,

[1] When Archbishop of Tuam he is often called O'Donnell, and in connection with his Irish Bible, why, I know not. In the College records, as in the original Charter, he is quite consistently called William Daniell. In the earliest accounts of the College (1593–5) he appears to have received and disbursed larger sums than any of his colleagues.

[2] He obtained the aid of several other Irish scholars.

[3] This New Testament, often since inaccurately reprinted, is shown by recent scholarship to be an excellent work, and is being republished under the able editorship of Professor Atkinson.

and there were Fellows who never received such salary; but in Ambrose Ussher's case we know he was both, and besides librarian, tutor and preacher. No man did such various service, and to judge from his extant MSS. no man was more fit to do so by reason of his learning. There is one brief Catechism of his printed, but the College Library contains many MS. volumes of his writings—sermons, essays, studies in Latin, Greek, Hebrew, and Arabic, above all a complete translation of the whole Bible from the original, and dedicated to King James, which seems to have been silenced by the appearance of the Authorised Version. Nevertheless this laborious scholar received no promotion. He had a long illness (apparently mental) during the present period, for we find his salary and an allowance for his commons paid to his brother on this account. But he was nevertheless one of the most important builders of the House, and one of those who from the first gave it the reputation it has since sustained.

He probably was far more useful in this respect than his brother James, who has shed such public lustre upon his country by his vast and not dissimilar learning. But during these years James Ussher had already chosen his career in the work of the Church rather than the University. He was at the beginning a working fellow, but presently obtaining a living, he only remained Professor of Theological Controversies, and therefore taught nothing but Divinity. His duties in Dublin were in his parish and in the pulpit; he was active for his College, buying books in London, Oxford, and Cambridge, and in promoting the solidarity between the English Universities and their Irish sister. He brought over Thomas Lydiat, and made him a fellow, apparently in 1609, so securing for the College the best teaching in chronology, then his favourite study. But he himself no longer appears to us as a College don, but as an European man of letters. However little he may have taught classes, the effect of such a man rising out of Dublin, and commanding the respect of the learned world, can hardly be over-estimated. The great danger before Trinity College was that it would degenerate, as the Royal College of Maynooth has done, into a narrow and exclusively provincial seminary, unrecognised and despised in its remote isolation. James Ussher was the first of a long series of men who have made their College not provincial but cosmopolitan; Ambrose may be put at the head of another series who have provided it with diligent teachers of varied and minute learning.

Widely different, but equally useful to the College, were the pair of Scotch laymen, James Fullerton and James Hamilton, who parted company with the Society soon after the accession of King James, and were advanced by him not only to knighthood, but to other substantial favours. Hamilton became Lord Clandeboye, and a great owner in the Co. Down. We may presume from the favours shown to Fullerton that it was only his death which prevented his attaining a like distinction. The earlier history of these men, who for a long time hunted in couples, is interesting, but obscure. They came to Dublin to work a school—this privilege being granted by the Corporation to Fullerton, who was the senior, in 1588.[1] Hamilton was his assistant, and to this school James Ussher was sent when a precocious child.

The immediate importance into which Fullerton blossoms on the accession of King James gives colour to the tradition that they were really political agents, sent by the Scottish king

---

[1] Cf. Gilbert's *Dublin Records*, ii. p. 219. The first entry appoints him schoolmaster to the city at £20 per annum and his diet, with the condition that city boys are to be charged no fee, liberty for private arrangements concerning others being granted. Next year the city finds this arrangement too expensive, and upon Fullerton's suit for payment of arrears due, alters the arrangement back to that made with his predecessor in 1587, viz., £10 salary (but this time sterling money) and leave to charge fees. Then in 1590 the citizens pass a resolution that they will strive to maintain the original bargain. After this Fullerton, so far as I know, disappears from the records of the city.

to watch his interests in Ireland during the last years of Elizabeth, and that their school afforded them a convenient disguise. Still their election to fellowships almost immediately after the foundation seems to show that their literary qualifications were not inadequate. But we know nothing of their efficiency in the teaching of the students—of course every fellow was required to lecture daily—we can only tell that they were both Bursars, and that both were employed on public missions for the College. For these services they required frequent leave of absence, and hence it is that we hear of lecturers, along with the fellows, among the authorities of the College, who elected Alvey (*Anon.* p. 63). Younger men must have supplied teaching while the Provost, Fullerton, and Hamilton were absent.

The latter[1] was first appointed agent of the College in the matter of the Archbishopric of Tuam, already spoken of, and we have his correspondence from the west in the spring of 1595. Then he was nominated by the Provost and fellows to go to York, and obtain the £100 bequeathed to the College by James Cotterel.[2] An extant note shows that he recovered this money, and paid the College £8 a year interest upon it for some years after. Apparently the realising of money was in those days a great difficulty. Thus we find frequent

---

[1] Cf. *Partic. Book*, p. 4: "No wages since his first coming nor comons for 2 whole years ending at Christmas, 1596, yet allowed = £8 14s.," does not say whether his comons dated from his first coming; so also p. 5, "whereof allowed to him for his wages since his first coming being two years which end at Midsummer, 1597," applied to Hamilton, gives us the date of his first residence as Midsummer, 1595, but he was a fellow since 1593, and the two entries do not agree.

[2] The act appointing him, signed by Travers, is still extant, and it is stamped with the original College seal. Unfortunately the impression is a careless one, and only makes this clear, that the Towers of Dublin were not yet adopted. There is a tall tower in the middle, with lower flanking towers, possibly the old gate of the College, and over it the book, lion, and harp. This unique specimen of the original seal has escaped the observation of all the earlier historians of the College; it is in the M. R. and catalogued C4.

references to Isham's grant, which was the purchase by the College from George Isham of part of a grant of £100 per annum from the Crown to him in Munster as an undertaker. But here again there were long delays, though there is an item in an old account for the entertainment of Isham during his stay in the College.[1]

If Hamilton had been the agent of the College for their first attempt to realise concealments in Connaught, Fullerton, Bursar in 1597, was the agent who travelled in the south with Crosbie and others to negotiate with the occupants of the concealments granted by the queen in that year. Crosbie in fact refuses to travel and work without him, and the last direct evidence of Fullerton's connection with College business is Crosbie's letter, dated 1606.[2] For immediately upon the new king's accession both he and Hamilton had gone to Court, and whether they were really accredited agents of the king in Ireland or not, had persuaded him of their usefulness and importance to his interests. The State Papers show clearly that during the closing years of Elizabeth's life, James, who was anxiously watching for her end, and planning to secure his own succession, was seeking to influence Ireland in his favour. Though the old queen was constantly protesting against it, and receiving from him dishonest assurances that he would meet her wishes, he was encouraging the immigration of Scots—Redshanks they were called—from Cantire, Mull, and from Argyllshire, to the north of Ireland. Elizabeth's first notion of a plantation in Ulster, for which she commissioned the elder Essex, was not to subdue the Irish, but to keep out the Scots. These people were not the Puritan lowlanders, but savages with bows and arrows, who spoke the same language as the Irish, and were closely akin in race and manners. Elizabeth authorises Essex to treat them as slaves, and put them to the galleys, if taken prisoners in arms. Yet they had secured for themselves a large and good territory, then called

---

[1] M. R., B4, verso 1.   [2] ibid., C, 6d.

the Route, between the Bush and the Bann;[1] they had occupied many other tracts in Down and Antrim, so much so that these two counties were carefully excluded by the Scottish King of England from his new plantation of Ulster. The encounter of Sir R. Bingham with these Scots, ending with their defeat and massacre at Ardnaree in Sligo (1586), shows them wandering with waggons full of wives and children, just like the Cimbri and Teutones in Roman times, and answering boldly that they recognised no right but that of the stronger to occupy land in any country.[2]

The secret encouragement by James of Scotch immigration —the MacDonnells of Antrim were the chiefs of this movement—was coupled with vague promises to the Roman Catholics of the towns that with the new reign a broad toleration of Popery would ensue. The faith in these promises showed itself at once upon James' accession, for Mountjoy, fresh from his subduing of Tyrone, was obliged to make a prompt campaign to Waterford and Cork, where the people had ejected the Protestant clergy, and openly celebrated the mass in the principal churches. His encounter with the Jesuit who led the Waterford revolt, and whom he silenced in controversy by producing a copy of S. Augustine from his tent, and thus proving the Jesuit's misquotation, is one of the most characteristic anecdotes in his great and striking career.

So far it seemed desirable to digress, in order to give meaning to the current story that these two fellows of the College were important political agents. The absence of

---

[1] S. P., 1596, pp. 52, 55, 227, 232. Sir A. Chichester was wounded with a Scottish arrow at Carrickfergus in 1597; cf. S. P., 1597, p. 466. They were hired as mercenaries by both sides in Tyrone's war.

[2] S. P., 1586, p. 175. These Scots "came with woman, boys, churls, and children, whereof they had many and great store of carriages," for the purpose of occupying Mayo. They fought with bows and arrows, and when defeated were massacred, not excepting their women and children (p. 183). Bingham's great difficulty in this campaign was that the kerne commandeered by the English not only fought badly, but communicated constantly with the enemy, so that he could keep no enterprise secret.

ALVEY (1601–9)

their names from the list of fellows who borrowed books from Challoner is a negative indication in the same direction. They were not scholars or College Dons, but men of action, probably invaluable as Bursars, but not as the promoters of learning. In the very first year of James the Irish Patent Rolls [1] show large grants of monastic and other lands in Connaught and Donegal [2] to Fullerton. He was knighted in 1605. In 1607 he is entitled Muster Master and Clerk of the Cheque for the army in Ireland. He was also a member of the Privy Council, and greatest of all, one of the seven Commissioners for the Ulster plantation, viz., the Bishop of Derry, Sir James Ley, Sir A. St. Leger, Sir H. Docwra, Sir O. St. John, Sir James Fullerton, and Sir J. Davis—all the highest and most important officials.[3] He also superintends the building of forts in Ulster, and was for a time in charge of the important castle of Sligo. He is perhaps the only official in the State Papers of that day who had no enemies and made no complaints. Even when the musters, for which he was responsible, were proved defective, there is a special letter (July, 1608), exculpating him. He is officially praised in another letter (p. 83) when going with important dispatches to England. But I can find not a single letter from his hand, during all this great and various public activity, though he signs, with others, many State documents.[4] Ultimately he was buried in

---

[1] p. 7 of the printed edition.

[2] Year 1, Jac. i., part 2 xiv.–xvi. These are followed up by new grants in year 2 (xvi. and lxvi.), and 5 (xxiii.) There is also a surrender of parts in 16, part. 4, lxx. The most interesting of these grants is that of the Abbey of Kilmacrenan in Donegal, which he obtained in 1603, but sold immediately to an adventurer, from whom the Earl of Tyrconnel bought it, but had not paid the money when he fled to Spain. In 1610 this abbey, counting as part of Tyrconnel's escheated lands, passed to the College.

[3] S. P., 1607, pp. 91, 397.

[4] Cf. on other Commissions and appointments, *op. cit.*, pp. 46, 113. He was an unsuccessful Candidate for the Provostship of Eton in 1624. Cf. Spedding, *Bacon*, vii. 407.

Westminster Abbey, as we learn from the statement that Archbishop Ussher was entombed with great pomp beside his old schoolmaster, Fullerton, in the Abbey. While the archbishop has no epitaph, the following can still be read over Fullerton's resting-place in S. Paul's Chapel (north ambulatory):

> Here lyes ye Remnant of Sr James Fullerton
> Knight, first Gentlemen of ye Bedchamber
> to King Charles ye first, Prince and King
> a gratious Rewarder of all Virtue, a severe Reproover of
> all Vice ; a profest Renouncer of all Vanitie
> He was
> a firme Pillar to ye Comonwealth, a faithful Patron to
> ye Catholiq Church, a faire Pattern to ye British Court
> He lived
> to ye welfare of his Country ; to ye Honour of
> his Prince ; to ye glory of His God
> He dyed
> Fuller of Faith than of Feares, Fuller of Resolucōn
> than of Paienes, Fuller of Honour than of Dayes.

Dr. Stubbs says in his History that he was sent as ambassador to France. He was at Court in 1629, when the Fellows prayed for his interference to preserve for them their liberty of electing a Provost, and died in 1631. Though the first large grant of the king to the College in his eighth year does not mention Fullerton, the fact that the lands were selected in the very counties of Munster, which he had examined personally along with Crosbie, leads us to the sure inference that to him this grant was due. It is clearly supplemental to that of Queen Elizabeth in Munster, and intended to complete her benevolence.

The action of Hamilton, the younger man, comes later, and is mainly concerned with the plantation of Ulster. During the period of Fullerton's great official activity, he only appears as a favoured recipient of large grants in the county of Down, quarrelling with McDonnell and others about delimitations and fishery rights. But the facts, as we know them, seem to justify us in saying that if these two Scotchmen had not been elected fellows, and become friends of the College, it might have remained to the present day a poor foundation.

We are not informed of the years of their birth, but as Hamilton (Viscount Clandeboye) lived till 1643, and Fullerton till 1631, they must have been in early middle life when they managed the affairs of the College in the interregnum between Travers and Alvey. It was they, together with James Ware and James Carroll, both of whom had financial dealings with the College for many years, who kept the inner life of the House, so likely to degenerate into petty provincialism or minute pedantry, in contact with the affairs of the outer world.

Provost Alvey's renewed residence in 1603 was not long; he again left from the beginning of June, 1604, to June 13, 1605, and this time for the distinct reason that a plague had broken out in Dublin, so seriously that the College was for a time broken up. Alvey's natural home being still in England, he is not necessarily to be blamed for this retirement, seeing that Challoner, Ussher, and others, whose homes were in Dublin, could watch the buildings and look to the safe keeping of the House till this time of pestilence was over.

The causes of this plague are but too manifest. The long war with Tyrone had only been finished (just like the recent Boer War) by a system of blockhouses, and by destroying all the food accessible to the Irish. Growing corn was cut with swords by soldiers, and the cattle which could not be driven away massacred. Those Irish writers who inveighed against Mountjoy's cruelty should be reminded that a determined guerilla war against a regular army, however superior, can only be stamped out in this way. Even in this humane and sentimental age the horrors of such a war are only diminished by the tenderer treatment of the non-combatants—the wives and children of the guerillas—and this change has brought with it, as we can see in the instance just quoted, a great and costly prolongation of

K

hostilities and with it of suffering. However, this devastation of the country and the "many dead lying in many places," bred not only famine but pestilence, and the crowd of starving creatures that wandered to Dublin to beg their bread carried with them the infection.

Challoner was as usual the active man to seek a remedy for this evil. The break up of the new College for such reasons must be avoided in future, if possible, and accordingly he set to work to obtain a site near the College and money to build a Bridewell for the restraining of vagrants and beggars. We may be sure that they would soon desist from camping on Hoggen Green, when this house of correction threatened them close by. The opening words of the petition[1] made to the city on January 20, 1603, are explicit—

"Divers well-disposed persons, considering the multitude of sundry sort of poor, many of them able bodied, and most resorting out of the country, who to the great disgrace of this worshipful city, and now the endangering of many by contagion, do abound among us, do willingly resolve to bestow the building of a place for a Bridewell, a house of labour and correction," &c.

And we know from Challoner's notebook that he acted as treasurer and paymaster to the workmen who set up this house upon the site granted by the Corporation. The petitioners' names show how closely the matter affected the College. They are Challoner, John King, James Ware (College auditor), and James Carroll. The fact that with the continuance of peace, and the recovery of the country under King James's enlightened rule, this Bridewell became useless and fell into such decay, and that it was devoted to another purpose in 1617, shows clearly that its foundation was to meet a temporary emergency, and to relieve a pressing evil. The plague in 1604 was severe enough to cause the closing of the College and the flight of the Provost to England. That we may call it a flight I infer from the fact that, owing to his hasty departure,

[1] M. R., D 9, and Gilbert, ii. 420.

the Matriculation book, wherein was set down "the Incorporation in the College, and the Matriculation in the University of Students," is stated in the P. B. to have been lost. It must have been under his care in the Provost's lodging. Unfortunately this negligence was no solitary act in the early history of the College. The early Matriculation books (before 1637) are all lost.[1] This is the more regrettable as there are in the Patent Rolls of James I. a large number of grants of Wardships of boys of important families, many of them gentlemen of the Pale, many others of great Irish houses, on condition of a fine, a rent for the ward's lands, and, lastly, an allowance from this rent of a yearly sum for the "maintenance and education of the boy in the English religion and habits, and in Trinity College, Dublin, from his twelfth to his eighteenth year." On these conditions, for example, the son of Sir Donald O'Cahan, and the son of Sir Neale O'Donnell, the most eminent northern chieftains remaining after the flight of the Earls, and both imprisoned for suspected treason, were kept by Chichester at Trinity College. The sums for these wards' maintenance are in some proportion, but not a fixed one, to the fine and rent; they vary from a few shillings to £20 annually, and are so numerous that if we could be sure the order was carried out we might recover the names of many early undergraduates. But as Carte tells us (*Life of Ormond*, i. 43) there was great negligence in watching the education of these wards, and many of them were rescued from the good intentions of the king by the Jesuits.[2] The fact remains that it was now the policy to favour the College, and that it received an increasing number of under-

---

[1] From the account in the *Particular Book* (p. 29) of the receipts of the Provost for *Detriments*, we can recover the names of some thirty-five graduates and undergraduates resident in the College, 1605-6. But the Christian names are in no case given, not even when three Pelhams and three Kavanaghs, probably groups of brothers, are mentioned.

[2] An analysis of the names of these possible students and the allowances made for them would be interesting, but would lead us too far from our plan here.

graduates who were not elected scholars, and not maintained by the House. The great variation in the maintenance seems to prove that there was a variation in tutorial fees, and other charges, and indeed the only fixed charge made by the College was that entitled *detriments*. There is an account from the cook in the M. R. (G. 2) which is dated May and June, but without a year, which seems to come from Alvey's time, and if so gives us the exact number of the Society. I date it in this time, because the number of fellows in the House for four successive weeks is only four, a number increased in Temple's time, though occasional vacation weeks may show this very small number. On the other hand the number of "schollers of ye house" is far too large for this period—41 the first week and 32 during the remaining time. I account for this by supposing that the cook included among the scholars of the House for his purpose those *scholarium commensales* (so frequently entered in the Matriculation book of 1637–41), whose commons were paid for by patrons of the College. Thus "for Sir James Carroll's scholar" is an entry we meet in the P. B. There are added in each week 10 fellow commoners and 20 Pensioners, who pay their weekly fees (detriments) through the cook, to whom they paid their commons account. Each pensioner pays $2\frac{1}{2}$d., each fellow commoner $4\frac{1}{2}$d. per week. Thus the Society consisted of about 70 members. We must, however, remember that Bachelors were then an important class, for their education proceeded regularly up to Master's standing. We also find in the Bursar's accounts that he received money for the commons of pensioners. Chamber rent is not mentioned. There were such stringent rules against students "transcending the wall, and sleeping in the town," that we may presume the practice of allowing lads to live with their parents in Dublin and come in daily to lectures had not arisen; nevertheless it is noticed that even earlier in the terrible gunpowder explosion of April, 1596, which wrecked many houses on and about the quay where it happened, a large number of students were killed. As Trinity

College had been granted the monopoly of University education in Ireland, it is hard to conceive these youths as belonging to any other establishment. The College records, such as we have them, make no reference to the explosion or loss of students, but these records are so scanty that the argument *ex silentio* has here no weight.

There is indeed a strange dearth of details about the life of the College during Alvey's Provostship. We only hear bare facts such as his tenure of, and salary for, the Divinity lecture in Christ Church, thus proving that he was a recognised clergyman, which in the case of these Puritans is often a matter of doubt. Some religious epigrams in Latin elegiacs in a MS. volume in the Library are ascribed to him, I know not on what authority; for some in the book are specified as Crashaw's. That his rule of the College was somewhat lax may be informed from the lists of *exiits* and *rediits* of scholars for the years 1603, 1606, and 1608 preserved in the *Particular Book* (pp. 207-10). In the first place the leave granted is very long—often from December or January till Easter, and so at other seasons. In the next place several of the *rediits* are not till months after the date fixed by the *exiit*. Thirdly, we do not find the formula usual in Temple's time, a few years later, *sub pœna amittendi discipulatum*, nor is there any penalty mentioned for outstaying the date fixed for return. The list in Temple's time produces a very different impression. The fact that after Alvey's retirement, and survival for many years, he left his larger bequests not to the College which chose him as a governor, but to St. John's College, Cambridge, where he had been educated, shows that, as in the case of Travers, he had not made himself at home in Dublin.[1] When in residence he did his official duties

---

[1] One solitary item appears in the Bursar's account of 1647-8 (under February 7), "Received for Mr. Alvey's College pott and salt which were pawned, £10;" and it is one of the last of such items, as if the Society had clung to this relic till all the rest were gone.

without blame, but he has left no mark on the College, though he once had been the head of a new party at St. John's (Mullinger ii. 324).

In the absence of direct information we may argue from analogy and infer that the life of undergraduates in the College near Dublin was similar to that of the same class at Oxford and Cambridge. A comparison of the salaries and charges for commons, battels, or detriments shows that Dublin was not then cheaper than the rest.[1] The very low prices of dinners arise rather from the scarceness of money everywhere. Twopence was a liberal price for a meal, and the fourpence allowed for the Provost's commons a handsome allowance.[2] The confusion produced by Queen Elizabeth's issue of base money for Ireland made sterling coin artificially valuable. Hence the importance of *sizings* in the early life of Colleges. This term, which is connected with *assizes*, in the sense of a conclave (*assidentes*) to determine prices of food, &c., means the provisions provided by the College at a regulated and wholesale price, just as many mediæval towns in England regulated by assizes the market price of victuals.[3] Sizings were therefore a privilege of students and other members of the College, saving them from trouble and fraud in procuring their food. But commons, being not only the chief meal of the day, but a parade and proof of constant residence, was never included in sizings. The *sizarius* (our sizar or the batteler at Oxford) was (and is) a student who obtained his commons free and paid for

---

[1] But the evidence on this is conflicting. While there are many complaints of the dearness of Dublin, a competent witness (Birchenshawe, S. P., 1606, p. 2) notes that food was quite cheap. He says that fat beef is a quarter, fat mutton half, and wheat half the English prices. A fat goose costs 6d., a chick 1d., a hen 2d., and a pig 8d. Clothes seem very dear.

[2] Thus when the Translators of the Bible at this time speak of the Good Samaritan taking out twopence and giving them to the innkeeper for the maintenance of the wounded man till his return, that sum did not sound absurd if an absence of a couple of days is intended. A penny a day is the usual allowance for all the food of a student outside his dinner.

[3] Cf. on this question Mullinger ii. 374, *sqq*.

sizings only. It being the duty of the sizars to attend at the fellows' table, each fellow was entitled to nominate one, the Provost four. Bedell defines *subsizatores* as those who attended upon the scholars' or undergraduates' tables.

As regards the other expenses of students, it seems necessary to assume that they brought with them what furniture was thought necessary, for I can find no mention in the minute outlays of these years of any furniture for rooms, except the table in a tutor's account (p. 106), and the new bed and bedding for Provost Temple, which was purchased on a grand scale, costing the great sum of £5 8s. 2d.[1] But the analogy of other Colleges shows that the amount required was small. The fashion was for two or three students to live with each fellow and sleep in his room on truckle beds. The great room was then the sleeping-room; if there were small rooms attached they were used for separate studies. But this was a luxury.[2] Firing and lighting were scarce and dear; the halls and the library were used by many students for their work. Beds and chairs in their rooms may possibly have been provided by each fellow for his immediate pupils. The caution money or bond taken from parents or guardians at matriculation implies that the student might possibly abscond with College property more valuable than what he had brought. William Kearney, the printer, was able (in 1595) not only to leave the College clandestinely, but carry off his printing press, benches, stools, &c., without the knowledge of the fellows. No doubt the College was then sparsely inhabited, but we must remember that if Provost Travers told Burghley there was room in three sides of one small quadrangle (140 feet

---

[1] P. B., p. 37. This means something like £50 nowadays.

[2] It appears from Bedell's Statutes (*de Decani officio*, sub. fin.) that this luxury had become general before 1628, for he there ordains that the Dean, with two or three fellows, shall constantly visit the rooms of students in the evening, shortly before bedtime, to see whether they are safe within and what is the condition of their rooms. It is very remarkable that in this ordinance there is no mention whatever of the tutors.

square inside) for 200 students and twenty fellows, he must have assumed tightly-packed dormitories, with hardly any sitting-rooms. Hence the importance of being allowed to work in the Library, and the jealousy with which the right was conceded to graduates only. It meant the use of a commodious study to those who had only sleeping-places in a room with others.

Ireland was now in process of being restored from war and devastation to comparative prosperity. The king had for the first time in Anglo-Irish history declared formally that he took the Irish under his royal protection and accorded them the rights of subjects, which meant, theoretically, equality with Englishmen, especially as persons in the eye of the law. Nevertheless we find in the Patent Rolls of the reign that the privilege was not granted for nothing, but was a source of income to the parsimonious king. There are hundreds of applicants for the declaration of the privilege by King's Letter, upon payment of a fee. Still there must have been a gradual growth of public confidence, especially after the lurking fear of a new revolt, which must have brooded like a dark cloud over the country so long as Tyrone and Tyrconnell were there. Hence the vast public importance attached to the sudden "Flight of the Earls." Even then there were still sudden alarms, which must have caused panics, such as the outbreak of Sir Cahir O'Dogherty, a young chieftain who possessed the education and polish of Tyrone, without his Jugurthine patience and his wiles. There followed, of course, large attainders and confiscations, and chieftains possibly innocent, such as O'Cahan, were imprisoned on suspicion and their sons handed over to English educators.

O'Cahan's son was ordered to Trinity College, but disappears, unless the conjecture of *Anon.* were correct, that the Cohonogh Dowin who was a scholar at this time was the youth in question. Some of the circumstances fit well enough, for he is censured [1] for various irregularities, and *for making*

[1] P. B., p. 222.

petitions to the State, and punished with the loss of his scholarship. This lad must therefore have been at all events the son of an Irish gentleman who was suffering under grievances from the Government. The entry is worth reproducing verbatim :—

"The 23rd of May (1608) it was agreed by the whole companie that Cohonnogh Dowin for divers grievous misdemeanours, partly by examination, partly by his own confession convicted, is censured to lose his scholarship, and to have a peremtorie admonition, that the next time he is found guiltie of his former misdemeanours, either to trouble the State by peticōns, to deale for priests, or disregard the governors of the house, be banished the same. And that one Daniel, for some such like carriage, provide him a place in the towne."[1]

But it can hardly be possible that Cohonnogh, or Conough Dowin, Latinised into *Conosius Dovinus* in his *exeats*, can be so well known a person as the heir of O'Cahan.[2] Moreover, Conosius Dovinus entered before December, 1605, as we know from the note of his tutor, Ambrose Ussher (appendix II. to Chap. II.), which is too early for the advent of young O'Cahan.

Along with many uneasinesses there were, however, rising hopes of new grants from the king, whom Fullerton and Hamilton were no doubt plying with petitions and arguments not only in their own interests but in that of the College.

There are clear evidences, even before Alvey's resignation, that the College was improving in its finances. In 1606 not only were the rents in Munster, but large arrears, paid up. In the quarterly accounts from this time to 1609 there is a gradual rise in the number at the fellows' and scholars' commons from an average of four and sixteen to nine and twenty-seven, in some quarters even more.

These facts make it very difficult to understand why Alvey,

[1] This last was probably an O'Donnell, as we find the fellow, William Daniell, when Archbishop of Tuam, also called O'Donnell.
[2] I find Coconaght (*i.e.*, Hound of Connaught) a Christian name only among the Maguires, and consider the youth to have been an O'Doyne, also written O'Duin, with a Maguire mother.

who had many years of life before him, and who had weathered the storm in Ireland, should have resigned when the sun of prosperity at last rose upon the College. He went to England again in 1608, and was concerned in the buying of books for the Library; the last quarter of his accounts in 1609 is no longer in his hand, but in that of Sir James Ware, and we might almost imagine that he resigned while in England and never returned, for in the autumn of 1609 preparations were already being made for the reception of his successor. But there are two enigmatical entries in the *Particular Book* which prove the reverse. There is an appointment made and signed by him of Challoner as pro-Chancellor during his absence, which he concludes: *rediturus, volente Deo*. This entry is at the top of the page, which contains matter of the year 1611, but is itself undated. At the top of the next page Challoner, going to England, appoints in his place as pro-Chancellor Charles Duñ, and this again, dated only May 5th, is over entries of 1612. Accordingly the historians have referred the two entries to these years respectively, though it would be far simpler to suppose them belonging to an earlier date, while Alvey was still Provost. But this simpler solution is upset by another entry fully dated, wherein Edmund Donnellan is elected a fellow (p. 189). It is signed by W. Temple, Provost, and attested, with their several signatures, by Henry Alvey *Procañ*, Thos. Lydyat, Ambrose Ussher, Anthony Martin, John Egerton, Wm. Byrd, and Jonas Frith. The date is June 3, 1611. Alvey was therefore certainly in Dublin and acting as Vice-Chancellor nearly two years after Temple had succeeded him, and if the other entry quoted dates from this year, he then intended to return. The matter becomes still more complicated by another entry in the P.B., p. 222, wherein Challoner is Vice-Chancellor and Vice-Master on January 29, 1611. Neither Alvey nor Temple can have been in residence at that moment. Temple, as we know (P. B., p. 203b) was prosecuting the suit of the College for a fixed pension at Court from June 20, 1611, to March 20th next ensuing.

These facts, which have hitherto been overlooked, afford an important correction to the current accounts of Alvey both in the histories of the College and elsewhere. But they also increase the difficulty of accounting for his resignation. The tide was indeed turning against the Puritans at Court on account of King James's difficulties with the Scotch ministers, but Alvey was not coerced to resign for this reason, seeing that his successor, Temple, belonged avowedly to the same party. The reasons for his departure will probably remain a mystery, for his quiet and unobtrusive rule caused but little remark, and he disappeared without any public comment.[1] Ussher kept him in memory, and hears about him from his correspondent, Samuel Ward. But he lived in obscurity, for even the recent diligent historian of S. John's College does not think him worthy of mention, though he died in the College, and bequeathed to it mementos of his affection.

The gradual growth of the College during his rule was due, therefore, partly to the advent of peace, with a new sovran of greater liberality to learning, partly also to the zeal and efficiency of Challoner, Ussher, and their younger colleagues. We also know from Ussher's correspondents that Alvey joined him in the enlightened policy of inviting learned

---

[1] On the same page of the P. B. (213) occur the two resolutions appointing Alvey and his successor (1601, 1609). But the difference of the language is perhaps significant. The first is in Latin : "Quod quum Mag. Gualterus Travers nuper Collegio &c., dignissimus præpositus esset, eodemque munere per quinquennium fidelissime fungeretur." The second in English : "That we that are fellows, lecturers, and M^{rs} doe approve the admission and election of Mr. Temple upon the resignation of Mr. Alvey." Yet the four principal names subscribed are the same in each. The coldness of the second towards Alvey must therefore have some significance. On page 60b of P. B. there is the further enigma, "For exceedinges after Mr. Alvey's departure, 2s. 6d." This modest outbreak of festivity, if that be the meaning, points to some mild satisfaction in the House at his departure ! Or else what does it mean ?

and pious men from Cambridge to settle and teach in Dublin both as college dons and parish ministers. In addition to Lydiat, mentioned already, we have Samuel Ward, of Ipswich, afterwards persecuted most unjustly by Laud, William Eyre, who actually came to Dublin, though he did not stay, Pearson, above all Anthony Martin, recommended specially by Eyre from Emmanuel College, who came in 1608-9, and remained to be an ornament to the College and the Church of Ireland. He plays a prominent part thirty years later, as will appear in Chapter VII. It has often been so in history—a body of undistinguished but zealous men govern better than a set of lay-figures led by one man of ability. The growth of prosperity under Alvey was shown by the increase of scholars and of fellows which we have mentioned. It is also shown by the early inventories of plate which are preserved in the *Particular Book* (pp. 202 *sqq.*). The laudable fashion had begun of presenting a "silver pott" or a "boll," or a great piece of plate with the donor's arms upon it. Either fellow commoners' parents or fellows, or public men of literary taste, led this fashion. There was a subscription for the bedell's staff, chiefly from fellows and masters, of £11 19s. 6d., then a considerable sum.[1] Three sums of 50s., received from students, were devoted to buying silver spoons, which cost £4 6s. 3d. per dozen. Two salt-cellars cost £3 4s. 4d. The summary of college plate at the end of Alvey's rule amounts to eight pots or cups, nine bowls, and three salt-cellars, one of them a trencher salt, and eighteen silver spoons. These gifts, and the names

---

[1] This mace was in the College, and in use, within the memory of the late Provost Lloyd, therefore till at least 1824. A larger and handsomer mace, dating from Queen Anne's time, then came into common use. This latter is shown in the *Book of Trinity College*, and has been carefully described in "Irish State and Civic Maces," &c., by J. R. Garstin (1898). The older and more precious staff was left in the bedell's possession, was forgotten, and disappeared. Possibly it may still be in the collection of some lover of old Irish plate.

of distinguished men who made them, show that the College was rising in estimation, and that at the fellows' table at least there were the beginnings of refined living.[1]

Perhaps the most interesting of the donors is Richard Latwar (Latewar), D.D., who gave not only a faire silver pott but a few books and MSS. to the library. This man, an eminent scholar and composer of Latin verses, and a former fellow of S. John's, Oxford, was taken by Lord Mountjoy from his living at Finchley to be his chaplain of the forces in Ireland. He seems to have been but too fit for this post; for, advancing eagerly into a skirmish near Benburb, in Co. Tyrone, in order to see the engagement, he was struck by a bullet (July 17, 1601) and died next day. This we have on the authority of Fynes Moryson, who was present in the campaign as Mountjoy's secretary.[2]

---

[1] Another excellent form of benevolence was the supporting of an additional scholar, whom the donor nominated.

[2] *Itin.*, Part II. p. 114. His *pater lugens* erected a memorial slab to him in the chapel of S. John's College, which is still extant, on the west wall, beside the door; but in his grief he has misstated both the year, the day, and the circumstances of his son's death! He dates it A.D. 1603, July 27, and *triduum* after his wound. But the epitaph, not erected till Mounjoy had been created Earl of Devonshire, is less trustworthy than Moryson's contemporary journal. The epitaph further states that Latewar was buried "in ecclesia aramathensi" (*i.e.*, Ardmachensi), which leads us to suspect that the stone-cutter had before him a text which he did not read accurately. Still the graving both 2 and 3 where 1 should have been before him seems hard to explain by any vagary of handwriting. Yet I know texts of the period where 1 and 2 are very similar. The epitaph is so little known that I will trespass on my space and save it from oblivion :—

RICHARDO LATEWAR LONDINENSIS HUJUS COLLEGII OLIM SOCIO ET ACADEMIÆ PROCURATORI OMNB^s HUMANIORIS LITERATURÆ (PRÆSERTIM POETICÆ) DOTIBUS INSTRUCTISS^o IN SACRA THEOLOGIA D^{ri} (DUM ILLUSTRISS, HEROA D^M MOUNTJOY NUNC DEVONIÆ COMITEM IN HIBERNICA EXPEDITIONE AD RES SACRAS PERAGENDAS SECUTUS EST) ICTU GLOBULI SAUCIO, ET POST TRIDUUM IMMATURE SED PIISSIME DEFŪCTO IN ECCLESIA ARAMATHENSI SEPULTO THOMAS LATEWAR PATER LUGENS ORBUSQ. FILIO CHARISSIMO HOC MONUMENTUM POSUIT. OBIIT JULII 27mo 1603 ÆTATIS SUÆ 41.

The fact that this remarkable man, during his few months of active service in Ireland, should have been a benefactor to Trinity College not only shows a friendship, either old or new, to have existed with some of the leading men, but that the attention of Mountjoy, a very bookish man, must have been turned to the College. The oration prepared for his visit, already referred to, suggests the same conclusion.

Latwar's gift to the little library of the College leads us to consider, in concluding the history of Alvey's time, the growth of that department, which was indeed very notable. The money secured by Sir James Carroll from the bills due to the officers who had given them to the College in 1592 only began to be realised in 1601. To judge from the extant College accounts, it was not received from Carroll till some years later, and then in small sums. Provost Alvey's receipts up to June, 1605, show £244 from Carroll, and in 1607 £350, one sum of £300 paid in England "by Mr. Treasurer's appointment." Carroll had so many intricate money transactions with the College and the State that we cannot be sure of our ground. But it seems more than likely that these constant payments were from the soldiers' bills, and intended for the Library. So far as the accounts can inform us there was no outlay for the Library in 1605 beyond paying for a catalogue. There is indeed one solitary document (M. R., A ii.) written in 1632, and containing financial matters about the repayment of old loans in copper, which states that the declarant (whose name is not given) lent £100 in silver for the buying of books for the Library in 1603. That this loan had some relation to the benefaction secured by Carroll is probable, and the mention of silver suggests that it was to be carried to England where the Irish copper was not current. But I can find no further account of the employment of this sum. The further fact that the first considerable catalogue of books is entitled (though inaccurately) the Catalogue of 1604 shows that there were then enough books to make a new catalogue necessary. In 1608, at all events, the buying of books was proceeding actively, for this was the year in which Challoner, Ussher, and the Provost were in England, and negotiating with booksellers and printers. Hence it was during Alvey's time that the future greatness of the Library was secured. In the many papers of his successors there is little or nothing about it, so that it is not too much to say that this noble feature in the College was the result of individual zeal on the part of three men at the right moment, and not of a general policy carried on during the early decades of the life of the College.

Of the books gathered by these early collectors many still remain, and will remain, upon the shelves as long as the Library lasts. But of all literature which has become antiquated, none is more completely so than the fifteenth or sixteenth century Commentaries upon the Scriptures or upon the Fathers. From a modern point of view these books are now absolutely worthless. The early collectors for our Library did not purchase any *incunabula*, any single specimen of the splendid printing of the fifteenth century. There are now many specimens of such books in the Library, as it were an ancient aristocracy, from the time that scholars printed for kings. But the first collectors neither valued these things nor would they have thought it right to purchase them for artistic and antiquarian reasons. The books of that time are bound coarsely in brown calf, with black labels, the mere working tools of scholars, teachers, preachers. The earliest press marks are not on the back, but across the front of the cut edges of the closed book. The earliest catalogue in the P. B. dates from February, 1600 (our 1599), and contains no more than forty volumes. The next has 1604 upon its front page and is doubtless the work of Ambrose Ussher, the first librarian, but there are many books in the list not printed till after that date, so that our copy must have been written up by a later hand. But here we have already a collection of several thousand volumes. This in itself must have made Trinity College a very different home for a scholar from what it had been ten years before. Leading men were beginning to send their sons to the College; Church preferment was in immediate prospect, for the Primate and the Archbishop of Dublin had been among the founders and patrons. The first attempt to amalgamate the warring races was received with acclamation and inspired radiant hopes. The Jesuit counterplot seemed to be foiled, and excited no fears in an observer so acute and experienced as Sir John Davis. The veteran Challoner and the rising Ussher were ample guarantees for the soundness of the teaching in the College. Fullerton and Hamilton were its powerful advocates at Court. The flight of the Earls had cleared the atmosphere of any dangerous thundercloud of rebellion. The State Papers of the day speak hopefully of the spread of order, of assizes held in wild country where no English law had ever been enforced, of a general feeling of peace and of security throughout the land. Such was the state of Ireland when Temple was called to be Provost of Trinity College.

CHAPTER IV

TEMPLE (1609–26)

IF the reasons for Alvey's resignation be obscure, the particular reasons for the selection of his successor are equally obscure. Of his general qualifications there can be no question. Born about 1555 of gentle parents, educated at Eton and at King's College, in which he was elected a fellow in 1576, an M.A. 1581, and presently incorporated at Oxford (as was then a usual practice), he gained an early and deserved fame as a teacher of the then fashionable Ramist logic, and published several open letters defending Ramus against the onslaught of the conservative Aristotelians.

It is now generally confessed that the Reformation in Logic of Ramus, though but a partial revolt, was the spiritual forerunner of the more complete revolution in philosophy due to Bacon, and constructed upon new lines by DesCartes. Ramus, and with him Temple, were still encumbered with the chains whose grip they had loosened, and so the new Provost has his place in the philosophy of the day as the acute and pugnacious supporter of a very partial, and therefore presently antiquated, Reform. Nevertheless, it was a Reform, and as such closely allied with Protestantism, and eagerly pursued by Protestant divines. In 1584 Temple had published his edition of Ramus' Dialectics with scholia—the first book (it is said) of the Cambridge Press—and it became a popular text-book. At that time he had gone down to Lincoln as master of the

Grammar School, from which he dedicates his book to the famous Sir Philip Sidney. In those days of student heroes there was no more effectual recommendation to a great man than learned authorship, even in the most abstract subjects. But the special boast of the Ramists was that they had made barren logic fruitful in applying it to all kinds of literature. Sidney made Temple his private secretary, took him to Flushing, and there died of his wound in Temple's arms, leaving him a pension of £30 a year as a mark of esteem. His success in life seemed now assured. He was successively private secretary to two high officials, and in 1594 even to Essex, then the foremost man in England, who obtained for him in 1597 a Parliamentary seat for Tamworth. The biographers state that he accompanied Essex on his unfortunate visit to Ireland in 1599. There is no evidence of this in the now published State Papers, and a phrase in the dedication to Cecil of a subsequent work (1611) implies that he first visited Ireland when appointed Provost.[1] In any case the disgrace and treason of Essex involved all his adherents in his fall, and it was with the greatest difficulty that Temple escaped, saved, as he says in the same dedication, *periclitantem de capite fortunisque omnibus*, by Cecil's favour. He naturally, however, disappeared from public view, and seeing his political career blighted, did not reappear till 1605, when he published, with a dedication to the then very popular Prince Henry, a logical analysis of twenty select Psalms.

This book, which has now only an antiquarian interest, was clearly intended to show that the logic of Ramus, applied to the sacred text, afforded a clear and reasoned-out *vade mecum* for the education and conduct of princes. It seemed also to remind the world, that if he had abandoned or lost his pro-

[1] *Quod mihi ob oculos proponebam, postquam invisere Hiberniam et Dubliniensis Academiæ moderandæ provinciam suscipere in animum induxeram.*

fession of private secretary, he was still competent above other men for a high post in the field of education.

All these reasons amply justify his appointment as Provost, though I can find no trace of his doings from 1605 to 1609, or his connection with any of the leading men of Trinity College, to explain his selection. One biographer of James Ussher says that Temple was invited and pressed to come by that weighty authority. I can find no evidence for this in Ussher's voluminous correspondence. The same biographer says the Provostship was at that time pressed upon Ussher by the fellows, and declined by him. This seems to me rather the expression of what the panegyrist thinks obvious, than any authorised tradition. Ussher, with all his learning, shows throughout his long life a singular inability for dealing with men. And of course we may be certain that practical affairs were distasteful to the man who lived with and loved books. Nor is it likely that it was he who selected Temple. Ussher was above all things a divine and a preacher; he shows no taste for logic whether Aristotelian or Ramist. If he had made the selection he would certainly have chosen an Evangelical divine such as Mede or Sibbes, who were afterwards solicited for the post. The well-informed Mr. Urwick says it was by the "importunate solicitation" of Challoner and Ussher that Temple came; I have not found the original of this expression. In Temple's second paper, defending himself from wearing a surplice, he says that he came over and brought his wife and children at great expense, owing to the "protestation" of Dr. Challoner that the Provost was a mere civil officer. This is an opinion so unlike what we know of Challoner, that he must have had very strong reasons for encouraging Temple. But even this does not prove that Challoner selected him. At the end of his protest against the surplice in Chapel, he says, when enumerating his literary and official claims to consideration, "by particular services done to the king before his coming into England." The crowd of people that curried favour with the king on these grounds was probably very great, and must have required some additional influence to make the suit effective.

This influence came from some independent source. Cecil, according to Temple's own statement, only approved of the nomination after it was made. The men most likely to have made it seem to me to have been Fullerton and Hamilton, now risen into favour at Court on the same ground that Temple alleges, but still deeply interested in the affairs of the College for which they worked in Ireland. Both of them had been pupils of Andrew Melvill, and he was an ardent promoter of the new Protestant Logic in Scotland. This science has from the outset been a leading study in Dublin—three of its Provosts have published text-books of Logic—and it may have owed its first importance to the close association of Ramus with Protestantism. There is every probability that the two Scotchmen were anxious to promote in Ireland the science in which they had been trained in Scotland, and therefore that they pressed the appointment of the man now confessed to be the leading Ramist in England. Though not a theologian, his recent work showed that he could apply his logic to Divinity. His earlier publications exhibit a wide knowledge of ancient languages and literature. He was as eager to expound the poetry of Homer as the piety of David through the medium of his universal method. So, perhaps by the influence of all the men suggested, rather than by any one of them, he attained to a post which was now growing in emolument and importance.

All the biographers have stated that he was made a Master in Chancery, which would have supplemented his income by £26 13s. 4d. per annum. The *Liber Munerum Hiberniæ* gives his appointment and patent under date January 13 and 31, 1609, and his successor's appointment in January, 1626.[1]

---

[1] In the State Papers of 1611 (p. 112), where there is a comparison of the salaries, &c., of the Law officers at the king's accession and his ninth

In all the Provosts' correspondence there is no allusion whatever to his holding the office. Being, however, a layman (and the first lay Provost) he could not hold the theological lecture at Christ Church, which then formed a considerable part of the Provost's salary, viz., £40.

We may presume that he undertook the care of pupils. The Provost's right to apportion pupils to what tutors he chose—a right which led to bitter conflicts between Tutors and subsequent Provosts—implies that he could assign them to himself, and this the Matriculation book confirms. And this source of income may have been considerable even in these early days. It seems likely that when the sons of great lords were sent to the College the Provost was expected to take charge of them. His statement that he brought over his wife and children creates, however, some difficulty. For we do not hear of his having any extern residence. The fact that several of Challoner's children were buried in the College[1] seems to show that even he was allowed to live as a married man within the walls, and if so Temple may have kept his family in the Provost's lodgings. Perhaps the allowance made for his Commons means that he did not dine in Hall. But alas! on all these interesting details we are reduced to mere conjecture. Still it is worth raising these questions, as they will suggest to some future inquirer, with fuller evidence, to find their answers.

From this time onward Temple's life was filled with administrative duties, and his latest publication, though dated 1611, may here be mentioned as the dying echo of his literary work. It is an exposition in Latin of the first thirty Psalms, dedicated in a somewhat fulsome language to his Chancellor, Robert Cecil, whereof the title-page names the author as Provost. It is the same application of Ramist logic to theology, as in his former "twenty select Psalms," and gives us a clear

year, there occurs among the Masters in Chancery, William Temple, in office 1602. This, of course, must be wrong.
[1] Concerning a birth in the College cf. below, p. 298.

insight into the character of his teaching, if he did still teach, in Dublin. Public lectures he probably did not give as Provost, but if he had pupils in his chamber he must have taught them daily, and he must further have stimulated Ramist teaching in the public classes of the College. This, his last book, was printed, and daintily printed, in London, for though there was printing in Dublin, we find from Mr. Dix's Catalogue that, except the Prayer Book and the New Testament of William Daniell, nothing but official proclamations, and the like, were as yet produced from the local press. Otherwise we should have expected a cheap reprint of his edition of Ramus for the use of the students. However, there is not a copy of this book even in our great Library, where early editions and commentaries on the *Dialectic* abound. Many of his other publications are also wanting, so that we may infer the absence in him of any ambition to leave the literary outcome of his life on record in the College. His wide classical knowledge, shown by the wealth of references and allusions in his early writings, suggests that he possessed many books, but this was quite general among the men of that bookish age. From henceforth this chapter of his history is finished, and we have to do with him merely as a shrewd man of business.

The *Particular Book* preserves Sir J. Ware's brief of the financial state of the College when the new Provost took the reins in December, 1609. Imprimis there was in the College trunk £137 13s. 11d. in ready money, no inconsiderable sum if we consider the scarcity of coin at that time. There were also due various sums from the Crown, from middlemen like Ware and Carroll, and arrears from local tenants, bringing the "sperata" assets up to £1,209 19s. 4d. The College was therefore now a solvent concern, and, moreover, there was every prospect of "increased entertainment from His Majesty," for the plantation of Ulster was in the air, and the learned king was sure to provide for the Established Church and the University.

He was already securing an increase of students to the College by the above-mentioned clause introduced into his sales of Wardships, and if the boy of twelve came up unfit to follow College lectures, there was a College schoolmaster (at that time one Woodward) provided, who took the place of the private coach or grinder nowadays, preparing backward boys for matriculation.[1]

For higher education the provisions were now ample. By the labours of Challoner and James Ussher an adequate library had been provided ; it had been catalogued and set in order by Ambrose Ussher and Sir Egerton (afterwards a fellow) ; the accounts of 1608–9 show constant items for additional tables, benches, and partitions to secure the safety of the books, and the convenience of readers.

The same pages tell us that the statutes, by which the fellows then governed the College, which were resolutions of their own, were written out in a faire copy. This, and the stately bed and bedding bought for the new Provost, seem to be the only preparations announcing that his advent was expected.

The teaching staff, whether fellows or lecturers, seems to have amounted to at least ten, for so many dined in 1609 at the fellows' table ; the scholars' table had risen to twenty-seven, and there are items in the accounts (p. 36) for new tables, additional table-cloths, new forms, which show that the numbers at commons had considerably increased. We know that there was now a fellows' table, a bachelors' table, a scholars' table, and a pensioners' table. The lower tables were served with trenchers, leathern jacks, and pewter cups. The fellows had already silver plate. At the same time the teaching staff had been increased by the importation, at Ussher's instance, of Thomas Lydiat, a very learned but not very successful chronographer, who came with the prospect of

[1] There is a note in the P. B. (215 b) specifying the date from which the matriculation of some of these boys was to be determined.

promotion to the school now rising at Armagh, but who was disappointed, and returned in a couple of years to England. His controversies with the great Scaliger, from which he emerged not without credit, show that he was a very considerable scholar. He was one of the earliest commentators on the famous Arundel Marbles.

Notwithstanding all this enlargement, the diet of the members of the Society seems to us worked on a modest scale. The allowance for this Provost's commons upon his arrival was about $4\frac{1}{2}$d. per diem. The very first page he has written in the *Particular Book*, after his mere acknowledgment of responsibility for the ready money in the chest, is a note of the daily cost of diet for the fellows and scholars.

It is worth adding that from this point the book, in which Temple for years made careful entries, is very comfortable to read owing to his clear and elegant Italic hand. It was the moment when the new handwriting was wrestling for supremacy with the old in consequence of the victory of the new Italic type over the old black-letter in printing. Travers, Alvey, Sir James Ware write the old difficult hand, which the Germans have perpetuated to their loss till the present day. Ussher, except in his early College notes, writes like Temple, a beautiful and clear modern hand. Challoner hesitates between the two. But Temple and Ussher are consistent, and write far better than even most of their successors, such as Bedell, who uses a sort of compromise. It is easy to see that there was then just such a conflict as has been going on recently in Germany between the advocates of the national and the European alphabets. Shakspere, for example, signs in the old script, which is regarded by those who are not versed in this question as evidence that he wrote with difficulty. If a document of any length is ever found in his hand, it will probably show an easy use of the modern script. This digression is therefore not without interest as regards the culture of the period.

TEMPLE (1609-26)

The document referred to is as follows [ob = ½d.]:

WHAT IS ALLOWED FOR DIET TO EACH FELLOW AND SCHOLLER.

Each Fellow is allowed for his diet weekly out of the kitchin ...	16d. ob	
Each Fellow is allowed in bread every meale an ob, and so for every day a 1d., and so for every weeke ...	7d.	3s. 3d.
Each Fellow is allowed to zize every weeke ...	8d. ob	
Each Fellow is allowed for beere every weeke	7d.	

Each scholler is allowed for his diet weekly out of the kitchin ...	10d. ob	
Each scholler is allowed in bread every meale an ob, every day a penny, and so every weeke ...	7d.	25d.
Each scholler is allowed in beere every meale a quart, for every day an ob, and so for every weeke ...	3d. ob	
Each scholler allowed to zize every week ...	4d.	

Each Fellow comoner payeth weekly for detrimēts ...	4d. ob since 6d.
Each Pensioner payeth weekly for detrimēts	2d. ob since [blank]
The Butler payeth weekly out of his gaynes	2s. 6d.

The new Provost here omits the gains from the kitchen paid in by the cook, which appear regularly in the older and in his own subsequent accounts, and amount to from four to seven shillings per week. One cause of this profit was certainly the habit of punishing students by excluding them from their dinner. From his allusion to two stated meals daily, it would appear that the sizings were additional food (for supper) which the student obtained at the cheap College rate to supplement the bread and beer in the above description.

There is in one of Challoner's notebooks[1] a specification of what food was thought reasonable to provide for this

---

[1] I cannot find the original. Stubbs refers to MS.D, I, 9 in the Library, but it is not there.

tariff.[1] The prices set down by Temple agree perfectly with the quarterly accounts of Alvey already often cited. Nor does the new Provost seem to have proposed any alteration till the king's munificence had produced, in 1613, a considerable and certain increase in the College income.[2]

The number and nature of the gifts to the College from the king—*Jacobo ejusdem munificentissimo auctore*, as the grace after meat still proclaims—have never yet been set down in order, though his letters patent and grants are all in the Patent Rolls long since catalogued. The first grant is in no way connected with Ulster, but is a grant to James Ware, as trustee for the Provost, fellows, and scholars of various townands (named) in Tipperary, Waterford, Kerry and Desmond, and Longford, either the estates of attainted men or of suppressed religious houses, such as Connall (in Kildare) and

---

[1] Stubbs, p. 41 : " The Colledge revenew of £400 st. per ann. will mayntayne yearly :—A Provost havinge a good diet dayley as after apeares £6 and £44 yearly.

" Ten Fellowes havinge a good diet dayley and £10 yearly ; forty Scolers having a good diet and 20s. yearly. The diet must be £133 6s. 8d. for which wee are to receive victuals at prices :—

" A mutton alive with the wool at 26½d. the pece, 320 a-year.
" A befe large and fatt alive at 16s. the pece, . 54.
" Corne at 5s. the peck, market mesure . . 200 pecks.
" half whete and bear malt ; half ote malt

" A Fellowes diet shall be 6 ounces of Manchet a mele, a pint and halfe of good bear the pece, three quarts in the mess [of four], and a sholder of mutton, and at night a good pece of beath * and porage, more than they can ete, enowe for ech, the bread [beare] a farthyng, of mutton 2d., befe 2d., and the heth [they had] a Second . . . they have £4 a-year a mess bestd, for the former make but £4.

" The Scolers diet is 6 ounces of good cheet [*i.e.*, second sort of wheaten] bread for ech, pint of ber the pece, pottell a mess, a joynt of mutton at supper a mess—and a good pece of befe at dinner at 12 peces in the quarter."

[2] The numbers dining at the fellows' and scholars' tables are higher in his first quarter (9 and 30) than they are for two years to come ; in 1612 they sometimes reach 9 and (but rarely) 34.

---

* Stubbs adds a note from Hallewell's Dictionary on this word, which is probably here misread for *bcafc*.

S. Peter de Rabio (in Longford), at a total Crown rent of £7 17s. 8d., "to hold for ever as of the Castle of Dublin, in common soccage." It is dated March 8th, in the king's eighth year, and is confirmed (secondly) by letters patent in his ninth year, also making a new grant of "such lands as the said Provost, fellows, and scholars now hold," thus confirming the gift of Queen Elizabeth in 1599.[1] It is easy to see in this grant the influence of Fullerton. We have already noted (p. 125) that he had investigated lands in Munster. This grant has never, so far as I know, been noticed, though it shows that the king was intent upon enriching the College before his Ulster plantation. The third grant is dated August 29th, year eight, and gives to the College the three great estates of Toaghy in Armagh, Slutmulrooney in Fermanagh, and Kilmacrenan in Donegal, together with the advowsons of nineteen livings in Fermanagh, Tyrone, Derry, and Donegal.[2] A letter from Fullerton[3] shows that he had been working in the interest of the College, and had secured for it about 20,000 acres of the best land in the north. The peculiar advantage permitted in the case of this and the Bishops' estates was that they are not required to disturb the native population already there settled, but allowed to give them leases, if they would pay a moderate head rent—an admirable security for these poor people, when their neighbours were being "expulsed" and transported to other and worse lands. If the College, as was usually the case, leased a large portion to a middleman, it was on the condition of his not disturbing the existing husbandmen. The fourth[4] is the large grant of chantry lands in Dublin, 10th of April, in his tenth year, which was the last great effort made by

[1] Cf. Patent Rolls, pp. 173 (*bis*) and 200, and S. P., 1610, p. 19, for details.
[2] It is noteworthy that no text of this great patent was ever enrolled in Ireland, nor was there any in the College M. R. till I recently procured a certified copy from the Record Office in London.
[3] Given by *Anon.*, p. 149. [4] Ibid., p. 222

Challoner for his beloved College. He made out a list of fifty-one holdings, small and great, in and about the city, which were escheated to the Crown by an Irish replica of the act of Edward VI., resuming these lands, bequeathed by dying Roman Catholics (as they now constantly bequeath money) to have masses said for their souls.[1]

The fifth is a small supplementary grant (21st of May, tenth year) of lands in Limerick and Kerry, the former property of Connor O'Connor, John Wolfe, and Devin McMorough, of Ballyknockane, attainted, with a head rent of 19s. 4d.

The sixth and seventh are the making perpetual of the yearly subsidy from the Crown of £388 15s., for which Temple went to England, and was long a suitor at Court, and for which he received liberal grants and rewards from the grateful College.[2] They are dated 12th February in the ninth and 22nd August in the king's tenth year.[3] The eighth, dated 12th May, in his eleventh year, is the patent giving the College power to elect burgesses and send them to Parliament. The ninth (year 13) is a letter empowering the College to plant the Ulster estates with the privileges granted to bishops.[4] The remaining two, which are not new grants

---

[1] This great and valuable gift (one item was 80 acres at Kilmainham), for which the College paid a rent of £22 16s. 7d., was surrendered in 1629. Entries about it in P. B. are on pp. 63 b, 101; a petition to be quit of arrears was made in 1628. This entry (171 a) shows an honest effort on the part of the College to realise the chantry lands, for it offers to pay to Mr. Garret Dillon a sixth part and three tenements of his choice out of whatever chantry lands the College shall recover by his direction. The text of the letter resigning (on April 15th, 1629) is given by *Anon.*, p. 174, and is there said to be among the College records.

[2] This grant in perpetuity, known as the Concordatum Fund, was enjoyed by the College till the reign of Queen Victoria, when Government, by very undue pressure, compelled the College to relinquish it in return for some electoral privileges. This injury, and the abolition of the celibacy clause in the fellowship oath, are the two items of "diminished entertainment" for which that reign is marked in the history of the College.

[3] Patent Rolls, p. 229.   [4] Cf. above, p. 155.

but modifications or changes of tenure in these estates, do not concern us at present.[1] Thus we see that during three years, roughly 1610–13, the king was showering favours on the College, and changing it from the poor and struggling foundation of Elizabeth into a wealthy corporation.

This large endowment was no isolated act of policy, no mere hobby of a pedant king, but part of a large measure which marks James I. as the sovran who has left the greatest impress upon Ireland of all English kings, from Henry II. to the present day. However severe may be the judgment of historians upon his policy in Scotland or towards Spain, there can be no doubt that almost all the real prosperity of Ireland dates from his plantation of Ulster, from his introducing on a larger scale that mixture of English and Scotch with Irish blood which has proved itself, from James Ussher and George Berkeley down to Arthur Wellesley and John Nicholson, the very elixir of the Empire's life. Earlier plantations in Leinster and Munster, not to speak of the old settlers in the sea-coast cities, had already produced some of this admirable blend; the wild stock of the mere Irish had been grafted, here and there, with nobler wood, but all these sporadic attempts are as nothing compared with the transformation produced by King James.

The reader will remember that twenty years earlier Elizabeth had taken similar advantage of the attainder of Desmond (who was in Munster what Tyrone was in Ulster) to plant undertakers and groups of English farmers and mechanics across the south from Youghal to Tralee. But this plantation was only ten years old when it was swept out by the appearance of Tyrone in the south, and though a certain number of the undertakers recovered their estates, and their descendants hold them to this day, the great body of the English middle and working classes disappeared from Munster for ever. Indeed there is ample evidence in the State Papers

---

[1] Cf. ibid., pp. 410–11.

of the time (1588–98) that even without the rebellion the enterprise was sickening for want of earnestness in the undertakers, and from the pressure of the surrounding natives upon a small population of settlers. The correspondence of men like Sir William Herbert, quoted in a previous chapter, shows clearly that the problem of planting Ireland with civilised English was not solved by Elizabeth and her statesmen. Her sporadic attempts to settle the north by means of adventurers—the elder Essex, Chatterton, Sir Thomas Smith, and others—had failed even more disastrously.

The great queen's failure is brought into clear light by the success of King James. No doubt the contrast arose mainly from peculiar historic causes, which had come into play in the north. But these causes would have produced little effect but for the enlightened policy of the king. We need but recapitulate the altered situation.[1] Long before either plantation the Scots had begun to filter into the north of Ireland as mercenaries, workmen, settlers. These people (unless when hired as mercenaries) had sided with Tyrone against Queen Elizabeth, but when King James succeeded, and Tyrone had submitted, they hailed with satisfaction the Scottish king on the English throne. When he came to invite settlers for his new plantation, he in the first place passed by Down and Antrim, where the principal Scots dwelt, though he might have included most of that land in his attainders. In the second place he invited not only English but many lowland Scotch to settle in the five adjoining counties. The settlers therefore did not come, as they did in Munster, to dwell among a wholly alien population; they had near them many old and established homesteads of kindred race. If any of the first grantees hastened to sell his land it was bought or leased not surreptitiously by an Irish native, but openly by an earlier Scotch settler.

These and other favourable causes also induced a much larger

[1] Above, Chap. I.

immigration than Elizabeth had been able to promote, and so the new population got a hold upon the five counties, which changed the aspect of them in a few years. Our evidence on this is full and conclusive. For the first time towns arose in the province of Ulster. For the first time mills and looms spread the sounds of industry through the country.[1] In thirty years Ulster was civilised, and how thoroughly appears from the following consideration. At the end of this period of prosperity the same calamity befel this plantation which had befallen Elizabeth's when it was only ten years old. As the Munster undertakers had been driven out with fire and sword by the Roman Catholic natives of Cork and Kerry, so the Ulster planters were set upon by the Roman Catholic natives of the north. There was horrible massacre and devastation. Nevertheless the towns held out; many single forts resisted, and when the rebels were defeated the remaining members of the fugitive families returned and resumed their civilised life. Many families in the north now trace their descent from the solitary survivor of a household in the massacre of 1641. But that survivor would not have persisted, unless he had felt that Ireland, not England or Scotland, was his home.

One more vital point must be urged to show the greater enlightenment of King James's Irish policy. He has been accused of giving the native Irish but a scanty allowance in his division[2] of their lands. That was the fault of his administrators, as Chichester earnestly complained. But it can be urged on the other side that he made more allowance for them,

---

[1] It is a mistake to give Strafford credit for having created the linen industry of the north. The country was known even before the plantation as very favourable for the growth of flax and as producing excellent yarn. This was pointed out as early as 1609 (S. P., *sub anno*, p. 208) to the London merchants as one of the "commodities" which made a settlement in Derry promising. And these merchants secured at the outset the monopoly of exporting yarn and linen from their ports.

[2] The figures given for the whole plantation (S. P., 1610, p. 581) are: Scotch and English undertakers 123 (and with far the largest individual grants), servitors 41, natives 63.

and gave them better terms, than any predecessor had dreamt of conceding them. And these details are as nothing compared to the new principle asserted by him, that he took the whole Irish race under his royal protection as his subjects. The effect of this great act in civilising the Irish, in raising their self-respect, and in protecting them from outrage, can hardly be over-estimated.

It was part of this great scheme to give the College a share in the plantation, to endow it together with the Church as the agent of higher civilisation, and to make it known to both natives and planters not only as a school of science and letters, but as the patron of livings, which sent learned ministers to live and preach among the people. The Puritan education of these divines made them from the beginning acceptable to the Scotch settlers in Ulster, and it is more than likely that the majority of the English planters were of the same theological temper. Thus the traditions of the College agreed with the spiritual wants of the people to whom it ministered.

From these large considerations we now return to the details of our history. The first matter to which Temple turned his attention was the establishing of definite College statutes. It is, of course, a mistake to say that there were none before his day. The extant rules were copied out for him before his arrival. In the March following there is a new item: "to Mr. But for writing out the statutes," and that this was a code amended or altered in some respects appears from the declaration made and signed as below:[1] The Provost's salary was not increased by this act

---

[1] "It is agreed, March 9, 1610 [O. S.] by the Provost and fellows whose names are hereto subscribed, that they all shall firmly join together in the maintenance of the Charter of the College, the Statutes of the same, the election of the new Provost, and all other things concerning the good of the said College. It is agreed also, the day and year above remembered, by the Provost and fellows aforesaid, that the new Provost shall from the time of his admission to the Provostship have and receive the yearly allowance of £100 st. of current money in England entirely for his

unless it be by specifying sterling money, and by making it the first charge on the College property, for Alvey had received nominally the same sum. But the statutes were doubtless modified, and the clause about maintaining the Charter shows that the policy of granting a new Charter, with separation of the College from the University, must already have been in the air. It will interest those to whom old College statutes are a curiosity, that the book (or rather loose sheets sewed together) of Temple's Statutes existed among the College documents till comparatively recent times. Now we have only the chapters from v. onward, which relate not to the College but to the University, each decree of which is signed in the margin by the Provost and four Senior Fellows. These ordinances are practically the *Regulæ Universitatis* ever since in force, for the University of Dublin as such has never obtained a Charter. But Hely Hutchinson had an earlier part before him, though he does not feel certain that it was the final redaction of it, because these earlier chapters were not numbered. He also notes that in Temple's own recital of the laws he had passed for the good of the College there was a statute respecting elections and one on the reformation of manners, which every recent search had failed to find. These he supposes to have been the first chapter (though they probably were quite distinct). The second in point of order concerned the use of the surplice, and is highly interesting, even in his second-hand report. This statute recited the use of the surplice to be ancient, but that it was perverted for many ages by the Papists and pretended Catholics to many superstitious purposes. The fellows express their aversion to this superstitious use; but cheerfully admit the use of it as received in the English church, especially as it has been enjoined by the authority of their most excellent prince; but its use is con-

fee, to be first paid out of such receipts as do come into the College out of any grants, rents, lands, or otherwise. Signed, William Temple, Ambrose Ussher, Anth. Martin, John Egerton, Th. Pillin, W. Byrd " (M. R., C 16, c).

M

fined to such Masters and Bachelors of Arts as are admitted or to be admitted into Holy Orders, and to others supported at the expense of the College. It is to be used on holy days at Morning Prayer, and the observance is enforced by the usual small pecuniary fines, increased on repetition of the offence. Hutchinson justly comments on the equivocal character of this statute as showing but an unwilling submission to the king and the Chancellor. The third chapter provided that all Masters of Arts not occupied with law or medicine shall preach constantly in Christ Church or some parish church in Dublin, under heavy penalties.[1] Thus the residence of clerical Masters in the College is taken for granted. Then followed a chapter on the number, salaries, &c., of scholars and fellows, and also concerning the expenses of the Society. All this we know from other contemporary documents. Then came two statutes whose loss is grievous to us; one against the use of tobacco; the other concerning the servants to be allowed in the College. On these Hutchinson gives us no detail.[2] I cannot but think that the College authorities stole a march upon the advocates of a new Charter by obtaining in May, 1613, letters patent empowering the College, *quum sit atque habeatur Universitas*, to send two representatives to Parliament. Thus the University powers of Trinity College were formally acknowledged, though the sheriffs of the city claimed the right of acting as returning officers, against which the College formally protested. But seeing that the members selected were the Provost and the Vice-Chancellor (Dr. Charles Dun) it is difficult to understand what returning officer they proposed to have for their elections.

But this set of rules is no Charter; and the University, having no incorporation or seal, can only be considered as a particular aspect of Trinity College. The seal of the College was then, and is now, affixed to all University documents such as

---

[1] This provision appears in both Bedell's and Laud's Statutes.
[2] Hely Hutchinson's MS., p. 170.

the Testimoniums for degrees; these documents are not signed by the Vice-Chancellor and Proctors, but by the Provost and Senior Fellows, and the University seal, granted in 1851, is a mere curiosity. The Caput of the Congregation of Doctors and Masters consisted in those days of the Vice-Chancellor and the Provost, for all candidates were required to visit and supplicate the Masters in their Regent House before the conferring of a degree. This is the preliminary which seems to have been transformed into the present practice of giving the Senior Master Non-Regent a place and veto in the Caput. The moment and reason for this change are mentioned in no document known to me. The printed statutes of 1728 already mention this Caput of three.

Turning to the proper College statutes, we find Temple's influence not less dominant. The increase of fellows and scholars from the old four and twenty-eight to sixteen and seventy was no sign of better management, as Dr. Stubbs and others have said; it was the direct effect of the large endowments of King James. But within each body Temple introduced momentous distinctions. He first separated Senior from Junior fellows, and took from the latter, as mere probationers, the right of legislating for the College. He made the distinction of natives, with special privileges, from the other scholars, thus carrying out the policy of the king, who was determined that the Irish should have the principal benefit of the foundation. We shall come presently to a most remarkable open letter of King James to the Church and University,[1] censuring their neglect of the mere Irish, and showing that the royal protection had been extended to the natives in all sincerity. The distinction of fellows into Senior and Junior, regarding the latter as mere probationers, the former as the Governors of the College, has dominated its history from that day till now. The principle was adopted, Temple tells us, from some of the

[1] Below p. 181.

Cambridge Colleges, and was natural enough, when youths were elected to fellowships not only before their A.M., but even their A.B. degree. With the celibacy statute enforced, and the many avenues of promotion then open, Senior Fellows were men of only seven or eight years' standing, and it was surely desirable that the Governors of the House should have some experience. It might further be urged that when the number of fellows was increased to sixteen, nay even in later times to twenty-eight, such a body of Governors would be unwieldy, and unfit to act with promptness and consistency. But the course of history has disclosed the unsoundness of the statute. The increasing wealth and comfort inside the College, and the competition in the learned professions, not to speak of the recent relaxation regarding celibacy, have naturally made the tenure of fellowships in most cases a life-tenure, so that the governing body consists generally of very old men. Had Temple been told that his innovation would result in men of thirty years' standing having no determining voice or vote in the government of the College, he would have recoiled from it with amazement. It would have been easy at the outset to make the Governors a committee of the fellows, elected for their efficiency rather than their seniority, seeing that seniority could hardly lose its due importance in a body of educated men. But all these difficulties were still in the womb of futurity, and Temple seems even to have established a second election for proper fellowship, after the first election of a probationer, for we have the very curious pair of entries in the P. B., p. 189, that Edmund Donellan being first elected on June 2, 1611, had according to an oath he then made, resigned on August 18th, in the following year, when he was re-elected, August 19th. But Hely Hutchinson tells us, I know not on what evidence, that Donellan obtained a Church living, when he was bound to resign, according to the statutes which he had sworn to obey; and that he was forthwith re-elected by an evasion which was not against the letter, though against the spirit, of the statute. Bedell, in his Statutes, has a probation of two months, and then a confirmatory election. Possibly the Charters caused some difficulty in making a second election of an elected person, and hence he was required to stipulate that he would formally resign, so as to leave the electors free to confirm their choice. This is the only explanation I can offer for this curious formality, unless it be that the preparation of new statutes was in progress, and it was thought unwise to have a permanent new fellow until the changes were complete. Unfortunately the dry facts of the P. B. are rarely supplemented by any explanation.

Conflicts about the powers of the Provost, and of the self chosen Senior Fellows, as against the whole body, were frequent, and fill the pages of the College histories to the exclusion of more important topics. The general lines of Temple's theory were ultimately adopted by Laud and Strafford, and were the basis, through Bedell's version, of the Caroline Statutes which still rule the College.

Next to the question of this government of the College, came that of the indefinite relations of College and University. Let us recapitulate the facts already mentioned. Queen Elizabeth had founded the College as the mother of an University, and given to the former the right to make all arrangements necessary for giving degrees, &c., in fact to act as an University, pending the future developments of education in Ireland. The foundation of other Colleges must have been regarded as quite probable, for in this age of learning and piety there had been frequent new foundations of the kind at Oxford and Cambridge, and the queen must have fully expected this good example to be followed in Ireland. But meanwhile the College acted as an University, appointed its own Vice-Chancellor and Proctors, held its Congregation of Doctors and Masters, and used the seal of the College for all University purposes. King James, in his letters patent of 1613, acknowledged these rights by giving to the College the privilege of sending two burgesses to Parliament, while he mentions the possible founding of other houses, as a reason why the present Society should have its interests protected in the legislature.

But there is evidence that everything in the College was disturbed by the shifting of the religious question in England, and the increased wealth and importance of the Corporation. King James was now setting his face against Puritanism, which had already shown its sturdy independence in Scotland. He does not seem to have paid attention to the appointment of Temple, a layman and a Puritan, who despised the ceremonies of the Church, and appeared in Chapel without a surplice. But it is more than likely that Ussher saw the danger, and began quietly, as was his wont, to take precautions against an excess of anti-clericalism in the College. For Ussher, though a strict Evangelical, was a stout defender of Episcopacy. His counter move to Temple may be found in the nomination of Archbishop Abbot of Canterbury to be Chancellor, in the room of the deceased Earl of Salisbury (1612). Hitherto Dublin had always followed suit to Cambridge, and as they had copied Cambridge Statutes, so they adopted the Cambridge Chancellor. Now, for the first time, while the latter chose another layman (Northampton), Dublin began the fashion of Archiepiscopal Chancellors, which led to such momentous consequences in the reign of Laud.

Archbishop Abbot promptly took action regarding the alleged neglect of decency in the Chapel services. He sent a very severe, almost violent, rebuke to Dublin, representing the king's indignation at the disuse of the surplice and neglect of the Book of Common Prayer in the Dublin College and the Cathedral services. Temple's defence of himself as a layman, acting in analogy with the lay precedents of puritan Cambridge, has been printed in abstract by Stubbs.[1] But in spite of Temple's arguments, and some

[1] p. 28.

threats of resignation, he promises obedience to the Chancellor.

We cannot tell whether the proposal to separate University and College came from Temple or from the new Chancellor. But it is clear that though they both favoured it, they were actuated by widely different motives. Temple was probably led by the precedent of Cambridge, and the anomaly of a College appointing its own Vice-Chancellor, and conferring degrees without any external sanction or revision of its standards. It is indeed most remarkable, and was hardly to be expected, that with this absolute independence Trinity College should maintain for centuries the high quality of its degrees. The Chancellor evidently (from the arguments urged against him by the fellows) had other schemes in view. He wished to encroach upon the fellows' right of choosing their Provost, to diminish or change the Visitors, and to curtail the fellows' privilege of making statutes for themselves. These were the very changes made by Laud. It was therefore made a *sine qua non* by the Chancellor, that before granting a new Charter for an University, the fellows should surrender the Charter of Queen Elizabeth. Logically he was perfectly right. It would have been absurd to found a new corporation with the right to give degrees, while the College retained this privilege in its original Charter. Supposing that the new University refused a degree, the College could confer it on the same person at their own Commencements, and seal it with their own seal. But when the fellows were approached upon this point, and asked to surrender their Charter as the preliminary step to the change of constitution, they objected that their property might be lost, their former legal acts questioned, in any case their oath violated, and they maintained their point. Several documents, containing their arguments, their concessions, their excuses, are still extant, and are given at great length by Hely Hutchinson, by *Anon.*, and by Stubbs. The fellows are perfectly ready to acquiesce in the king's desire to have his name mentioned in the title of the College as fellow-founder with Queen Elizabeth, and we wonder the new seal did not express that concession. They are quite ready, if any omissions or any improvements in their statutes can be pointed out by competent persons, to make changes or additions under their existing powers. They point out that as in the proposed University the Doctors and Masters were to have the power of legislation, there was no reason why the College, which contained all the leading members of the University, should not likewise legislate for itself. Hidden behind all these arguments lay the pregnant hint from Ussher (in London) to Challoner [1] that statutes sent from London would be dangerous. It may fairly be inferred that he felt little confidence in the new Chancellor (though of his own choosing), who, like so many other Englishmen wholly ignorant of Ireland, was hastening to legislate as soon as he was appointed. The fellows seem to have been particularly apprehensive of a change in the Visitors, such as that carried out by Laud, whereby seven high Irish officials, one of them the Mayor of Dublin, were replaced by the Chancellor and the Archbishop of Dublin, a close oligarchy consisting usually of two Englishmen, whose policy might run counter to the wishes of all the fellows. Nevertheless the separate establishment of an University was clearly regarded as inevitable—one of the many inevitable things which have never happened in Ireland. There seems to be a curious piece of evidence in the making of a new College seal. We have remains of two older seals, one the broad seal on wax,[2] and the other a small one for letters (above, p. 124). But it is certain that a new seal was ordered, for we still have the payment

---

[1] *Ussher's Life and Works*, xv. 55, "But I pray you, be not too forward to have Statutes sent from hence—*dictum Sapienti*."

[2] Attached to the appointment of George Raw as attorney of the College to take over the site from the Corporation of Dublin, Aug. 16, 1592.

of it noted in the accounts of December 27, 1611.[1] Aprill 1612 is on this seal. The only possible reason for this date on the permanent seal of the College would be the beginning of a new life, the original foundation of 1592 being regarded as that of the University. But when we consider the dates of the controversy, which seems to have followed upon the original proposal of Abbot in 1612, it is hard to maintain that any definite conclusion had been attained so early. It is barely possible that at the outset all appeared quite easy, and that a separate seal was ordered for the University, but that when details came to be considered unforeseen difficulties arose. Here again we are left to mere conjectures.

Contemporaneous with the earlier moments of this controversy were the successful efforts of Temple, Fullerton and Hamilton, and the unsuccessful one of Challoner, to secure the financial prosperity of the College. Temple went to Court (1611–12) and negotiated the changing of the yearly subsidy into a permanent one. Fullerton secured the increased endowments in Munster, and the grant of large estates in Ulster; Challoner made out the long catalogue of chantry lands, which was never realised.[2] All these enterprises were appreciated by the College; Temple was paid large sums of money (in all £110) for his energy; Fullerton was consulted as a sort of patron; Hamilton was granted a lease of the northern estate, which would have been disastrous to the College, had it not been broken, but even so he benefited largely by lesser money transactions with the College.

But before these larger endowments were realised, rival

---

[1] "Payd to Mr. Greene of Foster Lane in London Goldsmith for ye College seale weighing in silver 4 ounces and half and one peny weight at 5s. the ounce and 40s for the fashion . . . 3li 2s 9d.

[2] It appears from the State Papers of 1614, and from the heads of the Bill proposed in the Irish Parliament in that year, that the chantry lands in Ireland were not yet formally the king's property, though Edward VI. had resumed them all in England. Challoner must therefore have made them out in anticipation of the law.

plans were made for the larger usefulness of the College, and of these the most important were those of Challoner and of Temple. We know the former chiefly from the criticisms of Temple and of Archbishop Abbot, and are therefore not to be misled by the apparently obvious financial defects attributed to it by its adversaries. The point of interest in Challoner's plan is its likeness to that of Archbishop Browne already mentioned (p. 99). In the first place the conversion of all the chantry lands and holdings in Dublin, which Challoner actually obtained from the king, had there been distinctly pointed out as the natural endowment of the new University. In the second place the idea of having a very small number of fellows or lectors—Browne proposes four, Challoner six—and a very large number of students or masters, all supported by the funds (Browne 200, Challoner 160) is wholly at variance with Temple's plan of having a larger number of fellows, and a moderate number (seventy) of scholars, these forming the corporation, and monopolising the endowment, with fellow commoners and pensioners paying fees and decrements besides. The whole history of the College shows that this latter plan was feasible and practical, but we may well hesitate to condemn that of Challoner, whose experience of the College, and of Ireland, was far longer and more thorough than that of Temple. He probably saw that offering a free education to a large number would fill the College far more rapidly, and attract many whose parents were unwilling or unable to pay for them. Temple tells us in his criticism that to expect twenty new students yearly was altogether against their experience. During the ensuing years we find the want of popularity, and consequently small results attained with a large endowment, attributed by the Government to a faulty management of the College. In all probability the rejected plan was intended to meet this rising objection.[1] But most unfor-

---

[1] The details of the two schemes are well stated, with some details, by Stubbs, pp. 39-42, and are thus easily accessible to the curious reader.

tunately Challoner died in 1613, just at the time when his experience and authority would have been most useful, and Temple, with his Senior Fellows, his probationers, his native scholars, and open scholars, moulded the subsequent history of the College.

These are questions of large policy, and would be of high interest, if we knew all the details of Challoner's plan. Far less interesting are the various chicaneries and squabbles which took place regarding the setting of the new estates in Ulster. It was an obvious policy of the College to favour friendly middlemen accustomed to country life and ready to undertake the trouble of managing a large native tenantry, though with a considerable profit ; but it was clearly unsafe and unwise to make the Provost a College tenant, or to make large leases to a man of many speculations, such as Sir James Carroll. The proposal of Sir James Hamilton to have the whole of the Ulster estates on a lease for ever at £500 rent must have seemed at the time reasonable, for such men as Challoner and Ussher, who actually signed this lease, together with Temple, though they would doubtless favour an old colleague and benefactor of the College,[1] would certainly not have sacrificed to such considerations the welfare of their society. But the fact remains that the Junior Fellows, with Robert Ussher, whom they elected Vice-Provost, at their head, repudiated the bargain ; they saved the permanent lease from being carried out, though Hamilton was ready to increase

There are also in that passage the current prices of provisions, and this was worth quoting again, as the estimate of a practical farmer, and one who knew the proper diet for the Collegians of his day. See note 1, p. 154.

[1] The names of the College tenants in subsequent years show that it was a regular policy of the College to give profitable leases to ex-fellows on livings or in Sees in the North. Thus we find Dr. Robert Maxwell, Bishop John Richardson, and Temples and Bedells for some generations middlemen of the College. There is in the M. R. (E, 63) a complaint from Basil Brooke of Donegal, that Dr. Richardson is oppressing the natives on the College estate in the barony of Tirhugh adjacent to his own grant.

his bid to £650, and the estates were very soon found worth more than double his original offer. Archbishop Ussher, in a subsequent letter, acknowledges his mistake, in giving his cousin special credit for stout resistance to the Seniors on this occasion. The Junior Fellows maintained that, with the possible increase in the value of land, no lease should be made by the Society for more than twenty-one years, and they actually obtained an injunction from the Privy Council forbidding the Provost and Senior Fellows from making longer leases and from anticipating the renewal for the purpose of securing fines for themselves.[1] In the course they pursued they showed openly their suspicions of Temple's honesty, and they charge him with various other crimes, besides that of enriching himself from the College estates. They allege that he violated the Statutes of his own making by favouritism in the election of fellows, by laxity in his discipline, &c., &c. His long and angry reply to these charges is still extant.[2] It does not seem to me the defence of a man with his hands perfectly clean. That a section of the fellows should hold meetings without the knowledge of the Provost, and forward resolutions accusing him to the Government behind his back, was certainly a grave violation of all College discipline; but the facts that he

---

[1] Temple's reply to their arguments is preserved in the M. R., and it is amusing to note that the arguments of the Junior Fellows are stated in syllogistic form, and the objections framed in the same form. Here we see the old Ramist reappearing.

It is notable that a sudden rise (or fall) in the price of provisions is urged as a dangerous disturbing element, which might diminish or increase greatly the value of a fixed rent. Archbishop Abbot, in commenting on this matter to Ussher (*Works*, xv. 55) thinks that the College should take care to have some of the rents paid in kind to avoid this difficulty. It has been clearly shown by Mr. Bass Mullinger (*Hist. of Cambridge*, vol. ii.) that this form of rent turned out a real source of wealth to the Cambridge Colleges, when the price of provisions rose. Sizings could be kept at a low figure in such circumstances, and so the student could live with great economy.

[2] M. R., C 34, and Stubbs, App. xvii.

was unable to punish them, and that they even made good their case,[1] prove that appearances at least were strongly against him. There was a Visitation at Easter, 1615, in which inquiry was made into the alleged Puritanism of the College. All our books are silent about it. But Temple states triumphantly that this charge was then wholly disproved. It seems strange that the others should not have been discussed at the same time. The Junior Fellows' statement of their case and of the evidence is not preserved; it is therefore not worth while going more minutely into Temple's long and ill-composed defence. The whole affair was a discreditable squabble, and Temple's reputation, though he obtained the honour of knighthood from Lord Deputy St. John in May, 1622, never recovered. Hely Hutchinson, who had himself been subject to like charges from cabals among his fellows, and who had spent years in these angry controversies, speaks with bitter personal feeling concerning the persecutions of Temple, and spends much labour in his vindication. In the details of government, there seems no doubt that Temple was careful and diligent. Of this the P. B. gives us ample evidence. But these virtues may not make a man proof against the ambition of being a landed proprietor, and of providing for his family by favourable leases of the Corporation lands.

Immediately after his election in November, 1609, he enters the quarterly accounts in his own hand.[2] He notes the admissions of fellows, and puts down some of the *exeats*. It was in this year that the king made his great grants of three estates and of ten advowsons. But the formalities of the lawyers naturally occupied a couple of years before these increments were realised. In 1611 the Provost went to England to prosecute the suit of the College. During this time "Mr. Dr. Challoner and the rest of the fellows" manage the College, and Challoner is mentioned in private

[1] Cf. M. R., F 38.   [2] P. B., pp. 43b and *sq*.

bonds as chief or master. In March, 1612, Temple returned, and this year is full of important events for the College. The new Chancellor was appointed. Temple tells us all the law costs of getting the patent for the State pension, in which the lawyers' fees seem most exorbitant (£77). Anth. Martin gives an account of the College money, and Temple resumes his careful entries. But now for the first time a Bursar is appointed, and both he and the Senior Dean, as well as the Provost, have keys of the chest. Historically the most interesting note is that on August 7th, Dr. [Wm.] Chapell of Christ's College, Cambridge, is invited to come over at a salary of £20 per annum and his diet, as Dean and Catechist.[1] There are items in the accounts for the fitting up of his chamber. This was the tutor of Milton, the old Damœtas of *Lycidas*, who in course of time became Provost and Bishop of Cork. His fame as a logician was great at Cambridge.

As Anthony Martin was appointed Dean the following December, and Catechist, with a specification of the work he was to do, and as Chappell's name does not reappear in any entry of the following years, I take it that he returned to England in 1613, and resumed his Cambridge work.

But if we see in this choice the influence of Temple, it was only in harmony with the constant efforts of Ussher, and indeed of Alvey, to obtain good teachers and learned men to help the rising Colleges. Sam. Ward, a learned correspondent in Emanuel College, writes to Ussher in 1608 about the invitation to himself, and mentions Mr. Eyre and Mr. Pearson as suitable young men.[2] Ussher in a remarkable letter to Challoner mentions others. In this way the provincialism that has often in our day injured Irish Colleges was avoided, and that solidarity established which secured for the fellows of the Dublin College a high position in the learned world, and a hospitable retreat in their days of adversity.

We further learn that in this year the Ulster estates were

[1] P. B., p. 205. [2] Ussher's *Works*, xv. 56, and xv. 74.

actually leased to Sir James Hamilton at £632, in spite of the bond of the Vice-Provost and Junior Fellows to Sir H. Folliott and Sir A. Gore, that they would not agree to any lease under £700, and were then to give these gentlemen the preference.[1] But the lease to Hamilton was only for twenty-one years, which shows that a peaceable compromise was effected. Though we should not judge without better knowledge, it gives us an unpleasant impression of Hamilton that he forthwith (1613) sublet the whole estate to Sir James Carroll, a man with many irons in the fire, and even then showing signs of financial failure. Moreover, in 1618, the College had to accept a mortgage from him for the money he owed in rent to the College.[2] Luckily this Carroll, probably to pay some debt to the College,[3] surrendered to it his lease five years later (1618). Hamilton's rent began first to be paid in 1613, so that from this time forward the Ulster estate affected the College income. Hence it was in 1614, the year that Ussher was made Vice-Chancellor,[4] that Temple formulated his elaborate scheme for disposing of the enlarged College income of over £1,100 per annum by appointing more fellows and scholars, and by raising slightly the allowances for commons and sizings.[5] But these reforms do not seem to have been completed till 1617, when we have the following entry [6] :—

"It was agreed upon by the Provost and Senior Fellows that the Scholar's Cōmons at ech supper sh^d for eṽry seṽall mess receyve the addicōn of 2d. over and above their ordinary

---

[1] *Anon.*, p. 133. [2] P. B., 171.

[3] It is, however, equally probable that this surrender was connected with the surrender (*pro forma*) of the whole estate to the king in that year, that he might re-grant it in three separate manors, one for each county (Fermanagh, Armagh, Donegal), instead of having it all comprised under the manor of Kilmacrenan in Donegal. This second grant of 1618 is still among the College records, with a magnificent impression (on wax) of the king's great seal.

[4] He was re-elected 1617, and apparently remained Vice-Chancellor till his death.

[5] Stubbs, p. 39. [6] P. B., 171.

allowance out of ye kitchin. So as now the allowance for ech mess at supper out of ye kitchin wilbe 4d. This to begin July 26, 1617, and so to continew."

It might appear from an interesting discussion in July of the following year [1] that the increased outlay in the numbers and the entertainment of the Society was hardly warranted, if we could be sure that the plea of the College was one of reasonable caution and not of meanness. Let it be remembered that the College had already presented various of its students to fifteen livings in six years, and that two of them are asserted to be converts from Popery.[2] The new deputy (St. John) reports that in accordance with directions from England, he had proposed "the stay of the pension of £40 per annum for the College near Dublin for the maintenance of a weekly lecture in Christ Church, and to require the College to undertake the continuance of that lecture hereafter. I caused the Provost and fellows to come before me at the Council table, and acquainted them with His Majesty's pleasure. Those of the fellows that came with the Provost, being the best of their society, we found to be young men, and none of them able, as was said, to undertake that lecture, unless it were one or two that were beneficed, and had cures of souls within this city; so that it appeared to them that albeit they should receive His Majesty's former bounty, yet of themselves they were not able to continue the lecture without employing some other. The Deputy then "moved them, as a part of thankfulness for His Majesty's extraordinary bounty and liberal grants of great scopes of lands and a large pension,

---

[1] S. P., 1618, p. 201.

[2] P. B., p. 185b: Phelim O'Dogherty converted from Popery presented May 16, 1615, to vicarage of Tullaferny. Bernard Odenony (same date and circumstances) to Aghenis. As Tullyfern and Aughnish were in the old O'Dogherty country, and the College estate of Kilmacrenan was close by, the former convert may have been a local priest never educated in the College, and appointed to keep the new owners safe by his local influence. The two parishes have long been united as Tullyaughnish (Ramelton) in Co. Donegal.

that they should out of their own means entertain one or more able preachers to discharge that service, whereunto they pretended want of means to furnish such an extraordinary charge without the lessening of their Society, so that upon their failing, the lecture has since ceased, and will henceforth, unless they be quickened with an absolute commandment."

We have not the king's answer to this very discreditable report, but we know from entries in the P. B. that the lecture was resumed, for in 1621 (p. 193b) the famous Sam. Ward (now of Ipswich) was appointed Professor of Theological Controversies, and also to deliver the lecture, receiving a fee for each lecture, and in 1626 four Fellows were appointed to take the Friday lecture in Christ Church (p. 175b).

The facts here given are not so interesting as the reflections on the condition of the College which they suggest. They afford a curious commentary upon Temple's elaborate replies to the strictures of the Government that not only was the Irish Church neglecting its duty, but that the College had failed in its purpose, which was mainly to train up mere Irish and Anglo-Irish students to teach the people the reformed religion in their native tongue. Temple replies in one undated paper that already from its foundation Trinity had sent out ninety-three men fit for Church and State, and that all but five of them (who were dead) were still active. In another document, dated 1620, and therefore probably in answer to the king's great manifesto of 1620,[1] he states the number of Irish

---

[1] S. P., p. 277, and in the Patent Rolls, 17 Jas. xxxiv., printed p. 470 in the volume, from which I take the following passage (abridged) :—

And because the College of Dublin founded by Queen Elizabeth has since been plentifully endowed by him principally for breeding up the natives of Ireland in civility, learning and religion, and he thinks that by this time good numbers of the natives should have been trained up and employed as teachers of the ignorant among the Irish, if the governors of that house had not neglected their trust, and employed the revenues otherwise, he requires the visitors of that University to take care of that part, and directs that some competent number of towardly young men already fitted with the knowledge of the Irish tongue be placed in the

students at seventy-eight, of which fifty-four are Irish by birth, the rest Irish by indenising and habitation.¹

But all this fails to explain why he had no theologian ready to lecture in Christ Church, or why the College was compelled to invite Englishmen, one after another, to fill the chair of theological controversies after James Ussher. The impression produced upon us is that Temple was not only a layman, but a worldly person, and that he neglected the interests of the Irish Church, which he probably regarded as little better than the old Papal creed. When we consider the list of fellows he appointed, we fail to find among them names in any way so remarkable as the students at the foundation. If the names of Ussher and Temple recur, it is with feeble sons of strong fathers. Perhaps Anthony Martin, who was at enmity with his Provost in later years, was the best man among them. But the general

University, and maintained there for two or three years till they have learned the grounds of religion, and be able to catechise the simple natives, and deliver unto them as much as they themselves have learned. These men are to be thought of for small livings, and are to be provided for by ministers possessed of many livings, and partly from the fines of recusants.

¹ *Anon.*, p. 136. I am unable to reconcile Temple's figures, whose variations probably represent the variations of succeeding years. Stubbs (p. 42) quotes him as saying in 1613 that there were then twenty native Irish out of sixty-five students supported by the College. Temple writes on December 1, 1618, to Denis Bryen, the Munster agent, to apply to Lord Cork for £8 18s. 6d. of arrears, and adds : "The College has been at great cost for building [this, if meant to apply to recent years, was false] and is every year at a great and ordinary expense for the maintenance of eighty-six students with their sundry readers and officers." (*Lismore Papers*, ii. 2, p. 156). Stubbs (ibid.) quotes from another "undated paper" : Irish by birth, 44 ; Irish by habitation, 16 ; Irish Fellow Commoners and Pensioners, 18 ; strangers of Derbyshire, &c., 12 ; strangers of Cheshire, 8. This brings the total to 98. Temple says in the paper quoted in the text, that "no native of any towardness is refused, many though incapable of academical learning and instruction, admitted." I have not yet found all the papers to which Dr. Stubbs alludes, as he gives but few references. Those I have found are : M. R., A II. e, List of natives in the College, and remonstrance that the sons of preachers and undertakers are not treated as such ; A II. f, List of students according to nationality ; C 22 a and b, State of the College in 1617.

character of the College in Temple's declining years was decidedly second-rate. When the Deputy came in 1617 to be entertained with a theological lecture—a very solemn amusement [1]—James Ussher is still put forward as the chief disputant when the College should surely have shown its rising men. The pettiness of the individual complaints against the Provost is noteworthy, but the number of them, coupled with charges of grave malversation in the management of the estates, proves to demonstration that he had lost the confidence of his staff, and was no longer in spiritual touch with them. No intellectual ability on his part could compensate for that fatal weakness.

And yet then, if ever, there was need of a strong man with a whole heart to stem the tide that was turning against the College and the reformed faith in Ireland.

We are very well informed of the drift of opinion during these years, especially during the rule of Chichester (1604–16), whose long, accurate, and "painful" correspondence fully justifies the great confidence placed in him by the king. It is quite remarkable how colourless and merely objective the letters of St. John are in comparison with them. Moreover, Chichester had beside him his Attorney-General, Sir John Davis, whose letters are the very best and most lively of the period. The whole Irish policy of King James, and its execution, come before us with great clearness. No ruler of Ireland before him had ever understood the problem so distinctly, and none had ever devised better remedies. Plantations were, indeed, an old device of English statecraft, but they were confessedly plantations among "the Irish enemy." King James was clearly informed that there was ample land for both planters and natives as soon as the nomadic pasturing of the natives

---

[1] Messrs. Martin, Egerton, and Donnellan were the subsequent disputants; the questions were these: *Spiritus Sanctus in Scriptura loquens est solus infallibilis judex controversiarum. Jejunium pontificum neque Scripturæ neque rationi est consentaneum.* The Protestant flavour is here very strong.

could be replaced by decent agriculture.[1] Thus the American settler in the Far West could produce food for a population enormously greater than the Red Indians, who lived upon herds of roaming buffaloes.

But it need hardly be added that the displacing of even a part of the natives from the lands which they occupied, however much they neglected them, was an operation sure to excite strong resentment, and to be accompanied with many real hardships. What the king had to offer as a counterbalance to these griefs was relief from the "cuttings and cosherings" of the old chieftains, a secure freehold of the lands re-granted to the remaining occupiers, and a strictly just and gentle administration of the English laws. Lastly, the bulk of the escheated lands should have been re-granted to natives, whose interest would then have led them to dread the return of Tyrone, and the resumption of the old dues and exactions. Perhaps the only restriction to be put upon these large re-grants would have been to make conformity to the religion of the State a condition of remaining with a fixed tenure. No Roman Catholic State in Europe would have hesitated to enforce such a restriction on their side. But then the Reformed faith should also have been assiduously and zealously taught by a clergy conversant with the native tongue.

All these ideas were quite familiar to the mind of King James. Mountjoy, during the too brief time that he survived after his victorious career in Ireland, was undoubtedly the king's chief adviser upon Irish affairs, and Chichester, his lieutenant, had been brought up in the same school. But with the death of Mountjoy the master hand, which could have controlled errors and abuses, was gone, and both the king and his subordinates made mistakes of detail, which marred a large and philosophic policy.

In this policy the "college near Dublin" was to play a

[1] Cf., for example, what Sir Thomas Phillip says, S. P., 1632, p. 412.

leading part. While bishoprics and parishes were endowed with lands and glebes, the college was to educate an Irish Church clergy to do duty not only in the English and Scotch plantations, but among the natives. Here, however, as well as elsewhere, the plan failed in its details. Temple was evidently unequal to the task, and we cannot but regret that such a man as Daniell, now Archbishop of Tuam, was not kept in the College, and promoted to rule it at this crisis. It is evident from a letter of Ussher that pressure was being brought on Temple to resign during the last years of his life, and his case is but one of the many failures which King James had to endure. Neither Chichester, St. John, nor Falkland seem strong enough to subdue the greed of undertakers and servitors, the neglect and misconduct of Churchmen, or, on the other hand, to combat the vigour and persistency of Jesuits, seminaries, and priests, who utilised the grievances of the plantation to feed hopes of the return of Tyrone with a new expedition from the King of Spain.

The king was on the one hand urged by all those who hoped for grants of land to extend his plantations and make similar confiscations and settlements in the wild parts of Wexford and Carlow—Mounts Leinster and Blackstairs were haunts of Kavanaghs and other wild septs—and in Roscommon and Leitrim, where O'Rourke had always been a proud and obstinate opponent of England. On the other hand, the special Commission he appointed to report upon the alleged failure of the existing settlements, and to recommend remedies, point out the danger of such a course. " Though plantations made upon just grounds were very necessary for the securing of many disordered territories in that country, yet considering that works of that nature had been much perverted by the private aims of many particular persons to get only large scopes of land into their hands for their own profit, without any care of settling them for the strength and safety of the country ; and withal remembering that they are causes of much discontent and exasperation to the people whom they concern, and that these late plantations are yet in their infancy and far from being well settled, they deem it unreasonable to think effectually of any more plantations for the present ; yet the Lord Deputy's care, &c., should be acknowledged, and he might be let know that he will do good service if he can settle any disordered Irish country by breaking up the dependencies of the people from their chief lords, and disposing the lands in orderly manner upon the natives and possessors to their good content at profitable rents and tenures."[1]

Among the new landlords created by the Ulster plantation we do not hear a word of special complaint against the College, beyond the preferring of natives for the best scholarships. For in the first place neither here nor in Munster had the fellows displaced the actual occupiers ; and in the second the rents they required were always exceedingly moderate, so much so that great estates were acquired by the middlemen who held leases under them, without oppression of the natives. But the greed of speculators, and the king's evil habit of stopping the mouth of claimants for favour by grants of land in Ireland, became so great a terror to all previous holders that we have[2] a formal complaint from the undertakers to say that the whole enterprise in the north, which had begun most favourably, was now languishing through want of confidence in the king's gifts, which might any day be revoked on the ground that difficult or impossible conditions imposed upon the first grantees had not been fulfilled. Under these circumstances the fear arose that newer and stronger favourites would prove the lands to be again forfeited, and displace the first planters. Hence many were already selling their holdings at mean prices, and returning to England, while the natives were resuming occupation, and threatening the remaining English that they too would soon be driven out by the return of Tyrone.

[1] S. P., July, 1623, p. 427. [2] ibid., 1625, p. 518.

The State Papers of the day, especially under the rule of Falkland, who is ever complaining that he is shackled and thwarted, and unable to carry out his duty to the king, show clearly that with the partial blue sky of peace there were the lowering clouds and muttering thunder of the coming storm—public assemblies of priests and friars, missions of Jesuits, flying rumours of a great Spanish invasion, scattered occurrences of murders to resist the law—all caused, say the correspondents, by the vacillation of the king between his desire to uphold the reformed religion, and at the same time to temporise with Spain and the Pope. The news of Prince Charles's escapade to Spain set the minds of all the recusants in Ireland in a flutter. If the Prince married a Spanish princess it was surely impossible that her creed should be persecuted in Ireland. King James too often did retract his frequent orders regarding the expulsion of the Jesuits, owing to the pressure of the Spanish ambassador, so that the puzzled Viceroy never knew whether to tighten or to relax his rule.[1]

These matters are not a digression; they must be understood and kept in mind when we try to appreciate the religious and political atmosphere of the College in these early days. It is idle to say that the life of the students and their teachers stood apart from the great world, and had no concern with it. Such isolation in those critical times was quite impossible.

We have already suggested, regarding the wards ordered to be educated in the College, that but a small proportion of them was actually sent there. But we have lost the old Matricula-

[1] Cf. S. P., 1611, p. 246. The king does not wish to enjoin on Chichester the prosecution of recusants without exception, but leaves the whole question to his discretion, reminding him of the king's desire "that he should forward religion so far forth as it gave not any occasion to make any disturbance among the people." To this Chichester replies (Ibid., pp. 268, 446) that if the Jesuits and recusant lawyers were persistently prosecuted, "the rest of the people would soon banish the Pope out of their hearts." Accordingly some prominent people about Dublin were capriciously fined, while the masses of the people were left undisturbed.

tion book, which would tell us the facts, and therefore, beyond scholars, who were of the poorer class, we have only chance allusions to the fellow commoners and pensioners, of whom there seem to have been not more than fifteen or twenty on the books at any one time up to Temple's death. Nevertheless we know of some youths of importance, who were not wards, being in residence. An O'Donnell (son of Sir Neale), a Fitzmaurice (Lord Lixnaw's son), Lord Burke of Castleconnell, Captain Falkland, son of the Lord Deputy, and a son of Sir Turlough O'Brien are mentioned. The last occurs in a connection showing how respectfully these young aristocrats were treated. A student named Coyne was to be punished for going into the city without leave, when Sir Turlough's son went to the Provost and explained that Coyne had done so on urgent business for himself, whereupon the punishment is mitigated into a merely formal confession of the offence.[1] The other names appear in the State Papers of the reign.[2] Even in the time of Alvey the number of silver cups belonging to the College, evidently the gift of the parents or guardians of fellow commoners, show that the small number of paying students were people of quality.

The number of degrees conferred in the years 1614–25, of which an account is preserved to us by Temple,[3] shows an average of over twenty, which is very high, seeing that almost one-half of them, 112, compared with 119, are M.A. and higher degrees, implying a residence of seven years at the

[1] P. B., 215.
[2] Lord Burke of Castleconnell : "We have great hope of him, being Protestant, and bred in the College" (S. P., 1620, p. 282). "The Lords are glad to hear of the good education the Lord Lixnaw's son, *and others of quality*, are receiving in the College of Dublin, which they pray may be continued accordingly" (S. P., 1615, p. 66). "He is brought up with the Earl of Thomond, a Protestant, at the College of Dublin" (S. P., 1613, 459, also 1615, 102). I need not multiply quotations for the analogous cases.
[3] P. B., pp. 176, 184–5.

least. It is true that they came to College very raw, but they were not matriculated till they knew something,[1] being handed over to the College schoolmaster, one of the fellows, who taught them in the Chapel daily. The master in Temple's time was Ed. Donnellan, who was paid the large sum of £10 per annum, with an addition if the fees of his pupils did not bring him £10 more.[2]

Stubbs has given in his book (pp. 43–5) the details of the four years' course, with the important omission of all mention of the training in Latin, Greek, and Hebrew. Yet Bedell, from whose Statutes these details are taken, is quite express on the point. All the classes together were to be exercised in Greek and in Hebrew by a special lecturer, *si commode fieri potest*. This proviso is not explained. I presume that in the absence of a special lecturer, each tutor undertook this indispensable work with his pupils. But a Latin theme and a Latin description of the work of the week, as well as a weekly declamation, were also an universal requirement. What proficiency was expected of students appears from the Degree Examination, in which they were expected to translate any part of the Greek Testament and the first two Psalms from Hebrew into Latin. The latter might be merely an exercise in memory, but the former is an ordeal that nowadays hardly any of our ordinary candidates for the A.B. degree would care to face.

Omitting the details which may be read in the book referred to, or indeed in the Caroline Statutes, we think a general review of the education of that day and a comparison with our own will reveal many obstinate survivals of details, while the whole spirit and temper of University

---

[1] Cf. the P. B., 215b, the note beginning, "These are counted unmatriculated though in the College." The names follow with various dates, some of them a year back, fixed as those of their formal matriculation. This was in August, 1611, after the Midsummer Examination to test progress. There were then at least five fellow commoners in the House.

[2] P. B., 206b.

training has been modified by the fatal influx of text-books, which submerges much honest teaching and learning. The four classes of undergraduates remain to this day, and that the passage from Freshman to Sophister now known as the Little Go was an important step even then appears from the isolated note,[1] *post exam̄ habitas in grad. juni. Sophistarū ordin̄ cooptati sunt*, and eleven names follow. Had the failures been appended, we should have had an account of the Little Go of 1611, and of the size of the Senior Freshmen class in that year. The Professor of Theological Controversies, too, lectured then as he now does, on the Romish Controversy, but we do not find that the exposition now given by him of the Ritual of the reformed Church was required in this Puritan atmosphere. The main Commencements of the year were fixed at the end of Trinity term, and so they have remained till now, though that term has been shortened by a week. A summer term, in July and August, was then kept—now an approved innovation at Oxford and Cambridge, which some of us have in vain endeavoured to re-introduce into Trinity College.

But if in these points old traditions still survive, a great change has come over us since the time when the business of the teacher was to expound a subject and not a book, and that of the student was so to assimilate his lesson that he could reproduce it in a Latin essay, and defend his views in public disputation. If there was less to be known then than now, there was on the other hand an insistence upon that knowledge being ready for use, and defensible by argument. As a mental training our present University courses have nothing of the same value, and so far we have distinctly deteriorated. Most of us have endeavoured to mend the fault (very inadequately) by those debating societies which are so prominent in modern University life. But there long remained in Trinity College another valuable representative of the old spirit—that habit of requiring *viva voce* answering at Fellowship examination and

[1] P. B., 213.

for all the higher honours, which has only given way of recent years to the influence of the sister societies of Oxford and Cambridge and of the State competitions. There are men still living in Dublin who obtained their Fellowship by an exclusively *viva voce* examination, and not a little of the readiness of the Irish scholar is directly due to this excellent practice. It is known that Chatham trained his great son to fluency by making him read out Latin and Greek texts in English. Every scholar of Trinity College (from the foundation till late in the nineteenth century) underwent that very training. In the philosophy course for fellowship, *viva voce* still counts for half the examination.

The opening of the first year's studies with *Dialectic* points in its very title to a Ramist course. Though the pupils probably had no text-books, we may be sure that the lecturers used Temple's edition of Ramus, and the other commentaries upon this popular author. In the second year followed Logic; then in the third Physiology, or what we should call Natural Philosophy, such as it was before DesCartes, or even Bacon; in the fourth year this Physiology was combined with Ethic and Rhetoric. Even to this day, the insisting upon Ethics and Astronomy for the A.B. examination is a distinctive and valuable feature in the education of the College; and this astronomy is only a part of the physiology of the ancients, which corresponds to the mathematical physics still taught in our fourth year.

These details can hardly interest the general reader, nor is it very important to examine what was taught in the College, provided we know how it was taught, and that it was taught honestly. By the constant habit of inviting men of eminence from Cambridge to be Provosts or Professors, they secured that their standard should be that of England, not of the Ireland of that day, and James Ussher's influence, though he was now engaged in a wider sphere of work, must always have been used to promote real and serious learning.

Externally, the surroundings of the College were undergoing considerable change. At the first foundation Hoggen Green was really an open space, whereon the cattle and swine of the citizens used to graze. But in Speed's map (1610) it is already enclosed by a wall, and there are signs of buildings encroaching upon it. Let it be remembered, however, that, as Roque's map shows, the College of that day did not reach within fifty yards so far west or north as it now does. The old steeple, at the north-west corner of the original square, stood about half-way between the present gate and the belfry, and on that line. Hence there was considerable room between the College and the piece of ground acquired from the city by Sir G. Carey, Treasurer at War (in 1602), which skirted the water side of the green, and was afterwards acquired by Lord Chichester, whose residence there became famous as Chichester House. Sir Toby Caulfeild got another grant of the rising ground over against it between the Green, Grafton Street, and Suffolk Street, and built there a house afterwards (1632) occupied by Archbishop Ussher. These and other gifts began to encroach so much upon the public green, that there is a resolution passed [1] that no more shall be granted—a resolution, of course, presently violated. But the rise of fashionable residences about the Green must have been considerably affected by the Bridewell, situated about the foot of Trinity Street, which had been granted to Challoner and his associates in 1604.[2] The references to it in the City Records, which are few, are wholly distinct from those preserved by *Anon.* from the College papers, though not inconsistent with them. From both together we learn that the city, on petition from the lessees in 1604, consented to introduce words into the lease, widening the powers of the lessees. And in 1609 the city passed a resolution that as there was no longer any intention of having a Bridewell, the lessees might apply it to the other uses allowed by the original gift, notably for a free school.

[1] *Dublin Records*, iii. p. 303.   [2] Cf. above, p. 130.

Meanwhile Sir George Carey's house and holding had taken the fancy of Chichester, and at the close of his rule at the Castle, when he was about to remove to the north, he petitioned the Corporation to give him Sir G. Carey's lease with a long extension of years, that he might build himself a city residence. Very naturally he did not wish to have the derelict Bridewell facing his property, and so he proposed to the city to remit the fine of £50 imposed upon the citizens for the escape of a prisoner from the Castle, if they would make it over to Trinity College. This the city was willing to grant, but an unforeseen difficulty arose from the occupying tenant, George Breddam, who had evidently got a lease from Challoner and his fellows, and who refused to leave without compensation. Copies of the inquiries made by the city into his claims are preserved in *Anon.*, pp. 71–3, whence it appears that the Committee of inquiry conceded his claim for necessary repairs and glazing of the house to be £30. The case was decided by a court of law, and the Corporation was ordered to satisfy Mr. Breddam, and this is enforced by an order of Council in October, 1616, when St. John had already succeeded as Deputy. It was obvious that as the College was to get the house and ground, this charge might fairly be defrayed by them, and so we have from William Ussher, an official at the Castle, the following note, December 11, 1616, " Cossen Dr. Ussher. My Lord Deputy desires to know the resolution of the College whether they will pay £30 Eng. and take this Bridewell house or no—wherein you shall do well to repair to my Lord and that with some speed." Not one word of all this appears in the P. B., nor does the result appear anywhere in that book, but it is stated in *Anon.* that the city settled the house and plot on certain persons, who for the sum of £30 conveyed it to the College, and that it remained until the Rebellion of 1641 a place of residence for students under the name of Trinity Hall.

These tedious details are here given, because they were unknown to Gilbert, the historian of Dublin. If the Green had been somewhat invaded and curtailed the College had at least secured aristocratic neighbours, and a further house of residence.

It remains, in conclusion of this long chapter on Temple's rule, to estimate the discipline of the students from the notes of censures and punishments inflicted. But I protest against these being taken by themselves, and not in relation to the conditions under which the students lived. What scope or outlet had they for their energies, and what care was taken to given them innocent amusements as well as interesting studies? If human nature were not in some respects the same in every age, if youth were not gay and robust in every healthy race, we might well imagine that the educators of that day were absolutely ignorant of what we call innocent and wholesome recreation. The parks were not, as now, devoted to the use of the students for their games—all games in the courts or gardens being formally forbidden both in Bedell's and Laud's Statutes,—but divided by walls and fences into several compounds, and either let to the Lord Deputy for his horses, the Dean of Christ Church (Wheeler) for his orchard, or reserved for the fellows. Even these complain that the Provost had collected a heap of manure in the garden to which they were granted keys. The only legitimate reason a student could allege for visiting the city was to go to service at Christ Church, and yet there the seats reserved for him and his companions were exposed to cold and draught, and were so situated that to them the sermon was inaudible. There were indeed tennis courts in Thomas Street open to young blades like Lord Howth and Sir Roger Jones, even during Church-time on Sunday, where a famous affray between these gentlemen and their followers took place, but such pastimes were not provided for the College boys. The parades of the city, the bull- and bear-baiting, the processions round the circuit of the walls—all such distractions were forbidden and punished by severe measures—exclusion from commons for a week or two, the confession of the crime upon their knees, lasting all dinner time, and often the sharp correction of the rod. When the Junior Dean holds his "corrections" now every Saturday, he little dreams that his prodecessors in Temple's days applied the birch to the younger offenders, and even to those who had lost the privilege of *adultage* by frequent transgressions.[1] Is it any wonder then that we hear of some making free with the cherries that hung out temptingly over the Dean's orchard wall, that others escaped early from Sunday Chapel to roam in the country, that others "transcended the College wall" to visit the town, and even effected their return by night through a window in the ground floor of the steeple? To any one fond of boys there seems little harm in any of these escapades save that of going to alehouses in the city, where the women who served were, according to the city records, of more than doubtful character. Playing cards with the porter in the steeple, and carrying off bacon and fowl from the College larder, was no heinous offence for those who had been excluded from commons for some trifling transgression. I see no more serious flaw in their conduct than the habit of breaking windows and getting over walls, which a little reasonable laxity would easily have cured.

We close our chapter with the fact that Temple, whose health was long failing, and whose vacancy was being eagerly watched by many prospective Provosts, died on January 15, 1626 (O. S.) and was buried under the Provost's seat in the old College Chapel.[2]

---

[1] We are told in Bedell's Statutes (Cap. II) that students were freed from the rod at the age of eighteen, but as the normal period of education was from the twelfth to the eighteenth year, the use of the rod is parallel to that in the English public schools of our day.

[2] I remember, when a boy, that the opening of foundations for the present belfry disclosed the ancient burial of some person of importance. A paper was read in the medical school upon his skull, which was of a singularly low type. We have no authentic portrait of Temple to help us in this respect, but it seems likely that he was the person exhumed, and if so, this spot gives us the site of the west door of the chapel, where the Provost would sit. This indication moves the original quadrangle far into the present court, as already suggested.

CHAPTER V

BEDELL—ROBERT USSHER [1] (1626-34)

TEMPLE, in spite of his leases of College lands, and the appointment of his son as seneschal, died considerably and discreditably indebted to the College. The money claimed against him amounts to £450, and we know that there was great difficulty in recovering it from Lady Temple and his sons. But though the Provost's salary was still only £100, the indirect profits must have been considerable, for Ussher is full of fears [2] that some adventurer will obtain the post for the sake of lucre. We have still the letter of one of the aspirants, Edward Clark, who had succeeded another plunderer, Sir William Ryves, as Commissary of Prerogatives, &c., a lay post which much troubled the bishops and clergy, and in which great injustices

---

[1] With the entry of Temple's death commences the earliest official Register of the College, it being enacted in the following, August 19 (Reg., p. 15): "The Register's place and the custody of the Library is devolved to one of ye Senior ffellowes in perpetuū; his stipend is six pound per annum." There are some later resolutions and some lists thrust into the first few pages. But from henceforth we have something like a continuous record of public events in the College. The entries in the P. B. overlap this book up to the great Rebellion, and are often identical with it, but both are independent, and each of them often supplies what is missing in the other. The remaining authority is the Bursar's book.

[2] Cf. his letter of February 9, 1626-7, quoted by Stubbs, p. 51, and the king's mandate, M. R., F 46.

to ecclesiastical property were common. This man suggests [1] that the fellows may favour him, as his official post gives him so much control over their benefices and glebes in the country.

Such were the people whom Primate Ussher dreaded. He had also made up his mind that a lay Provost was inexpedient. Temple's rule, so far as the College was intended to provide an efficient clergy, was distinctly a failure. He bethought him of two pious men, Joseph Mede, a fellow of Christ's College, Cambridge, and Rich. Sibbes, a well-known preacher at Gray's Inn. The Senior Fellows actually elected Mede, and sent over two of their number to fetch him. But meanwhile the juniors, who claimed by the Charter a voice in the election (a claim admitted by the Visitors), chose Robert Ussher, for years back Vice-Provost (if that office was permanent), and actually swore him in. This proceeding, followed by many similar quarrels, shows what good reason there was for a complete reform in the government of the College. Primate Ussher's attempts to secure a proper man had not been successful. Mede sent over his resignation, which is in the Registry; Sibbes refused to come over.[2]

The two archbishops then bethought them of William Bedell, probably far better than either of the others, and he was specially recommended to the fellows in an extant letter from Abbot, wherein he mentions that Bedell had been abroad, and

[1] S. P., 1625, p. 39. "The provost is very aged and sickly. Pray secure my nomination if you can. Perhaps the fellows will favour me as I have power by the prerogative to examine the dispensations and titles of the clergy of their benefices."—Letter to William Boswell.

[2] The facts are not quite clear. There is a letter from Abbot to Ussher (*Life*, xv. p. 375) written when he was sending over Sibbes. Hely Hutchinson says that he was proposed for election in the College, but that the fellows voted in equal numbers for and against him. This statement I have not been able to verify, and I do not believe it, as all the records are silent about it. Another contemporary letter says that Sibbes was appointed Master of S. Katherine's Hall in Cambridge, which he no doubt preferred to the Irish College.

had large experience of men, as well as College learning.[1] We have also[2] a recommendation of him from Sir H. Wotton, whose chaplain he had been, at the embassy in Venice. This is not the place to speak of the highly interesting condition of Venice when Bedell resided there. The republic was tainted with the principles of the Reformation, and openly refused to submit to the dictates of the Pope. Their theological leader was Fra. Paolo Sarpi, who would have undoubtedly carried through a revolt to Protestantism, had he possessed the temper of a Luther together with his own profound learning. Bedell was this man's constant adviser in theology, especially in the meaning of the Greek and Hebrew originals of the Bible, and was so zealous in his endeavours to spread the light, that he learned to speak and write Italian fluently, and even translated for Sarpi and his brethren in revolt the English Book of Common Prayer, which they were ready to adopt, if their State had maintained its opposition to Rome.

The experience of a great struggle against the Papacy in Venice was a very suitable prelude to a commission in the campaign against Popery undertaken by the English Government, and its Protestant College, in Ireland. But this Venetian experience was not Bedell's only qualification. He was the younger son of a squire of old family in Essex, and had been educated at Emanuel College, Cambridge, where he was elected a fellow in 1593. About 1602 he went out on a living at Edmondsbury, from which he went in 1604 to Venice. After a stay of a few years there (I cannot find how long) he returned to his country living, where he remained in comparative obscurity till called to Ireland. This delay in his promotion is said to have been due to his Calvinistic opinions, though he was distinctly a Churchman, and not a Puritan; a

---

[1] This eminent man has found many biographers. Apart from articles in Dictionaries there are two sketches by his son and son-in-law, recently republished by Mr. Shuckburgh (Cambridge, 1902), and lives by Bishop Burnet, Monck Mason, and others.

[2] Bedell's *Life* (Mason), p. 89.

more serious obstacle was his modest and retiring character in an age when most appointments were given to men who brought themselves into public notice. At all events, the king, the Chancellor Abbot, and the Lord Deputy directed the Senior Fellows to elect him, which they did, not without protest from the juniors. Abbot in his letter says that having examined the College statutes, he finds that the election belongs to the ancients or seniors.[1] The answer of the juniors was of course that no College statutes could override the original Charter wherein this right was given to the fellows generally, and before any distinction between senior and junior existed, and this was the opinion of the Visitors to whom they appealed, " but because the Prime Visitor, their Vice-Chancellor Ussher, was absent, nothing was done."[2] Robert Ussher indeed stood upon his election, even when Bedell came over, and refused to accompany him and the other fellows to see the Primate at his Palace of Termonfechan near Drogheda. But Robert Ussher was no man to hold out in opposition, and so Bedell was formally sworn in as Provost on August 16, 1627. Bedell's diary gives us the exact dates of this part of his life.[3] He took care to secure himself in case the place did not suit him :—

"Item, that the place here being litigious, and my family untransported, I meant not presently to give up my living, but when with the convenience of my affairs I might so do. Then I took the oath, and had the keys delivered to me. After, I exhorted every man to do his duty, and to live according to the statutes, by which I was strictly bound by oath to govern. After began the Divinity Lecture. After dinner I viewed the hall, Provost's lodging, library, gardens, &c. At 2 of the clock was a meeting of the Senior Fellows. It was

---

[1] Unfortunately this is one of the chapters of Temple's Statutes which has been lost. Very possibly it was torn off from the rest to be sent over for Abbot's perusal. At all events we have lost the particular wording of all that related to elections.
[2] M. R., F 56, dated June 2, 1627.
[3] Now accessible in P. B., p. 97 *sq*.

resolved the next Lord's day to have a Communion; and to that end to provide a Communion table, carpet, cloth, napkin, &c., and an *amnesty* of all former quarrels."

These details show how completely Puritanism had eaten into the habits of the College. Not only when Temple became old, but for eleven years back, there had been no Holy Communion in the Chapel. Well might Ussher see the necessity of appointing a clerical Provost to maintain the doctrine and discipline of the Church. Bedell seems merely to have had a look into the College and its disorders, and to have drawn up and passed a copy of the statutes,[1] when he departed again for England, leaving the College in charge of the Welsh Vice-Provost, John Floyd, without even waiting for the election of new fellows and scholars. This is what Bedell tells us in the highly interesting letter to Sir N. Riche on the disorders of the College.[2] The finances he could not attack in this short visit, seeing that there was debt[3] and looseness of business habits amounting to dishonesty.

The reason of his departure was to bring over his family, but as he stayed away eight months, and made many efforts to resign, we may suppose that his wife and family refused to come, though that reason, beyond the six weeks' illness of a son with ague, has not been stated. His conduct in staying away seems to us reprehensible. He heard presently that the College was in disorder. The Vice-Provost, who then seems (as acting Provost) to have had a veto, refused to elect any further fellows, because his own cousin, William Floyd, was not chosen. Randal Ince was the only fellow elected.

[1] P. B., 98b, September 6th :—" Mr. Temple's case, and the statute *de Ecclesiastico Beneficio* was treated about, and after much deliberating differred till the Provost's return. 7th. The statutes which in all this time had been degested and brought into order in a new booke were finished, consented unto, and agreed they should be read. 8th. The statutes read in the Chapell," and so on for some days, till the Provost, after waiting at Ringsend five days for favourable weather, put to sea September 18, 1627.

[2] Stubbs, Appendix, xxviii.   [3] ibid., p. 395.

BEDELL—ROBERT USSHER (1626-34)

Several candidates then petitioned Lord Falkland to admit them as fellows on the ground that a lapse of time had occurred, which gave the election to the Crown. Falkland accordingly issued an order to admit three of them, Cottingham, Vesey, and Floyd, but the fellows called a Visitation and showed clearly that they had not lost the right of election by lapse. The Visitors even deposed the Vice-Provost, and declared him no fellow, though allowing him to remain a tutor and have commons. Falkland thereupon retracted his order.[1] The fellows were so busy quarrelling that they even forgot to inform the Provost of current events. Of this he complains in his letters, and bemoans his own incapacity. The one thing obvious—a speedy return, was the course he did not take. At last, in answer to a most respectful and affectionate, but pressing Latin missive from the fellows,[2] and the command of the king and Chancellor, he made up his mind to return to Ireland.

He was only Provost for about two years, when he was promoted to the combined Sees of Kilmore and Ardagh, but in these two years he had more influence upon the College than

---

[1] These three men, charged in the Visitation with making false representations to the Lord Deputy were therefore not fellows, and should be erased from the list which appears in the College Calendar. Neither H.H. nor *Anon.* seem to know Falkland's formal retractation of his mandate, preserved in the M.R., F 53. The terms in which the major part of the fellows complain (*Anon.*, 161) show us clearly one feature in the form of election, which had already disappeared from Bedell's Statutes, adopted a few months before, but which was evidently acknowledged as still dominating the election of 1627. Bedell notes that these new statutes were subscribed and appointed to be read formally the following July (P. B., 99b), though it had been done the previous September. "The fellows took objection to the Vice-Provost for *propounding whom he pleased*, and that *he denied to propound natives*, who were candidates, because his relative was denied." It was therefore the privilege of the Provost (or Vice-Provost) to propound a list, on which the Senior Fellows voted. But if they rejected the list they had no power to nominate others. Vesey and Cottingham had been candidates at a former examination, and not apparently at the recent one.

[2] Given by Stubbs, p. 397.

Temple in his eighteen. He has left in the *Particular Book* entries in the form of a diary, which are most instructive regarding the life of the place. On the other hand, he neglects to tell us (what Temple does) the names of the scholars elected each year, so leaving a serious gap in this part of the College Register. He also re-handled and reduced to literary and connected form the College statutes, "which being part Latin, part English, and in sheets of paper some stitched together, some loose, and a heape w̄out order, with long p̄ambles, and sometimes unnecessary, and in many places defective, digested into a new form, and published in the Chapell."[1] Of these at least two copies in his handwriting are extant. They not only give us the general outline of the older book, for he made no unnecessary innovations either in matter or style, but also the model upon which the Caroline Charter, which ever since has governed the College, was drawn up. A comparison of the work of Bedell with that of Laud will show how conservative the latter was, and how closely he followed his predecessor in all points which did not call loudly for reform.[2] There can be little doubt that as Bedell was a friend of Laud, and as Ussher was so also, the changes introduced by Laud and by Strafford were suggested, or at least approved of, by the Bishop of Kilmore.

The one salient fact in the history of the College was the disorder of its government, and the fact that fellows, engaged in wrangling, neglected their proper work. A letter of Ussher (xv. 575) has indeed been quoted from that day to this, to the effect that these statutes were copied from those of Emanuel College, Cambridge. No one seems hitherto to have verified this statement, for a comparison of the two codes shows it to

---

[1] Note from a letter to Sir Nath. Riche, quoted in Stubbs, p. 395.

[2] The copy of Bedell's Statutes which I use for my review of his work is one in his own hand which I bought at a book auction some years ago for a few shillings. There is another in the College Library, another copy is in the Muniment Room. From these I have printed them in Appendix I. to this volume, and for the first time.

be quite wrong. It is indeed clear from the history of the College that Bedell's Statutes were in the main those of Temple, and they bear no more likeness to those of Emanuel College than they do to the statutes of any other College in Cambridge, with the one exception of the standing required from candidates for fellowship—at least seven terms from their B.A. degree. This is, of course, the point to which Ussher refers, though he speaks generally. The somewhat rhetorical preamble, and the first chapter *de Cultu divino* are probably composed by Bedell, for the statutes of other Cambridge Colleges show that the composition of this preface was a thing of display, wherein the author showed not only his Latin prose, but his historical and literary conceits. Laud repeats it verbatim, but to copy such a thing from another book of statutes would be regarded as we now regard copying another man's sermon. The duration of a fellowship seems to have been but seven years from the M.A. degree, for we find at this time senior fellowships frequently declared vacant, or claimed on the ground that they ought to be vacant,[1] but in Bedell's book the question is deliberately left open, and there is a distinct allusion to a new Charter on this point about to issue from the king. The care of Divine service is marked by making it the subject of the first chapter, and here no doubt there were many particulars introduced. In Laud's book this matter is postponed till the ninth chapter.

A further examination of these statutes may be postponed to the sequel, in which Laud's rehandling of them will be considered. There are two significant explications set in the forefront of the book and dated September 23 and 24, 1628, that is to say after Bedell's return. The first defines the "Ecclesiastical Benefice" which a fellow was sworn not to hold save within three miles of the city. It receives its widest meaning, whether with or without a cure of souls. At this very time a fellow, Parry, was accused of holding such a

[1] P. B., 97-8.

benefice, and removed. The second defines whether the disqualification of marriage (*si uxorem duxisse compertum sit*) was to be retrospective, or only to apply to cases after the date of the statute. The latter interpretation was adopted, which suggests that during the reign of disorder this licence also had crept into the College. As a matter of fact there was a Senior Fellowship claimed by Mr. Price on the ground that Mr. Thomas was married, and had so forfeited it according to the statute, but the official interpretation, as he had been married long before the promulgation, was held to save him from the forfeiture.[1] There were also accusations of malversation against both Vice-Provost and Bursar, of neglect of duty, and disregard of natives by the fellows; moreover, not one of the staff at this period appears as an author or eminent teacher. The chapter on the choice of a Provost says that *cæteris paribus* an alumnus is to be preferred to a stranger.

There was little chance of this suggestion being adopted honestly, when we compare the eminence of Bedell with the obscurity of his staff. The popular man in the College who was again elected when Bedell resigned was Robert Ussher, but his great cousin in recommending him has little to say of his learning or his eloquence. Ambrose Ussher was still alive, but evidently no longer employed in the College. He died suddenly in 1629, the last of the old Society of better days. I have found indirect evidence that James Ussher felt this decadence, for he no longer entrusted lads of importance to his old College. There are letters to him from Exeter College, whither he had sent James Dillon, his relative, and whom the rector, evidently proud of such an honour, proposes to take into his own chamber. He is to associate with three sons of earls, and with the son of Lord Caulfield, an Irish peer and a member with Ussher of the Privy Council in Dublin.[2] There was evidently no tutor in Trinity College to whom Ussher would now entrust the education of a youth under his

[1] Reg., 18.   [2] Ussher, *Works*, xv. pp. 417, 419.

care. He was a timid man, who would not face the odium of mending things by a trenchant visitation, but he must often have suggested to Abbot and to Laud, now Bishop of London, and rapidly rising in power, the reform of the Irish University.

The disorders of the students, so far as we know them from Bedell's diary of punishments, were trivial in comparison with those of the fellows, but there was one fraught with such consequences to the city that it is well worth studying in some detail. We find in Gilbert's *Records of Dublin*,[1] an entry of a lease by the Corporation to Alderman Arthur of a strip of land running along the west wall of the College, for the purpose of building. Such a grant was one step towards turning the common of Hoggen Green into streets, producing ground-rent to the city, and there is evidence in resolutions of the citizens [2] that it was against the feelings of those who desired to keep open places of recreation to the inhabitants of the city. S. Stephen's Green, and the broad expanse of Blackhall Place (Oxmantown Green), show how far this jealousy of old rights produced its effect. But Hoggen Green, now already sometimes called College Green, was in more imminent danger. Great people had obtained plots on each side of it, and men of influence in the city like Arthur were making further encroachments with the consent of those who wished to raise the revenues of the city. But no sooner did Arthur, in the spring of 1629, set up hoardings to begin his building, than the College protested to the Lord Deputy that the proposed houses would interfere with the light and comfort of the College, and stop a gate westward which they had intended to make towards the city. They also petitioned the Corporation in a curious document printed in the appendix to this chapter. The dispute was referred to a Commission of the Privy Council, who recommended that Arthur should sell his lease to the College. But upon his refusal the students sallied out, and carried off the boards of the enclosure into the College.

[1] Vol. iii. p. 207. [2] Above, p. 188.

The Provost reprimanded them after Evening Chapel for this violence, and ordered them to bring the woodwork out of their rooms into the court, where it was piled up in a great heap, and a message sent to Arthur that he might take it away if he chose. This he did after some hesitation. Nor did he feel strong enough to take legal action against the College, whose turbulent acts must have had many sympathisers in the city. But as he persisted in his refusal to sell, the ground remained vacant. The memory too of this successful resistance to encroachment was fresh for many long years, for in 1683[1] we find allusion to the adjoining ground remaining vacant owing to certain "turbulent scholars." It was not till that date that the College petitioned the Corporation to break the lease, now held by Arthur's descendants, on the ground of neglect of conditions therein, and grant it to the College, which promised to keep the thoroughfare from S. Stephen's Green to Lazy Hill open, and the road in repair. Thus this piece of ground, under condition of being planted and kept open westward for the benefit of the citizens, became part of the College, and it appears as the garden along the west front in the picture annexed to Brooking's map (dated 1728).[2]

These consequences are, however, long subsequent to the days of this history. Suffice it here to say that if the College owes the Corporation a great debt of gratitude for the gift of its present site, the Corporation also owes the students of the College some consideration for saving it from its momentary lapse in public spirit, and keeping open that central spot in the present city, without which the great west front of the College, and the splendid Parliament House, now the glory of architectural Dublin, would never have been undertaken.[3]

We can perceive Bedell's earnestness by the prompt way in which he introduced improvements in the education of the

---

[1] Gilbert, *Records*, v. 274.   [2] Cf. Stubbs, 189.
[3] The papers on this controversy (A iii. a, 1, 2, 3, in the M. R.) are given in the appendix to this chapter.

House. He not only instituted at once the speaking of Latin at commons, which we may compare with the speaking of French at girls' schools at meal-times nowadays, but he was the first to give reality to the Royal desire regarding the training of a clergy able to teach the natives in the Irish tongue. Immediately upon his return (June, 1628) he directed "an Irish lecture to be read publickly in the hall, when all the natives that have the £3 a year are enjoined to be present; as also at Irish prayers in the chapell, upon holy days."[1] On the following 15th August it is ordered "that the natives lose their weekly allowance, if they be absent from their Irish prayers upon the Sunday," and in September, 1627, "an Irish chapter to be read in the Testament, by one of the natives at dinner in hall; and so to continue between twelve of the most proficientest, until the rest be able to perform it; which we enjoin them all within half a yeare, or, in default thereof, to be deprived of their natives' stipend."

These entries make it plain that the better-paid place of native scholar, who received a salary of £3 instead of the 10s. of the rest, had not been honestly given away,[2] and the study of the native language no more practised than it was at Maynooth College, till the present century. The names of the native scholars do not appear to be Irish (Kerdiffe, Conway, Baker, Davis, Burton are some of them), and the scholarship exam. does not seem to have included any test in that language, occasionally only does an unmistakable name occur, such as Teig O'Heyne.

Being in earnest and a good linguist, Bedell gave the example

---

[1] Reg., pp. 15, 17, 24.

[2] The following note (P. B., 99 : "Je 26, 1628, the same day, the natives' exercise was appointed for the first month to learne and write ye Ld : Prayer" seems to show that the natives were either wholly illiterate, or perfectly ignorant of Irish. A month at the Lord's Prayer seems otherwise absurd. Twelve Testaments for the Irish were presented a few months later by Sir William Ussher (P. B., 99b). Then service books are bought and bound for the natives (ib., 100).

by learning Irish himself, had advanced as early as March, 1628, to Psalm 88 in his translation of the Psalms, which had not been included in the Irish Book of Common Prayer, already printed some years before.

All these facts are fully set forth in the lives of Bedell; but when the biographers add that he was warmly encouraged by Archbishop Ussher, they seem to me not to understand the evidence. The earlier history of the College shows plainly that the greatest of the Anglo-Irish looked upon the native language even still as a great obstacle to true religion and civility. Their policy was to make English necessary, and spread the knowledge of it through their benighted country. The great founders, and Ussher with them, never thought of establishing an Irish lecture, till urged to it by repeated messages and orders from England. Both at this period, and after the Restoration, it was from English, and not from Anglo-Irish Provosts, that the impulse towards Irish studies arose. Among all the languages which James Ussher knew, I cannot find Irish enumerated, though we hear that his uncle, Henry Ussher, could preach in the language. We hear of sporadic cases of the favouring of Irish-speaking converts, and of aspirants to orders, by James Ussher, but of any continued efforts, like those of Bedell, there is no trace in his well-known life or in his voluminous correspondence.

We turn, in concluding our account of Bedell's brief but effective rule, to his Diary regarding the daily events in the College. Signs of laxity in the teaching and discipline were everywhere apparent. Here is a significant entry, July 16–18 (1627): 'At Examinations each forme censured. Agreed that none shall ascend out of one forme to another, however absent, till he be examined.' The annual summer examination test for moving up a class had therefore been evaded, and the teaching neglected. Various boys not students were being fed in the kitchen, but were now "interdicted fire and water, bread and beere" (ib., 100). Despite the ample income of the College, the chest was in debt, rents were unpaid, and sundry economies became necessary. The native places were reduced to twenty. The Provost, with characteristic honesty, set an example by undertaking to pay for his own commons. An entrance fee in the form of argent was established, or enforced. For an examination of the chest showed that apart from arrears, and money which "was perhaps never put in," there was £495 actually short of the money known to have been received. It was apparently the alarm at this excess of expenditure over apparent receipts that produced the disastrous petition (April 18, 1629) to be quit of arrears for the Patent of the Chantry Lands, which ended in the loss of that Patent (above, p. 118). The constant breaches of discipline, fighting, haunting the town, &c., which are noted from day to day are best explained by the following melancholy entry (July 11, 1629), "The fellow commoners complaint of Mr. Price (Dean) for the forbidding them to play at bowles in the orchards. They were blamed, and it was shown that by Statute they might not play there." Here are the terms of this fatuous prohibition repeated in the Caroline Charter: *Nulli lusus discipulis in area vel hortis Collegii permittantur*,[1] and this in the midst of a chapter threatening penalties for transcending the walls, breaking the windows, robbing the orchards, playing dice or cards, keeping sporting dogs, singing birds or hawks, and pursuing field sports; the boys were not even to talk in the halls or court, except when they were drinking their beer at *merenda* (breakfast). The following outrage is peculiarly interesting, because the student acted strictly according to a proclamation of the City Fathers: "Booth, for taking up a pig of Sir Samuel Smith's and that openly in the day tyme before many, and causing it to be dressed in town,

[1] The one exception was a theatrical representation by the students, to which there are a few enigmatical allusions in the Registers, *e.g.*, December 23 (1629): "The Senior Sophisters exercise dominion over the junior sort this Christmas, a comedy acted by them, and a play by ye bachelors." But even this was banished out of College by the next Provost (Stubbs, p. 63)

inciting Mr. Rollo and Sir Conway, who knew not of it, condemned to be whipped openly in the Hall, and pay for the pig."[1] There is not a word preserved of the lad's defence, but we can supply it from the order quoted below, one of many similar in the old Records of the Corporation.[2]

There was some debate between the Provost and the Chancellor, whether students should be required always to wear their gowns when they went, by permission of their tutors, into Dublin. Bedell thought not, "because the streets were very foul," the Archbishop suggested the undignified alternative of "taking them under their arms." I presume, from these gowns costing so much, that they were ampler than they now are, and that he meant tucking them up under their arm.

But Bedell's educational policy went farther and higher. He felt that it was a narrow thing to confine the House to be "a poor College of Divines," and promoted the study of both Law and Medicine. There is even a proposal mentioned[3] to found a College of Physicians in Dublin—an anticipation of the idea carried out by John Stearne a few years later.

No precise statement is extant concerning any rapid increase of students, owing to Bedell's excellent and enlightened reforms, but we may infer it from many distinct signs. He approaches the Chancellor on this point, whether it were not well to admit to lectures students who are matriculated, *even though they live with their parents in Dublin*, thus opening the door to a far-reaching change in the education of the college. This points to an excess of students in residence, which was relieved, or the relief at least attempted, by the founding of halls, to which

---

[1] P. B., 104–6.

[2] Gilbert, ii. 377 (1601): "yf eny sowe, hogge, or pigge shalbe found or sene, either by daye or nyght, in the streetes within the cittie walles, it shalbe lawfull for everye man to kill the same sowe, hogge, or pigge, and after to dispose the same at his or their disposition, without making recompence to such as owneth the same."

[3] S. P., 1626, p. 148.

we shall return presently. Trinity Hall, to judge from a single stray notice,[1] still existed, but we have no mention of students living in it. The increase of students must also depend to a great extent on the prosperity of the Protestant plantation in the north, and of this prosperity there is the most convincing proof in the offers made to Bedell by the middlemen, such as Lord Claneboy (Hamilton), Dr. Richardson, and others, whose twenty-one year leases were drawing near to their close (1629 or 30).[2] All these people were now seeking renewals, and most of them offering, when the College made difficulties, to double their rents.[3] Such offers speak for themselves, and must have made Bedell feel that whatever his difficulties had been, owing to the neglect or dishonesty of the previous management, the College would presently not only be solvent, but rich.

Yet all these healthy symptoms were accompanied by the growth of a counter-influence likely to destroy not only the College but the whole plantation, if not stayed. This was the increasing power and pretensions of the Popish priests, Jesuits, and friars, whom the weak policy of Charles, and still more his marriage with a Roman Catholic princess, were encouraging with the prospect of State connivance, if not toleration. These missionaries, whose zeal deserves our admiration, had hitherto been content to deter the youth of Ireland from going to the dangerous College, and in this they had to a great extent succeeded. Now we hear for the second time [4] of an offensive movement, and an attempt to seduce young men from Trinity College to escape to Spain for their education. On April 2, 1629, Bedell notices that "the proclamation against Priests and Jesuits came out;" it seems not to have been too soon, so far as the College was concerned, for in the July of the same year [5] we have the interesting inquiry

---

[1] P. B., 104 b.   [2] Cf. especially Reg., p. 23, for these offers.
[3] Cf. P. B., pp. 102-3.
[4] I think the older evidence (above, p. 32) doubtful and at all events from a hostile source.   [5] P. B., 104.

into the conduct of three students—Trafford, Walworth and Smith—whose irregularities in going into the city and "frequenting suspected houses" seemed to arise from some more serious cause than mere idle amusement. These students, and one Camber Griffiths, were examined by the Dean (Bedell had appointed but one Dean in his statutes), and the Provost, and confessed that they had been at the house of Bodkin, a broken merchant, and a Galway man, where they had met two friars named Birmingham and Plunkett—both names of old gentry of the Pale—and one Nugent, who plied them with arguments in favour of Popery, and offered to convey them secretly and safely to Galway, and thence to Spain. The depositions of the young men (August 7, 1629) are preserved [1] and are highly interesting in their details. I print that of Smith, which is the fullest, in the appendix to this chapter. We can still identify the house of Plunkett in Lower Bridge Street, and can stand in the little court within, now paved, but in those days an arbour, of which more anon (p. 215). The lads did not know that Nugent was an active Capuchin, working with Plunkett for the transportation and education of students abroad.[2] Neither did they know that round about the arbour was a College of Capuchins and a Mass House, which was seized by the Government a few months later, perhaps owing to this very evidence.

In these latter days, when we read the Roman Catholic bishops' fulminations against proselytising as a crime,[3] it is well for the historian to remind his readers that so long as men believe that their own creed is the only way of salvation, they will move heaven and earth to make one proselyte. Nor will they admit that the means they employ can be reprehensible, provided the grand object of saving souls is attained. There

---

[1] M. R., Box A iii., c. 1 and 2.

[2] This appears from a curious paper which got into Wentworth's possession, described in the S. P. for 1634, p. 37.

[3] *E.g.*, the daily papers in Dublin of December 22, 1902, contain a document of this kind from Archbishop Walsh.

follows even naturally the absurd consequence, that what each side does zealously as a religious duty is imputed to its opponents as a crime.

But while the Papist side were now strenuously pursuing this course at the risk of persecution and death, we do not hear any self-congratulations from the heads of Trinity College that they have reclaimed many of the recusant youth and brought them within the pale of the State Church. A few cases of priests converted outside, and obtaining on that ground support in the College, or promotion to a living, are recorded. Controversial lectures were constantly given, as they are now, to the Divinity students, but the saving of souls by "practising" does not seem to have been in fashion in the College. Meanwhile the feeble and spasmodic action of the Irish Government towards the recusants and the Romish clergy was doing its natural work, in spite of the protests of Falkland and other experienced men; the Irish officials were for strong and thorough measures, but were restrained by the king and his Privy Council. "The things we wish to suppress," says Falkland,[1] "are the extension of the Papal jurisdiction, the erection of Colleges and the unlawful [monster] meetings, for which purpose we have issued the accompanying proclamation : . . . *We will meantime not touch the secular priests, or the abused laity*, except by the proclamation; but we hope to reform them. We look to your Lordship for help in correcting the contagion of Popery, which is always more apt to grow in peace than in war time, for during war, the military and Protestant party has a free hand to weaken and spoil the Papists"—a naïve and interesting admission of injustice. The accompanying proclamation commands all colleges and monasteries of the Roman Catholic orders to dissolve and separate upon pain of seizure and expropriation.

The practical results were of some importance to the College. From this letter, and from many others of the period, it appears that while the friars and seminaries were beguiling or

[1] S. P., April, 1629, p. 446.

exciting the populace with continual promises of Spanish invasion, they saw (as they now do) that a quiet but zealous propaganda, under the connivance of a weak Government, was a far more successful policy. Bishop Bedell, when resisting the impudent demand for a plurality of livings from Dean Bernard (Ussher's chaplain), tells us that in his diocese there were sixty-three Romish ecclesiastics for thirty-three of his Church; letters in the S. P. for 1630 (pp. 512–3) show that even the Protestant plantation was not safe, for several Scotch noblemen in Tyrone, notably the Earl of Abercorn, were Papists, held great meetings of priests, and attended mass. The whole desire of the king and his advisers was not to suppress these things, but to obtain money from Ireland. It was believed to be a rich country, yet did not pay its own expenses of government; if this could be remedied by indulging the Papists to a certain point, well and good; if subsidies could be obtained from them without calling a Parliament, still better; but at any price, money must be raised. So the country was in apparent peace, with the fires of rebellion *suppositos cineri doloso.* But this peace was sufficient to encourage men to send their sons to Trinity College.

Here are the judgments of two men, the one a veteran politician, an astute man of the world, with a great fortune consisting of Irish land and Irish manufactures. Lord Cork, writing to Lord Dorchester,[1] adds to an official letter these reflections :—

"I cannot say—and no statesman in this age can say it—that I know Ireland well. Bad communications and the Papist influence keep the body of it estranged from us. But I have known Ireland for forty-three years, and never saw it so quiet. What may be the intentions of our never-sleeping enemy (Spain) I know not. . . The only present danger is the priests, who communicate much with their brethren abroad. The great lords of the Irish, who formerly had a great following, are all gone. The rebellious spirits have grown old and the

---

[1] S. P., 1630, p. 589.

kearne and horsemen are not to be seen, and have no arms. There is no more barbarism and plunder. The Irish gentry have got titles from the king, or by currency of law, and no longer depend upon their great lords. If we have a few more years of peace I think the king ought to be able to command a levy of English and Irish, reformed in manners and religion, more powerful than any force which the disloyal party could raise. There is a marvellous change from the state of things which old inhabitants can remember. Buildings and farming are improving, each man striving to excel the other in fair building and furniture, and in husbanding, enclosing and improving their lands. I wish there were foreign employment to keep the well-born Irish youth busy, and trades to occupy the young men of meaner sort.[1] The walled towns are almost altogether inhabited by the ancient English, and these old colonists are, I think, more loyal than otherwise, and they like peace, which is good for their trade and estates. Contentment is, in fact, general."

Lord Cork, then Lord Justice for Ireland with Lord Loftus, had means of knowing all that official people knew in every part of Ireland, together with his own intimate experience of the south.

Here is a contemporary expression from a gay young nobleman, Lord Conway, settled in the north near Lisburn (Lisnagarvy). The letter is written to the same Lord Dorchester[2]:—

"This is a curious place, you will think me best in it. Two faces are never alike. Greater stormes are not in any place, nor greater serenities—foul ways, boggy ground, pleasant fields, waters, brooks, rivers full of fish, full of game; the people in their attire, fashion, language, barbarous; in their entertainment free and noble. I end with the snatch of an old song—

    Pone sub curru nimium propinqui
    Solis in terra domibus negata."

Such was the general state of Ireland, and of the College, when Bedell was promoted to the Sees of Kilmore and Ardagh, and resigned his Provostship on September 18, 1629. The

---

[1] The professions and Collegiate education were therefore no large factor in the problem as he understood it.
[2] S.P., 1630, p. 521.

Lord Deputy had already informed the College of the king's intention in the previous May,[1] and had warned them, as usual, on no account to proceed to the election of his successor till the king's pleasure be known. To this the fellows demurred so strongly that a deputation of them went to England to move their friends at Court (among whom Sir James Fullerton is mentioned perhaps for the last time), to assert the sanctity of the Charter with its right of election vested in the fellows. The effort was only partly successful; the king assured them that it was only from a sincere regard for the good of the College that he insisted upon interfering, yet so far yielded, that if their nomination received the approbation of Primate Ussher, he would sanction it. The second nomination of Robert Ussher proves his continued popularity, but also perhaps the desire of the meaner section of the fellows to be ruled by an easy-going man. For such the new Provost is said to be even by his cousin, the Primate who recommended him. In the entry of the Register (October 3, 1629) mentioning his election by the fellows, two of them record their refusal to subscribe to it. But we do not know whether this was owing to the dictation of the Crown, which they desired to protest against, or to their objections to the new Provost.[2] He certainly carried on zealously the policy of Bedell regarding the Irish lecture, and regarding the general discipline of the College [3];

[1] Reg., p. 21.

[2] The fact that in the following February letters about the election are sent to the Archbishop of Canterbury, the Bishop of London, and Sir James Fullerton, points to the former alternative. Freedom of election in future was evidently the grave question of the moment.

[3] The best evidence of this is to quote a page (27) of the Register, which exhibits some very quaint items :—

Jan. 30. The Batchellors absent from yesterday's Sermon are to make a theame and ten disthicks of ũses to yᵉ Provost twice this forthnight. So yᵉ fellowe-comoners for yᵉ same reason are alike punished.

The Sophisters who are adulti are to loose their adultiship. The juniors who are not adulti are to be whipt.

Mr. Th. Andrews is to gett Perkins Catechisme wᵗʰ out booke, and is

in some respects we even see a Puritanical flavour in him, when he objects to theatrical amusements inside College. Another point in Bedell's policy, that students should be allowed to live with their parents in the city while attending lectures, was evidently not approved of by Robert Ussher, for just after Bedell's resignation we find the order [1] "that all schollers and ffellowes commoners that lyeth abroad in towne are to come into comons by Satturday next, or to loose the benefitt of their chambers and studdyes in ye College." This was probably a measure to prevent rooms from being held by non-residents when there was increasing pressure for accommodation in the College. The obvious way of supplying the want, by new buildings in the College, seems not to have been mooted,[2] for at this moment another very interesting solution seemed possible, which belongs to the public history of the time. Falkland's proclamation against the religious orders having been quietly disregarded and he himself recalled, the Lords Justices (Cork and Loftus) determined to take active

---

to repeate a principle evy 2ᵈ day to yᵉ end of yᵉ catechisme. The Bible clearke shall examyn him openly at dinner tyme after grace ;
Jan. 31. The Butler admonisht for bad beare.
Feb. 1. The manciple admonisht for bad meate.
   Given by consent to a poore man for an almes 11s.
Feb. 3. Geo. Berne, a late convert, a forward good scholar, and altogether destitute of any friends, being recomended unto us by the Lo. Primate, hath his Comons allowed him untill the next election of schollers wᵗʰ this caveat that it be noe president for any others for the time to come.
Feb. 17. The Fellows and Schollers are to make ũses for the Countess of Corke's funerall. Sir Conway Tho. Andrews, and Charles and Adam Loftus are to stand in yᵉ hall tomorrow wᵗʰ potts of water before yᵐ. Sir Conway is to gett Eccles. in hebrew and yᵉ 1 book of Homer's Odysses.
Bolton and Andrews to declayme agˢᵗ drunknes, and Loftus after dinner to get Pkins' Catechisme, and withall none of them must keep company together for a year's space.

[1] Reg., 25.
[2] What use was now made of Trinity Hall we do not know. I can find only one allusion to it at this time, Reg., August 3, 1629, "Dermoitt yᵉ Sadler denyed to build on Trinity Hall Wall."

measures, and on S. Stephen's Day, 1629, directed the Archbishop and mayor and some officers to seize one of the mass houses and lay hand upon the friars. They tried the experiment on a house of Carmelites in Cook street. They were at once resisted. The priests were saved by a mob which gathered 3,000 strong, and stoned the mayor and Primate, so that they had to take refuge in any house they could.[1] They were only saved from greater violence by the Lords Justices, who were returning from church with their retinue. "Seventeen public houses of massing priests have been set up in the four months which have elapsed since the proclamation, four of several orders, collegiated in distinct houses, and one of them Jesuits."[2] The outrage led to further acts of repression. The house in question was razed to the ground by the Lords Justices,[3] and a very prompt petition of the College (February 11th, Reg. 28) was entertained for one of the mass houses which had been cleared of its clergy. On March 2nd Lord Cork writes that two of these houses have been handed over "to the Provost and Colledgioners of the College neere Dublin, their own Colledge being grown incapable to receive the number of students resorting thither."[4] The Register says that "the possession and custodium of two mass houses in Bridge Street, and soon after one in ye Back Lane, was granted us." The two Bridge Street houses, knocked into one house of residence, were entitled S. Stephen's Hall—no one tells us why, but possibly on account of the assertion of the law on that saint's day which obtained it for the College—the second in Back

---

[1] The fullest account is in the curious book of J. Nalson, *Foxes and Firebrands* (1685).
[2] Wilmot to Dorchester, S. P., 1629 (O.S.), January 6th.
[3] The order was given by the English Council at the request of the Lords Justices. This house in Cook Street, of which the site is still quite clear, communicated at its back with the house in Bridge Street given to the College. The document F 64 in the M. R. recites the grant of the house in Bridge Street on the previous 15th of March, and grants (May 19th) the Jesuit house in Back Lane.
[4] S. P., 1629, p. 522.

Lane, being the property of the Earl of Kildare, was named Kildare Hall. The sites are easily determinable. A small iron gate in Lower Bridge Street (east side) leads into a little court, now surrounded with old houses and in tenements. Another similar gate leads in from Cook Street, the old Carmelite house just mentioned, over which is now a large inscription of *Roman Catholic Schools, founded in* 1758, showing that the property long remained in Recusant hands. The other is the very similarly situated Tailors' Hall in Back Lane, to which an iron gate through the houses leads, so that it is hidden from the thoroughfare. That these houses were not intended as new Colleges, but mere halls in connection with, and controlled by, Trinity College, appears from the following important letter[1] :—

"July 27, Trinity College.
"*Provost Ussher of Trinity College, Dublin, to the Bishop of London.*
"The Lords Justices have been pleased as we have so little room here to answer the great resort of scholars coming hither out of England and all the parts of this kingdom, to give us two of the superstitious houses lately seized by the King. We have settled several scholars in them according to the enclosed scheme. We should be very glad if in the event of a new plantation, the King would grant some lands for maintaining this house, and would ease us of charge for some arrears of rent due upon some Chantry lands which we got from King James, but of which we have not ever yet made any profit or indeed got possession, in spite of a lawsuit and other means adopted to get it. We hope the King will carry out the undoubted intentions of his father by enabling us to continue solvent and comply with these requests. Wherein I, in the name of this society, do humbly beg your noble favour unto this poor house, as heretofore we have continually tasted, and in all humility shall remain —Your honour's most obliged servant, Robert Ussher."

Here is the scheme :

July 17.
1. *Project for settling scholars in the House of Back Lane, granted to the College by the Lords Justices and Council.*

---

[1] S. P., 1630, p. 560.

(1) The undersigned think that the best course is that the first class which is in Trinity College be sent thither yearly, wherein they are to continue for the space of two years to be instructed in the Greek and Hebrew tongues, in Rethoricke and Logicke, and after they are to return to ye College to learn other sciences, and leave it indifferent for the Fellow Commoners to go or stay.

(2) We hold it fitting that any of the scholars sent thither should be allowed to sit for scholarship in the College at the times of elections.

(3) The tutor should have £E. 2 per annum from every Fellow Commoner for tuition and £E. 1 from every scholar or pensioner.

(4) Every Fellow Commoner should, we think, pay 2l., and every pensioner or scholar £E. 1 per annum towards " reparations, utensils and officers."

(5) A Rector should be set over this house and should be responsible to the Provost of the College and the Vice-Chancellor for its Government and expense. His salary should be paid out of the money subscribed by the Fellow Commoners and Pensioners towards the maintenance of officers.

(6) There should be a steward to provide bread, beer, victual, utensils, and necessaries for reparations of the house. His wages should arise from the stipend of the Fellow Commoners and Pensioners.

(7) All the lecturers and the steward of the house should be chosen by the Provost as is the use in the College.

(8) We conceive it is most necessary that all the students should be kept diligently to their books in the public place appointed for lectures from 7 of the clock in the morning, and from 1 till 5 in the afternoon by their several lectures.

Robert Usher, pro.
Rich. Jordan.
Joseph Travers.
David Thomas.
Will. Fitzgerald.
Thad. Lishag(t).

Fellows.
" Ye Lord Primates approbation is on ye next side of ye leaf."

On back. 17 July 1639.

This order for disposing scholars in the New House, I hold to be very convenient, and if any Fellows object to it as drawing their pupils from them and diminishing their fees, I hope that the Lords Justices will interpose to take order that the private profit of a few shall not give impediment to the public good, whereof many, by God's blessing, are like to be partakers. Ja. Ardmachanus.

An entry in the Register of July 1st shows that the matter had been under discussion in the College. The Provost and fellows have lent £20 for the furnishing of the new hall. It is further agreed that the two last classes (*i.e.*, juniors) shall "remayne there for two yeres (except fellow comoners) the Rector is to be their Tutor and out of the stipend of ye schollars and fellow-comoners the steward is to have £20 per an. as he is manciple cooke butler and porter." The rest to be given to the Rector.

There follow on August 8th, "the Rector's place in the New Colledge is elective yearly, and Mr. Boswell is elected this year." And on September 14th the (to me) enigmatical entry: "Sir Guñ and Sir Brererton appointed M^{rs} in Bridge Street are allowed 12 artists [*sic*] to reade to y^m and their place is elective yearly." Further on in the Reg.[1] we find :—

"Sir Harrison by consent of the Board and major part of the Senior Fellows was appointed lecturer of all the schollers (undergraduates) in the house in Bridge Street, and is to receive quarteridge from them accordingly. And it was for this consented and agreed upon that he should have from each ffellow-comoner and pentioner there studyinge such rent quarterly for their Chambers and studyes as is payd by ffellow-comoners and pentioners out of their Chambers and studyes here in this Colledge, viz., 3s. 4d. per quarter for a ffellow-comoner, and 1s. 8d. per quarter for a pentioner."

Thus, by a side wind, we learn what no other entry of the time tells us, that the students in College had not only chambers (for sleeping, probably holding several lads), but studies, and that for these they paid the rent above named. But it is also evident from James Ussher's endorsement that there was opposition to this extension into halls, and that there were tutors who then made considerable profit by the overcrowding of the College. Sir William Brereton[2] found about eighteen scholars in Bridge Street in July, 1635. Other details are given from the accounts of 1630 by Dr. Stubbs.[3]

[1] p. 43, Ap. 18, 1634.   [2] *op cit.*, p. 142.   [3] *Hist.*, p. 63.

The evidence at this moment points to Kildare Hall as being the more important of these halls. It had a Rector, and Lord Cork endowed a theological lecture there on Tuesdays, which he and the Court used to attend. We have in the S. P. of the year 1630 (p. 509) a remarkable letter from Lord Cork (to Dorchester), wherein he says, in explaining his own vigorous action, that the respectable Roman Catholics of the country are hostile to the Friars, and think they should be put down, adding :

"They have Dublin in their hands at present, are masters of the walls, and have found a secret way by which at full tide or low tide they can bring what men they like into the city. There are two posterns by which such men can be introduced, and their houses can contain 5,000 of them. The Jesuits' house owned and claimed by the Dowager Countess of Kildare (being one of the ten seized into His Majesty's hands), is a new-erected and goodly fabric, the chapel whereof, which her ladyship calls her hall (though neither chimney, table, nor window that any may look out of) is 75 feet long by 27 broad. It is seated round about, with an altar with ascents, a curious pulpit and organs, and four places for confession neatly contrived, galleried above round about with rails and turned ballasters, coloured, a compass roof, a cloister above with many other chambers, all things most fair and graceful, like the banquetting house at Whitehall, and ways out of their house to the town walls, turrets and flankers at their command."

Brereton, visiting this house, after he had seen that in Bridge Street, gives a briefer but perfectly consistent account.

The annals of the College are in other respects very meagre under Robert Ussher's government. Here is an entry perhaps characteristic of it (1632) : "It is agreed that every one under the degree of Master of Arts (Noblemen's sonnes and Privie Counsellours' heyrs excepted) shall in token of his respect to the Provost bare his head when he shall see him in the inner quadrangle." There was a quarrel over the appointment of a new auditor in place of Sir James Ware, who had proved unsatisfactory, and so the Provost's desire to appoint Ware's son failed, and the fellows audited for themselves. There was an agitation about the election to fellowship of William Newman, a person of influence, who, being once rejected, thought it beneath his dignity to compete again, but obtained a mandate from the Lords Justices, countersigned by the Primate. This last signature, which surprises us, was coupled with the threatening letter from the King[1]: "And for whose (Newman's) election you the Provost and some others consented, only some that combine themselves to oppose government opposed: We therefore, resolving hereafter to have the proceedings of such opposers examined, and censured as it shall deserve, do require and comand you so to elect the sayd William Newman." So he was elected, and seems to have been accepted quietly, being an alumnus and M.A., and not a stranger imposed on the Society.

However, when such interferences were tolerated, we are not surprised to find the Primate, upon the death of Abbot, procuring the appointment of Laud, already Chancellor of Oxford and undertaking great reforms there, as Chancellor of Trinity College. He had Robert Ussher on his side; also the Professor of Divinity, Joshua Hoyle, one of Alvey's importations from Oxford long ago, and now holding a high place both in the College and as a preacher in S. Werburgh's. But the Primate adds that some of the Fellows are so factious that nothing could please them that came from their superiors.[2] So Laud was elected by the Provost and Senior Fellows, according to their Charter, on September 4, 1633. Moreover, the appointment of Wentworth as Lord Deputy had already been decided upon—the two strongest men in England, bound together by ties not only of public policy but of private friendship, were now to control both the Church and the University in Ireland. The removal of Robert Ussher was effected by a modest promotion to the Archdeaconry of Meath, and afterwards to the See of Kildare.

[1] Reg., 39.   [2] *Works*, xv. 398.

220 AN EPOCH IN IRISH HISTORY

His actual resignation was dated August 11, 1634; but his influence upon the history of the College was already effaced by the advent of greater forces. The only personal trait I can quote to give the reader an image of the man is his curiously bombastic letter and verses to his cousin James Ussher.

APPENDIX I.

LETTER OF R. USSHER TO JAS. USSHER (*Works*, xv. 95).

Duas fulgentes et insignes stellas, vir ornatissime, firmamento nostræ ecclesiæ nuper decessisse, Cimmeriæ, et horrendæ, quibus miserrima hæc insula, et in occasum vergens Academia involvuntur tenebræ promulgant: ad quas dispellendas te fulgenti scientiarum splendore omnibus prælucentem, admirabili morum candore coruscantem, summoque honore coronatum, Deus elegit, ut studiorum tuorum habenas, ad emolumentum nostræ Ecclesiæ Babylonica superstitione infectæ, ad salutem patriæ mentis cæcitate laborantis, et ad dignitatem Academiæ in præcipitem ruinam irruentis, expedite flectes. Miseris succurrere te didicisse, ter nobilis illa pugna nunquam satis laudanda nuper cum superba, et septemplici Romanæ gentis hydra, sub Christi vexillo inita, pro maturata ætate, ac illibata despectæ Ecclesiæ castitate, palam testatur; quam pæne oblivio, vel potius cruenta tyrannorum rabies etiam spirantem absorbuit et sepelivit. Perpetuas hujus peregrationes, duraque exilia, terribilem Draconis faciem fugientis, ab ultima antiquitate, qua incunabulis fuerat, ad nostra fere tempora vivis coloribus depinxisti. Nunc igitur facessant nostris finibus mendaces Romanæ synagogæ Cretenses, quos olim abyssus turmatim evomuit, facessant (inquam) non sine hac novitate, qua perfidam, et obscænam Babyloniæ meretricem salutent: ferreo tui ingenii ariete Antichristiani regni fundamenta concussa, vel potius convulsa, nova restauratione indigere; veram Christi sponsam demum tenebrosis umbris extulisse caput; teque istius gravissimæ controversiæ et contentionis palmam reportasse. Hinc omnes, quos liber tuus, varia sane lectione et doctrina perpolitus, vel saltem ejus fama a limine salutavit, uno ore te solum in hac materia Apollinis lyram attigisse, constanter perhibent; hoc idem insignis tua fama stipulatur, quæ nullam Europæ partem insalutatam reliquit, idem industriæ et ingenii tui fœtus, quem omnes avide arripiunt, summoque prosequuntur amore. Filium equidem parentis causa omnes fovent, parentem filii gratia omnes admirantur; sic cunctos te cum admiratione amare, cunctosque te cum amore admirari facile percipias. Immortales Deo grates, propterea quod te per devios antiquorum campos vagantem in penetralia suæ veritatis deduxit, benignitatis suæ thesauros tibi aperuit, teque patriæ incolumem, patriamque tibi restituit: tibique, amantissime sobrine, justissimas habeo gratias, quas me tibi diu debuisse immensa tua erga me gratia comprobat: cujus cubiculum tuum mihi creditum minimam non esse tesseram ingenue fateor. Sed ne chartacea hæc salutatio te gravissimorum negotiorum mole obrutum, molestia afficiat, vela contrahem; hoc interim ab te flagitarem, et hoc audaciæ meæ symbolum, pariterque amoris, serena humanitatis fronte accipias.

tuæ salutis, et felicitatis studiosissimus,
Rob. Usserus.

[The letter unfortunately has no date, but is put by the Editor among those of 1616.]

Then follows:

ad obscænam meretricem septem insidentem
montibus, de tuo libro carmen.

Frigore cur pavido trepidas, Babylonica Thais;
  Cur trepidæ præbes turpia terga fugæ?
Fluctibus Hesperiis emergit lucida stella
  Qua veniente fugis, quaque oriente cadis.

Purpuream lucem vitat caligo profunda
  Dagon sic arcam concidit ante Dei
Hac radiante patent cunctis genitura nefanda
  Gorgoneusque tuus partus, uterque parens,

Mordaces anni, violataque fædera lecti
  Et Stygio suboles carcere spurca fluens
Fulgenti nuper cecidit tua gloria cælo
  Nunc eadem terris in loca nigra cadit.

[We may well wonder how James Ussher preserved this, we hope undergraduate, effusion among his serious correspondence.]

APPENDIX II.[1]

To the Right Worshipful our good Benefactors the Major, Sheriffes, Aldermen and Comon Council of ye Citty of Dublin.

We, the Provost, ffellows and schollers of Trinity Colledge nere to this Cittie, humbly show to y^r Wo^r: That wheras a certayne enclosure is begū to be made upon a peece of ground, nere to ye gate of ye said Colledge w^h an intencōn to build thereupon (as is already signified to ye right Honble the lord Deputy of this kingdome) which is like to be verie p̄judiciall to the sayd Colledge, as well in stopping up the ordnary way wherby they doe now bring all their provision of coales, sand and other like carriages from ye water's syde; and water for their brueing; as also in taking in the passage where aunciently there was a gate and way leading into the scite of the house where the Colledge is built; which they have resolved to renew to avoyd the comīng in of horses and hoggs from ye greene into the Court of ye Colledge upon the ordinary opening of their great gate. And further by stopping or straightening the water course which runeth along by the wall of the Colledge, whereby upon any outrageous fflood the walls wilbe borne downe as happened in the same place which is now inclosed about eight years since, although the same was not then soe straight as it is like to be by building upon it and inclosing it. And lastly inasmuch as the building being in all likelihood for mean people, wilbe too neere a receipt for ye scholars of ye said house, and p̄judiciall to ye manners of ye students; as geñally of ye whole kingdome; soe among others which are ye youth of this City brought up in ye said Colledge, of which number there are at this p̄nt above XX the most whereof doe also receive maintenance from ye said House. The Peticōners soe humbly desyre that the said inclosure may not be p̄mitted to proceed, and doe offer to levele ye said ground at their own charge, and to enlarge ye Causey which is sett w^h stone frō the Colledge gate to ye city w^hout inconvenience to any, and to ye ornament of ye said citty and Colledge. And they shall daily pray for ye peace and welfare of ye said citty, and ye blessing of God upon ye governmñt and inhabitants of ye same.

---

[1] M. R., A. III. a, and cf. Gilbert, Dublin Records, III. 207, and Reg., p. 15. (Summer 1628, exact date uncertain.)

To the Right Honble Lord Deputy and the High Council of this Kingdom.

The humble Petition of the Provost Fellows and Scholars of Trinity College near Dublin,[1]

Humbly sheweth, that whereas of late an inclosure near to the gate of the said College hath been set up with purpose to build thereupon concerning wch your suppliants petitioned to the Citty (that it might not proceede) showing the wrong and great inconveniences which would grow thereby to the said College. Which petition was referred to be considered by certain persons named by the Citty and the (worke) for a time left off. Till now within these 3 days the sayd inclosure is afresh set up and in part upon the ground of the sayd College to the great nuisance of the same.

It may please your Honors: Inasmuch as the protection of the said College is by their charter in special manner recommended to your honors and that some disorder (which your petitioners shall not be able to prevent) may (otherwise) happen if the sayde inclosure should be thrown down by the unruly multitude of the scholars of the said College, to inhibit the said inclosure and building until the inconveniences thereof shall by your wisdomes be considered. And they shall ever pray for the peace of this Kingdom and your Honors' prosperity.

Ulto January 1628.

We pray and require the Lord Primate the Lord Archbishop of Dublin the Lord Dillon and the Lord Docwra or any three of them that view the place where the inclosure within mentioned is intended to be sett up and having considered of the inconveniences p̃tended to arise thereby to your Petitioners to certifie unto us their opinions concerning the same. And in the mean tyme the sayd worke is to be stayd whereof we require all persons whom it may concern to take notice and to forbeare proceeding therein accordingly.

H. Falkland
T. Loftus, Chan^r.
Hon. Valentia   More Dom Kilmallock
                   R. Ranelagh
Balfour   Arth. Midensis
W. Caulfield   E. Blayney
Shurley   Laur. Esmonde.

---

[1] The words in brackets are inserted above the line.

19 Feb. 1628.

May it please your Lordships : Upon view of the inclosures in the petition mentioned and examination of the Nuisances arising to the Petitioners by the going forward of the work, we are of opinion it would proove very inconvenient and prejudicial to the College and for ought yet appearing a wrong and incroachment uppon their rights that the intended building should be raised in that place, it being proved before us in [presence] of the several pties interested that by the said building a passage would be taken in where anciently there was a gate or way leading into the site of the said College ; and although for the present stopped up the Petitioners allege they intend to renew and open again for divers necessary uses. Wherefore after we had in obedience to your Lordships' commands informed ourselves the best that we could of the true state of the difference, we propounded diverse meanes of a friendly accord for preventing all further contestations between your Petitioners and the Defendant Robert Arthur merchant who hath gotten the lease from the City of the said inclosed piece of ground at ye rent of 3^s 4^d per annum. But for the time we could not prevaile with the s^d Defendant to listen to any composition. Yet at a second meeting between them before two of us the Referees, at which the Mayor with divers Aldermen and citizens were present, the said Arthur and Petitioners by mutual consent submitted themselves to an agreement then moved, viz., that the said Arthur should sell and make over unto the Petitioners all his whole interest in the said inclosed ground, for such a price as should be awarded him by two to be chosen of either side for that purpose and in case the said orderers did not agree thereon, that then the Right Hon^l. the Lord Chancellor should as umpire lay down the same and thereby conclude all parties. Which agreement notwithstanding it was so solemnly assented to on both sides your Petitioners complain that the said Arthur doth fly from and now standeth upon terms as at first. All which we humbly leave to your Lordships' honorable consideration.

Jas. ARMACHANUS
J. S. DILLON
Henry DOCWRA.

This refference was retourned to my L. Primate and at his lodging here April 2° delivered.

Memorandum upon the 24th of Feb^r. at night betweene supper and prayers tyme the schollers of the Colledge pulled downe the poles and railes which were standing upon the ground, and there being 2 pistolls shot of, the noise whereof was heard into the Provost's Lodging. The Provost going to chappell met a litle boy of the City with 2 pales in his hands (going out of the Coll.) who sayd a scholler had given them to him. Whereupon the Provost after prayer blamed the disord^r and wished that whosoever had any of the pales or timber they should lay it in the quadrangle in the Court that the owner might have his own. The next morning there was a pile set up in the midst of the quadrangle besides divers posts and pieces here and there. The next morning word was sent to Mr. Arthur by Sir Kerdiff, one of the City, that there was much of his tymber layd in the College Court and if it pleased him he might send for it away. Which same thing was given notice of by the Provost meeting his brother in the way to St. Patrick's Church the same day. At evening he sent for the timber away.

Jan. 31.

(Endorsed) The humble Petition of the Provost and Scholars of Trinity College of Queen Elizabeth near Dublin.

APPENDIX III.

The Examination of William Smith, August 7, 1629.

[The variants of Walworth's evidence are given in notes.]

He saith he and Wallworth first met with Mr. Bodkin at Mr. Cullen his house in Castle street about the last of July, whom they considering to be a man of good parts and very fair carriage and perceiving him to be a traveller fell into discourse with him. Mr. Bodkin perceiving them to be scholars of this College, entered into a high commendation of Spain of Civill^{ty} especially of the Colleges therein, commending their lives, their strict form of government and the books which they use, which discourse continued long till they parted that night. Upon Saturday the first of August, they met again ith' evening when their discourse was much to the same purpose; that night they lay there. Upon Monday the 3rd of Aug. they met again and then both of them made their desires known and their grievances unto Bodkin, affirming that they were troubled in conscience about their religion, whereupon Bodkin offered them his best endeavours for their satisfaction in any scruple that arose unto them, whereupon he procured them an access to a friar, one *Plunkett,* who labored to encourage them in their intended resolution of being Roman Catholics, but resolved them in their doubts (according to his ability) very slenderly. The same afternoon they met again, and [he brought them to friar Nugent, who W.] demanded whether they were constant in their resolution and what was the cause of their revolt, they to indeare themselves unto him, tould him that they were fully resolved in their course, and the causes them moving were some errors maintained in the religion of the Protestants and the great disagreement between them ; Nugent replied upon this answer very discreetly and with reasons which seem unto him very weighty. The same afternoon by the help of the said Bodkin they were brought to one Friar Barnewell, a Capucine, who discoursed (as he conceives) very learnedly of the non errabilyty of the Church, producing arguments against the Lord Primate very sollidly, and thus having promised them a pardon frō the greatest censures of the Church and having promised them a form of confession for a reconcilement to their church they parted.

Upon the 4th of August Bodkin brought them to Plunkett and father Browne, the Provincial of the Carmelites, as he takes, with whom they had some discourse to little purpose, but fair encouragement, and thus they parted. The same afternoon as they were going to Father Bath (?) they met with Nugent, who brought them to one Mr. Plunkett's house in Bridg Street, where he used the conveniency of an arboure in the garden for their better privacy; being thus accommodated he fell into dispute of certain points controverted between the Protestants and Papists, viz., of the Sacrament of the Altar ; of the Supremacy of the Pope ; of the mariage of Priests ; of the translation of the Bible, of which and many others he discoursed very largely, commending him in his objections, as if the hope were the greater which he conceived of his conversion. Then commending unto him Spain and the College there together with their exquisite government and form of discipline and having intreated him very courteously, he wished him to address himself often unto him, who (as he saith) was exceedingly tender of his case and exceedingly solicitous to lay downe a safe course for the accomplishing of his intended journey for Spaine.

And as for Bodkin in all these passages he behaved himself with all love and courtesy,[1] offering them the command of his horse for their conveyance to Galloway,[2] whither if need were he promised to accompany them and to make them acquainted with the friars there,

---

[1] Labouring to have the plott compassed with all secrecy for their sakes (W.).

[2] From whence there went shipping daily to Spaine (Walworth).

and that he would furnish them with horses to ride up and downe the country for their pleasure, and for their procuring of the benevolence of well disposed Catholicks, bearing them in hand that they should not want for anything and that when they should be resolved for their intended voyage, that he would procure them the conveniency of a ship in which they should be transported for Spain or France as they should desire.

This I do affirm, as witness my hand,

WILLIAM SMITH.

CHAPTER VI

CHAPPELL AND THE CAROLINE STATUTES (1634–40)

The promotion of Laud to the English Primacy and of Wentworth to be Lord Deputy were of mighty import to the history of Ireland, and in the history of Ireland Trinity College played no insignificant part. The whole country was in great need of social and religious amelioration, and in this the College must co-operate. Critics alleged that hitherto it had failed to supply the country with a learned and zealous clergy, and that so it had missed its main purpose. But in the many complaints brought against individual bishops and clergy for simony, for neglect, for malversation of Church property, I cannot find the Fellows presented to College livings or promoted to bishoprics among the culprits. They were no doubt inefficient in preaching to the Irish in the native tongue; they were most probably infected by the abuses which they saw around them, but the great culprits, the men who ruined the influence of the reformed Church in Ireland, were either the Irish priests, whose conformity was dishonest, and who made away with the property of their sees or livings for the purpose of endowing the Romish faith, or else the numerous English adventurers, not students of Trinity College, who came to Ireland for the purpose of plunder, and were not ashamed of holding a number of benefices, without residing in, or caring for, any of them.

How deep-rooted these malpractices were appears from the honest efforts of Bedell to reform them in Kilmore, and the resistance offered by men like Bernard, Ussher's chaplain, without censure from the Primate. But there is no reason to think that many respectable and resident rectors had not been sent out from the College to its livings in the north. As far as the gentry of the country were concerned, they had begun to send their sons freely to Dublin for education. Lord Falkland (as we said above, p. 84) had a son there; Lord Cork (in 1630) sent two sons; Lord Docwra had sent two sons long before, and among less known names, the number of donations of plate, with the name and arms of the donor, shows that fellow commoners, of families with the privilege of escutcheons, were coming up in increasing numbers. Even from Cheshire and from Wales students came over, and the list of fellows and scholars shows many unmistakably Welsh names.

So far the College was distinctly prosperous, and increasing in popularity, yet observers as competent as Primate Ussher, and even under the Provostship of his cousin, complain that the discipline among the fellows was bad, and that factious opposition was constantly made to any enforcing of strict rules. This was his reason for proposing Laud as the new Chancellor, a move he must afterwards have bitterly regretted. The Provost had no power to punish except with the consent of four Senior Fellows; this majority could not elect without the consent of the Provost; thus a deadlock in the constitution was constantly impending, and was only avoided by avoiding the enforcement of unpopular duties. Ussher, therefore, was clearly in favour of a strong Provost, with greater powers than the statutes allowed.

But Laud and Wentworth had an additional policy to promote, for which such reforms were merely a convenient lever, and this policy they concealed from Ussher. Both Laud and Wentworth were clear-sighted enough to see that the real obstacle to the assertion of absolute royalty lay not in the Roman Catholic but in the Puritan opposition. The assertion of the right of private judgment against the dictates of authority, in faith, naturally suggested a similar assertion in politics, and as this revolt against the Stuart notions of the Royal Prerogative was rife in Scotland, its proximity to Ireland, and to the many Scotch settlers, not only in the Plantation but even more in Antrim and Down, might lead to a dangerous increase of the Puritan opposition. Even the Church of Ireland had been trained, so far as Trinity College could do it, in the creed of Puritanism, and had already assumed that strictly Evangelical complexion which it has retained to the present day. In order to stay this danger, Bramhall was brought over by Wentworth and made Bishop of Derry, from which he could supervise and report on the north, and insist upon that distinction between Churchman and Dissenter which Ussher would willingly and wisely have overlooked. The policy of Laud and Wentworth in matters ecclesiastical, carried out now for a short while by Bramhall, interrupted by rebellion and war, but resumed again by him as Primate at the Restoration, was the policy which created the deep chasm between the Protestant communions of the north, subsisting to this day, and working incalculable mischief. The strong man was sent to the north, as the seat of the principal danger, but for the south some other High Churchman must be provided, and for this purpose Dr. William Chappell, of Christ Church, Cambridge, was promoted, against his will and inclination, to the Deanery of Cashel. It is likely that even now his appointment was not intended to be permanent, for in Cashel, though there were many ecclesiastical abuses, there was no Protestant dissent. Chappell's long residence in Cambridge as a fellow and tutor pointed him out as qualified to succeed to the Provostship of the Puritan College, and there stop the efflux of Evangelical principles into the parishes of the north. For it is certain that he was known to Laud as a High Churchman, and as such sent to Trinity College. But (as usual) when we come to explain the situation in detail, many difficult problems offer themselves for solution.

Chappell has left us a Latin iambic autobiography,[1] wherein we read that he was born in 1582, obtained a scholarship and the degrees of A.B. and A.M. at Christ's College, Cambridge, and (when he was at a loss whither to turn for a profession) a fellowship in 1607, which he speaks of as the goal of his ambition. The text then passes into religious effusions and reflections, and begins its narrative of facts again with his appointment as Dean of Cashel in 1633. There is thus a great gap of twenty-five years in the autobiography, only to be accounted for by the loss, or the suppression, of a page of two of the original manuscript, for we can show that the missing period was by no means devoid of passages, which the author could not fairly omit from the confessions of his life. He was invited on August 8, 1612,[2] as already told (above p. 74), by Temple and his fellows, to teach theology and act as Dean and Catechist; and various entries in the P. B. during 1613 prove that he was actually in residence. In 1614 he is gone, without leaving a trace behind him in Dublin, except that Anthony Martin is appointed in his place as Catechist, November 16, 1613.[3] But in 1615 he is reported to have exhibited his acute intellect in so brilliant a disputation at Cambridge, in presence of the king, that his adversary fainted, and the king paid him the highest compliments. Of all this there is not one word in the autobiography! Nor is there any account of his making the acquaintance or obtaining the confidence of Laud, who says, indeed, that he did not know him personally before his promotion. And yet all this was worthy of explanation, for Temple and Ussher had surely invited him to Dublin, not only as an acute Ramist logician, but as a theologian of their type. In the subsequent years he was a well-known tutor at his Cambridge College, and has saved

[1] Printed in Leland's *Collectanea*, vol. v. [2] P. B., p. 205. [3] ibid., p. 206.

his name from the oblivion even of the English public by having chastised the boy John Milton, his College pupil.

As I said already, he gives us at the close of the period a supplication to God to pardon his faults, and this must have come at the end of the missing narration. When appointed Dean of Cashel he says that God knows, and the world knows, what he had to endure; but when he comes to the offer of the Provostship he bursts out into such violent language about the College that I cannot think it intelligible, if he had not already given us (in the lost portion) some account of his experiences of 1613.

If this middle portion of his life was suppressed by himself, which is also possible, we must look for some serious cause. It is certain that he was regarded in early life as a Puritan, and as such he must have been acceptable to Temple in 1612. Ussher must then have known him well. He came back to Ireland a High Churchman and an Arminian in doctrine. This conversion, which accorded with his worldly interest, and obtained him promotion, certainly earned him the determined hostility of Ussher, and may have been to Chappell a disagreeable passage in his former life.

However, Wentworth, having got rid of Robert Ussher with an archdeaconry, a cheap bribe as compared with the bishopric he expected Ussher to claim, brought Chappell, who had endured some months' residence at Cashel, to Dublin, and had him elected Provost by going down in person to the College, and telling them they must elect him, otherwise he would inhibit their choice, and refer the matter to the king. The Lord Deputy's cynical contempt of charters and privileges as against the royal will appears in many of his letters. He purchased the favour and admiration of his miserable king by promising to make him as absolute a sovereign as any in Europe. And so long as he remained in power in Ireland, he was as good as his word. He violated over and over again, not only the old statutes of the College, but those he had procured from Laud, to compass a personal object. The former disorders of the country enabled him to find flaws in the title for every property, or dishonesty in acquiring it, and so to extort large sums by way of composition to avoid confiscation. There was but one personage whom he feels compelled to treat with consideration, and whom he is unable to depose. That was Primate Ussher. Yet even upon him he contrived to force in Convocation the acceptance of the English articles in place of those drawn up by Ussher for the Irish Church. But the Primate, though personally unassailable, was a weak leader, and not on good terms with his bishops. His closest friend and adviser, who was supposed by Wentworth to lead him, was Anthony Martin, Bishop of Meath, a very able and determined man. But Bedell, his most pious and learned colleague, was often at variance with him, and for the most serious cause.[1] Bramhall of Derry represented the policy of Wentworth. The rest seem mere cyphers, and not even of one mind in public affairs.

Under these circumstances the appointment of a High Church and an English Provost was a great move in the game against the Evangelical and national cause in Ireland. For I need hardly say again that the Anglo-Irish sympathies were then as decidedly opposed to the English as they have been to this day. These were the reasons why Ussher, as Vice-Chancellor, took no pains to admit Chappell formally as Provost, not because he was offended that the new Provost had not waited on him at Drogheda.[2] Both Hely Hutchinson and Anon. speak of Chappell as a first-rate man in learning, piety, and character. Wentworth always praises him, and thinks him the best man to promote in Ireland, probably owing to the punctuality of his obedience. Yet his many blunders in the management of the

[1] All the Lives of Bedell are very full regarding these disputes of Bedell with grasping clergy and officials, and the very lukewarm conduct of Ussher, or even his screening of the offenders.

[2] This is what Chappell says in his autobiography.

College, which he was wholly unable to keep at peace without obtaining absolute powers, his conversion to Laud's views, his own querulous complainings in his autobiography, and the catalogue of complaints against him when his protector Strafford was disgraced—all this is strong evidence that Laud made a bad choice, and without sufficient knowledge of his man.[1] He only published one insignificant logical book, the *Ars Concionandi*, at the very end of his life. There is not one note of contentment in all his confessions, save at the moment he got his fellowship, and again when he had carried the new Charter, and was Provost, with almost absolute power, and an income of £500 a year. Yet even then he was required by his Master to take a bishopric, and hold the Provostship *in commendam*, in violation of his solemn oath.

But he was no mere pawn in the great game which Wentworth was playing for King Charles. And Trinity College became an important corner of the chessboard. Not only did Wentworth force upon the College a Provost of his own choosing; he did not scruple to impose on them Fellows, and even Senior Fellows, to carry out his policy. And he tells Laud that it were well to send over a few suitable Englishmen every

[1] When mentioning his resignation of the Provostship to Laud (S. P., 1640, August 7th, p. 244), Chappell speaks with satisfaction of his reformation of the College, and that having found it £200 in debt he had left it £2,000 in credit. He adds that he would willingly have ended his days there, but for the objections of his being an absentee from his see. There is nothing like this in his autobiography. Amid the conflict of opinion concerning Chappell's character, the following passage from a letter of Bedell to Samuel Ward (*Lives of Bedell*, ed. Shuckburgh, p. 362) is well worth citing.

Touching my lord of Corke, I never changed a word with him about your difference [probably his variance with Ussher], but, as I wrote in my last, he hath proferred, nay, performed much kindness to me. I do much approve his reformation of the manners of the College, improving the rents, enlarging and beautifying the buildings. In the service of God many account he hath brought in too much ceremony; others esteem the condition of this country and tyme do require it; and I think it may do more good here than in England." This evidence, from a man of unimpeachable honesty, who had himself been Provost, is the best defence of Chappell known to me.

year, and make them scholars and fellows, promising to promote them in the Church of Ireland next after his own chaplains. All this policy had one clear object, to defeat and discredit the Protestant party in Ireland, who would naturally take the part of the Puritan Opposition in England and Scotland, and to create a High Church party by means of imported Englishmen, who would submit to the Divine Right of Charles, and who would not carry on any extreme controversy with the Roman Catholics, who were now to be conciliated. For the first need of the king was money; there must be subsidies obtained, either by voluntary offers from the gentry or from an obsequious Parliament, and for this purpose the Roman Catholic gentry of the Pale and the remaining Irish lords must be humoured. It was even part of Wentworth's policy to play the loyalty of one against the other, and make them bid at his auction of the king's favour.

These are the general considerations which explain the tedious history of the petty squabbles in the College, which now assume such strange official importance. The great struggle to impose the new Church views upon the Protestant party was by no means confined to carrying through the English articles in Convocation. The heads of that party must be discredited. The opening move was the attack upon the great monument which the Earl of Cork had set up at the east end of the chancel in S. Patrick's to his wife, her father, Sir Geoffrey Fenton, and her grandfather, Chancellor Weston. It was the lady's dying wish to be laid near them, and the Earl carried it out with splendid loyalty. He purchased the site from the Dean and Chapter, sent for the best workmen from England, and set up a great monument at the cost of £1,000 in what is known as the Jacobean style, in the place reserved by Churchmen for the reredos. All this was done with the knowledge and approval of not only the Dean and Chapter, but of the two Archbishops, and suggests clearly enough that there was no altar or communion table at the east end, and that the service was of a very Puritan sort. This was all reported by some one whose name is withheld—probably by Chappell—to Laud, who set Wentworth to work to abate the scandal, and he took it up so eagerly that Lord Cork at once attributed his action to personal hostility. He appealed to the Dean and Archbishops, and a committee of inquiry sat to consider the matter. But Laud was firm, and insisted upon the removal of the tomb, to Lord Cork's intense mortification. But so much was ultimately conceded, that its new place was as near as possible to the old, at the east end of the south wall of the chancel, still overlooking the communion table. In that place the older among us all remember it, before a restorer who had probably never heard of the controversy removed it to the far end of the nave, beyond the south entrance.

All this debate, which occupies large room in the correspondence of both Wentworth and of Laud, was intended, along with the assertion of greater decency and ceremony in the keeping of churches, to discredit not only Cork, but Ussher, who had tolerated such violations of decency. Presently a much greater accusation was brought against Cork regarding his fraudulent appropriation of the old abbey of Youghal and its revenues. But Ussher was not so easy to upset, even though Wentworth reports that when entertained by the Primate at his fine palace in Drogheda he found the private chapel without even a communion table.[1] For however

[1] Sir William Brereton (*Travels*, p. 135, Cheet. Soc. Ed.), visiting Drogheda about the same time, and visiting this "pretty little plain and convenient chapel," also finds the great parish church, where the Primate preaches every Sunday when resident, "with the communion table placed lengthways in the aisle, over against the pulpit; the body of the Church in good repair; the chancel, as no use is made of it, wholly neglected." Such, then, were Ussher's notions of ritual. It is also stated (S. P., 1636, p. 142) that the King received news that the bishops only wore their rochets and episcopal robes when they went to church in the Lord Deputy's presence, or to preach before him; but that when they went to any other church they wore no robes at all, as if they were ashamed of their calling, and that this was an old practice in Dublin. The King and Laud ordered that all ministers shall say prayers in their surplices.

learnedly Ussher might defend episcopacy, the influence of Travers and his college days was still upon him.

Meanwhile Chappell was labouring to reform the life and discipline of the College in his own way. The Irish lecture was at once abandoned, and all care to promote natives, according to the intention of the second founder, ceased. On the other hand, daily chapels, with surplice on Sundays and holy days, were imposed on the students, but tacitly resisted by the fellows, who had been accustomed to laxer discipline. The favour of Wentworth, who sent (in 1637) his own son (a mere child of eleven) there under the charge of Harding, a tutor imported from Cambridge, brought the College into greater fashion. For, of course, students were not alarmed by the impending change of statutes, on which Laud and Wentworth had determined. A clear indication was the refusal of the new Provost to take the oath to obey the existing laws —a refusal causing much debate and dissatisfaction in the College, but justified by Laud and permitted by Wentworth. The bowing of the Provost whenever he passed the chapel door was noted and taken, as Irish Protestants now take it, for a sign of Popish superstition. In Ware's *Bishops* we read that "in order to give the juniors a taste of government, he established a Roman Commonwealth among them, to continue during the Christmas vacation, in which they had their Dictator, Consuls, Censors, and other officers of the Roman State in great splendour." If this account be accurate, Chappell was so ignorant of the Roman Commonwealth as not to know that the Dictator superseded all the other officers, and suspended the constitution at the moment of a crisis.

Meanwhile, it seems plain that Wentworth had no liking for the College Halls in the city, and that the Government did not offer any serious opposition to the legal action taken by the former owners of these Halls before the Council, that their property should be restored to them. The seizure by Lords

Cork and Loftus was represented either as wholly illegal, or as only applying to the priests or friars who occupied these premises. Very probably some middleman had leased them, and they had been turned into monastic houses without the formal knowledge of the owners. At all events it was made an accusation against Strafford at his trial, that he had allowed the Papists to reoccupy these houses to the injury of Trinity College. His reply may be formally true, but is disingenuous. He says that they were recovered from the College by suits at law, and that he had objected to the decisions. It takes small knowledge of the man and of his Government to know that if his objection had been serious, the actions at law would have failed. He was absolute despot at his Council, and could have quashed all such proceedings by a mere appeal to the royal prerogative. But it was another way of humiliating Cork, whose action was made to appear hasty and illegal. We know from two dockets requiring the Provost and fellows to give evidence, that the Dowager Countess of Kildare was the plaintiff in the one case; the prosecutor in the other case we cannot tell. The middleman was probably the Plunkett before mentioned, but a man called Edward Jans gives a receipt[1] to the College for £5 rent for the part in the hands of the College, the other half being payable by Richard White, to whom it was formerly let.[2]

On the other hand, Wentworth, while allowing these houses to go, was by no means lacking in zeal to promote the College. It is probable that they were alleged to be causes of lax discipline; in any case the Provost could not watch them as he did his own Society. Wentworth inaugurated afresh the proper policy of enlarging the College buildings by private subscription, and his donation of £100 was followed up by many other gifts on the part of those who sought his favour. Two Fitzgeralds, an Archdeacon and Dean, built a whole bay of buildings. Sir Chas. Coote

---

[1] April 20, 1637.   [2] Reg., 100.

gave £50;[1] Sir Geo. Radcliffe, £20; Sir George Scott, £20; George Baker (by bequest), £500—in all at least £2,000. This was the real and practical answer to Wentworth's indifference about the Halls, but it was not urged in his defence. Yet it was the moment when the College first began to expand beyond the two small quadrangles towards the north, and occupy the ground nearer the river with new chambers. None of these additions are now standing, but they can be clearly seen on Rocque's map.[2] An interesting brass (now in the Library) with an inscription in very loose iambics by the Provost, records Baker's gift as follows:—

>   MDCXXXIX.
>   D M S.
> " Georgius Bakerus, Cantabrigiæ incola
>   Dublini vixit hospes quoque diu
>   Moriturus urbi prætulit Academiam
>   Ubi vivet hospes eminens et excipiet
>   Tuos, Apollo, filios chara capita.
>   Ædibus quas sumptu suo paravit splendidas
>   Vivet et amplo fruetur laudis præmio
>   Alii dum sua perierint pecunia
>   Qui satis magnum haud putet Bakerum
>   Majore magnus esto beneficentia.
> Gul. Chappell Cork. et Ross
> Episcop. Hujus Coll. Præpositus."

But all these external aids, of which the accurate dates are not known, but which probably extended from 1634 to 1639, were of little use while the College was being wrecked by the internal dissensions of the fellows. The dislike to Chappell and his new régime broke into flame upon the first election to

[1] There is a stray note out of its place in the Bursar's Book, written upside down to the receipts of 1676 (the book is not paged), which gives us information somewhat different: " 1636: Money^s collected for ye building Jan. 6 Receaved of Sr Charles Coote £95 0 0 Receaved from Sr James Ware £10 0 0 Receaved from Archdeacñ Maxwell £100 0 0;" cf. Stubbs, p. 79, who had not seen this, for other items.

[2] Stubbs, p. 191.

Senior Fellowships after his appointment. There was notice of one impending vacancy, for a Fellow called Boswell (a Cheshire man) had been appointed to a distant living. Meanwhile another Senior Fellow (Ince) died, so that there were at least two vacancies to be filled up within the space of two months, according to the existing statutes. This gave time for discussions and cabals. There had been seven junior Fellows elected in 1631, of whom the senior had gone out, the next two (Kerdiff and Conway) were already Senior Fellows, and the choice lay among the remaining four in order of seniority, unless some grave cause of complaint authorised the electors to pass over the senior men. Assuming that the order of admission is observed in the entry of these fellows' simultaneous election, Arthur Ware, a young man of important and influential family, was the junior. Nevertheless, he formally claimed the seniority against the other three, on grounds which none of the many papers about this matter have condescended to mention.

The Provost showed his first weakness in not determining this question at once. The late Provost Ussher, who had admitted these fellows, was within reach; similar cases must often have occurred to serve as precedents. Nevertheless Chappell asks all the candidates to state their claims in writing, and when they all (except Ware) declined or refused to do so, kept postponing the election in the hope of some settlement. But ultimately he was pressed for time, and proposed the candidates, disregarding Ware's petition, in the order given in the Registry, viz., Hoyle, Pheasant, Cullen, Ware. Hereupon the second point was raised, not by the Provost formally, but surely at his suggestion: were these men free of all serious blame in their College life? Now the conflict between High and Low Church views at once came out It was notorious that the senior three had been utterly neglectful of daily chapels. Hoyle even refused to wear a surplice. This being a *gravis causa* to Chappell, the case was presently put to the Visitors in a very different form : [1] " whether a fellow of the College, living in the town the far greater part of a year and a quarter (*e.g.*, since Chappell's arrival), for which no cause is rendered but want of sheets, and in all that time not once reading prayers, disputing, commonplacing, nor procuring any to do duty for him, do not vacate his fellowship." But the Visitors had not been appealed to by Chappell for a remedy against this disorder for over a year, and not till this election quarrel had begun. At all events, some of the electors judged the surplice question a *gravis causa*, while others did not, and did not reject Hoyle till another Sunday had passed, upon which his continued refusal to wear the surplice set three of the electors against him on the ground of contumacy, and against the others for similar causes, and none were elected that day. Before the adjourned election took place, the three rejected fellows had appealed to the Visitors to inhibit it. The only ground they state is the false assertion of precedence by Ware as against the act of the late Provost in admitting them, and many subsequent recognitions of it.[2] The Visitors, in this case the two archbishops, Bishop of Meath, the Mayor, and Lord Loftus promptly acceded (February 13, 1635), and ordered a Visitation, which was held on the following May 18th.

The Provost's contention was twofold : (1) The three junior Fellows, in appealing to the Visitors without the consent or knowledge of the Provost, had been guilty of a graver breach of discipline, for which they should be expelled, and not promoted. (2) The Visitors had no power to interfere with the election, seeing that the only duties assigned them by the Charter were to settle differences which the Provost and fellows could not settle (a point not admitted in this case), and to punish grave crimes. But the Provost was worsted. After much heated altercation, in which the Primate, who was Vice-Chancellor, showed a violence quite foreign to his

---

[1] S. P., 1637, p. 146.   [2] *Anon.*, p. 210.

mild and quiet nature, the petition of Hoyle, Pheasant, and Cullen was justified, and the Provost and Senior Fellows ordered to elect them in that order at the next election for senior Fellows, the last election having led to no result, owing to the inhibition. Meanwhile other vacancies upon the governing Board had taken place, and in June, 1636, there were only three Senior Fellows remaining : Newman, Conway, and Kerdiff.

It was during this interval that the Provost took the more than doubtful step of abrogating a clause in the chapter concerning elections. To elect Senior Fellows was necessary for the conduct of the House, which must have been in great difficulties with only three Senior Fellows to hold the College offices restricted to them. On the other hand Bedell's statute, then in force, mentioned the majority that could elect as at least four (out of seven, the normal number of Senior Fellows). Chappell's expedient was to abrogate the words *nempe quatuor* from the statute, which was done by an undated act written in at the close of the official book of statutes, signed by the Provost, Newman, and Conway. It is more than likely that this act was sprung upon the remaining senior Kerdiff, just before the election. For when the day came, and he found what was intended, he left the Provost's lodging, in spite of the Provost's threats, and informed the candidates who were waiting outside. Meanwhile the electors within had decided to pass the three senior men over on the ground of contumacy, and to elect Ware. But before he could be admitted formally, by kneeling before the Provost, the rest rushed in a disorderly and insolent manner into the room, and claimed their right according to the recent decree of the Visitors. The Provost, however, stood firm, conceding only that if they signed a paper confessing their fault, there would be another election held for the remaining places. They refused and appealed at once, not this time to the Visitors, but to the Privy Council. All this happened on the 18th of June, and the case was heard at once on the 20th, and then at an adjourned meeting. On the first day the Council, seeing that the order of the Visitors on May 18th had been openly disregarded by the Board, asked the Provost to comply with it. The Provost urged that the Visitors had exceeded their powers, but that if the complainants, who deserved expulsion for their insubordination, would confess their fault, he would admit them junior to Ware. When the Council met again this had not been done, and the Provost still defended his position. His action in electing without four Senior Fellows, by changing the statute, he apparently excused on the ground of necessity. The Provost and fellows protested against the interference of the Council, complained that all discipline would have subverted, and appealed to the Chancellor. Nevertheless, the Council (among whom were several of the Visitors) authorised a second visitation, held on July 20 by the two archbishops, the Bishop of Meath, and the Lord Mayor. On this occasion there was no uncertain sound. The Provost was censured in severe terms by the Primate; the two Senior Fellows who had conspired with him to alter the statute were deprived of their fellowships. Messrs. Pheasant and Cullen were made Senior Fellows, senior to Ware, and the punishment of the Provost referred to the king.

This sentence, with the defence of the Provost, was sent to the king, who naturally referred it to Laud to decide. Most unfortunately Wentworth had been absent during these months from Dublin. Had he been at the Council he would have made a prompt decision and seen it enforced. But now he is very glad to submit to his friend Laud, though Laud is equally anxious to refer it back to the Lord Deputy. There is no dispute mentioned in Laud's correspondence, on which he hesitated so long, and prayed so eagerly for a peaceable compromise. Apart from questions of etiquette, or discipline, or the interpretation of statutes, there was on the one side his nominee the Provost, sent to Ireland to reform College and State, and a devoted instrument of his and Wentworth's policy. On the other the great Primate and the Council had decided the case in solemn judgment, and to reverse their acts would be a matter of jeering to the many Roman Catholics who were watching the conflict. Laud writes out the whole case, thirty-three folio pages,[1] and sends it to the disputants to agree upon the facts before he will decide, but urges Wentworth to arbitrate, and writes a most serious letter to Ussher which seems to imply that his sentence will probably be against the Visitors and for the Provost. This was evidently Wentworth's view also, to whom justice was nothing, the supporting of his creatures everything.

We have no formal account of the result. But Laud's anxious pleading for a settlement, and his hints of the result of a formal decision had their effect. The acts of the Visitors were mostly ignored. Pheasant, the ringleader, who had even gone over to see Laud, but had produced on him a bad impression, was expelled; Newman and Conway were restored to their fellowships. But Hoyle and Cullen were made Senior Fellows, senior to Ware, though Cullen was so long absent from College that the Primate interceded to have him retained.[2] The Provost therefore won most of his battle by Wentworth's "persuasion," and so far the great Ussher was discredited—another item in the policy of lowering all prominent men, and of crushing out all independence, in Ireland.

The Provost's hands were even strengthened by a violent ukase against the keepers of alehouses harbouring students and allowing them to run bills, which gave moreover to the Proctors the same power of visitation of houses, under the Provost's orders, which they possess in Oxford and Cambridge. This inroad upon the rights and liberties of the citizens of

---

[1] Of this a very full abstract will be found in S. P., 1637, pp. 145-9. This is the document of which Stubbs regrets the loss. Wandesford's letter, to which Wentworth refers as going to the root of the matter, is unfortunately not in the collection.

[2] Reg., 62.

Dublin was made about a year after the great quarrel, and seems intended to magnify the importance of the Provost and his discipline. He had probably represented to the Lord Deputy that the habit of going to alehouses, and even ot spending the night there, was beyond his control, especially in the case of boys who lived with their parents in the city. Both the order and one case of the violation of it are related to us at length, in extant documents, and printed by Dr. Stubbs.[1] That the Privy Council should assume the duties of police magistrates to aid the discipline of the College appears sufficiently strange, but stranger still is the astounding severity of the punishments inflicted on the student Weld, who is found harboured by the widow Jones in a suspicious alehouse, and late at night. The erring widow is fined £40, and has to stand in the market-place with an inscription on her, "For harboring a student contrary to the Act of State, also, that she shall make public acknowledgment of her offence at the College, where and when the Provost shall direct," &c., &c. Dr. Stubbs has not printed the full text of the action of the College in this matter. The Privy Council had ordered "that the said Daniel Weld shall stand fined £40 to his Majesty—a fine equivalent to £250 in our day—that he be left to the Provost of the College to inflict such further exemplary punishment on his person, whether by expulsion or otherwise, as the Provost shall think fit." A fortnight after this sentence (June 11, 1638), the Registry (p. 66) gives us the following entry :—

We may not conceive the fault light, which our most honoured Governors have deemed so heavy. And therefore whereas Mr. Weld (for so he may yet be called) hath { contemned the Act of State / scandalised this } { College as a / University as an Inceptor this year, } { student in it / member of it } I, William Chappell, Provost of this College, do by order of the Right Hon. the Lord Deputy and Council, censure him as followeth :

---

[1] App., xxxii.

In regard of the College	as a student to be deprived of	his study therein
		all testimonium of good carriage.
	as a scholar to	to be deprived of his scholarship
		to have his name erased in the College books
In regard of the University	to be suspended from his degree of Master of Arts not to be restored till he bring sufficient testimony from the place where he shall live one year at the least of his	honest conversation
		conformity to the orders of the Church.

All this is very neat and logical, and quite in the style of the Provost's *art of preaching*, which is full of these logical paradigms. We must also remember that punishments in those days were far severer than our modern humanity would tolerate. But when all reservations, explanations, and palliations have been made, who can justify such a sentence as anything better than a piece of pedantic absurdity?

Such judicial violences were sure to deter young men, not only from this crime, but from the College. Wentworth must have consulted with the Provost about it, and the pedant agreed with the despot, who was becoming more and more truculent, as he felt his enemies' power waxing, and the protection of the false and feeble king waning. By this time he and Laud had secured for the Provost all the powers necessary to rule his College and the University at his ease with despotic power. Such a sentence as that just noticed would have been impossible under Bedell's Statutes without the consent of four Senior Fellows. But now there was a new order of things, which almost deserves a separate chapter.

The practical prelude to the introduction of the new Charter was the insolent imposing on the College of two Masters of Arts from Cambridge, Messrs. John Harding and Thomas Marshall, *vice* Newman, whose place had expired, and Pheasant expelled [1]—not merely as fellows, but as Senior Fellows. Thus the Provost obtained two votes to aid him in forcing the acceptance of the new Charter. These orders or Wentworth were issued on April 20 and on May 10, 1637; the Charter was accepted on the eleventh of the same month with a solemn ceremony in the chapel, at which Ussher, as Vice-Chancellor, was present, probably in no good temper. But Bedell was there also, and approved highly of the change.[2] Quite apart from these arbitrary acts, the whole policy of both Wentworth and Laud, to neglect Irish and Anglo-Irish for the benefit of imported Englishmen, appears clearly not only in the names of the fellows, but of the scholars elected in these years. Not a single O or Mac appears among them; the natives' places are not even filled by youths of English names well known in Ireland. So far as Ireland was concerned its University was being rapidly denationalised.

The passing of the Charter took place almost exactly in the middle of Chappell's Provostship, which lasted six years. The latter three years, which offer little of note, may be despatched in this history before we proceed to analyse the new Charter. From the day that he was installed as absolute master of the College we hear of no more insubordination among his subordinates, for obvious reasons. The violations of the new statutes came from his superiors. Harding, the imported Senior Fellow, who was tutor to Wentworth's son, having accepted a living, and consequently having voided his fellowship, was forthwith reappointed Senior Fellow by Letters Patent from the Lord Deputy in manifest violation of his own code (Reg. 61). Dean Margetson, a friend of the Deputy, was ordered to have a D.D. degree. The Provost, being promoted (June, 1638) to the bishoprics of Cork and Ross, and offering to resign his place, was directed by Wentworth and Laud to hold it *in commendam*, though even the king was known to be opposed to such a practice. In one letter from Laud

---

[1] Reg., 56, 57.   [2] Cf. Shuckburgh's *Bedell*, p. 340.

to Wentworth [1] he says indeed that Primate Ussher's dislike of the Provost made it desirable to remove the latter, if another fit man could be found for the College. But Wentworth would not hear of it. On this occasion Ussher, though ousted from the government of the College, as will be explained in the next chapter, thought it right to protest. Here is his letter [2] :—

"I was very sorry to see that clause of his Maj. letter whereby the Provostship of the College was granted to be held *in commendam* with the bishopricks of Cork and Ross; of which the party himself, whom it concerneth, is sensible enough that it can hardly stand with the solemn oath which he took upon the sending over of the new statutes, especially this clause being thereunto added, *non impetrabo nec procurabo directe vel indirecte dispensionem contra juramenta mea praedicta, aut contra ordinationes aut statuta collegii vel ipsorum aliquod.* The eluding of oaths in this manner I do conceive to be a matter of most pernicious consequence; and the party himself, as I hear, is not unwilling to give over that place unto his brother, who now keepeth with him at the college. Whom, if your grace should not think to be so fit a man for that place, you have a very worthy man of your own there, Mr. Joseph Mede, who was heretofore nominated unto the self-same place, and that with the good approbation of the council table in England."

The great Irish Primate speaks with undisguised contempt of "the party whom it concerneth." But Wentworth would not yield, and it was not till eighteen months later, when both Wentworth's and Laud's actions were being called in question, and their enemies were declaring themselves both in England and Ireland, that Chappell again sought and obtained leave to resign.

When he resigned all things were still nominally subject to the tyrant of Ireland, and the following entry [3] expresses the outside appearance of the facts as Wentworth wished them to appear :—

[1] Strafford's *Letters*, ii. p. 120.
[2] Ussher's *Works*, xvi. p. 37.
[3] Reg., 70.

"July 20, 1640. The Right Revd. Father in God, William Lord Bishoppe of Corke and Ross, being chosen Provost on the 21st of August, 1634, after he had gratiously reformed the students, happily promoted new Statutes and rich amplifying of the buildings, beautifyed the Chappel, Hall, Provost's lodgings and Regent House, with the garden and other places by ye good advice and assistance of our worthy learned and pious Vice-Provost, Mr. Doctor Harding, and wonderfully increased the College Plate[1] and stocke, reduced all things into a blessed order, and faithfully governed by the space of sixe yeares as a glorious pattern of sobriety, justice and godlyness, the 20th of July, 1640, resigned up his Provostshippe in writing under his hand and Episcopall seale. [Witnessed by the Vice-Provost and Senior Fellows.]

The reader of the events rehearsed in this chapter will be amused at this encomium, especially at the adverbs and qualifying adjectives. It is true that the buildings were increased, fine pieces of plate acquired, young men of fashion educated. But what did all that avail when the high-handed despot under whom he served goaded the country promptly into a rebellion, which within five years swept away all this order?

The Registry of these blessed years is very scanty. The pompous punishment of Weld, and the State recognition of Harding's official perjury are the longest it contains. There is in the M. R. (F. 77) a curious petition (dated July 26, 1638) to recover books borrowed or lost from Kildare Hall, "now given up," and from the College Library. The witnesses summoned are Barry the Librarian, Mr. Boswell, rector there, and Mr. Hoile after him, and the names of the borrowers, viz. :—

To the Right Honble. Thomas Viscount Wentworth, Lord Deputy-General.
    The Humble Petition of the Provost and Fellows of Trinity College, near Dublin,
Humbly showeth that whereas divers books of good worth, some from the College Library, others by the gift of persons well affected,

---

[1] It is to be noticed that the clause in Bedell's Statutes directing that fellow commoners should at entrance contribute a piece of plate was expunged by Laud.

were for the use of the Students, while Kildare Hall was possessed by the College, there bestowed, and by the carelessness of some and rapacity of others are kept from your Petitioners,

And whereas also divers books have been borrowed out of the College Library and lost or detained from your Petitioners to private use to the great diminishing of our Library,

And whereas also divers persons whose names are underwritten stand indebted unto the College in divers sums of money, and most of them a long time,

May it please your Lordship that such as are here undernamed may be examined upon oath for the clearing of the first, and they who shall be found to have had them in keeping caused to produce and restore them.

That those who have borrowed from the College Library may be caused to make restitution.

That those who stand indebted to the College may make satisfaction.

And your Petitioners shall pray, &c.

To be examined for Kildare Hall—
- Mr. Barry, keeper of the Library.
- Mr. Boswell, Rector there.
- Mr. Hoile, Rector after him.
- Mr. Carter.
- Mr. Wilkinson.

The names of them that have borrowed from the College Library.
- Doctor Arthure.
- John Binnes.
- John Wiggett.
- Charles Johnson.
- Richard Bourk.
- Rowland Eustace.
- Mr. Puttock.
- Mr. Baskervile.
- Mr. Brodeley.
- Chris Coburne.
- John Allen.
- William Newman.

The names of those that stand indebted to the College.
- Robert Ashwood, £19.
- Richard Bourk, £7.
- Henry Jones, £10.
- John Watson, £3.
- Willm. Newman, £12.
- Garrett Mead, £18 13s. 6d.
- John Allen, £5.

DUBLIN CASTLE, 26th July, 1638.

The parties within complained on are hereby required to appear forthwith before us to Answer these several complaints,

WENTWORTH.

There is also a petition from the Provost and fellows dated March 24, 1639, to have their Crown pension of £388 15s. commuted for lands of equal value in the proposed plantation of Connaught, and the king's letter to Wentworth sanctioning this change.[1] There are many papers relating to suits of the College with tenants, or tenants with one another, on the College lands, especially in Co. Limerick, in which Thomas Clanchy (or Clancy) of Craiggard, who seems to have acted as an agent for the College, plays a prominent part.[2] Among all these papers are but few with personal touches. In the midst of Thomas Clancy's business letters I found two of no historic but of much social interest, for they enable us to feel sympathy with homely people across the span of three centuries. Here they are :—

(M. R., D 62.)

"My most deare Joye and one Love,—I knowe it is tedious to you my absence, and soe it is for mee; but God be thanked, my business is done, and I looke everie daie to come home. I thought not to have written to you before I came my selfe, but for feare y^u should thinke some accident befell mee, I have written this to be of good comfort. I sent you a good gowne, pettycoate and gorgett in Mr. F. trunke; looke to y^r home busines, tender my dutie to y^r father and mother, and to all my friends my love, not forgetting y^r selfe. I remaine Thine one onlie Loyall while I live to bee

"M. Purdon.

"Dublin, *Junii*, 1638."

[There is no endorsement or address.]

(M. R., D 63.)

"Dublin, *this 29th of Maye*, 1639.

"Cossen Thomas,—I beleeve yor greefe and sadnesse comes of the love that you beare unto me—of which I doe thinke that it is the feare of y^r parentes makes you not to marrye mee, but if you had expresse your minde unto mee at the first tyme of your acquaintance I would never desire yo^u to be mine, but, deere hart, seeing that it is late to repent it and that I have gott ill will for you and that yo^u have drawen my love soe farre upon you, and if it bee

---

[1] M. R., F 70, 70a.   [2] ibid., C 53–68; D 48–53, 62–75.

your intent to marrye elsewhere I will never hinder you howbeite it is the overtrowe of my fortune. I would desire you to come to see me, for I am not well this daye.

"Soe I rest yo^ur loving cossen,
"Munday morninge at Ormonds armes,
"MARY BROWNE."

[Address: "To my very loving cossen, Mr. Thomas Clansie, thiese be
att"

There is also an important document,[1] dating just after the new Charter in 1637, giving the conditions of new leases with tenants. It is plain that the material prosperity and order under Wentworth had sensibly affected the value of land, and that the College rents were now being raised. But here is an entry in the Register of which the humour has escaped previous historians. It illustrates the pedantic side of the "close Ramist," as the Provost is styled. I give it in English, though the Latin original puts it on higher stilts :—

"To all the faithful in Christ to whom these presents may come— Know ye that we the Provost and Senior Fellows of the College of the Holy and undivided Trinity near Dublin of the foundation of the most Serene Queen Elizabeth, by our unanimous consent and assent according to the Statutes of the College have elected, co-opted, and admitted Master John Pemberton to be butler of our College, and hold and confirm him as so co-opted and admitted by these presents furnished with our seal, and the subscription of our names. Given this 28th of February, 1639.

Wm. Cor et Ross, Pps.

Joh̃as Harding	Alex. Hatfield
Nath. Hoyle	Chr. Pepper
Th. Seele	Chr. Beckwith
	Guil. Clopton

At the same time William our College cook had his place confirmed to him in ye same manner, signed and sealed as above said."

We hear from the historians of Oxford Colleges that the inferior officers were regarded "inferior members" of their

[1] M. R., D 73.

College, and not unfrequently took degrees. This man called *Magister* may have been such, but I do not think so pompous a recognition of it will be found in any of their records. In this obscure body of insignificant Dons one name only stands out in after history—Thomas Seele, who had already gone out on a living, but finding it intolerable petitioned and obtained leave to resume his fellowship and College life. He lived to be an active and distinguished Provost after the Restoration.[1] The whole history of the College during these six momentous years reflects and explains the history of Ireland. There was external prosperity, an increase of the means and materials of life, many solemn thanksgivings for the righteous and merciful rule of the dread sovran, who was robbing the landlords of their titles and the people of their liberties. Natives and settlers, chieftains and undertakers, all alike were suffering. But all complaint was crushed out by the Dublin Star Chamber. Wentworth was sitting on the safety valve, and when recalled to England to aid his tottering king all the elements of discontent burst forth. The higher classes in their Parliament, the Anglo-Irish nobility and gentry, Protestant and Catholic, began the attack. But behind them lay greater and more ungovernable forces, that swept away constitutional discussions with an avalanche of rapine and murder.

But we must insist upon the fact that externally Wentworth's rule was one of great prosperity. The Dublin of his day, according to the evidence of Sir William Brereton, was a brilliant city, comparing most favourably with Edinburgh, which the traveller had just visited. We find that in 1637 he travelled leisurely from Belfast to Dromore, and through the mountains to Newry and Dundalk, and presently through the

---

[1] The formal act re-admitting him, sanctioned by six Visitors, is given in Reg., 49, and occurred in 1635, before the great disturbance. Seele was elected Senior Fellow in January, 1637 (O. S.), and therefore the first under the new Charter.

O'Byrne, O'Moore and Kavanagh country, west of the Wicklow Mountains, without ever incurring the smallest personal danger from wood kerne or outlaws. During his stay in Dublin he meets various distinguished men of Trinity College, the Primate, who entertains him twice at dinner, Richardson, now Bishop of Ardagh, who at this very time presented to his old College the stately chalice and flagon still in use in the Chapel, and Hoyle, whom he hears preaching at S. Werburgh's. Brereton's taste was for sermons, of which he heard many, and liked those of Ussher (at S. Andrew's) best. The Lord Deputy was probably away, for the chief thing admired in the Castle are the stables, of which we hear often in Wentworth's letters.

The whole impression the traveller has of Dublin is that of a thriving city:—

> "This city of Dublin is extending his bounds and limits very far, much additions of building lately, and some of these very fair, stately, and complete buildings; every commodity is grown very dear. You must pay also for an horse hire 1s. 6d. a day; here I met with an excellent, judicious, and painful smith. Here are divers commodities cried in Dublin as in London, which it doth more resemble than any town I have seen in the King of England's dominions."[1]

The extension of the city towards the College was at the moment the most important. We have already noticed the new residences on College Green (p. 201). It was in Sir Toby Caulfeild's house that Lady Cork died when on a visit in 1629. There is an allusion in the Register to the students having attended her funeral. The house is, however, to us of higher interest in that Ussher bought it, and petitioned the Corporation (in 1632) to have a garden round it, as he desired to settle there on account of his old affection for his native city.[2] This was the house in which Brereton dined with him, and found the study removed from the rest, perhaps in the garden, for the Primate would not be disturbed at his literary work,

---

[1] *Travels*, p. 144.   [2] Gilbert's *Records*, iii. p. 260.

which commenced daily at 5 a.m. and lasted till 6 p.m., with the exception of two hours (11–1) for relaxation, when he saw his friends.

But in spite of his assiduity, Ussher must have had time to visit the College and its Library constantly, and must have been profoundly disgusted when he saw the High Church practices of Chappell. It is remarkable that when visiting the College, Brereton merely mentions the Provost, and speaks sneeringly of the Library and its MSS. whose value he thinks greatly exaggerated. What would Ussher have said to this judgment? These trifles are only quoted to show the ease and affluence of life in Dublin under the strong rule of Wentworth.

The Caroline Constitution (1637).[1]

Nothing is more usual and more false than to state that Laud gave the College a completely new code of Statutes. They were indeed appended to a new Charter, but even that did not abrogate the old, but recited it with some modifications in its Preamble. Similarly the new Statutes were mainly, both in substance and in form, those which we have in Bedell's hand, and these again are, according to Bedell's own statement, put together and arranged from the older code which had been sanctioned by Temple and his fellows. There is no copy of these oldest laws of the College extant, but the rules of the University, which govern, with hardly a change, the acts and meetings of the Senate to this day, are in the Muniment Room, each rule signed by Temple and his fellows, and they begin (as has been said above) with Chapter V.

[1] I have thought it right to give the whole of Bedell's code in an appendix to this volume. These Statutes have never yet been printed, and are highly interesting in many ways. A few notes have been here added that the general reader may mark the principal changes. The Caroline or Laudian Code is printed next after the Elizabethan Charter in the book of Statutes, published by the College in two vols. (Dublin Hodges and Foster, 1844, 1898).

But as Bedell must have added and changed a good deal, so Laud, reading Bedell's book carefully, and with a view to the recent troubles in the College and the Irish Church, and having regard to his friend Wentworth's wishes, not only introduced several new principles, but gratified several old animosities in his retouching of the code. The general intention of both Laud and Wentworth was to make the College distinctly English in tone and Anglican in creed, and in this they ran counter to the policy of Bedell, who had striven to make it Anglo-Irish, if not Irish, and of Ussher, who had made it Evangelical, if not Puritan. Both these pious men had sought to make the College life religious, Laud sought to make it ecclesiastical. But the temper of the times, and the fierce attacks which were being made on his policy, kept him very cautious to avoid offence, so that it requires a minute collation of his text with the earlier code to see the mind of the man behind apparently trivial alterations of form. The preamble opens with Bedell's words, until the new circumstances of Charles' Charter come to be stated by Laud. But in the forefront of the regulations Bedell had naturally put the chapter *de cultu Divino*, which Laud degrades to the ninth chapter, though there repeating words only suitable to its original place.[1] Where the use of the Irish Church had been ordered in the Chapel, that of the Anglican is substituted, with the special permission of a shortened Morning Service, " in order that the students may get earlier to their lectures." What the use of the Irish Church had been in Temple's time I cannot tell, but I do not believe that the Puritan fellows read the Anglican liturgy daily, and Bedell does not speak of his having made any innovation in this respect. The short chapter of the Bible read (sometimes in Irish) before commons, and the recitation of a verse or passage during meat by a

---

[1] " Hinc igitur admoniti *primo* de iis præcipiendum putavimus "—no the only instance of careless re-editing I have found in Laud's generally careful work.

scholar, in order to suggest a religious conversation, was changed by Laud into the mere reading of a chapter during meals till stopped by the *tu vero* of the Senior in the hall. The Graces now said before and after meat are those of Bedell, changed only in one word by Laud.[1] Bedell (and probably Temple) had ordered that daily prayers should be conducted by the fellows and resident masters. Laud adds: provided they be ordained, and at least in Deacon's orders. The fellows and scholars are to take their oath, *tactis sancrosanctis Christi Evangeliis*, an addition quite foreign to Puritan manners. Likewise the limits of the four terms were now marked by Saints' days instead of the simple dates in the older statutes, and Trinity Sunday and Monday are brought into prominence on account of the title of the College. On that Sunday there is a largely increased allowance for Commons, so that it must have been a veritable *gaudy*, and on that Monday the new fellows and scholars have been elected from Laud's day till now. On the other hand there was a compulsory fast slipped in parenthetically by ordering "corrections" by the Deans to be held on Fridays at five o'clock—*cœnam enim ea nocte nolumus*. Bedell had ordered these corrections to be held after supper. Another indulgence seems to us more strange in a man of Laud's temperament, and is ascribable to his dislike of Puritanical asceticism. To the clause forbidding absolutely the games of dice and cards, on pain of expulsion after the third warning, he adds, "except at the time of Christmas and in the public Hall of the College." Otherwise all sports are forbidden as strictly in the later as in the earlier code. Amid the general straitening of conditions and increased severity of punishments it is to be noted that while Bedell has ordained the same oath for the fellows and the scholars, and in both a declaration of adherence to the Protestant faith as con-

---

[1] Oculi omnium in te *respiciunt* B. *sperant* L. Even the *Carolo conservatore* of the second Grace is already in that of Bedell, and had therefore no reference originally to the new Charter.

tained in the Bible, and a repudiation of Popery, Laud makes the oaths distinct, and abstains from making the scholar declare his creed (cap. vi.), but merely puts to him the solemn acknowledgment of the king's supremacy, and the abjuring of the allegiance to any foreign prince or priest. It is here quite plain that the new statute provided for the admission of Roman Catholics into scholarships, though their College duties would afterwards entail going to the Anglican service in the Chapel. The use of surplices and hoods was strictly enjoined. Bedell had made the Fellow swear that the object of his studies would be theology, that he may be of use to the Church of God, unless God inclined his mind otherwise (cap. viii., *sub. fin.*). Laud, leaving this clause, with the further exception of the Jurist and the Medicus, inserts at the end of cap. vii. another clause requiring every fellow with these two exceptions to be in priest's orders within three years of his election, or else to lose his fellowship. The survival of Bedell's clause in cap. viii. is evidently an oversight. For the contrast between the tone of the Puritan and the Priest is here very plain. We feel in the earlier the voice of Travers or Temple, in the latter the voice of Laud. It was a direct rebuff to Bedell, that his clause ordaining the scholars who obtained Irish places to prosecute their studies in Irish, and show proficiency in the language, was expunged, though it was enacted that the sons of citizens of Dublin and of the College tenants (mostly northern planters) should be preferred. But then Bedell had since given Wentworth considerable annoyance by joining the gentlemen of Cavan in a protest against the exactions of the State, and showed a dangerous sympathy for the Irish poor and the local interests, which made him suspected and disliked by Wentworth. Accordingly care was taken to suppress Irish teaching in Trinity College. This change was noted at the time and included by Parliament in the charges against Chappell.

An anti-Irish policy was manifested, not merely in the matter of studies but in the constitution of the highest authorities of the College. Strange to say, in the letters patent preceding the Statutes, the Provost and Senior Fellows are still empowered to elect a Chancellor, Proctors, and other University officers, thus showing that Laud did not differ from the original conception of the College as a corporation endowed with University powers, and not the first of a number of Colleges to be placed under a controlling University. Probably it was assumed that the Provost, who was from henceforth to be a nominee of the Crown, would always choose as Chancellor some great personage of influence at the English Court, for the importance of the Chancellor was always to mediate between the College and the Crown. And from henceforth the Chancellor was to be no mere ornamental head. Laud, in view of recent quarrels, made himself the primary Visitor, to whom all serious questions are to be referred by the resident Visitors, whom he restricts to two, instead of the previous seven.

This was a change which gave great offence, and which can hardly be understood as less than a direct insult to Ussher. He had been for years the Vice-Chancellor, and as such primary Visitor and Chairman of a Board of seven, consisting (with him) of the Archbishop of Dublin, Bishop of Meath, the Vice-Treasurer, the Treasurer at Wars, the Lord Chief Justice, and the Mayor of Dublin. So long as Ussher lived he would dominate that Court, which was distinctly of an Anglo-Irish complexion. Probably Laud and Wentworth thought it too unpopular to remove him, but they gave him, as his only colleague, the Archbishop of Dublin, who would almost always be an imported Englishman, and not only if they differed but when they agreed, their decisions on all important questions were to be void, unless approved by the Chancellor. The result was that Ussher took no more interest in his old College. He came down indeed to the Chapel to hear the new Statutes read, probably with a very sore heart. He protested to Laud next year [1] against Chappell being allowed to

---

[1] Cf. above, p. 248.

violate the new statutes. But neither Laud nor Wentworth heeded him, and from henceforth he withdrew completely from any part in the direction of the College. Being in England at the outbreak of the rebellion of 1641, when his houses and lands were wasted, and a war of many years ensued, he never returned to Ireland again.

The critics of the day seem not to have appreciated the gravity of this deliberate thrusting aside of the most learned and eminent of Irishmen from his supervision over the College wherein he had lived and worked so many years. They complain of the offensive treatment of the Mayor of Dublin, who represented the city that ranked first among the great benefactors of the College. But no doubt the Mayor and citizens spoke out, whereas Ussher kept silence, conscious that the insult had come from the man whom he had himself urged to become Chancellor and brought in by his persuasion over the unwilling or indifferent Society.

The greatest innovations were, however, decidedly in the position of the Provost. We can well imagine the contempt with which Laud expunged the preamble to Bedell's fourth chapter, on the permanent Senate of the College consisting of the Provost and Senior Fellows : "*quia in Academica societate bene constituta ea ratio plerumque tenetur societatis administrandæ quæ ad Aristocratiæ formam proxime accedit, existimavimus non potuisse nos huic Collegio melius consulere, quam et in eo gubernando ad modum Aristocraticum procederemus,*" according to which Bedell proceeds to put the whole power of determining all matters in the College according to the statutes into the hands of the Provost and major part—*nempe quatuor*—of the seven Senior Fellows. But Laud was a monarchist, and determined that the shackle of the four Senior Fellows, which had hitherto often paralysed the Provost's action, should only survive in name. The chapter *de cultu divino* is moved away in order to allow that " on the Provost's quality and position " to stand in the forefront. The general description—a man of blameless life, a theologian, at least a Bachelor in Divinity, at least thirty years of age, holding no more that one benefice—is all adopted from Bedell; but Laud adds that he may hold any ecclesiastical dignity short of a bishopric, consistent with his duties according to the statutes. We may remember that Chappell was Dean of Cashel when appointed Provost. Furthermore Laud adds that he must be unmarried and must resign if he marries. But the three great differences are these: (1) Though the words of the older statute remain that a son of the College is to be preferred to a stranger, the clause is rendered nugatory by the abolition of the old election by the fellows, and the reservation of the appointment to the Crown. It'is quite certain that it was the intention of both Laud and Wentworth to fill the place with imported Englishmen. (2) Wherever the statutes have not laid down a fixed punishment, all the discipline is in the Provost's hands. He consults upon grave crimes with the two Deans, who are put under his control; and can expel any member of the College on his own authority. If he chooses he may propose to the Senior Fellows what censure they think right in any case, and then may go with the majority; but in this he is like the king in Homeric society, who generally and for appearance' sake consulted his nobles, though the power of life and death was in his hands. (3) In elections under the older statutes the Provost and major part of the Senior Fellows, if they agreed, decided the result, but if that majority after three scrutinies remained opposed to the Provost, the election for that occasion was declared abortive, and nothing was done. Laud retained the first two scrutinies in the same form, but made them idle by adding that on the third scrutiny whosoever the Provost (or in his absence the Vice-Provost) had voted for, should be elected. Thus the majority was of no consequence whatever to the Provost. He need merely vote three times for his nominee to elect him.

This statute is to the present day the law of the College, and whenever a majority cannot be obtained in a fellowship election the Provost decides. But a great change was introduced into the reading of the statute by the Visitation of 1791, whereby the majority of Senior Fellows can elect in spite of the Provost. To translate the words *quem major pars Sociorum Seniorum una cum Præposito elegerit* as " whom the major part of the Provost and Senior Fellows *together* shall choose" (instead of: *having the Provost with them*) was no doubt a most safe and excellent translation for the purpose of protecting the College from the acts of an arbitrary Provost; to argue that either the history of the Society, the tenor of the statutes, or the Latin words, justify such a rendering, is to my mind a task only fit for a lawyer working for his fee; yet this was the decision of a first-rate judge, Lord Clare, and has since governed all the elections in the College.[1]

There was one somewhat immoral provision for assisting the Deans in their duties which was even more pronounced in the older statute than in Laud's. Bedell had ordained that some of the scholars should be appointed as *observatores occulti* to report to the Deans all cases of negligence or disorder they noticed among the students. Laud preserved the clause, omitting the two ugly words, and the ordinance lasted down to about 1820.[2]

---

[1] This constitutional point, arising out of a quarrel of Hely Hutchinson with his Senior Fellows, excited such interest that one of the fellows, Matthew Young (afterwards a bishop) published a special treatise called *The Provost's Negative* (2nd Ed., Dublin, 1792), wherein all the arguments against such an absolute veto from the analogous cases of Deans and Chapters and Mayors and Corporations are admirably marshalled. There are added, as an appendix, the opinions of several learned lawyers, all in favour of Young's reading of the statute. As a matter of policy, he and Clare in his decision were undoubtedly right. But I do not believe that Laud, were he brought back from the dead, would have agreed with this interpretation.

[2] At which time a porter whispered every week to three of the scholars, "You are *Morum*, sir, this week," *i.e.*, *magister morum*. It was the duty of these three to fine at least eight persons 2s. 6d. each, by way of increasing the income of the College. Hence strutting in the courts, wearing boots, &c., were made pretexts for these fines. There was no

It is not desirable in this history to give further details regarding the management of the College. Without a knowledge of the statutes no reader is likely to take an interest in such matters ; and however the specialist in College lore may delight in a minute collation of these two codes, and of them with sister codes prevailing in the Colleges of Cambridge or Oxford, such researches either assume considerable special knowledge, or require a printing of long Latin texts in parallel columns. We may concede that without such researches all accurate and thorough history is impossible. But the writer who desires to bring the annals of his College into relation with the history of the country must refrain from inflicting his labours on the reader, he must be content to give the results of these labours, so far as they are strictly germane to his subject. For this reason I suppress a host of minor details, and return to the public history of the times.

appeal from them. The scandal was stopped by the three scholars appointed for one week combining to fine each of them eight of the fellows. The fines were paid, but the *Magistri morum* dropped for the future. This item of more recent College history is nowhere in print, so far as I know. It was told me by my father, who was a scholar in 1821, and one of the actors in the farce.

CHAPTER VII

THE GREAT REBELLION AND THE CIVIL WAR IN IRELAND

THE years 1639-40 show in our old Matriculation book a considerable increase in the number of entering students. Everything seemed prosperous in the College. Wentworth reports to the king that despite the constant intrigues and insinuations against him at Court, and the allegations that he was hated in Ireland, all the various sections of the population were contented and happy under his government. He does indeed mention by way of exception in the winter of 1639-40 that some wood kerne had begun again to burn down gentlemen's houses in the remote country, and that he was taking special precautions to put this kind of outrage down. He also knows that there is some excitement among the Irish exiles abroad; but he shows no sense of any serious danger, and urges the expediency of holding a Parliament in Ireland (in March, 1639), which would give the example to England in voting liberal subsidies for the king's needs. This supremacy of Wentworth, with his known patronage of the College, must have acted powerfully upon its material prosperity. We can still see in the Matriculation book, which begins with his little son's name, how many of his friends and dependents—Englishmen—also sent their sons thither. He tells Laud that the Provost, now Bishop of Cork, but still kept in the College by his order, is passing well content. The inner annals of the

College, as we have said, are dumb. The Primate and the Bishop of Meath had been silenced, and when the Parliament came together, even without the Lord Deputy's presence to direct and intimidate them, he found them sitting on his arrival (March 23rd) in perfect docility to his wishes. They practically voted all the subsidies he required, they accepted with effusive thanks all the nominal graces offered by the king. They even went out of their way to assure King Charles of their extraordinary contentment with the government of Wentworth, now Earl of Strafford and the king's most trusted minister.

Yet within the year this universal satisfaction had turned into an universal outcry against his tyrannies, injustices, and cruelties; he was a prisoner in the Tower, on trial for his life. Within a year and month he ended his career upon the scaffold (May 11, 1641) with the approbation of hundreds of thousands of Englishmen, and the satisfaction of almost all classes in Ireland. This astonishing *peripety* of fortune is not easily paralleled in history. The fall of Sejanus, Tiberius' confidant, has been celebrated by a great historian and a great satirist. But Sejanus was a poor creature in comparison with Strafford, and Sejanus belongs to a long past century. Among the contemporary men, if we may compare very small things with very great, the Provost of Trinity College affords another example of the wheel of fortune. But he was not without some warning. When the Irish Parliament reassembled in June, 1640, after the bold resistance to arbitrary taxation made by the Short Parliament in England during the interval, any intelligent observer might perceive that the autocracy of Strafford in Ireland was a thing of the past.

There is no policy upon which it is so easy to unite opposing parties and factions as on the policy of refusing to pay money. The lavish votes of March seemed madness to the stingy arguments of June. Many of the members already repented them of their effusiveness under the dreaded scowl of the great Lord Deputy, and were becoming ashamed of this their extravagant resolution :—

'And particularly in placing over us so just, wise, vigilant and profitable a Governor as the Rt. Hon. the Earl of Strafford, who by his great care and travail of body and mind, sincere and upright administration of justice without partiality, increase of your Majesty's revenue without the least hurt or grievance to any of your well-disposed and loving subjects, and to our great comfort and security by the large and ample benefits which we have received and hope to receive by your Majesty's Commission of Grace for the remedy of defective titles procured hither by his Lordship from your sacred Majesty, his Lordship's great care and pains in restoration of the Church, the reinforcement of the Army within this kingdom, and ordering the same with such singular and good discipline, as that it is now become a great comfort, stay, and security to this your whole kingdom, which before had an army rather in name than in substance ; his support of your Majesty's wholesome laws here established, his encouragement and countenance to your Majesty's judges and other good officers, ministers and dispensors of your Laws, in the due and sincere administration of justice ; his necessary and just strictness for the execution thereof ; his due punishment of the contemners of the same, and his care to relieve the poor and oppressed. For this your tender care over us, showed by your deputing and supporting of so good a Governor, we your faithful subjects acknowledge ourselves more bound than we can with tongue and pen express.[1]

This obsequious spirit lasted in the College a little longer than in the House of Commons. But when Chappell saw clearly both that his patron's power was waning, and that the king's need of Wentworth would certainly prevent his constant residence in Dublin to protect his friends, this prudent Provost retired (July 20th) to his bishopric, resigning his government of the College with the laudatory resolution already quoted (above, p. 249), the Collegiate parallel to the Parliamentary effusion of the previous March. With the fall of Strafford came the fall of his minions. But for the rebellion of October, 1641, Chappell's fate might have been even a lesser tragedy of the

[1] Carte's *Ormonde*, i. p. 93, from the House of Commons Journals.

same kind. For the Irish Parliament, as we shall see, was determined on punishing him, and though they would hardly have taken off his head, he would certainly have suffered years of imprisonment.

Meanwhile upon Chappell's resignation a new appointment was made by the Crown, no doubt at Laud's recommendation as Chancellor, but of this not a word transpires. For at this moment both Strafford and Laud were busy with far weightier matters than appointing Provosts of Trinity College. Nevertheless the action of the Crown in filling up the place was exceedingly prompt. The king's letter to the Lord Lieutenant is dated June 20th.[1] Chappell's formal resignation is dated in the Registry July 20th. In the same book under August 1st, Richard Wassington, B.D., and Senior Fellow or Vice Gerent in University College, Oxford, is sworn in by the Vice-Provost upon receipt of His Majesty's letters.

There is an absolute silence concerning this Provost, his character and his policy. The elections of fellows and scholars for the year had been already held on Trinity Monday by Chappell. Before the next Trinity Monday the new Provost was inhibited by the House of Commons from proceeding to any further election. And this was only the culmination of a long series of debates, reports and resolutions which are formally noticed in the Common's Journals from February, 1641, onward, but which were of course the common talk of men from the moment that English agents came to Ireland to seek out complaints against Strafford. When everything he did was canvassed and condemned it was impossible that his alteration of the government of the College should escape notice. What the new Provost therefore found upon his arrival in the College was the excitement of a coming counter-revolution. Thomas Pheasant, the expelled fellow, was evidently busy in fomenting it, for he ultimately (July, 1641) presented a petition to the House against the late Provost.

[1] S. P., 1640, p. 242.

The whole policy of Strafford regarding the College was attacked in the person of the now Bishop of Cork, the new statutes were declared a great grievance, and without doubt, had not the rebellion broken out in October, 1641, and absorbed the whole country, Chappell would have been impeached, the statutes would have been abrogated, and those of Bedell (or most of them) restored. Laud too had fallen like Strafford into disgrace with the Parliament, and was under impeachment for similar reasons. The kind of news, in the absence of newspapers, which reached Dublin must have been enough to fill Wassington's heart with dire alarms. I think it well to quote an unknown document as giving a lively picture of the gossip of the day.[1] The acts of the Irish Parliament regarding the College from February to August, 1641, are worth repeating here.

"4th March, 1640-1. That the Government introduced into the College by the late Provost, now Bishop of Cork, and used there

M. R., D 71.   [1] "London, 2nd *February*, 1640 [O.S.].

"This weeke were published some notable treatises, the one is called the Jury or Inquisition de jure divino, whether by divine right it is lawfull to inflict punishment upon the Lordly offending Bishops yea or noe. The other is penned by the judicious Lord Verulam, and was presented by [? to] King James when he came first to the Crowne, under the name of Certaine Considerations touching the better purification and edificacon of the Church of England.

"We receive noe good newes out of our Northen quarters, for the English army, taking it very il that the Scotts are sooner provided with monies than they, are fallen to a great muttiny and are like to disband themselves. The Parliament sate about the busines to-day for the speedie remedieing of these orders, and for the preventing of the Inconveniences for the time to come. Satterday, Munday, tuesday was spent in the consideracon after what manner to pass the bill of subsidies, whether they should use the woord of Comons alone, or add alsoe that of subjects, Comprizing by it the Nobilitie. Itt was discussed with that vehemency that it was thought there would happen some difference betweene the two houses. But the matter was taken up at last by admitting of both these words.

"The bill for calling of Parliament, hath in like manner bin indifferently discussed, some ptended it should be held yearely, others once in three

since the procuring of the late Charter, 13 Charles, hath subverted the ancient and first foundation thereof, and doth wholly tend to the discouragement of the natives of this Kingdom, and is a general grievance.

"It is ordered upon question, that the Committee appointed to consider the grievances of the College shall draw up a charge against the late Provost, now Lord Bishop of Cork, since his time of government in the College, and present the same to this House; and that the Clerk of the Rolls shall deliver unto the said Committee copies of the several charters and other writings that belong to the College, *gratis*. And the now Provost and Fellows of the College are to deliver *gratis* copies to the said Committee of all such statutes, charters, and writings as the said Committee shall demand, and think fit to be copied for their better information; and that *William Newman* and *Robert Conway* shall be forthwith sent for by the Sergeant-at-Arms, and answer here unto such matters as shall be objected against them.

"It is ordered that the Committee formerly appointed to hear the grievances of the College of Dublin, shall forthwith repair to the Lords, and humbly desire that the Lord Bishop of Cork may be speedily sent for to answer such things as by this House shall be objected against him, concerning his evil government and practice

---

yeares. Nothing is yet concluded in it. His Matie declared himself upon the last of November very gratiously under his hand to the Scottish Com^n that they should have full power to examine all his Ministers and that hee was resolved noe waies to protect any of them or to foster them in his service, if they were found delinquents by the Parliament. Hee sent alsoe to the house of Comons a gratious message in encouraging them to goe on in examining all their grievances.

"The Comittees sitt daily, in examinacon of witnesses against the Deputy and Sir George Radcliffe, though they have already matter enough to condemn them both. On Wensday a new terrible charge was made by Mr. Prynne ag^t the Lord Lieut., the proffes of some of them were soe odious and filthy specified by his owne letter, that the house would not abide to heare of them, yet of late they are not soe invective as formerly, they being loth to displease his Matie.

"Upon the same day the tobacco grievances were taken into consideracon. It was given out that my Lord Gorring who is said to have a principell hand in these and other monopolies, had hid himselfe or fled the country. But I am certaine there is noe such matter. Itt continues that Portugall's ambassador is on the way, and our English m̃chants have b^n signifying that 30 saile of shipps coming from the West Indies not knowing of the result were seized upon by those of Lisbourne. The Parliament takes special notice of these great Concurances of the Ruining

used at the College, at the time of his being Provost there, and voted in this House to be grievances. (i. 349.)

"27th Feb., 1640. A statute lately made, 'that if any student or member of that Society shall offer to exhibit any complaint concerning the misgovernment or grievances of the said House to any other than the Provost and Fellows of the same, that he, or they, so complaining shall be forthwith suspended or expelled'—by which means none of the said students dare exhibit any complaint of their grievances. It is therefore this day ordered that if any such statute there be, the same should be in this particular void and of no effect, and that it should be free for any of the said students, scholars, or others, to present and exhibit to the said Committee all manner of grievances concerning the misgovernment there, or any manner of rights belonging to the said College either wrongfully detained or unjustly made away. And it is further ordered that no student whatsoever shall suffer under the penalty of that, or any other statute to that effect there established, for informing, setting forth, or discovering the several evils, grievances, and misdemeanours under which the College now groaneth." (i. 332.)

"Feb., 1640. (p. 353.) *The state of the case of the College of Dublin, for so much as hath been reported to the House for the grievance thereof:*—

"Queen Elizabeth by a CHARTER dated the 34th of her reign on

of our wicked Ministers of State, and the King of Spaines monarchiall designes.

"There is noe more talke of Amboina busines, but excessive rejoycing for the arivall of the Holland Embassador and transfactacon of the knowne mariadg. Yesterday they had a most stately solem audience in the Banquetting house, the Queen and the royall children being there present. The Bpp. of Lincoln his sermon is put of, the Lord Primate preaching before the Kinge the last Sabath day in divers Churches in London, the people would not abide the readeing of service, but instead thereof fell to reading and expounding of whole Chapters and singing of psalmes. The Arch Bpp of Canterbury being of soe meane a parentage will scarce have the hon[r] to be brought into the Tower, but rather to the Gat house or to Newgat; the Articles are ready against him, but the Chardge is not yett given up. Amongst other aggravacons of his   against forraigne Churches three spetiall testimonies are alleaged against him which are yet of fresh memory. The one is for denying the prince Elector's chaplain to preach at Court. For altering the forme of the last briefe of the palatine collecons, a cause Intimateing the reformed beyond the seas to bee of another religion, and lastly for disturbing of the Dutch and French Churches in their antient and soe long continued liberties."

[No endorsement or address, but clearly from an Irish correspondent in London.

supplication made by Henry Usher in the name of the Citizens of Dublin, did erect and found the College near Dublin to be a College and University ;—and among other things gave them power, by that CHARTER, of electing their Provost when voidances should happen of that place, and also power of making laws and statutes for the better government of that College, to be made by the Provost and Fellows of that College.

"And likewise appointed them thereby Visitors, viz. : the Chancellor or Vice-Chancellor of the University, the Archbishop of Dublin, the Bishop of Meath, the Vice-Treasurer, the Treasurer at Wars, the Lord Chief Justice of His Majesty's Court of Chief Place, and the Mayor of Dublin.

"Statutes were anciently made, whereby the election and the whole government were reposed in the Provost and seven senior Fellows, who were to take an oath when called to their places : and by the said statutes the natives of the Kingdom were directed to be preferred to Scholars'-places, and to Fellowships in that College, before any other the subjects of His Majesty's dominions, *caeteris paribus.*

"About Aug., 1634, Mr. Chappell became Provost and continued Provost unsworn until Trinity, 1637.

"About May, (13 Charles, 1637), a Charter was procured to the Provost, Fellows and Scholars of the said College, by which charter the ancient charter seemed to be confirmed in part ; but the nomination or donation of the Provostship thereby was reserved or resumed to His Majesty.

"The statutes formerly in force by that Charter were annulled, and statutes annexed signed with his Majesty's hand, with the hand of the Archbishop of Canterbury, and thereby it was further commanded that these new statutes and none others should be observed, unless his Majesty should be pleased to add to them or to change them as to his Majesty might seem meet.

"The Chancellor, or in his absence the Vice-Chancellor, and the Archbishop of Dublin were appointed Visitors, with assent of the Provost, Fellows and Scholars ; yet there appeareth but two of the Fellows that consented to that act and deed—*Wm. Newman and Robert Conway ;* so that those two, together with the Provost, seem the only persons of the College that wrought that change, and by their consent would bind the whole College, and those two, such fellows, as by the Visitors, at a visitation held 20th July, 1636, were deprived of their Fellowships.

"By the late statutes it also appeareth that the Provost should not hold a Bishopric while he continued Provost ; and the natives ought to be preferred, as they were to be by the former statutes.

"Upon acceptance of the late Charter and Statutes, the Provost on Trinity Monday, 1637, took his oath to the new statutes, which oath, during the continuance of the former statutes he would not take.

"The Provost put back the natives who ought to be preferred to Scholarships or Fellowships, and fetched strangers of his pupils in Cambridge, though less learned than the natives, and preferred them to the Fellowships and offices in the College, and Scholars' places, less worthy than the natives; those that were preferred to Fellowships, having spent little or no time in their studies in this College, were suddenly so put into them as though they seemed to have been sent for to accept of them; when the natives which expected them were prevented by them.

"The Mathematic Lectures and the Hebrew Lectures were by the said Provost put down.

"The natives of the kingdom by such practices have been infinitely grieved, discouraged, and disheartened to follow their studies.

"The Mayor of Dublin, at whose instance the College was founded, and the site and lands on which the College stands by him given, was ungratefully put forth from being a Visitor.

"And the two Visitors appointed are not able to redress the grievances, for by express words in the new charter, the Vice-Chancellor and Archbishop of Dublin can do nothing without the approbation of the Chancellor, who is now the Archbishop of Canterbury, and if they shall it must be void.

"The Provost, after his acceptance of the Bishopricks of Cork and Ross, continued Provost of the College above two years, contrary to those statutes to which he was sworn.

"There is not among the Senior Fellows who govern with the Provost but only one native now there; and whereas by the first Charter Fellowships were to be but for seven years, by the new Charter they are to continue their Fellowships for life, so as the averseness settled in those strangers towards the natives is not to be removed in their lifetime, if not extraordinarily redressed.

    JOHN DUNGAN,   ADAM CUSACKE,
    JOHN BYSE,   PAUL REYNOLDS,
    BRIAN O'NEALE,   ARCHIBALD HAMILTON,
    ROBERT BYSE,   WILLIAM PLUNCKETT.

"That the Committee of the House now in England, with the advice and assistance of the Archbishop of Armagh, should supplicate his Majesty for speedy redress; and that the same may be done by an Act of Parliament to be passed in this Kingdom, discharging the new Charter and Statutes, and re-establishing the first foundation and Charter.

"9th June, 1641. (p. 414.) It is voted by the House, *nullo contrad.*, that all and every the proceedings of William Chappell, late Provost of Trinity College, Dublin, and now Lord Bishop of Corke, since he assumed upon himself the office of being Provost of the said College, and during his continuance in the said office are great grievances and fit to receive redress.

"That the Provost and Fellows of Trinity College, Dublin, shall this Trinity Monday next, and also hereafter, forbear the election of Students to Fellowships and Scholars' places, until this House gives further direction therein.

"Aug. 2, 1641. (p. 521.) For as much as information has been given that Malachy Horgan, John Lissagh, and several other natives of this Kingdom have presented themselves to sit for Scholars' places, and by means of the said former order, the Provost and Fellows may not accept any the natives for such Scholarships, it is ordered that the Provost and Fellows should forthwith take the several natives now ready to sit into their consideration, and preferring those natives bred in the schools of Dublin before other natives, they, according to their several abilities in learning, may be allowed the benefit of Scholarship from Trinity Monday last; to the end the nation may not suffer by neglect.

"Aug. 7th, 1641. (p. 535.) Whereas a complaint being made against the late Provost, that he made several leases of the College lands to the hindrance of the College and the disimprovement of their revenue; ordered that the new Provost shall make no lease of any of the said College lands, nor confirm any such leases already made, till this House gives further order therein."

Hely-Hutchinson, in his MS. (p. 159), has no difficulty in exposing the rash injustice of this attack. The statement about two fellows only having accepted the Charter is false. The protest against the tyrannical rule of preventing appeals to extern tribunals is absurd, for it is the law of every College. The holding of the Provostship with a Bishoprick was legally condoned by the special dispensation of the Crown. The general outcome of the matter is quite plain. Chappell was a creature of Strafford, and therefore everything he did was a grievance.

T

What could the new Provost do, a stranger to Dublin and the College, but sit silent, and watch the current of events leading to an upheaval of the country, and with it of his authority and of the whole College discipline? With such a prospect his nonentity during these anxious fifteen months is not 'surprising.

There must have been also mutterings of rebellion and disorder throughout the land, though not sufficient to alarm the easy-going Lords Justices, who had been forced upon the king's choice. The vigorous and soldierly Ormond, whom Strafford had recommended, would probably have saved the situation. People in Dublin seem to have been like the people in Pompeii, who in spite of sundry rumblings in the mountain, lived on in carelessness and ease till the day came when the eruption swallowed them up. These signs had not escaped Strafford, who had an efficient army at hand, now disbanded by the insistence of the English Parliament. The friars and priests must have been organising their followers actively all throughout the year.[1] There must have been plenty of preaching of treason, plenty of secret seditious meetings, and other preparations for war. But the peace established by the great Deputy for the last seven years had spread a feeling of security throughout the country. The Scotch settlers in the north were occupied in concerting with the Recusants for a redress of the grievances inflicted on both by the bishops of the Anglican Church. Strafford had played them one against the other; they were now disposed to combine against him as the vice gerent not only of the English king but of the Anglican policy of Laud.

---

[1] There are two documents, dated March 31, and September 28, 1639, in the M. R. (D 60, 61), the former a licence from Joanes de Soria, Provincial of the province of Castile, to brother Jacob Lacy, to go to Ireland "for his health's sake"; the latter from Lacy asking the Provincial leave to go from Askeaton (Co. Limerick) to Cork to see his friends, and endorsed with address to Mr. John Barnewell, apparently a false name for the Provincial then in Ireland. Such documents give us very broad hints of what was going on.

On the 23rd of October, 1641, the storm broke, and though the attempt on Dublin Castle was foiled at the last moment, the whole of Ulster was in a blaze. The army which Strafford had kept at Carrickfergus being disbanded, the larger part of it, the seven thousand Irish, were ready to join the insurgents for the sake of both patriotism and plunder. Even where massacres did not ensue (and they were frequent enough), the English of the plantation were driven naked from their homes in winter, to find their way as best they could to a place of safety. And in that crisis places of safety lay far away and far between. Like an oasis in that great desert of human crime was the respect with which Bishop Bedell, and those who sought his protection, were treated by the natives who felt that here, indeed, was an Englishman without guile who had sought to understand and benefit the people intrusted to his care. There is no passage in modern history which affords us a closer parallel to this Irish rebellion than the outbreak of the great mutiny in India, where the contrasts of religion and of race were not unlike those of Ireland in 1641, and where the half-civilised majority of subjects wreaked horrid vengeance upon the minority of masters, excusing to themselves every brutality under the cloak of devotion to religion and of ardent patriotism. Worse than all the rest were the outrages upon women and children, as the hateful brood of foreign usurpers; and these crimes led in both cases to shocking retaliations. War, said Thucydides long ago, is a stern taskmaster, and makes men's feelings as hard as their circumstances.

These miserable conditions of the country are necessary to explain to us the few facts we know about the College at this crisis. It is hard to imagine a society more helpless. Their Chancellor, Laud, was in the Tower, awaiting his trial for High Treason against the Protestantism of England. Their Vice-Chancellor, Ussher, was in England and weaned by many incivilities and rebuffs from caring for his old College. The Provost had run away, having "embarked himself for England" with the first flight of fugitives from Dublin. The Vice-Provost, Harding, who was involved in the same persecution which had fastened upon Chappell, had also disappeared.[1] And here comes out the fatal weakness of the policy of Laud and Strafford in Anglicising the College. There was but one Anglo-Irish fellow in the College, according to the complaint of the Committee, and that was Seele. The rest were all English strangers. There was no longer a body of local Visitors, such as the Mayor of Dublin, to take an interest in the life of the College. The autocracy of Laud and the Provost had apparently reduced the fellows to mere creatures of the Anglican policy, having few connections in Dublin, and no popularity in the city. This is the real gravamen of the charge made by the House of Commons against Chappell and his policy. Moreover, it was certain that all the income of the College from its northern estates was for the present cut off. There was every chance of the rebellion spreading to the south. The livings in the College gift were worthless. They were indeed vacant, left vacant because the incumbents had

---

[1] This fact, which no historian of the College has mentioned, is certain. *Anon.*, who is careful and well informed in these matters, states (p. 249), without citing his authority, that on November 20, 1640, the following were the Senior Fellows: N. Hoyle, Vice-Provost, Seele, Hatfield, Pepper, Beckwith, Clapton, and Cocke. Accordingly the two English nominees of Strafford, Harding and Marshall, had already disappeared. If we are not deceived by homonymy, this very John Harding, D.D., who had come to promote Laud's policy, turned Puritan with the rise of that party, and is specially complained of by the king in a letter to the Lords Justices (S. P., 1643, p. 384). "We are informed by the Archbishop of Dublin that of late some factious and seditious preachers have appeared in Ireland, &c. We hear that John Harding, D.D., Sub-Dean of our Cathedral Church, is one of these preachers, and that, in the absence of the Dean, he allows similar preachers to ventilate their doctrines in his church. There is to be a Commission to punish these delinquents," &c. We can easily understand the College, in a fit of loyalty, probably when the Lords Justices were deposed in 1643, degrading this man, and taking from him his degree, of which more presently. He reappears as an active member of the Cromwellian Committee for the restoration of the College in 1650 (below, Chap. VIII.).

been driven away, and the rectories burnt. Ruin stared them in the face.

The House of Commons, however, behaved with commendable promptness. Not a week had elapsed since the outbreak of the Rebellion, when the Lords Justices and Council issued (October 29th) the following order :—

"Whereas we are informed that the Provost of the College hath left his charge there and hath embarked himself for England, we do pray and require the Lord Bishop of Meath and the Master of the Rolls to repair unto the College, and to take a present account of the state of the same, and withal to take care to see all such plate as they have remaining there, to be carried into the Castle together with such sums of money as they can spare, to be there safely kept for their use. And we do appoint Dr. Teat to take the government of the College upon him, until it shall please His Majesty to make choice of a new Provost, requiring all there to give due respect unto him," &c.

It then appears[1] that the Lords Justices appointed Dr. Faithful Teate and Dr. Dudley Loftus, Master in Chancery, as *temporarii subrectores*, and authorised the former to occupy the Provost's lodgings in the College. About this Teate Mr. Urwick has gathered some interesting facts.[2] He was a D.D. and educated in the College. I find that a lad of the same name, Faithful Teate, son of a local physician in Cavan, entered in 1640, hardly a year before these events.[3] We do not hear one word further of Dudley Loftus' share in these transactions. But Teate turned out a failure. Dr. Stubbs[4] has printed a petition to the Lords Justices and Council showing that notwithstanding their

---

[1] Stubbs, p. 84, without reference.

[2] Urwick, pp. 50–2, who shows that he was a consistent non-conformist, frequently persecuted, and also keeping up his connection with Dublin, even after the Restoration.

[3] Nahum Tate, scholar of the College, poet laureate, and known for his version of the Psalms, was his son. The name is spelt in various ways.

[4] App. xxxiii (2), p. 411.

lordships have graciously provided for the maintenance of the College—

"Yet so many and so great are the distempers of the said College, through the defect of government and all collegiate discipline for the space of these seven months past, few acts performed therein, for want of a Provost, &c., whereby it is much feared that the said College will return to its former chaos unless sustained by a governor of extraordinary ability,"—

they ask that Anthony Martin, Lord Bishop of Meath, heretofore for a long time a worthy member of that College, may be prevailed on to undertake its guidance. This is signed by thirty-three names, including, I think, all the fellows and some scholars. The answer is dated, June 14, 1642, and summons Dr. Teate to be heard before the Council. The report of the Council to the king must have supported the petition, for the next document (xxxiii (3)) is a missive from the Lords Justices and Irish Council to this effect: Whereas his Majesty's Letters of March 27 (1643) signifying that "he is given to understand that the person who has now the oversight of His Majesty's College near Dublin, hath many ways manifested himself to be ill affected unto the present established government under His Majesty's subjection, and is thereby liable to a further inquiry made into his life and conversation, and principally as now His Majesty's kingdoms are full of seditious spirits who have occasioned the great distractions in them," the king therefore orders the Bishop of Meath to take charge of the College, until he shall send over a Provost, and he orders Dr. Teate to surcease any further direction of the College. The Council directs him, as well as the Vice-Provost and fellows, to obey the bishop, and render him all respect and observation.

It is plain that Teate was attacked because of his Parliamentary and Puritan tendencies. We may from the same causes explain the degradation from his degree of D.D. of Harding,

Chappell's Vice-Provost, who had once been of the opposite school. We do not find one word in the Registry or in the State Papers about this degradation; we only know of it from a curious paper (M.R., C 75), wherein the fellows vindicate themselves from the charge of having affixed the College seal to this act of degradation by the Senate without having the right to do so in the absence of a Provost.[1] The affair therefore took place during the interregnum (1641–5), and the reasons given are so inadequate that we cannot but suspect it to have been merely the persecution of an unpopular man. Probably it was the Collegiate pendant to the Parliamentary attack on Chappell. But as the Lords Justices, Parsons and Borlase, are usually considered to have been on the Parliamentary side, we find it hard to explain their antipathy to Teate, and must suppose that the Royalist feeling in the College pressed them to cancel his appointment, but that it was not done till 1643, when Ormond's influence replaced theirs in the Irish Government. Still there can be no doubt that College and Council agreed to replace this Puritan preacher by a Bishop of known steadiness to the Crown and Anglican Church, though certainly no High Churchman.

We have met his name frequently in this history. It may be well, now that he assumes the control of the College, to review briefly his life and character.

He was a native of Galway, and possibly born a Papist, for he is said by Ware (I know not on what authority) to have spent the early years of his education in France, whither Galway Roman Catholics generally went. We next find him at Emanuel College, Cambridge, and specially recommended to Ussher by his learned correspondent, William Eyre, who says (in Latin) :—

"Antony Martin dwelt here with us as you know; you know him sufficiently well; I know him intimately. Nationally and in dis-

---

[1] I have printed the text in an appendix to this chapter.

position he belongs to you, and he would be ours, not only in disposition and our desires and by his own merit, but also by position in the list of our Fellows, if he had been ours by nationality. Why do I say this? I will explain in few words. Since this my Martin (for so in fact he is, under my care and in a manner guardianship) declines to be ours, I would congratulate him and you if he can be yours and win a place of Fellow in the College of his country. I have lately heard that some are shortly to be received into the roll of the Fellows of Dublin College; I know also your desire to gather into your seminary the upright and the learned who may rise to be of use in teaching arts and instructing youth, or in gathering in the Lord's harvest in Ireland,—that is the most important. For if you have in your seminary those who can laudably and successfully train your youth in philosophy and literature, such as I know well you already have, it will come to pass with God's blessing, that a better class of youth may be kept in Ireland without going beyond your range to Rome or elsewhere. Such an one I trust our Martin will become; he is indeed such an one as many wish to be taken for and both in *literis humanioribus* and in integrity of life, a most genuine Nathanael, without guile."[1]

There is no answer from Ussher, or any mention of his being brought to the College extant, but he appears as "Mr. Martin," "reading and moderating" in Hilary term, 1609,[2] with a salary of £2 per quarter. As he was never a scholar of the House, he was appointed a lecturer on his coming to the College. This was evidently Ussher's doing. These wages, as they are called, are regularly entered every quarter till March, 1612. In that year he receives and accounts for College money in the absence of the Provost, as if he were Bursar, as appears more fully in an audit of Ware's.[3] In this year he goes to England on the business of the College, apparently[4] the buying of books for the Library. But he is lecturing again in College at the end of this year. And on June 3, 1611,[5] he signs with Alvey (as Procanc.), and his fellows the election of an Edmund Donnellan. He must therefore have been himself a fellow before this date. In 1612 he signs next to Temple,

[1] Ussher's Works, xv. 22, 23.   [2] P. B., 34b.
[3] ibid., 75b.   [4] ibid., 80b, 82a, 87a.   [5] ibid., 189.

and frequently alone with him, as representing all the rest, in money matters (ib., 204–5). If he was Bursar, he resigned in 1613, when Egerton was chosen. But in that year (November 13th) he is appointed Catechist and Lecturer in Divinity in place of Chappell, who had left. This he held till February, 1615, when we find the following entry, which signifies to us that he was leaving:[1] "Agreed that Mr. Martin should have his fee of fellowship for one year and a half beforehand, amounting to £12 sterl., provided that he did renounce under his hand all challenge and clayme to any sum of money dew unto hym before he was sworn and admitted Fellow. And further that he be give an acquittance for so much received beforehand for his fellowship.—W. TEMPLE, Prov." This entry implies that his salary as Lecturer was not paid him completely, or that there was some bargaining with him, when he came over; also that the questionable habit of giving fellows who went out after their seven years a "Viaticum," as it was called, was maintained in this way with Martin. He was paid some unearned salary when he was leaving. This most genuine Israelite without guile was a hot-tempered man, as appears from a letter of Temple to Ussher, in which he sends his kind regards to all the fellows except Mr. Martin, and from several later allusions. But when he passed into the Church, its annals show us that he was indeed an Israelite, seeing that he at one time held four ecclesiastical benefices simultaneously. His advancements are as follows: First, a prebendary of S. Patrick's (Jagoe); then Archdeacon of Dublin, holding with it the treasurership of Cashel; Vicar of Galbally in Limerick, and Rector of Battersea, near London! Then Dean of Waterford, and a prebendary of Tuam, and lastly (1625) Bishop of Meath. He also paid the College £40 yearly rent for the estate of Bundruis (Co. Donegal) as a middle man, with tenants under him.

This was the man to whom the College was entrusted in so great a crisis. He had been driven from his house at Ard-

[1] P. B., 207.

braccan early in the rebellion, his property looted, and he himself in a petition quoted by Ware estimates his losses at over £8,000, showing how prosperous a profession the Church was in Wentworth's time. It is added that he was disliked by the Lords Justices, and seldom summoned to Council, till they passed a resolution asking the members thereof to subscribe some of their plate to meet the crisis. Martin jeered at the notion, saying that he, whose palace in Meath had been looted, had nothing left but a few old gowns. He was then actually imprisoned by the Justices for some time, when he wrote the petition to the Crown just referred to. It must have been as an indirect protest against this rough treatment that the College demanded to have him set over them.

The Fellows had not waited for his appointment to petition the Council for their yearly allowance, which was now the only income upon which they could count, and regarding this petition the Lords Justices and Council had made the following minute, unrecorded by the historians, which I quote from a very illegible copy in the M. R. (D 78) :—

"May it please y^r Lo^p.—As the losses of many thousands of particular p̄sons Brittish and Protestants by occasion of this Rebellion begetts in all good men m^{ch} pitty and c̄opassion, so ye calamities which have thereby fallen upon this k^{g}dome in generall and therein upon publique Societies, and amongst them upon ye Colledge neare this citty, one of the greatest ornaments of this Kingedome, we cannot but take to heart with much disquiet of mind, wherefore we crave leave to offer to y^r L^{dp}^{s} considderation ye enclosed petition of ye Fellows and scholl^s p̄sented at this board, and doe earnestly beseech y^r Lp . . . . p̄vention of ye dissolution of so royal a foundation, whence so many p̄sons eminēt in learning and pietie have issued, that y^r Ldp^s would so pvide as treasure may be sent, whereby we may be inabled to pay thē their annuall pention of 400^{ll} p. st. now due for a yeare ending at Easter next and so for the future, seinge noe revenue can yet be gotten in yet heare for his Maj^{tie} to this or any other debt of his Maj^{ties}, and noe rent due to ye Societie by their tenants can yet be had, but all th^r lands remaines in hands of the rebelles, so as unlesse ye pention be paid ye Societie will be forced to dissolve, which would be so great a p̄judice to this Kingedome as we wish and hope by y^r L^dp's noble favour it may be p̄vented, and so we remain. Frō His Maj^{tes} Castle of Dublin, Ult° Martii, 1642, y^r L^dps to be cōnded Wm Parsons, Jo. Borlase, Ormond and Ossory, C^h Lambart, Ad Loftus, Jo Temple, M. Rotherā, Fr. Willowby, Ro. Meredith."

And in the margin below :—

"To ye Right No^{ble} Rob. Erle of Leicester, Ld Lieutenant Gen. and Govern^r gn̄rall of Ireland."

The first and most obvious attempt to satisfy this petition was the proposal of Ware in the Irish House of Commons (August 16, 1642) to appoint a Committee to find out what lands about Dublin belonged to rebels, wherewith they could now support the College. This inquiry, however, seems to have been fruitless.[1]

The old Bursar's book verifies these items, and tells us that of the £344 received, £82 was by way of contribution from the State, and £120 borrowed upon deposits of College plate.

We also have, not in the Registry, which is a blank for this year, but in a loose sheet (D 81), the list of officers chosen on November 20, 1643 showing that the life of the College and its official acts were still subsisting. Yet I can find no formal appointment of Anthony Martin as Provost, though he signs himself *præpos. Coll.* in the act appointing Ormond as Chancellor, dated March 12, 1644 (O. S.). In the document (M. R., C 78), in which Ormond appoints him and Ware to report on the College, March 13, 1643 (O. S.), he was not yet formally Provost, though he had been appointed nearly a

[1] A page of rough accounts of Gilbert Pepper, Bursar from November 20, 1642 to 1643 (B 98), shows that the petition had some further effect, for he gives a list of sums received in that year, viz., sixteen items amounting to £344 12s. 7d. and £301 4s. 9d. taken out of it for expenses. He notes that the baker and the brewer respectively had been paid £47 3s. 5d. and £54 8s. 6d., deducting 1s. in the pound, apparently for the Bursar. He also states the quarterly expenses in four sums, showing an increasing economy, viz., £100 12s. 1½d., £90 4s. 0½d., £87 7s. 3d., and £66 5s. 4½d.

year before (April 25, 1643), to take charge of the College. In Kerdiff's petition (M. R., F 83) to be restored to his fellowship by the Chancellor (which was done), he says that the delays in legally appointing Martin Provost, which are not yet over, urge him to make this application. His petition and the order are dated December 9 and 13, 1644 (O. S.), therefore only three months before Martin signs as Provost. Thus his formal appointment must have been somewhere in January or February, 1644 (O. S.). Barrett says that in a Plate book (which I have not yet found) he signs as Provost on February 18th. As he had succeeded to Chappell's work in 1613, so now he succeeds him, not only as Provost, but as a bishop holding the post, which was distinctly against the Statute. But if this did not prevent him from accepting the appointment officially, it was a violation of the letter only, not of the spirit of the law, for his See was non-existent during the Rebellion, and he was forced to live in Dublin with his family in great poverty.

In the absence of other documents, the silence of the Registry, and the general panic and confusion which seems to have seized the Government of the country, we have but one source to fall back upon, and that is the old Bursar's book, which contains the receipts of the College written in one direction, the amounts taken out by each Bursar in the other, each item signed by his name from 1626 to 1680. Unfortunately, the Bursars only register the money as "taken out of the College trunke," and do not in this book give any details of its expenditure, such as I have above quoted from a loose paper. Still the general financial condition of the College is to be reconstructed from this book. Chappell had written to Laud, after his resignation,[1] that having found the College in debt, he had left it £2,000 in hand, and there must have been credit, for the sums received in the year ending November 20, 1641, that is to say, into the opening of the Rebellion, are in round numbers £1,370, whereas the expenses are about £1,760. The details of the

[1] S. P., 1640, p. 242.

income—rents, the Crown allowance, and the rest—are all specified, except the money received from students. In the year following (counting always from November 20th) there is only £70 obtained, and under the following entries: "Aug. 27, 1642. Borrowed of ye M^r of ye Rolles twentie pounds, ye Coll. stock being then all spent. Sep. 15th Borrowed frō Jacob Kirwan which was received from Mr. Boote fiftie pounds for which there lieth deposited with him in lew therof for the space of nine months the worth therof in plate, the names wherof are written in the Coll. Booke of plate."

These entries are immediately followed by those of Gilbert Pepper, which have already been mentioned, and which continue the disastrous pawnings of plate, which scattered or destroyed a collection quite unique. When even the remains which the College still possesses form the finest collection of Irish plate known, what would it have been if almost the whole of it up to 1641 had not been melted down, sold or coined during the dire distress of the Great Rebellion?[1] It seems all the worse because in Gilbert Pepper's year public sympathy for the College had been excited in England, and various sums amounting to £183 came from London and from Cheshire by way of contribution.

The appointment of Ormond as Lord-Lieutenant (November, 1643) marks a change of policy in the management of the State, and also a great improvement in the hopes of Trinity College. The Lords Justices were evidently thought guilty of trafficking with the Puritan party, and Royalist officers were appointed under Ormond (now Marquess), and from the following May an allowance of £3 10s. weekly from so-called dead pays in each company appears in the accounts, which was

[1] The only pieces now remaining from before the Rebellion are the flagon and chalice for the Chapel presented by Bishop Richardson in 1632, and a companion flagon given by Moses and Arthur Hill (of Co. Down) in 1637. These are still in constant use, and are noble specimens of the work of the period.

ordered by him. This, together with £110 from England and £50 worth of plate, make up, with a few little rents of parks about the College, the income (£234 14s.) of November, 1643, to November, 1644. The same sad story is repeated in 1664–5, except that we find now the first mention of tithes granted to the College, and that Ormond supplements the weekly £3 10s. by some small additional benevolences, *e.g.*, for one month's commons (July 21st to August 16th) £14. This implies that the daily fare of the College amounted to 9s. 3d. In these days of low prices and scarcity of money, when daily diet could be provided for two or three pence, the Society may have numbered about forty. In a petition of "the students," dated June 20th (without year, F 81), that they have kept watch (as guards), and are in arrear fourteen weeks of the 6d. a day granted each of them from the State, it appears that this was at one time the allowance, and it would account only for twenty students. To these the fellows must be added. On January 6th an order of Parsons and Borlase (therefore not later than 1642 O. S.) forbids the quartermaster to billet soldiers under any excuse in the College (F 81).

Regarding the sale of plate this year gives us a few interesting details. Under the date April 19, 1645, we have this entry "received of the overplus of the plate coyned by Mr. Scout (Schoute) £6 8s. 4d.," and the note is added : "This plate was pawned 1642 to Albert Butts and J. Price, and afterwards by y^m made o͞v to Mr. Schout 1643, who uppo͞ nonpayment of ye moneys coyned the plate, and ye principall and interest being paid, there remayned the above named sum͞e."[1] But from January 29th to the following August no additional plate was sold. The reason appears in a petition of the fellows dated August 19, 1645, to the Lord-Lieutenant, which after the usual

[1] Theodore Schoute was a Dutch merchant settled in Dublin, important enough to be an M.P. His associate was Wybrants, whose descendants are still well known and respected in Dublin.

self-commiserations goes on to say that "there being some few small parcels of plate, not hitherto upon exigencies expended, which uppon the utter failing of other supplies y^r Pet^s thought they might make use of, the R^t. Rev. Fath. in G. An. Lo. Bp. of M. (to whom the authority of the House is comitted) will in noe wise give his consent," &c., &c. They "therefore pray that y^r Lo^{ps} would be pleased to persuade ye s^d Ld. Bishop Provost to give his consent for the maintenance of us by the s^d plate."[1] This may possibly apply to the plate of the Chapel, which thus escaped sacrilegious destruction.

The petition was, however, successful, for the sale of plate begins again in the next month (September 13th) with an item of £17 10s. 7d., and in the opening of the next year (November 20th to February 12th) £43 are obtained from this source, though amongst other gifts from the State were four barrels of herrings, which they sold for £4, and the contributions from the impropriate tithes of Naas, &c., granted to the College.

The catalogue of the precious pieces, both intrinsically and historically, absorbed by these years of want would be worth making, in order to show the wealth and dignity the College had attained before its disastrous jubilee.[2] Meanwhile the execution of Laud had left the post of Chancellor vacant, and the new Provost and fellows, with great good sense, appointed Ormond. The deed of appointment, with the College seal attached, is still preserved in Kilkenny Castle.[3] Thus a great Irishman, and a layman, replaced the English prelate or politician who had hitherto occupied the position—a matter of all the more importance, as by Laud's statutes the Chancellor was

---

[1] M. R., D 89, a mere rough draft with many corrections, and very difficult to read.

[2] The last item is on April 2, 1648; cf. Stubbs, pp. 85-7.

[3] Cf. *Book of Trinity College*, pp. 11, 32, for facsimile of seal and for the text.

to interpose constantly in the government of the College. There can be no question that Ormond performed this, as he did every other public duty, with dignity and generosity. He contributed, and made his officers contribute, to the wants of the College. His last benevolence before his exile was £20 given to the College, July 13, 1647, and from the officers of the army in September, £21 2s. 6d.

On February 25th, on the next page, we find a new patron and protector: "Received by vertue of a warrant from the Governour, Coll. Jones, £12."

In the previous May and June the Irish Parliament had been discussing the revival of the charges against Bishop Chappell, and the Provost and fellows were asked, "was it inconvenient to proceed against him,"[1] and members were invited to give the House of Lords details about a new petition of the College.

But the Society was too anxious about its daily sustenance to urge prosecutions against the misdeeds of ten years ago. In those agitated times the government of Wentworth must have seemed a thing of the far past, and the violences of his rule a matter of ancient history. It was more important to secure the sympathy of the Parliamentary party, which could easily be done by informing them of the early Puritan history of the College. That this was accomplished successfully appears both from the friendly and practical patronage of Colonel Michael Jones, Governor of Dublin till Oliver Cromwell's arrival, and also from the many sums collected among pious people in London, and sent over for the relief of the College.[2] Though the College rents from the north and from Munster had absolutely ceased, and though we hear of no new students, no Commencements, no public acts beyond petitions for money, we find the Bursars, who change every November 20th, husbanding their little resources (about

---

[1] House of Commons Journals on May 24 and June 2, 1647.
[2] Cf. Stubbs, p. 87.

£200 per annum), and even beginning the years '47 and '48 with a few pounds in hand.

Who were these men that steered the College through such a series of disasters?

With the Provost we are already acquainted. He was evidently not a man of letters, but a vigorous man, a learned man, and an effective preacher. When the Puritan Government in 1649 ordered the suppression of the Book of Common Prayer in Churches, and the use of the *Directory*, he disregarded their order, on the legal ground that the old act of Uniformity, ordering the use of the Common Prayer, had not been formally repealed, and preached, we are told, to crowded congregations in the Chapel on the heresies of the day till the plague, which stops all the records of the College abruptly on May 11, 1649, carried him off, and he closed his chequered career in great poverty but in high repute, and was buried under the old steeple beside his Chapel.

The Bursars we can enumerate, as we have their entries— Nath. Hoyle, Gilbert Pepper, Thomas Seele, James Bishop, John Kerdiff, Will Raymond, James Bishop, Thomas Locke, and Thomas Vale. Only the last, with three others, had been elected Junior Fellows in 1646 by special king's letter to Martin,[1] and this shows that the Corporation were hopeful enough to supply their losses in governors. Every Senior Fellow was therefore Bursar in his turn, and they all dated their election from the days of prosperity. Not one of them is in any way celebrated. Seele, the most successful, having been elected in Wentworth's days, lived to be Provost and Dean of St. Patrick's under the Restoration. Kerdiff, too, was an active manager of College finance, and was entrusted by Cromwell with the re-letting of the College lands in 1657. He had resigned to avoid accepting Laud's Statutes, had been readmitted during the Rebellion, and even made a Senior Fellow, with Raymond Bishop, by special act of the Chancellor

[1] Reg., 72.

(July 17, 1647) to fill up the necessary number of Senior Fellows, of whom, at the moment, Seele only was in residence. Some were dead, and some were fled. Moreover, "for sufficient reasons set down in the Registry" Hoyle had left on July 20, 1646. The Registry is silent on this point, and Hoyle reappears among the Senior Fellows under Winter, the Cromwellian Provost in 1652. It is stated by Urwick (p. 60) that he went to Oxford, and that he obtained a fellowship at Brasenose College in 1649. He was probably invited back to Trinity College on account of his long experience there. And yet this scanty record occupies six or seven pages in giving all the minutes of the evidence against Richard Coughlan, elected but one year before (1646) with Vale to his fellowship. He turned out a very uncomfortable person, resuscitating the traditions of Pheasant, coming unasked into the Board Room, cursing and swearing, and saying openly that the Provost was a fool and a knave and that he would kick him. No defence of Coughlan is given. The three pages of evidence have been partly torn out, I imagine, by some act of violence of Coughlan or one of his friends. But the formal expulsion given with such explicitness and ordered to be put in the Registry some months after the sentence, shows some timidity, or fear of prosecution for illegal action, in the Provost and Senior Fellows. In spite, however, of these jars, the new rule of making fellowship permanent enabled the same small band of otherwise obscure men to follow a prudent and patient policy, which the old rapid change of governors would have rendered impossible. Of students and studies during these times of alarm we hear hardly a word. The Matriculation book gives us the number of lads that entered each year, and from November, 1641, to November, 1657, we have 4, 7, 4, 3, then a chasm till 1652, and again 4, 1, 12, 6. In 1657 prosperity returns and twenty-six lads enter.

Yet even in these stray entrances the high quality of the lads does not disappear. Henry Dodwell and Anthony Dopping enter together in 1655, Michael Ward (from Shropshire) in 1656. In 1657 a lad born in New England, and in 1659 one born in the island of Providence, in the Eastern Indies, appear in the list. Many of these were the sons of pious ministers, whose missionary zeal had carried them first abroad and then to Ireland, where crowds were reported to be thirsting after the Gospel, and during these years John Stearne was teaching his splendid philosophy of resignation in books of great and curious learning, to which we shall return. But for the moment the incipient and slow fusion of the nationalities in Ireland was rudely interrupted. To be an Irishman now was to be a Papist, a rebel, and a murderer deserving all the vials of God's wrath upon his head. And in this disastrous quarrel Trinity College was unavoidably upon the English side.

M. R., C 75. APPENDIX. [Cf. p. 279.]

Reasons moving the Sen. Fell. to put the Public Seal to the certificate of Mr. Harding's degradation :—

1. The clause in the statute prohibiting the Seal to be put to any instrument in the Provost's absence relates to things which concern the College only. This was a particular concerning the University, which having no other seale than what is of the House when it is required in things concerning the University altereth its propriety and cannot be denied.

2. In things signed by the House w^n it is presupposed to be the College seal only the ordinary form of instrument goeth *Nos Præpositū and Socii Sen.*, &c. In this certificate it was only the declaration of an University Act without any such form.

3. The Vice-Provost having consented to the reading of the Proposition for Mr. Harding's degradation in the University included his own vote in the House, and being conscious to the business as far forth as it concerned the House, we could not expect his negation to the certificate for what before his own eyes was done in the University, espec. having formerly frequently consented to the sealing of the Revd Father in God the Lord Bishop of Meath, to whom the care and charge of the College is by his Maj. committed, being one of those by whom the seal was commanded, we suppose in a matter (the omission whereof would be scandalous to the

College and the doing of it no way inconvenient) his Lordship's authority, though in other things not actually exercised yet being in this express, and by us not in anything ever denied, was sufficient, being *consentiente Præposito* to conclude our obedience.

Lastly. In a thing wherein there was no apparent inconvenience to the House. The Fellows were desirous rather to approve their obedience to the commands of the Pro-Vice-Chan^{cellor} in the name of his Maj^{ties} Commissioners than to stand upon the nicety of a statute the literal observance whereof in the absence of the Provost these two years they conceive would not but have been much prejudicial to the College.

[It appears from this that His Majesty's Commissioners actually influenced the Pro-Vice-Chancellor to hold a Senate and degrade Harding, and that the Vice-Provost, sitting with him as the second member of the Caput, made no objection at the time, though afterwards he raised difficulties. As there had been no formal Provost for two years the date must be near the close of 1643.]

CHAPTER VIII

THE PROTECTORATE—WINTER (1652–60)

THE plague and the Provost's death were the last and worst calamities which interrupted even the regular recording of the Bursar's work. From May 11 to November 20, 1650, there is absolute silence. Then six months of entries from Neylan, Bursar, then a huge gap with only two entries of Miles Symner, till 1655. So likewise the receipts, which in those first six months amount to £276, of which £100 was a bequest or Mr. John Collins of the City of Dublin, vintner, were chiefly grants from the Parliamentary Commissioners, and they stop abruptly; so does the Registry. We must seek, in the external circumstances of these eventful days, the explanation of this strange collapse and silence among the men who had held the College together so long under such adversity.

No historian of the College ever threw any light on this chasm till Mr. Urwick, in his pamphlet, gave us extracts from the acts and documents preserved in the Dublin Record Office. The exact date of Provost Martin's death does not seem to be known, but it happened, as I believe, in May, 1650, when the English Parliament had already commenced (March 8th) to take new action regarding the management of the College. This is the document :—

"All castles, lands, tenements, rents, which did heretofore belong to the late Archbishop of Dublin, the Dean and Chapter of St

Patrick and the farm of Ardbrackan, with the parsonage of Trim, shall be vested in HENRY IRETON, WILLIAM BASILE, attorney-general, Col. ROBERT VENABLES, Sir ROBT. KING, Col. HENRY CROMWELL, JOHN COOK, Dr. HENRY JONES, Dr. JONATHAN GODDARD, Col. HIEROME SANKEY, Dr. JOHN HARDING,[1] JAMES WHITELOCK, JOHN OWEN (clerk), ROBT. STAPLETON, JENKIN LLOYD, and RALPH CUDWORTH (clerk), to hold in trust for the settling and maintenance of the Colledge now in or near the city of Dublin, commonly called TRINITY COLLEDGE, and of a Master, Fellows, Scholars, and officers therein; and for the erecting settling and maintenance of one other Colledge in the said city of Dublin, and of a Master, Fellows, Scholars and officers and of publique Professors in the UNIVERSITY there; and also for the erecting, establishing and maintenance of a FREE SCHOOL, and of a Master, Ushers, Scholars and officers there, in such manner as by the said Trustees, or any five or more of them, with the consent and approbation of the Lord-Lieutenant of Ireland, shall be from time to time directed. And the said Lord-Lieutenant is hereby authorised and appointed, by warrant, to place in the said University, Colledges, and Free Schools respectively, such persons to be Governors, Masters, Public Professors, Fellows, Scholars, and officers, and to appoint unto them such yearly stipends or salaries out of the premises during their respective lives, or for such lesser time as he in his judgment shall think fit. And likewise to remove and displace such of them as he at any time shall hold expedient. . . . And the said Trustees, with the consent and approbation of the said Lord-Lieutenant, are authorised to consider of and put in writing such rules, directions, statutes, as they shall think fit, for the erecting, maintaining and government of the said University, Colledges, and Free School, and of the Masters, Professors, Fellows, Scholars, and officers there, and the same to send over in writing to the Parliament of England, there to receive such alterations, addition or confirmation, as by the Parliament of England shall be thought fit."

And in the mean time the said Lord Lieutenant is hereby authorised by warrant to put in execution all or any of the rules, directions, statutes, as shall be so agreed upon and put in writing as aforesaid."[2]

It does not appear from this document that of this Committee Owen was the leading member, but Mr. Urwick

[1] Apparently Wentworth's nominee of 1637, above p. 247.
[2] Henry Scobell, *Collection of Acts,* anno 1649, cap. 74; part 2, p. 104.

shows it from his memoirs and letters. There follows a most interesting letter from the Trustees, also brought to light in this connection by Mr. Urwick :—

"To Mr. John Owen, Minister. We have enquired into the present state of the Colledge of Dublin, and do find it furnished with very few officers, the consideration whereof (and the house being at present visited with ye pestilence) move us to dissolve that Society until it shall please God to remove the sicknesse, and some means found out to establish a course which may probably conduce to those good ends. We desire you (whom we find to be one of the Trustees of the Colledge) upon advice with Mr. Thos. Goodwin or others will seriously consider what laws, rules, are fitt to be established in the said Colledge, wherein we desire that the education of youth in ye knowledge of God and principles of piety may be in the first place promoted. . . . What God shall direct you in this matter we desire you to communicate to us with all convenient expedition, and likewise what qualifications are requisite in ye admission of persons according to the course now used in your University. Dublin, 2nd July, 1651."[1]

From this it appears that Owen was regarded as the proper authority to draw up regulations and make suggestions about the College, now practically dissolved owing to the plague, which seems to have raged in Dublin for a whole year. It appears that the other clerical trustee, the famous Ralph Cudworth, was also in Dublin for a short time, and may have helped Owen with his Cambridge experience. It is to be regretted that this man was not chosen to remain as Provost, instead of Winter, as his name would have added no small lustre to the history of the College.

The documents in the Record Office tell us that the letter to Owen, just quoted, was followed promptly by the appointment of Samuel Winter to control the College. But it was not his formal appointment as Provost, which, as in Martin's

[1] *Public Record Office, Dublin, Commonwealth Records*, Vol. A-39, fol. 10. There is on f. 120, a letter to Mr. Harrison : encouragement for him and his friends in New England to settle in Ireland ; promises of religious freedom, suitable lands, &c.

case, was delayed for a considerable time. This latter, however, is copied in the Registry, under the date June 3, 1652, and was signed by Oliver Cromwell. Yet in a previous entry, wherein the conferring of the degree of B.D. on him is registered, he is already called Provost.[1] The entries (already quoted by Mr. Urwick) show how the reconstruction was begun.

The first of them, and one of public interest, was to appoint Major Miles Symner (an old scholar of the College) Professor of Mathematics, in order to instruct intelligent young men in the art of surveying lands—an enormous work at that moment, for which there was no efficient staff at hand. Even soldiers were allowed to attend his lectures.[2] Another has a great permanent interest to members of the college, the appointment of John Sterne as Fellow. His matriculation is in the book, at the age of fifteen, on May 22, 1639, and he is even then remarkable as being the first student in the book styled *Pensionarius*.[3]

There was evidently a prudent desire to bring back or keep such of the older fellows as were willing to work under the Cromwellian rule. Nor was this unreasonable to expect. The College had from the beginning been Puritan in spirit and traditions. The High Church irruption of Laud and Chappell was superficial; it had only lasted for a few years, and had passed away like an evil dream. In the complexities and confusions of parties that distracted Ireland for eight years, the College had been from its very nature spared all trafficking with either of the Roman Catholic parties. The only question for the Fellows to solve was whether they would be Royalists or Parliamentarians. And even in this

---

[1] Reg., November 18, 1651.   [2] ibid., 95.
[3] Up to that time there are only three classes occurring in the book (which, unfortunately, begins only with 1637), viz., *Sociorum commensalis* (fellow commoner), *scholarium commensalis*, and *Sizator*. From 1639 onward pensioners occur more and more frequently, and *scholarium commensales* less and less, till 1662, when the latter disappear.

THE PROTECTORATE—WINTER (1652-60)

dilemma there were not wanting elements of mediation. For if they were a Royal foundation, aristocratic in sentiment, they were distinctly friendly to the Parliament in their Evangelical doctrine. Ussher, as we know, commanded to his death the respect of Cromwell and his Independents. No English bishop held that position. If Bedell had lived, with his contempt of vestments and of organs in church, he would probably have been similarly appreciated. Henry Jones, Bishop of Meath and Vice-Chancellor, was a brother of Michael Jones, the Cromwellian general, and dropped his title of bishop for the time, while remaining in his position of Vice-Chancellor.[1]

Hence the College had hardly to change its views on religion, and was only required to acknowledge the new Government, which caused no great heartburnings. Moreover, as has been said above, the new Government came in bringing back old friends. Joseph Travers, who had been made fellow in 1630, was summoned from England and made a Senior Fellow and Professor of Civil Law. Nathaniel Hoyle, who had gone to Oxford for some years, came back as Vice-Provost. Stearne and Cusacke belonged to old Dublin families, known for their Protestantism. Both names were connected with the Usshers, and appear constantly in the records of Dublin City. Norbury and G. Marsden were educated in the College. Ed. Veale

[1] He showed his interest in the College at the moment of its revival by furnishing, with fittings, the interior of the library then existing. From this older building, now gone, two graceful staircases have been transferred to the present one, with the handsome brass which commemorates the gift :—

MS
Coat of   R.D.D. Henrici Jones S T D.
Arms.   Hujus Academiæ Vice Cancellarius
Qui propriis sumptibus hanc
Bibliothecam pulcherrimo graduum
Apparatu fenestris classibus
subselliis cæterisque ornamentis
instruxit auxit collocupletavit
Ann° Æræ Christi MDCLI

(or Veele) had connections with Ireland, and a Veele is actually entered (in 1641) as *natus in hoc Collegio* (a strange birthplace!) in the year 1624. With an additional sprinkling of ministers from famous Puritan families in England, like the Marsdens, or New England, like the Mathers, Owen and Winter might fairly expect the derelict College to be well furnished with new guests.

Why Winter was appointed, and not Owen, we cannot tell. He was summoned to attend the Commission sent to Ireland in 1650 "for the settlement of that most distracted and ruined kingdom," as a godly, able, and orthodox Divine. For this call he left a valuable living at Cottingham, near Hull, where he was comfortably settled with a rich wife, who was most unwilling to cross the sea to Ireland. But he was a devoted and zealous minister, whose "opportunities were his riches," as he often said, and the want of Gospel teaching in Ireland was then notorious. The biographer who writes the *Life and Death of the Eminently Learned and Pious and Painful Minister of the Gospel*,[1] describes him as from his youth subject to fits of exaltation, in which he heard voices, saw visions, and felt in personal and intimate communication with God, with whom he wrestled in prayer, as Jacob did with the angel at Peniel. He had devoted himself from the age of twelve, in answer to a heavenly voice, to the work of the ministry, and took every pains at school and at Emanuel College, Cambridge, to qualify in learning for his profession. The Puritans of that day still kept up the noble tradition of Travers and of Ussher, that those who built their faith on the words of the Scripture were bound to know it in the original, as accurately as possible. Thus he was fitted to take his place as the head of a seat of learning. He confined himself, moreover, to teaching theology, and to constant preaching both in the College and the city, and the volume of sermons, or rather the heads of sermons, which he

[1] By J. W., London, 1671.

had preached before Lord Deputy Fleetwood and Henry Cromwell show the wideness of his learning and the subtilty of his arguments.[1]

He is said to have "given several considerable sums yearly for the support and encouragement of some poor scholars in the University of Dublin, besides a large sum of money disbursed out of his own purse towards furnishing the Library there with books."[2] His general character makes this very credible, though the Registry is silent about it, and though the Matriculation book does not bear out in all its details the statement "he, out of his zeal, &c., in a short time encouraged and procured the return of divers fellows and students to the College, as also the coming over from England of several hopeful young scholars, whereby the College was suddenly replenished with many religious and hopeful young men," whom he taught and prayed with assiduously both in chapel and in his lodgings. The remark must apply to the pious preachers he brought over and made fellows. For, as already noted, the Matriculations do not show a rapid increase of students till 1657.

But Winter was not to blame; he was not only a zealous Christian and a learned man, but a thorough gentleman. He evidently had no strong feeling against the Episcopal Church. Nothing is clearer from our scanty documents than that both H. Cromwell and Winter were afraid of abolishing the Established Church in Ireland before another set of ministers could occupy the charges of the Episcopal clergy. Winter gives in his

---

[1] Gilbert says (*Hist. of Dublin*) that Fleetwood being an Anabaptist, even kept a preacher at Christ Church to controvert Winter. There is no trace of any such opposition in the Dedicatory Epistle to Fleetwood and Cromwell prefixed to the Sermons. The book was published in 1656 (Bladen, Dublin). The notes teem with quotations from Greek, as well as some from Hebrew. By one of his College ordinances preserved in the Registry, Winter makes a knowledge of Hebrew necessary for the M.A. degree.

[2] *Life and Death*, &c., p. 36.

notebook [1] the thirty-fifth article of Cromwell's orders relating to the Church on the maintenance of able teachers, and providing that till provision for the clergy be made, the existing maintenance for them shall not be disturbed or impeached. The succeeding article gives liberty of conscience to all those holding varieties of opinion, provided such liberty does not extend to popery and prelacy. Accordingly, in another part of the notebook (pp. 1 *sq.*), Winter carefully enumerates all the benefices in the diocese of Meath and their yearly values, also such Rectories as would soon fall out of lease. He enumerates with equal care the advowsons granted to the College by James I., and in 1659 the Provost and Senior Fellows formally appoint Mr. Robert Auld by a mistake to the combined Rectories of Cleenish and Derryvullan, and presently separate them and appoint Mr. John Dale to one of them,[2] and also master of Enniskillen school. Dr. Stubbs quotes another case of a blunder of this kind made by these inexperienced men. Winter's policy was clearly expressed by that of his Senior Fellow, Samuel Mather, ordained at Drogheda December 5, 1656, and then preacher in Dublin. "Though he was a Congregational man," says Wood, "and a high Non-conformist, when the Lord Deputy (Henry Cromwell) would send him to Munster to displace Episcopal ministers, he declined, as he did afterwards the like in Dublin, alleging that he was called to preach the Gospel, not to hinder others from doing it."[3] Of course he had soon learned that the Evangelical clergy of Ireland were little removed from his own doctrine.

These men never seem to have thought about the Romish controversy. Winter's great and earnest trouble was with the Anabaptists, against whom all the arguments in his published

[1] Called *Collections*, p. 35, in the Library, MS. 804, 6. Cromwell pensioned many of the deprived Irish bishops.
[2] For these accounts cf. *Reg.*, 94 and 97.
[3] Quoted from Urwick, p. 78.

sermons are directed. Hence in his notebook he is particular in telling us the number of infants he baptized, and this ceremony (he dared not call it a Sacrament) he held to be one of the greatest means of grace. He also gives numerous lists of marriages, for performing which there was a great deficiency of clergy. He is said to have impoverished himself greatly by coming to Ireland, and to have left the College much indebted to him, and the latter is probably true. The love of good horses was his one weak point, and some of them, which he had brought over with him, the Irish army stole from him on one of his journeys with the Commissioners. The accounts of his later journeys, which he carefully kept, show us constant and considerable items for the keep of his horses—shoeing, grazing, frost nails, &c.[1] There are also liberal allowances for his servants, such as "Tobacco, Tom 3s., and Zachary, a pott, £1 10s." Tom may possibly be his nephew. In any case it seems a worldly item. Happily we can learn from his extant will that he recouped himself for his losses by acquiring considerable estates in Ireland—one in King's County of 1,000 acres and another, still larger (Agher) in Westmeath, which he bequeathed to his sons and nephew, and which their direct descendants still enjoy. These must have been grants of confiscated lands from the Commissioners to make up for the loss of his comfortable English living. We also find in his accounts a number of small rents for houses, &c., in Dublin and Drogheda received for his mother, who did not die till 1659. This must have been a State grant for her support, and amounted to over £100 per annum.

Entries of the public acts of his rule in the College are but scarce in the Registry. Soon after Henry Cromwell came to command the army in Ireland[2] he was elected by Winter

[1] There is a peculiar breed of very large horses still kept at Mr. Winter's place, Agher, in Westmeath. It would be interesting to know whether they are derived from the Provost's importation.

[2] A stray line on a blank page (83) in the Registry, with no signatures states the bare fact that Cromwell was made Chancellor on March 16, 1653.

and his fellows Chancellor of the University—an act absolutely ignoring the fact that Ormond, though in exile, was alive and indisputably the legal Chancellor, who accordingly resumed the post with the Restoration. The affair seems to us almost ridiculous, but had its practical uses, for this Cromwell proved a kind friend to the College. If we may conjecture the practical excuse for doing it we shall find it in the proclamation of the new Chancellor that strict obedience shall be given to the Provost.[1] This document clearly points to some disturbance in the College—a sign of returning life, and Winter may have felt that he wanted the support of the head of the Government as Chancellor. His support in matters of finance was not less useful. The Bursar's book shows that in 1656 the Crown grant of £388 15s. was again recognised and two quarters of it in debentures of £96 15s. 8d., as well as a year's arrear, paid to the College. The Commissioners had also attended to the petition of the College and admitted the representations of their Senior Fellow, and now agent, John Kerdiff, who was able to identify the College estates and save them from confiscation among the Cromwellian adventurers and soldiers. The former tenants, if not killed or outlawed, began to pay rent and arrears to save their interests. Numerous

This is earlier than we should have expected, for Fleetwood was still Lord Deputy. But I have found in Thurloe (ii. 162) a letter from Dublin dated March 13, 1653, giving a lively account of the landing of H. Cromwell at Ballock (near Kingstown) and his enthusiastic reception by all classes except the Anabaptists. The writer adds : "Yesterday (March 12th) he visited the College, where his Lordship was entertained with copyes of verses, speeches, and disputations." This shows that there was organised life there, but says not a word about his being made Chancellor that week. I suspect, therefore, that the date of the appointment in the informal note to be false and that he did not become Chancellor till some years later (1658?). The act of making Stearne Hebrew Lecturer lacked his confirmation till 1659, though made in 1657. There is the copy of a petition (M. R., F 87) made by the Provost and Fellows to him as "Commander of the Forces and Chancellor of the University of Dublin," which is endorsed February 16, '55. But I do not think this title and endorsement conclusive.

[1] Reg. 84.

THE PROTECTORATE—WINTER (1652-60)

new leases were made by Kerdiff in 1654-7, and the sums "taken out of the trunk" in these years (1656-1660) amount to over £900 per annum.[1]

There was therefore now again an ample income to support a large Society. What evidence can we find in the records to show the numbers of Junior Fellows, scholars, or students? The only serious complaint the historian has to make against Winter and his rule is that there were no regular annals kept of College events, exeats, fines, elections, &c., the Registry only containing isolated entries. So also the Bursar's book, containing an accurate list of the monies taken out by the Bursars, has no accompanying details of the expenditure, and there is an almost complete absence of all those stray papers in the Muniment Room, from which the present history has derived so much information during the earlier years of the College. Winter was not careful of these things, and whatever papers he had, apart from his little book of *Collections*, he probably kept in his own lodgings and carried away with him when he was displaced by the Restoration. Of the lives of his fellow-workers and compeers we have only one side recorded—their

---

[1] We have in the Mumiment Room (F 86-90) a series of papers containing a petition to H. Cromwell for power to collect rents (Feb. 27, 1655), an order authorising Kerdiff to do so (Sept. 6, 1655), an earlier provisional lease to Robt. Maxwell (afterwards Bishop) of some lands in Armagh at a rent to be presently fixed for the rest (1654). There is also a Report (March 8, 1656) on the evidence produced by Kerdiff as to the title and conditions of the College estates in Munster given in the appendix to this chapter (cf. also M. R., A, iv. a), and lastly a list of the tenants and their rents for Kilmacrenan, let to them in 1656 for three years, in Winter's own hand. The Provost seems to have confined his attention as to leases to the Ulster estates. He has given us (*Collections*, p. 58) the gradual improvement in the College rents in the years 1652, 3, and 4. In Donegal alone the rents in 1654 improved by £300 in spite of the heavy duties required by the public purse both on land and stock, viz., out of Dr. Richardson's lease in Tirhugh total rent £116, public rent £28 10s. 8d., College rent £87 9s. 4d. This was very different from the old Crown rent, and is quoted from his note upon the true value to the College of the estate. The conditions of lease in Kilmacrenan are given p. 65, showing that there was a cess charged on all the stock of the farms.

religious labours and experiences, while their dealings with the world, often shrewd and practical enough, are studiously ignored by their pious biographers. We have already cited the case of Winter in this respect. There are, however, a few items in the Registry on a great public movement among the soldiers in favour of Irish learning, which are interesting symptoms of the spirit of the times, and to which we shall presently return.

It is but common justice to Winter, who has been treated with great contempt by the writers in the Restoration and those that have copied them, to enumerate some other yet unnoticed entries. At the very outset (September, 1652) the porter is commanded on no account to allow the drying of clothes in the Quadrangle or the free entry of women without an order from the Provost or fellows. In the same month comes the appointment of Joseph Travers to the professorship of Civil Law, showing that secular studies were not to be neglected. During May, 1654, twelve students are granted the B.A. and seven the M.A. by consent of the Provost and Senior Fellows. On May 4, 1655, one B.D. and fourteen A.B. degrees are thus consented to. Nothing is said about any formal Commencement, nor is the consent of either Chancellor or Vice-Chancellor set down. But how dangerous an argument from the silence of the Registry may be appears from entries in the Matriculation book—which is quite the wrong place to put them—to the effect that on June 2, 1659, John Tailor, seven years a student at Magdalen College, and John Clearke, also of Oxford, are admitted M.D., being recommended by the Chancellor, Henry Cromwell, *in pleno Senatu Academico*. On the same day Thos. Crompton from Brazenose takes the M.A. *omnibus exercitiis præstitis*. John Thompson, a few months later, is admitted M.A. *ad eundem* from Glasgow. There were therefore solemn meetings of the Senate held in 1659, and most probably from the beginning of Winter's rule. In 1654 it is agreed to give Dr. Robert Maxwell a lease of lands in Co. Armagh.[1] On

---

[1] Corroborated by M. R., F 88, in September.

THE PROTECTORATE—WINTER (1652-60)   305

February 2, 1654, formal leave of absence is given to Joshua Cowley, M.A., for six months. We are not told what his duties and emoluments were. In the same month John Stearne, the Registrar, is granted leave to sleep in the city or elsewhere, for the practice of his profession of physic. In November, 1656, Stearne is appointed Professor of Hebrew at a salary of £30 for life, which act is confirmed, with modifications as to salary, by the Visitors in later acts.[1] In May, 1658, a deed was signed with one Robert Stearne to let and dispose of to the best advantage the College lands in Co. Limerick on leases of twenty-one years, getting a salary of £30 for the first year and £20 for the remaining twenty. In June, 1659, the regulations are passed (Reg., 89) requiring from all candidates for B.A. and for M.A. a competent knowledge of Greek, Rhetoric, and Hebrew. There is no mention made of examinations, but merely of certificates from the lecturers in these subjects. The election of annual officers on November 20, 1659, is recorded (Reg., 91), and on February 23rd in the same year (O. S.) that one James Clelow[2] has been co-opted in the fourth class, viz., a Senior Sophister—one of the curiosities of false perspective in a book that omits most of the important occurrences in the College. Such is also Winter's last act (April 2, 1660), to remit the commencement fees (£1 4s.) to two students on the ground of their good behaviour and proficiency. There immediately follows (Reg., 92) the first stroke of the death-bell of the Protectorate in the College. "March 29, 1660. By the general Convention of Ireland, upon reading the petition of several scholars of Trinity College, Dublin, and consideration had thereof, it is ordered that Dr. Samuel Winter, Provost, and the severall fellows of the s^d College uppon sight hereof

---

[1] 1657 and 1659. Reg., 90 and 87-8.

[2] This Clelow, a curious name, had entered from Chester on July 17, 1657, and was raised to this, the fourth class, before his proper time Hence the special entry.

X

deliver into the hands of Mr. Cæsar Williamson and Mr. Francis Saunders or one of them the originall Charter of the s^d College and that the s^d Mr. Saunders doe deliver to the s^d Petitioners a true coppie of the oath mentioned in the locall Statutes of the s^d College which the respective Provosts thereof did usually take at their admission, to the end the s^d schollars and their Councill might peruse the same.—Signed, NICH. BARRY, Clerk of the Gen. Convention of Ireland."

Though we are told nothing more, the situation is plain enough. The political pendulum had swung back to Royalty, the Restoration of Charles II. was imminent, and those who served the times must hasten to make their peace, if they would bask in the rising sun. It is obvious that Cæsar Williamson and Francis Saunders were the promoters of this petition among the scholars, though they were Senior Fellows, and associated with Winter in his daily work. They knew perfectly that such a petition was directly contrary to the statutes, which confined appeals of students to the hearing of the Visitors. Though Henry Cromwell was gone, they might lawfully have appealed to the Chancellor Ormond, whose return was to be expected. But there was probably no time for these legalities, or compunction in violating them, in the great hurry to declare for the Restoration. So Winter disappears silently, without protest or complaint, displaced, it is assumed, technically, for not having taken the Provost's oath— as the petition plainly suggests—leaving behind him a good reputation, and taking with him his title to the Irish estates, which he was able to secure for his descendants.

Before we conclude our estimate of the condition in which he left his College, we must review the action of the Protector regarding the promotion of higher education in Ireland outside the College. There can be no doubt that Ireland was now more completely pacified than it had ever been since the English Conquest. The strong hand of Cromwell, and the thorough sweeping out of the religious fomenters of native rebellion, together with his enlightened treatment of Irish industries, were rapidly healing the terrible wounds of his ruthless sword. Even the confiscations of land, and transplantations of natives and Anglo-Irish gentry to Connaught, cannot have been either so thorough or so cruel as they are painted by prejudiced historians. The following facts are established with certainty from Winter's private notes of his life and work in Ireland. He travelled frequently through the remotest and wildest parts of the north (Tyrone and Donegal) and also to Kerry—counties inhabited generally by the natives, with some English settlers scattered among them. Excepting the stealing by "the Irish army" of his horses, we cannot find that he ever incurred the smallest danger or annoyance. He never speaks of requiring any escort, or taking any precautions, yet he does tell us that he carried large sums of money, apparently College rents, which he had received. But if we should gather from this that the native population had been extirpated, such an inference is refuted by the fact that more than half the new tenants of such an estate as Kilmacrenan in remote Donegal were people of unmistakably Irish names, paying small rents, and thus in peaceable occupation of their homes. On the other hand I can trace no attempt to induce Irish Roman Catholics to come and reside at Trinity College, as was the policy of earlier Governments, in the hope that they might adopt the creed of their educators. The Puritans were too uncompromising for that policy and indeed the massacres of 1641 had placed a great gulf between the races, and had rudely checked the assimilation which had long been doing its quiet work.

But as far as native tenants were concerned—and these were not the ditchers and delvers with property less than £10, who were specially exempted from transplantation—the College estates had always favoured them, and favoured them still. As was said in a former chapter, the Church and the College were not bound by the conditions of the original plantation to exclude Irishmen from their farms, and the names of these tenants, in Limerick and Kerry, in Fermanagh and Donegal, show that either directly, or through middlemen, the original inhabitants still held their lands from the College.

We are told on the one hand, by Prendergast, that nothing could exceed the horror and desolation produced by the Cromwellian Settlement, which cleared the country of its inhabitants, the seaports of their merchandise, the country houses of their traditions.[1] On the other hand, we are assured that a great material prosperity arose in the land, as soon as peace prevailed, in spite of the large confiscations and outlawries, and the replacement of the old by new proprietors. From a Roman Catholic point of view, the former statement must appear the more probable. For that Church was persecuted and swept out with a consistent rigour very different from the vacillating and intermittent repression of the Stuarts. But to tell us that the enterprising English and Dutch settlers in the ports did nothing to revive trade, and that ships no longer visited Galway or Waterford, because the Recusant merchants had left, is to maintain what is in itself incredible, though for some years there was really a deficiency of population in these cities. The *Thurloe Papers* contain a good many letters on this point, (*e.g.*, v. 508) which show that here the recovery was slow.

But on the other hand the peaceably inclined rural population, which is always the majority, had been suffering from the swordsmen employed in the various armies or raiding for themselves, much in the same way that Germany had been suffering from the Croats and Pandours under Tilly or Wallenstein. These self-styled gentlemen (like the *cadets Gascons*), the ancestors of the squireens and buckeens that infested Ireland till the present generation, were above any industry or labour, and

---

[1] Prendergast was a native of Tipperary and knew little of the North. He went by the letter much more than by the fact. For him an order given or even contemplated was an order carried out.—R. B.

THE PROTECTORATE—WINTER (1652-60)

regarded loafing and license as the *summum bonum*, to be obtained only during the cessation of law and order. We are told that 40,000 of these were exiled, or exiled themselves, to seek their fortunes in wars abroad. The relief caused by their disappearance more than compensated for all the harshnesses of the Cromwellian Settlement.[1] The General who paid for all that his army required, and hanged one of his soldiers for stealing a fowl, was a new and strange phenomenon in Ireland. People might now till their ground, and graze their cattle in safety, and accordingly many of the Anglo-Irish Protestants returned and bought farms from the Adventurers.[2]

These considerations seem to me to explain the peaceable journeys of Winter, and the rapid rise of the College rents largely paid by native tenants.

But quite apart from this financial support of the College the efforts of Cromwell and his advisers to promote higher education in the Irish capital are shown by two proposals, of which the shortness of his rule marred the fulfilment. These were (1) the founding of a New College of equal size and endowment with Trinity, and in its immediate vicinity; (2) the endowing of Dublin with a great public Library. The documents have been gathered with commendable care by Mr. Urwick, whom I gladly quote :—

> Running through the records of the Commonwealth period, we find a deliberate and growing design to establish a second College in connection with the University, to be called New College, with its Master or Provost, its fellows and its scholars.
>
> This design is mentioned in the Act of March 8, 1649-50. Doctor John Owen, when consulted by Henry Cromwell (who asked him for the Oxford Statutes), advised the establishment of this New College on the broadest basis, restoring the University to its primary standing as a clearly national institution. The site selected for the New College lay between the College Park and S. Stephen's

---

[1] Cf. Fleetwood to Thurloe, iii. 559 and Gookin to Cromwell, ibid., v. 646, writing in 1655 and 6.

[2] Gookin, *loc. cit.*

Green and Baggot Street; and "the Houses commonly called Cork House with its gallery leading towards the Castle Bridge and some ground contiguous thereto" were transferred for the purposes of a Library from Dr. Robert Gorge to the Lord Deputy, Henry Cromwell, on March 20, 1657.

"Ordered that the Trustees of ye Colledge at Dublin meet the Com[tee] of Stores in Cork House to consult concerning the ruinous condition of the said House, and how the same may with most speed be repaired. Also to consider of a lease of the said House, November 16, 1654." [1]

Among the letters and papers relating to Henry Cromwell during his residence in Ireland, inherited as heirlooms by Mrs. Prescott, is the following interesting account of this scheme as planned and carried out in 1658. It is a letter on a single sheet of parchment, and from the Commissioners to the Lord Deputy, Henry Cromwell.

"May it please your Excellency, In pursuance of your Excellencies order of Dec. 1st, 1658, we have considered of the Act of Parliament and the several particulars mentioned in the said order, and finding that your statutable allowances for Trinity Colledge, Dublin, were in some particulars very slender and meane, we have sett down some small additional allowances thereunto, as by account of the particulars thereof hereunder mentioned may appear, for the payment whereof some of the lands and tithes now vested in the Trustees may be settled on Trinity Colledge. And we humbly propose to your Excellency that the like allowances of sallaries and commons as they now stand with the additions, may be settled and made for the New Colledge as soon as it is erected. We have also in the said accompt set down several allowances for publique Professors, and for the publique Library and Free Schools. And finding that the said allowances soe set down by us (although they be very moderate), doe by near two hundred pounds exceed the several yearly revenues of Trinity Colledge and of the Trustees named in the said Act, besides such part of the Trustees' revenue as may prove non-solvent; And what must be allowed out of the tithes for serving the cures of several parishes which cannot amount to less than £400 in the whole, unless upon application to the Parliament, which is desired, some lands equal in value may be granted in lieu of the said tithes, and the tithes restored to the several parishes;—We humblie propose and desire that the lands and possessions of the late Viccars-chorall and Petti-canons of St. Patrick's, Dublin, be granted and confirmed by the State for compleating of a competent revenue for the ends in the said Act mentioned—in regard it is conceived the said lands and possessions were intended to be granted by the said Act. And in the mean

---

[1] Public Record Office, Dublin, Cromwell Records, A-5, fol. 34.

while that the Trustees be suffered to receive the rents thereof for the ends aforesaid. We further humbly propose that the several allowanees soe set down for Trinity Colledge and for the publique Professors and others mentioned in the said account, be respectively paid out of the said Trustees' revenue to Trinity Colledge and to such of the said publique Professors during life as are already appointed ; and the allowances for the other persons to commence as they are or shall from time to time be appointed and settled. And that the overplus of the said Trustees' revenue be layd aside for the building of a new Colledge. And if after the erecting of the said new Colledge, it shall appear that the several revenues of Trinity Colledge and of the said Trustees shall fall short to answer the several allowances set down in the account as aforesaid, and then such proportionable deductions to be made from the respective sallaries in the said accompt mentioned, as shall be thought fitt.

"Wee also humblie offer to your Excellency that the ground near Trinity Colledge bordering on Baggottrath Land, Stephen's Green, and the highway, are a convenient place for building of the aforesaid New Colledge, and that St. Sepulchre's, by St. Patrick's church, is a convenient place for settling the Free School therein, and for affording house-room for the Schoolmaster and Usher.

"And seeing your Excellency hath been nobly pleased of your free bounty to become the first benefactor by consenting to bestow your interest in Corke House and Gallery adjoining for a public Library and Schoole, we are humbly of opinion that the said House and Gallery is the most convenient place for those uses; and we doe humbly propose that the Books and Manuscripts formerly belonging to the late Lord Primate of Ireland and purchased by the State and Army to their greate and lasting honor for a public good, be placed in the said publique Library.

"And not doubting but your Excellency's noble and pious example will be attractive to many others to become benefactors to soe great and good a worke, we doe with all thankfulnesse acknowledge your Excellency's expressed zeale for the publique good and advancement of the Gospel and Learning, the ends of the said Act. And doe humbly propose that by publique authority a Booke or Books may be provided and by certaine hands thereunto to be appointed by your Excellency, be tendered for the subscriptions of such whose harte God shall move to follow your Excellencie herein, and that by such ways and meanes of recommendation to the Judges of the Four Courts and in the Circuite to the Nobility, Justices of the Peace, and the chief men and others of the several Provinces and Countys, and to the inhabitants of the City of Dublin and other Citys and Townes in Ireland; and to ye Army, as may be further agreed upon and best advance the same. All which we humbly submit to your Excellency's further consideration togeather with the ways and meanes how the said lands proposed for the erecting of a new Colledge may be contracted for and purchased from the parties who have interest therein and procured from his Highness if he have a title thereunto. Dated the 18th day of January, 1658."

Hereupon follows this table of Charges[1] :—

AN ACCOMPT OF THE YEARLY CHARGE OF THE COLLEDGES, PUBLIC PROFESSORS, LIBRARY, AND FREE SCHOOLE ABOVE MENTIONED.

		Ye Statutable Allowances for Trinity Colledge, Dublin, Yearely.			Additional Allowances by the Comittee, Yearely.			The Yearely Allowances including the Additions.		
		£.	s.	d.	£.	s.	d.	£.	s.	d.
	The Provost	100	0	0 ..	50	0	0 ..	150	0	0
	The Vice-Provost	000	0	0 ..	20	0	0 ..	20	0	0
	Seaven Senior Fellowes at 9l. 13s. 4d. each..	67	13	4 ..	72	6	8 ..	140	0	0
	Nine Junior Fellowes at 3l. each	27	0	0 ..	81	0	0 ..	108	0	0
	70 Schollers—									
	30 Natives at 3l. each ..	90	0	0 ..	30	0	0	} 220	0	0
	40 Schollers at 10s. each	20	0	0 ..	80	0	0			
	Divinity Lecturer	40	0	0 ..	000	0	0 ..	40	0	0
	English [Div.] Lecturer	40	0	0 ..	000	0	0 ..	40	0	0
	Catechist	13	6	8 ..	000	0	0 ..	13	6	8
	Bursar	10	0	0 ..	5	0	0 ..	15	0	0
	Senior Deane	4	0	0 ..	000	0	0 ..	4	0	0
	Junior Deane	2	0	0 ..	000	0	0 ..	2	0	0
	Senior Lecturer	4	0	0 ..	000	0	0 ...	4	0	0
TRINITY COLLEDGE DUBLIN.	Six Junior Lecturers at 4l. each	24	0	0 ..	000	0	0 ..	24	0	0
	Library Keeper	3	0	0 ..	3	0	0 ..	6	0	0
	Auditor	6	13	4 ..	000	0	0 ..	6	13	4
	Register	3	0	0 ..	000	0	0 ..	3	0	0
	Bible-Clke	4	0	0 ..	000	0	0 ..	4	0	0
	Butler	2	0	0 ..	000	0	0 ..	2	0	0
	Cooke	9	0	0 ..	000	0	0 ..	9	0	0
	Manciple	9	0	0 ..	11	0	0 ..	20	0	0
	Gardner	16	0	0 ..	000	0	0 ..	16	0	0
	Laundresse	4	0	0 ..	000	0	0 ..	4	0	0
	Porter	6	6	0 ..	000	0	0 ..	6	6	0
	Provost Commons	13	13	0 ..	13	13	0 ..	27	6	0
	16 Fellewes Commons at 13l. 13s. each	218	8	0 ...	000	0	0 ..	218	8	0
	70 Schollers Commons at 6l. 14s. 4d. each	470	3	4 ..	75	16	8 ..	546	0	0
		1,207	3	8 ..	441	16	4 ..	1,649	0	0

		£.	s.	d.
NEW COLLEDGE.	THE LIKE ALLOWANCES OF SALLARIES AND COMONS FOR THE NEW COLLEDGE	1,649	0	0

£. s. d.
3,988 0 0

---

[1] I will add here that a paper in the M. R. (G 8) gives, after a list of the College tenants and rents, at this time amounting, with the Government allowance, to £1,462 8s. 4d., the full summary of expenses :—

	£	s.	d.
The full number of fellows and scholars allowed statutably	698	9	4
Fellows' and officers' sallaries come to about	330	0	0
The natives' sallaryes to	90	0	0
The scholars' sallaryes to	35	0	0
	1,153	9	4

Thus showing a good surplus. This paper, to judge from the names of the tenants, &c., dates about 1658.—I. P. M.

THE PROTECTORATE—WINTER (1652-60)

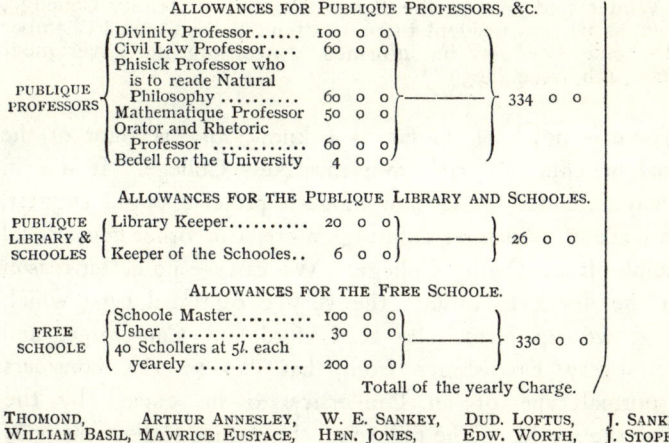

ALLOWANCES FOR PUBLIQUE PROFESSORS, &c.

PUBLIQUE PROFESSORS	Divinity Professor	100 0 0		
	Civil Law Professor	60 0 0		
	Phisick Professor who is to reade Natural Philosophy	60 0 0		334 0 0
	Mathematique Professor	50 0 0		
	Orator and Rhetoric Professor	60 0 0		
	Bedell for the University	4 0 0		

ALLOWANCES FOR THE PUBLIQUE LIBRARY AND SCHOOLES.

PUBLIQUE LIBRARY & SCHOOLES	Library Keeper	20 0 0		26 0 0
	Keeper of the Schooles	6 0 0		

ALLOWANCES FOR THE FREE SCHOOLE.

FREE SCHOOLE	Schoole Master	100 0 0		330 0 0
	Usher	30 0 0		
	40 Schollers at 5l. each yearely	200 0 0		

Totall of the yearly Charge.

THOMOND,	ARTHUR ANNESLEY,	W. E. SANKEY,	DUD. LOFTUS,	J. SANKEY,
WILLIAM BASIL,	MAWRICE EUSTACE,	HEN. JONES,	EDW. WORTH,	J. STOPFORD,
JA. WARE,	PAVL DAFYS,	FRAN. ROBERTS,	EDW. ROBERTS.	
JOH. HARDING,	JO. BRIDGES,	ROBERT GORGES.[1]		

It is interesting to note the items in which the Committee thought the allowances in Trinity College adequate, and where they recommended an increase. In no case did they propose to diminish, still less to abolish, a salary or allowance.

Following up this plan we find the following orders :—

"Whereas an Act of Parliament dated 8th March 1649, intituled an Act for the better advance of the Gospel in Ireland, Wm. Basill, John Cook, Esqrs., Dr. Henry Jones, Dr. John Harding, Col. Hierom Sankey, are appointed Trustees in behalf of Trinity Colledge, Dublin. Ordered that the said Trustees be desired to attend the Commissioners of Parliament on Friday at 2 p.m., about the lands settled for maintenance of the Colledge, and Free Schools, in and near Dublin, and Mr. Barry, the clerk, is then to be present. And Dr. Gorges is desired to bring with him the report and proposals presented to the late Lord-Lieutenant about the said Colledge.

"The said Council taking notice how that it is a duty incumbent upon them to consider all due ways and means for the advancement of learning and training of youth up in piety, have thought fitt to appoint Wednesday next, being the 14th inst., in the afternoon, for

---

[1] MSS. belonging to Mrs. Prescott, 13, Oxford Sq., London, W. See *Hist. MSS. Commission*, Appendix to 2nd Report, p. 98 :—" 1658, Jan. 18, Return signed by the Earl of Thomond and others of the Revenues of Public Institutions in Ireland."

Dr. Winter and five of the Senior Fellows of Trinity Colledge, Dublin, as are now resident there, to attend at the Council Chamber to the end they may be informed concerning the government thereof; 9th Dece., 1659." [1]

There is nowhere, so far as I know, any account of the special benefits expected from this New College. It was in no way intended, as certain modern projects might suggest, for a place of education differing in creed or other educational principles from Trinity College. We can see no better reason than the desire to imitate the very exceptional type which had grown up historically at Oxford and Cambridge, and which every Englishman from that day to this considers the normal type of an University to be copied by the rest of the world. The failure of the earlier Halls mentioned in this volume does not, however, imply the failure of this experiment, had it obtained a fair trial, and it is interesting to speculate how the history of Dublin would have been changed, had another College filled up the space proposed, including part of Merrion Square, and bordering on S. Stephen's Green, and the present College Park.

The other attempt of Cromwell to promote learning in Dublin was to set up there (not in the College) the famous library of Primate Ussher, who had received the honour of a public burial in Westminster Abbey on April 17, 1656, and whose books were forthwith offered for sale by his impoverished daughter, Lady Tyrrell, the grand-daughter of Luke Challoner. The facts have been thus gathered by Mr. Urwick :—

In the Minutes of Council (Oliver Cromwell present), June, 12, 1656, we read :

"That it be referred to Dr. Owen, Mr. Caryll, and Mr. Sterry, or any two of them, to peruse *the Catalogue of Bookes in the Library of Dr. Ussher, deceased*, late Archbishop of Armagh, and to certify their opinion to the Counsell what manuscripts or other books, part of that Library, are fitt to be bought by the State, and in the meantime the

---

[1] Public Record Office, Dublin, Cromwell MSS., A–17., fol. 67, 92.

sale of the said Library and of every part thereof is to be forborne; whereof all those whom it may concern are to take notice and to inform themselves accordingly." [1]

Mr. Urwick proceeds to give eleven extracts from State documents regarding the sale of Ussher's books. From these I shall only quote the last three :—

(9) In the Letter of the College Commissioners to Henry Cromwell, they say :

"Seeing your Excellency hath been nobly pleased of your free bounty to become the first benefactor by consenting to bestow your Interest in Corke House and Gallery adjoining for a Publique Library and Schoole, We are humbly of opinion that the said House and Gallery is the most convenient place for those uses; and we doe humbly propose that the Books and Manuscripts formerly belonging to the late Lord Primate of Ireland, and purchased by the State and Army, to their greate and lasting honor for a public good, bee placed in the said publique Library." [2]

(10) "Ordered that it be and is hereby referred to Sir Hardresse Waller, Major-general of Foot, the Lord Chief Justice Basill, Baron Sanchey, Dr. Gorges, Capt. Dean, Capt. Hopford, Capt. Warren, and Capt. Standford, or any three of them, who are desired to take a view of the Gallery at Cork House, and ye Armory Room neer ye Castle, and having called before them such persons and workmen as they should hold fitt, they are to consider which place shall be most convenient for placing ye late Dr. Ussher's Library, and to present an estimate of the charges for making presses and chaines for ye Books, in order to use and security. And ye Secretary attending this Board is to attend ye Major-General that the meeting may be hastened and report made unto ye Board for further consideration. Dated at ye Counsell Chamber, Dublin, ye 29th of June, 1659. Tho. Herbert, Secretary." [3]

(11) "Ordered that such of ye Trustees for Trinity College as are in or near Dublin, as also Dr. Winter, Dr. Gorge, and Mr. Williamson, be desired to attend ye Board upon Thursday, ye 3rd instant, at 3 in ye Afternoon, and to consider together how ye Library, formerly belonging to Dr. Usher, purchased by ye State and Army, may be disposed and fitted for public use. And also to take into consideration a lre. from Dr. Bernerd, as also a paper delivered by Dr. Jones, concerning ye publishing some part of ye said Library or Manuscripts, and of recovering some part of ye said Library, being at

---

[1] R. O. (London), Dom. Interregnum, I. 77, p. 175.
[2] Dated January 18, 1658. MSS. of Mrs. Prescott, Historical MSS. Commission, *loc. cit.*
[3] Cromwell MSS., as before, A-17, fol. 6.

present abroad in some men's hands, albeit, they ought to have been returned hither with ye bookes already received ; and to inquire whether ye present Catalogue comprehend all ye bookes which were purchased, or such only as were sent hither and are in custody of Mr. Williamson or others ; and to informe themselves in what condition ye said Library at present is ; whether since ye coming of ye said books hither, any of them have been lent out, or otherwise disposed of ? To whom ? When ? And by whose order ? With what else may concerne that business. Dated at Dublin, ye first of November, 1659.[1] Tho. Herbert, Secr."

I need but remind the reader that Dr. Bernard, in his funeral sermon on Ussher at Westminster Abbey, had suggested this benevolence of Cromwell's soldiers by mis-stating the circumstances of the first foundation of the College Library. Still it remains true that soldiers had joined in the earliest endowment of the College ; he might have added that in recent years Colonel Michael Jones and his officers had contributed to its support, when it was starving under the scourge of the Rebellion. But before the books, which had reached Dublin, could be deposited in Cork House the Restoration supervened, and in 1661 they were deposited in the Library of Trinity College, as "the gift of His Most Serene Majesty Charles II."

It is therefore in transferring the gift intended for the city to the College, and in this respect only, that Charles II. (besides his Act of Settlement) benefited the Society. Probably the transference was suggested by the Duke ot Ormond, though he had not yet returned to Ireland.

The Restoration is beyond the limits fixed for this volume. But the words just cited are a good example of the credit taken by the returned Royalists for the large ideas and generous plans of the officers of the Commonwealth. Thus the Charter and establishment of the School of Physic was due formally to Charles II., but the whole basis had been laid by John Stearne, who as early as 1654, when the College was making no proper use of Trinity Hall, and when the Corporation threatened to resume it, made the beginnings of

---

[1] Cromwell MSS., as before, A-17, fol. 83.

a medical college by residing there, probably with some students, and promoting the foundation of that famous Corporation, the College of Physicians, which is even now not wholly divorced from Trinity College. But these obscure beginnings, and long unrewarded labours, are forgotten. So also the Free School, which the Cromwellians would probably have founded beside St. Patrick's, suggested the foundation of the King's Hospital and Free School, known as the Blue Coat School in Blackhall Place, Dublin. In Ireland at least the Protectorate was no mere interval of republican usurpation, when unauthorised and incompetent people exercised authority and did public mischief to the exclusion of the legitimate officers of the Crown. It was rather a period when a group of very able, though narrow, men managed to restore order and then set themselves to the improvement, materially and morally, of the country they had conquered. If they made mistakes, they also had great successes, and above all, they brought fresh ideas to bear upon the subject of education, by which the Restoration largely profited. Thus the Trinity College which Ormond found again upon his return as Chancellor was no decayed and impoverished Society, whose learning and whose prosperity had disappeared during the political turmoil of the Rebellion and the Usurpation, but a well-ordered home of learning and piety, with its old estates secured, its privileges protected, and some of the very governors he had left in possession when he went into exile still at the helm, and ready to serve under the restored royalty.

It is this unbroken continuity through many generations that constitutes the nobility of a family, a Corporation, a State, and this quality no art or mystery has ever been able to counterfeit. It is the ἀρχαῖος πλοῦτος καὶ ἀρετή of Aristotle, hereditary wealth and ability telling upon many generations, each one of which keeps drifting from the crudities of youth, and acquiring that mellowness of age which is indeed the rich autumn of human civilisation. The men of the Restoration did their best to obscure this noble continuity.

Bishop Jeremy Taylor, the new Vice-Chancellor, a great man of letters but a most mischievous politician, gives an account of the College as he found it to Ormond,[1] which seems a direct contemporary contradiction to what I have been writing. He says he found "all things in perfect disorder, indeed so great as can be imagined to be consequent on a sad war, and an evil incompetent Government set over them." He thought "there were no University Statutes, no established forms of conferring Degrees, no Regius Professor of Divinity, scarce any ensigns academical." The good Bishop was talking Restoration rubbish, and maligning his pious and able predecessors. Had what he said been even approximately true, Trinity College would not have become in a few years what he himself calls "the small but excellent University of Dublin." But as the assailants of Strafford would prove that everything Chappell had done was a grievance, so the assailants of Cromwell would prove that anything Winter had done was disorderly. We can judge these things more calmly now. Bishop Jeremy Taylor, though he did lasting mischief in the north by persecuting the Presbyterians, did much good for the studies of Trinity College. But Winter did so also and did not persecute.

Of the men gathered round him in the College, few have left us books whereby we may judge them. But there is one who well deserves to be viewed as an author, inasmuch as his literary work must have been done during Winter's rule, and before he devoted himself to the practice of his profession in Dublin. John Stearne had been exiled when an undergraduate by the Rebellion, and prosecuted his studies at Cambridge. But as soon as Winter became Provost and peace was restored, he returned and was admitted a fellow. Amid the dearth of details about the social life of the

[1] Stubbs, p. 107.

College, and of the city beside it, under the Commonwealth, the books remaining to us from John Stearne's pen are a valuable and little known source of information. He tells us, in the Preface to his *Animi Medela* (Bladen, Dublin, 1658), that his father was an immigrant, married to a niece of James Ussher, and that after good schooling (which he does not further specify) he entered Trinity College (1639, aged 15, according to the Matriculation book). He was evidently among those who fled in panic to England, at the outbreak of the Rebellion, without time to pack up his possessions (and indeed, he says, he had none to pack) and then owing to the influence of his grand-uncle (then in England) with Samuel Ward, the Primate's old and learned correspondent, now master of Sidney Sussex College, he was there entertained and educated, till the troubles of the time reaching Cambridge also, he migrated to Oxford, where he was likewise treated with all hospitality by Seth Ward, then Savilian Professor of Geometry. But the distress of the Civil War also invaded Oxford, and he felt himself a burden to his hospitable entertainers. He seems to have been brought up with royalist people, and the king's execution evidently threw him and his friends into the greatest trouble and perplexity. Then, he says, in his sore mental distress, he sought and found in the Stoic philosophy a spiritual haven, which he confesses with shame might have been found long before in the Christian religion. This autobiographical note he puts in his book, as one that has escaped shipwreck sets up his votive tablet. However, in this philosophy, he "found peace," and now convinced that wealth and promotion were of no consequence to happiness, he returned to his own people in Dublin, where an unexpected good fortune awaited him. Taken up favourably as a Dublin man, and recommended by his teachers from England, he was presently made a Fellow, Tutor, Senior Fellow, Registrar in Trinity College, and successively Professor of Civil Law, of Hebrew, and of Physic in the University. He was besides a physician in large practice in the city. He was after the Restoration the founder and first President of the College of Physicians.

But all these official duties, ably as he may have performed them, are but the outside of his life. His inmost soul, his peculiar and special love, was for theological ethics, for the problems of the soul and its connection with the body, for the search after the *summum bonum* here and hereafter. The anxious speculations of his time of trial at Oxford, where he had been converted by the school of Chrysippus, were brought into order by him and produced as *The Healing of the Soul*, to which title is added a list of the grave problems discussed—Free Will, the efficacy of Prayer, the origin of Evil, the nature of Repentance, besides the psychical causes for tears and ecstasies—in fact a whole philosophy of practical life. He followed up this curious book, which teems with the learning of the ancients, with a pendant on the Cure of the body, called a Dissertation on Death, on its nature, and the means of delaying it, and seven years later with a book of aphorisms for life, chosen from many great sources.

It is beyond the scope of this work to enter at any length into the views and theories of Stearne on these vast problems. His combination of Stoicism and Christianity is ingenious, his use of corroborative texts from divers sources an evidence of great and varied learning. But we are much enlightened on the spirit of the day in educated Dublin by the external aids which he invokes to obtain a hearing for his theories. And let us note in passing that he is absolutely silent on the medical side of his education. It is known from other sources that studies in anatomy were being carried on at that time in Cambridge, and from the fact that he himself tells us the religious world looked on the medicus as *atheus*, and moreover resented his incursions into theology, we can see that these studies on the human frame were best kept secret. The founding of a separate house for medical studies points to the same conclusion. Stearne was evidently anxious to secure himself from the persecution of the Calvinistic bigots. His first book begins with the *Imprimatur* of the Government, signed Thomas Herbert (clerk of Council), April 17, 1657, a year before the work was published. Then follows a somewhat fulsome Dedication to Henry Cromwell, now Lord Deputy and Chancellor of the University, whose benefits are *tot et tanta, tanta et tam divina*, that without him as Chancellor the atrophied Society would hardly have retained the privileges, certainly not the appearance, of a College. Then comes the autobiographical open letter already noticed, and then complimentary letters and verses *from three bishops*—Raphoe, Ossory, and Kilmore. Was there ever greater care taken to establish the orthodoxy of a book? But the notable thing is that now, under H. Cromwell, he appeals not to preachers, not to his Provost Winter, but to bishops. Educated public opinion was evidently turning in their favour; prelacy was no longer a bugbear, and even stately Church services were again tolerated. Thus Langley, writing to Thurloe [1] under the date August 14, 1658, speaks with some contempt of " great stories told here of the retinue and great state the Lord Deputy of Ireland (H. Cromwell) takes upon him, they say far beyond what Strafford did—his stately march to the church, with maces borne on horseback, the mayor of the cittie and all other persons of state attending him with great majestie ; his sitting above in the church in a stately seat, his wife opposite to him in as much ; the sumptuous chairs belonging to these seats, with cullor and fringe, is not left out." When such ceremonies were in fashion, the Puritan spirit must have been much diluted in Dublin.

Stearne's second book, Θανατολογια *seu de Morte Dissertatio*, published in Dublin and London, 1659, shows the same features in its preamble. There is a rhetorical imprimatur signed by William Petty, clerk of Council on January 31, 1658–9. The

---

[1] *Thurloe Papers*, vii. p. 335. H. Cromwell was never much of a Puritan. Mrs. Hutchinson calls him a "debauched, ungodly cavalier." He wanted to marry the delightful Dorothy Osborne, afterwards Lady Temple.—R. B.

dedication is no longer to Cromwell, who had departed, but to the Trustees appointed to look into the finances of the College, and work out the scheme of founding a New College. Then comes a letter of commendation to his brother Robert, and then an open letter to the reader, which is remarkable for an outspoken attack upon the ignorance and intolerance of the preachers who only knew Calvin's system, and had dared to criticise him. In this spirited passage he ridicules these cobbler-theologians, who think themselves fit to profess that science, and he warns the Professors of Logic that they will be the next attacked. Stearne's attitude is therefore declared, and then follow not only verses from his old patron Robert Maxwell, Bishop of Kilmore, but a letter of commendation from Jeremy Taylor, at the moment living in his delightful retreat at Portmore, near Lisburn, whither Lord Conway had invited him to lecture and preach. So we have Stearne in the very best High Church company. It need not surprise us that his aphorisms (in 1666) were dedicated to Ormond, the restored Chancellor, in language similar to the earlier dedication to Cromwell. He even says that he had chosen a similar patron for his former book. It is somewhat pathetic that so earnest and scientific a student of longevity should have had his own life cut short at the age of forty-five.

This curious piece of forgotten literary history seems to prove that the Church of Ireland, with its Evangelical temper, was not at daggers drawn with the Government of the Protectorate, and that society in Dublin, during these ten years, must have regained much of its gaiety and its charm. The country was perfectly safe. Ludlow could have a country house at Moncktown (as he calls it) several miles from Dublin, without any danger of a raid from the O'Tooles in the Dublin mountains. Winter, as we have told, could travel where he liked without risk, and so there was time to study, peace to meditate, and the conditions of University life were not unfavourable. We have in Dudley Loftus another man who was piling up erudition, and making translations of Logic from the Armenian, during these very years; and from Loftus's editing of the posthumous work of Stearne, we knew that they were personal friends.

These are the few stray evidences I have been able to gather of a deeply interesting but almost wholly unrecorded decennium in the life of Dublin and its College.

The elder John Stearne[1] is remarkable above his fellows in many ways. He shows us what excellent teachers Winter gathered into his staff. He shows how superior the Anglo-Irish intellect, when properly trained, was to the pure English so largely imported in those early days into Trinity College. Next to Ussher, he is the most remarkable Fellow produced in this period by the College, but differs from him widely in being the first example of that peculiar type which distinguishes Trinity College, Dublin, to the present day. Instead of devoting all his life to one study, he mastered several branches and, so far as we know, taught each of them as ably as any of his colleagues. From that day to the close of the nineteenth century this manysidedness has been the peculiar fashion of the College, and has produced men whom specialists have acknowledged as masters in each of their studies. This quality was originally stimulated by the circumstance of a small staff being compelled to teach many subjects; but its strange success in avoiding superficiality must be due to some deeper cause than this, or the many and stringent requirements of the Fellowship Examination. The real cause seems to be the versatility of the Anglo-Irish intellect, that type represented all over the world in so many successful soldiers, traders, lawyers, statesmen, that it may fairly be regarded as the most valuable strain in the very composite Anglo-Saxon race. Trinity College has been from the beginning the College of this Anglo-Irish breed, and that is the reason why it has flourished and

[1] His son, John, became Bishop of Clogher and Vice-Chancellor, and a great benefactor to the College.

produced great results in the face of great obstacles, in spite of many rebellions and revolutions. With this recognition therefore of John Stearne, as the first notable example of a permanent type, we may fitly close the history of the first seventy years of a famous Society and of its influence upon the history of Ireland.

APPENDIX.   (M. R., F 89.)

To the Right Honble. the Lord Deputy and Council.

May it please your Lordships,

According to your Lordships several references to me directed, the one dated the of March, 1656, and the other dated the xiith of May, following upon the Petition of the Provost, Fellows, and Scholars of Trinity College, near Dublin, touching their interest in certain Lands and tithes in the Provinces of Munster and Ulster, I have examined the business to me referred in the presence of Mr. John Kerdiff, Agent for the said College. Who produced unto me Letters Patents under the great seal of Ireland, dated at Dublin the xxviiith of June, in the 39th year of the reign of the late Queen Elizabeth, whereby she did give, grant, and confirm to the then Provost and Fellows of the College aforesaid the towns, villages, hamlets, lands and hereditaments particularly mentioned in the said letters Patents, and also in a particular or Schedule thereof hereunto annexed, To have and to hold the premises to the said Provost and Fellows and their successors for ever, for and under the several and respective rents in the said letters Patents expressed and reserved, which in all amount to the sum of xxiv^{li} x^{s} ix^{d} Irish yearly at the feast of St. Michael and Ester by even portions, with a clause of distress therein contained for non-payment of the said rent.

And there is also a proviso in the said letters Patents contained to this effect, that if the said towns and lands, or any part thereof, should be wasted, depopulated or destroyed, by reason of any Rebellion, Insurrection or any other means, so as the said Provost and Fellows of the said College should not enjoy the same, that then, during the time of such wasting, depopulation, &c., the said Provost and Fellows should not be bound to pay any rent for the premises so wasted, &c., as by the said Letters Patents appeareth.

And the said Mr. Kerdiff also produced unto me a letter directed to the Commissioners general of the Revenue in Ireland, and subscribed by Walter Thomas and Whithall Brown (which he affirms to be the Com^{rs} of the county of Kerry) and which is dated from

Tralee the 10th of August, 1655. In which letter is expressed, that for the years 1654 and 1655 mentioned in your honor's order of the 14th of April, 1656, The College lands in that County were in the year 1654 set for xxiv^{li} paid into the public Treasury, and in the year 1655 were set for about £73. As by the said Letters (thereunto annexed) appeareth.

The said Mr. Kerdiff also produced unto me another writing, stil'd a List of such Landes within the County of Limerick as do belong to the College near Dublin, Endorsed with the name of John Teige, who is affirmed by the said Mr. Kerdiff to be Clerk to the Commissioners of the Revenue of the Province of Limerick. Whereby is expressed, that the College landes lying within the County of Limerick were for the year 1655 let for the use of the Common Wealth for the sum of cxxxvi^{li}. As by the said writing hereunto (also annexed) appeareth.

He also produced unto me another writing, dated Sept. 1655, subscribed by William Purefoy, affirmed to be Governor of the Province of Limerick, and by Robert Cox affirmed to be one of the Commissioners of the Revenue there, Requiring that the rents of the Lands specified in the said list or Schedule should be paid to the said Mr. Kerdiff for the use of the said College, and desiring the Receivers, Surveyors, and all others concerned to take notice thereof. As by the same writing (also annexed) appeareth.

The said Mr. Kerdiff also produced unto me another paper signed by William Hartwell, affirmed to be then Receiver of the precinct of Limerick, dated at Limerick 14th Sept., 1655. Whereby the said Hartwell (though acknowledging the rents within his charge to appear due to the said College) yet certified: That in regard the same, with others in a rent roll, were returned to the Commissioner General as a charge upon him the said Hartwell. And for that he was by his instructions not to issue out any part of the Public Revenue, but by special warrant, with a Letter of Advice from the Commissioners General, he therefore refused payment thereof. As by the same writing (which is also hereunto annexed) appeareth.

But it being demanded of the said Mr. Kerdiff, who were in possession of the said Lands and premises before and when the rebellion began, He acknowledged, that after the passing of the said Letters Patents and long before the beginning of the rebellion the most part of the said Lands and premises were granted to divers persons in fee farm, who were since acting in the late Rebellion. The names of which fee farmers, together with the Lands to them granted within the several counties of Limerick, Kerry, and other counties and also the rents reserved to be paid for them, are mentioned in a List or Schedule hereunto annexed. But the said Mr.

Kerdiff affirmed unto me that in all and every the conveyances so made there was reserved to be paid yearly to the said Queen Elizabeth her heirs and successors all chief yearly rents and annual profits going out of the premises so granted, which to the said Queen or her Ancestors were of right due, or to be paid, with a Covenant also from every such fee farmers to pay the same. And that there was also by every such conveyance reserved to be paid to the said Provost and Fellows a certain yearly rent with a Covenant also from every such fee farmers that the same should be paid accordingly at the daies limited, and certain sums (*nomine pœnæ*) thereby reserved for the non payment thereof. And that there was also in most of such conveyances a condition contained to this effect, that if the rents and *nomine penes* (sic) aforesaid should be unpaid for one year after the days thereby limited for the payment thereof, that then upon Notice and certificate thereof to be given by the said Provost for the time being to the Lord Chancellors of Ireland, the Lord Chief Justice of the chief place and Master of the Rolls for the time being, or to such of them as should be in Ireland, and by the consent of them or any two of them under other hands, It should be lawful for the said Provost and Fellows and their successors at their wills and pleasures into the same lands to re-enter. And after such re-entry every such conveyance should be void.

And the said Mr. Kerdiff also affirmed unto me, that in most of the conveyances aforesaid there is a covenant from the said Provost and Fellows to each fee farmer to this effect : That if by reason of any rebellion, invasion, or insurrection the lands so granted or any part thereof should happen to be waste, so as the Grantee should not receive the profits thereof, and should continue so waste above one year, That then for every year after such first year, there should be allowed and abated to the Grantee the seventh part of the rent of the premises so wasted. If the said Queen her heirs and successors should allow the same to the said Provost and Fellows according to the said Letters Patents.

And the said Mr. Kerdiff produced unto me a deed purporting to be a counterpart of one of the fee farm deeds, and which was made between the said Provost and Fellows and one Daniel Ferris . . . and which I find to be made according to the effect and purport aforesaid. And affirmed that though he could not, for the present, produce the rest of the counterparts unto me, yet within a short time he would produce them. All which I now humbly certify unto your Lordship (as I would have done far sooner, according to your Lordship's references), but that the said Mr. Kerdiff (being otherwise busied abroad about the occasion of the College) did not thoroughly attend the business before this time.

24th Feb., 1657. WILLIAM BASIL.

APPENDIX

[These Statutes were brought into order, amended, altered, and imposed upon the College by Provost Bedell and his Senior Fellows in 1629. I have added a few notes on the changes made by Laud, and on some technical terms.]

STATUTA COLLEGII

SANCTÆ ET INDIVIDUÆ TRINITATIS JUXTA DUBLIN A SERENISSIMA REGINA ELIZABETHA FUNDATI

Septembris 23, 1628.

Quod quæsitum est in Sociorum juramento Cap. 7, quid Ecclesiastici Beneficii noïe intelligatur, post varios tractatus, reque diligenter consideratâ, universaliter quodvis Beneficium Ecclesiasticum cum curâ, sive quod sine curâ dicatur, eo nomine intelligi censemus.

Guiliel. Bedell, Præp.

Septembris 24, 1628.

Quod dubitatum est de Clausulâ Cap. 6ti, *Quod si quem Uxorem duxisse compertum sit*, ei an ad Matrimonium quoque initum, antequam illud Statutum conditum esset, extendatur: cum Leges (quod dici solet) non respiciant; id de Uxore tantum post eam Legem ducta intelligendum judicamus.

Guiliel. Bedell, Præp.

APPENDIX

IN NOMINE SANCTISSIMÆ ET INDIVIDUÆ TRINITATIS

In Statuta Collegii Dubliniensis

PREFATIO.

Permagnam vim in doctrinarum studiis existere, ad excolendos hominum Animos, et a ferâ agrestique vitâ ad humanitatis et Religionis officia traducendos, vel inde facile constare potest, quod non solum priscis temporibus, apud Hebreos, Ægyptios, Græcos, et Romanos, Literarum politiorum disciplinæ viguerunt, sed etiam posterioribus hisce seculis, eædem (postquam Barbarorum incursionibus profligatæ aliquandiu a communi hominum consuetudine exulassent) revocatæ sint, et apud plerasque nationes in magno honore constitutæ. Ut exteras nationes omittamus, intuemur ANGLIAM nostram, in quâ tot passim extructæ Scholæ et tam illustres Academiæ testantur, omnium Artium quibus Sapientiæ Præcepta continentur rationem et disciplinam summæ curæ clarissimis Principibus et Magnatibus fuisse. Neque vero dignas tantum existimârunt quæ ab indigenis Anglis studiose colerentur, sed cum in iis tantum ad Pietatem et Humanitatem momenti situm esse perspicerent, de literarum quasi Coloniâ aliquâ in HIBERNIAM (in quâ olim floruerant) reducendâ cogitarunt. Et factum est singulari præpotentis Dei Providentia et misericordia erga Gentem Hibernicam Antichristianæ Religionis Tyrannide oppressam, ut Serenissima Princeps Elisabetha Collegium SANCTÆ TRINITATI juxta Urbem Dubliniensem extruendum curârit: quod et annuis redditibus dotavit, et ACADEMIÆ privilegiis ornavit. Id exemplum ejus ut Solii ita Pietatis successor JACOBUS (Regum quos unquam viderat BRITANNIA longe doctissimus) secutus, magnis id proventibus et Latifundiis auxit. CAROLUS vero ejusdem pietatis ex asse hæres, Diplomate ad

Proregem scripto privilegiorum a Decessoribus suis indultorum se conservatorem indulgentissimum professus, studium insuper suum erga id Collegium tanquam veræ Religionis Cultusque civilis et bonarum Artium Seminarium, clementissime testatus est : Quoniam vero inter privilegia a Serenissima Regina ELISABETHA Collegio indulta illud præcipuum est, quo Præposito et Sociis ejusdem Collegii Leges, Statuta, et Ordinationes, pro eodem pie et feliciter gubernando, condendi potestas conceditur ; quod etsi tentatum, nondum perfectum et absolutum est : Nos Præpositus et Socii quorum nomina subscripta sunt, pro facultate nobis concessa, officio nostro consentaneum duximus, quæ a decessoribus nostris recte et utiliter sancita sunt, quæque ad Collegii regimen accommodatissima videntur, in unum corpus conferre, et separatis quibusdam Capitibus comprehendere.

De Cultu Divino.

Caput Primum.

NEMINI obscurum esse potest, quam infeliciter succedant omnia cum præpotenti Deo debita veræ Pietatis officia minime deferantur. *Primum,* inquit CHRISTUS, *quærite regnum Dei, et justitiam ejus, et ista omnia vobis adjicientur.* Hinc igitur admoniti, primo [1] de iis præcipiendum putavimus, quæ ad Religionis officia pertinent. Preces Deo publice in Sacello offerantur mane et vesperi. Qua autum hora preces inchoandæ sint, de eo Præpositus Collegii et major pars Sociorum Seniorum statuito. Formula sit ea, quæ in publica Ecclesiæ Hibernicæ Liturgia præscribitur. Et quoniam locorum sacrorum respectus ipsi quoque religioni reverentiam conciliat, Sacellum anterius et interius decorè semper habeatur, non modo in sartis tectis, et fenestris, ac pavimentis, sed mensa sacra decenter cooperta sedibusque a situ et pulvere

---

[1] Laud overlooked this word in adapting his Chapter IX. from this.

detersis. Neque in Sacello quicquam nisi sacrum personare fas esto.

VOLUMUS autem et statuimus, ut e Collegii studentibus singuli Artium Magistri, sive Socii fuerint, sive Sociorum Commensales, sollenne illud publicarum precum munus per se aut per alium diligenter obeant. Quod si quis vicem suam neque ipse obeat, neque per alium supplendam curaverit, ita ut preces ad horam constitutam omissæ fuerint, nolumus illi ullum vel invaletudinis vel negotiorum prætextum sufficere, quominus quinque solidis Anglicanis continuo et absque ulteriori causæ examinatione mulctetur.[1] Multam impositam delinquenti Præpositus, vel in ejus absentia Vicepræpositus, aut Decanus exigito, idque pro ratione præscripta in Statuto de Multis exigendis.

Si quis Studentium qui non sit in illustriori aliqua facultate Baccalaureus, a precibus abfuerit, puniatur quemadmodum aliis deinceps Statutis præscribetur.

Ante cibum quotidie in Aula prælegatur Caput aliquod veteris aut novi TESTAMENTI. Lectores sunto Scholares, Baccalaurei et Sophistæ qui stipendiis Collegii aluntur, quisque secundum ordinem senioritatis suæ. Initio cujusque lectionis precationem fundat Lector ad hanc formulam. DOMINE, *revela oculos nostros, ut intuemur mirabilia de Lege tua.* Finita Lectione, subjungat alta voce ; *Da nobis Intellectum,* DOMINE, *et observabimus Legem tuam ; toto Corde observabimus eam.* Inde benedicat mensæ hac formula :

Oculi omnium ad te respiciunt Domine, tu das iis escam eorum in tempore opportuno : Aperis tu manum tuam, et imples omne animal benedictione tua. Miserere nostri te quæsumus Domine, tuisque donis, quæ de Tua benignitate sumus percepturi, benedicito, per Christum Dominum nostrum.

Finito prandio et cæna, Gratias agat hac formula :

Tibi laus, tibi honor, tibi Gloria, O beata et gloriosa Trinitas. Sit nomen Domini benedictum, et nunc et in perpetuum. Laudamus

---

[1] This absolute fine if the reader disappoints is still inflicted.

APPENDIX

te, benignissime Pater, pro serenissimis, Regina Elisabetha hujus Collegii conditrice, Jacobo ejusdem munificentissimo auctore, Carolo conservatore, cæterisque benefactoribus nostris : rogantes te ut his tuis donis recte et ad Tuam Gloriam utentes in hoc Seculo, te una cum fidelibus in futuro fœliciter perfruamur, per Christum Dominum nostrum.[1]

Porro Lector post medium prandii aut Cænæ sistat se coram Præposito aut ejus locum tenente, et Sententiam aliquam e Lectione memoriter recitet clara voce, unde occasio nascatur Sermonis religiosi. Atque ut Sacræ Scripturæ contextus omnibus fiat familiaris, volumus ut quisque si non BIBLIAM saltem NOVUM TESTAMENTUM habeat de proprio.

Sacrosanctum Eucharistæ Sacramentum secunda ad minimum Dominica cujusque Termini celebretur ; præter diem Natalis Domini, Paschæ, Pentecostes, et Dominicæ quæ dicitur Trinitatis. Assistat celebranti quispiam e sociis, in ordine saltem Diaconatus, quem Præpositus ad id munus advocaverit.

De sanctificandis per quosvis studentes diebus Dominicis, qui Collegio præsunt, ii solicite et diligenter providento. Locum igitur et tempus sacris concionibus habendis constitutum singuli in Collegio studentes seposito omni prætextu semper obeunto, et in eisdem audiendis, se quanta cum Reverentia et Attentione fieri potest gerunto. Si qui abesse deprehendantur, ii pro qualitate delicti et personarum puniantur, Quin etiam si qui diebus Dominicis otiose in plateis substiterint, aut ingrediantur Tabernas, aut ludicris cujuscunque generis exercitationibus intersint, in eos severe animadvertatur.

Volumus insuper, ut Præpositus vel quispiam e senioribus Sociis ad Catechistæ munus quotannis eligatur. Is quolibet die Sabbathi hora secunda pomeridiana, per singulas Anni Septimanas, in aliquo Catechismi Capite adhibitis interroga-

---

[1] These graces are still in daily use with Laud's variants that *sperant* is substituted for *respiciunt*, and *recte ad Tuam*, &c., is said omitting *et*. Laud adds an English Collect to come after the 3rd Collect at Morning Prayer, *pro Benedictione Studiorum*, and also directs a shortened Form of Morning Prayer.

tionibus et respensionibus Scholares erudito. Quinetiam per singulas cujusque termini septimanas, die et hora a Præposito et majori parte Sociorum Seniorum præscriptis, Catechismi Caput aliquod oratione continua accuratius tractet et persequatur. Quo in munere sic Catechistam versari placet, ut intra spatium unius Anni singula Catechisticæ institutionis Capita percurrat, et interpretetur. Hujus Auditores sunto tam Baccalaurei quam studentes juniores.

Porro Præpositi et Sociorum Seniorum erit, videre, ne quæ Pontificiæ, aut alterius hæreticæ Religionis Opinio. intra Collegii fines alatur, aut propugnetur, sive publice sive privatim. Quod si acciderit, volumus ut quam primum impiæ Opinionis progressus intercipiatur. Præterea nemo in Sociorum numerum eligatur, qui Pontificiæ Religioni quatenus a Catholica et Orthodoxa dissentit, et Romani Pontificis jurisdictioni per solenne et publicum juramentum non renunciaverit.[1]

De Qualitate et Officio Praepositi.

Cap. 2^m.

Exigit Politici Corporis ratio, ut ante omnia Caput constituatur a quo cetera membra dirigantur. Statuimus igitur ut Præpositus a Senioribus sociis eligatur, moribus probus, vita integra, et fama inviolata, annos natus ad minimum triginta. Et qui deinceps eligetur non solum Magister in Artibus esto, et ad binas Prælectiones Theologicas quovis termino publice in Sacello præstandas alligatus, sed etiam Baccalaureus in Theologia, vel Professor in eadem facultate et in sacris ordinibus constitutus. In ejus Electione volumus et Statuimus ut, cæteris paribus, extraneo educatus in

---

[1] Though retaining some details, this Chapter is largely modified in Laud's Chapter IX. He specially directs that no other than the Anglican Catechism shall be taught. The Holy Communion is to be celebrated by the Provost, or senior Doctor of Divinity in the College, though he may be assisted (even in Laud's statute) by a deacon.

Collegio præferatur. Nec habeat quicunque electus fuerit, quamdiu Locum et munus Præpositi supplet, Ecclesiastica, ut vocant, Beneficia uno plura, idque non alibi quam intra tria milliaria a Collegio ad Ecclesiam parochialem Ecclesiastici beneficii. Sit porro in re familiari providus, res Collegii et negotia ita administret, ut non suum, sed Collegii commodum quærere videatur. Et neque gratiæ in causis cognoscendis decernendisve, neque odio, neque ulli animi perturbationi pareat, sed æquitatem ducem semper sequatur. Huic volumus singulos Socios, Scholares, et Collegii Ministros suo Ordini subesse; eique in licitis et honestis, exercitium Scholasticum, aut dicti Collegii Regimen, aut commodum, aut honorem tangentibus, sine murmure obedire et parere. Officiariorum et Lectorum imprimis curam habeat, ac illos si muneri suo desint (uno ex Sociis Senioribus consentiente) pro arbitrio suo puniat : nisi pœnæ aliqua expressa mentio pro ea culpa in Statutis fiat. Quo in Officio eum manere volumus, quoad bene se honesteque gesserit, et secundum Statutorum præscripta vixerit.

NOTE.—Laud, adopting this Chapter generally, makes the following modifications :—(1) The Provost is allowed to accept any Ecclesiastical dignity short of a Bishoprick, provided it does not interfere with his residence and duties ; (2) His power of punishment is made more explicit and absolute in that (*a*) the Provost need not have the consent of any Senior Fellow, (*b*) in all cases not specified by the Statutes he has power to inflict what he deems a suitable punishment ; (3) he is required to be celibate, and to resign the Provostship if he marries.

DE JURAMENTO PRAEPOSITI.

Cap. 3.

Statuimus, ut qui ad Præposituram Collegii eligatur, hoc juramentum sequens publice in Sacello præstet :

EGO, G.C. huic Collegio SANCTÆ TRINITATIS hoc sacramento meipsum adstringo, ac DEO teste promitto ; primo me veram Christi religionem ex animo complexurum ; Scripturæ Authoritatem hominum judiciis præpositurum, Regulam

Vitæ, et summam fidei ex verbo DEI petiturum ; cætera quæ ex verbo DEI non probantur pro humanis et non necessariis habiturus ;[1] Auctoritatem Regiam in omnibus summam, et externorum Episcoporum jurisdictioni minime subjectam æstimaturum, et contrarias verbo Dei opiniones omni voluntate et mente refutaturum. Deinde me omnia dicti Collegii beneficia, fundos, prædia, possessiones, dominia, proventus, jura, Libertates, privilegia, omnia denique bona sine imminutione et vastatione quantum in me situm erit, conservaturum, et administraturum. Statuta hujus Collegii pro virili mea in omnibus servaturum, iisque omnibus quæ ex eorum præscripto gerentur meum assēsum accommodaturum. Omnesque et singulos Socios, et Discipulos, Pensionarios, Sizatores et subsizatores,[2] et cætera Collegii membra, ex iisdem Legibus et Statutis, sine ullius generis, aut conditionis, aut personarum respectu, gratia aut odio recturum et defensurum : atque ut prædicta omnia legitime et salutariter ab aliis administrentur ac defendantur curaturum. Tum, me neque in meis, neque in alienis negotiis (quia præsentia Præpositi necessaria judicatur) amplius sex in Anno septimanis [3] a Collegio abfuturum, nisi vel Collegii, vel Regni negotia, vel Regia Auctoritas me alio avocaverit, aut vis, morbus, contagium, aut alia quæpiam causa necessaria, a Sociis senioribus aut majore eorum parte,[4] intra sedecim dies ante vel post dictas sex septimanas expletas approbanda, impediverit. Denique si loco motus fuero, aut si sponte cessero, me omnia Collegii bona quæ in mea potestate sunt, aut esse debent, Præsidi et Quæstoribus sive Thesaurariis Collegii vel statim si id fieri potest, vel intra quindecim dies sine controversia et imminutione redditurum. Postremo juro, si munere Præpositi jure et legitime abdicatus fuero, me nullam Litem Actionemve Collegio, aut his qui me legitime abdicarunt

---

[1] This clause was omitted by Laud as smacking of Puritanism.
[2] There were no subsizars in Laud's time.
[3] Laud allows two months.
[4] In Laud's book this power is reserved for the Chancellor or Archbishop of Dublin, Visitors.

ea de causa unquam in posterum intentaturum. Item quod non impetrabo dispensationem aliquam contra juramenta mea prædicta, aut contra Ordinationes et Statuta Collegii, vel ipsorum aliquod, nec Dispensationem hujusmodi per alium vel alios publice vel occulte impetrari aut fieri procurabo, directe vel indirecte, nec impetratam qualitercunque acceptabo.[1]

Hæc omnia et singula observabo, ita me Deus adjuvet, in CHRISTO JESU.[2]

De Senatu Collegii, Constante ex Præposito et Sociis Senioribus.

Cap. 4.

Quia in Academica Societate bene constituta ea Ratio plerumque tenetur Societatis administrandæ quæ ad Aristocratiæ formam proxime accedit, existimavimus non potuisse nos huic Collegio melius consulere, quam si in eo gubernando ad modum Aristocraticum procederemus. Ac proinde cum potestas nobis concessa sit, sanciendi eas Leges quæ ad hujus Collegii gubernationem aptissimæ judicabuntur, et cum nihil de numero Sociorum ad Collegii regimen Præposito adjunctorum definitum adhuc habeamus, Volumus et statuimus ut quos Præposito vel charta fundationis, vel Collegii particularia Statuta, ad meliorem rerum singularum procurationem adjunxerint, ii Sociorum septenario tantum numero constent, sintque ex iis qui suo gradu et ordine senioritatem inter alios Socios obtinent, et idcirco Socii Seniores appellentur ; reliqui vero Juniores. Senorium Sociorum authoritas qualis esse debeat, partim Chartæ prædictæ legibus, partim variis Collegii Statutis expositum est. Volumus igitur ut Præpositus et horum Seniorum pars major, nempe quatuor, rem quamvis in deliberatione positam definiant et concludant. In Seniorum numerum

---

[1] This clause is omitted by Laud.
[2] *Tactis sacrosanctis Christi Evangeliis,* Laud. This taking of oaths was against Bedell's Puritan principles.

si quando locus aliquis prorsus vacaverit, e Sociis Junioribus proximus suo ordine et vice succedat, et deinceps honestiora stipendia accipiat : ita tamen ut judicio Præpositi et majoris partis Seniorum probatus, intra duos menses secundum Chartam fundationis nova Electione, sive admissione inter hos septem (quos solos proprio nomine Sociorum in Charta fundationis accipiendos decernimus) cooptetur.

NOTE.—This Chapter was wholly rewritten by Laud, to whom the idea of an aristocracy ruling the College was abominable. He made the Provost absolute in his control, but using the seven Senior Fellows as assessors. If any of these was absent after any summons from the Provost, the latter was to command their votes in addition to his own.

The confirming election of a Senior Fellow two months after his formal selection was also abolished.

Moreover, in all acts of the governing body the Provost (or Vice-Provost) must be present, and apparently consenting. He was given an absolute and explicit veto in matters (such as leases) which required the College seal.

DE SCHOLARIBUS.

Cap. 5.

Reliquum Collegii corpus e Scholaribus constat; quo nomine tum Discipuli, tum Socii Juniores comprehenduntur. In Discipulorum electione volumus et statuimus, ut præcipua ratio habeatur Ingenii, doctrinæ, virtutis et inopiæ. Et quo magis quisque ex eligendorum numero his rebus excedit, eo magis, ut æquum est, præferatur. Omnes qui Discipulatum in Collegio petunt, ab electoribus ab hora octava antemeridiana ad decimam, et ab hora secunda pomeridiana ad quartam, per duos dies diligenter quid in Grammatica et literis humanioribus possint, examinentur. Atque die electionis, omnes qui Discipulatum petunt nomina sua et comitatum Regni in quibus nati sunt, Præposito et Sociis Senioribus tradenda curent, quæ coram omnibus electoribus recitentur. Sumantur autem potissimum et eligantur ex eorum numero (si modo idonei sint, et cæteris pares reperiantur) qui in Scholis Dubliniensibus educati sunt, aut nati in hujus Regni comitatibus ac locis, in quibus Collegium prædia, fundos, proventus ac reditus habet : ut quorum labore ac sudoribus Collegii membra omnia et singula sustentantur, eorum potissimum liberi in eodem educentur, et virtute ac humanioribusque literis ad reipublicæ utilitatem instituantur. Alioqui ex aliis regni partibus, aut Dominiis Coronæ Magnæ Britañiæ subditis indifferenter ad numerum supplendum qui maxime idonei videbuntur, semper sumantur. Nullus hæres qui jam sit, aut patre mortuo futurus sit hæres, cujus hæreditas summam decem librarum excesserit, in hunc numerum cooptetur. Nemo eligatur in Discipulum, qui non sit ad Logicam in aula discendam idoneus. Sociorum et Scholarium Electores iidem sunto. Post Electionem a Præposito quam primum commode fieri potest, omnibus Electoribus præsentibus, in Discipulos admittantur. Senioritas Discipulorum tempore admissionis præscribatur a Præposito et majore parte Seniorum Sociorum, sed habita ratione ætatis, doctrinæ, et virtutis. Discipuli autem stipendia nemo diutius accipiat, quam donec Magistri in Artibus gradum adeptus fuerit, aut per Leges Academiæ annuarias adipisci poterit, aut in Socium eligatur.

NOTE.—This Chapter was adopted by Laud, adding an annual day of election (Trinity Monday) and expunging the clause by which the seniority of the scholars was determined by the Board on the day of election. Seniority on the College books was the determining cause till 1851 ; since that time, the list is arranged in order of merit.

In Laud's Statutes the next Chapter (VI.) gives the oath of the scholars, swearing allegiance to the king, and obedience to the laws and Regulations of the College, *but containing no declaration of creed.*

DE SOCIORUM ELECTIONE.
Cap. 6.

Volumus et statuimus ut in Socios Probationarios sive juniores ii solum cooptentur quorum de Religione, Doctrina, et moribus, tum Præpositus, tum Socii Seniores honestam et bonam spem Animis conceperint, quique septem minimum terminos, post susceptum Gradum Baccalaureatus in Artibus, Studiis operam dederint. Discipuli ipsius Collegii semper præferantur, atque similiter tenuiores ditioribus, doctiores indoctioribus, et probiores minus probis; modo cætera respondeant. Eligendi potestas sit penes Præpositum et majorem partem Sociorum Seniorum. Præpositum semper tum domi esse volumus, nisi morbo aut aliqua causa gravissima præpeditum. Cujus locum post viginti quatuor dies (si Præpositus interesse non possit) suppleat Vice-Præpositus. Modus autem erit hujusmodi. Primum omnes Electores memores juramenti Collegio jam præstiti, provideant et statuant, se neminem in Socium electuros, qui sit Infamia notatus, de Hæresi probabiliter suspectus, aut moribus et vitæ consuetudine dissolutus, sed eos duntaxat, quos teste conscientia idoneos judicaverint. Et quo magis libere in hoc versentur, volumus ut si ad eos aut eorum quemlibet literæ vel nuncius a quacunque persona in favorem alicujus candidati mittantur, is pro ea vice omnino inhabilis ad capessendum locum Socii judicetur. Quod si quispiam eorum quibus eligendi potestas tributa est, vel munere donatus, vel spe muneris inductus, cuiquam suffragatus esse deprehensus fuerit, et coram Præposito reliquisque Sociis Senioribus de eo legitime fuerit convictus, Collegio expellatur.

Quatuor diebus proxime præcedentibus electionis diem, ab hora octava antemeridiana ad decimam, et ab hora secunda pomeridiana ad quartam, omnes Electores diligenter exquirant, quid singuli eligendi, sive sint Baccalaurei, sive sint Magistri, in bonis Literis efficere possint: Primo die in Dialectica et Mathematica; secundo in Philosophia tum naturali tum morali; tertio, in linguarum cognitione, in historiis et poetis, et in toto genere humanioris literaturæ; quarto, in scribendo de themate aliquo et versibus componendis. Qui autem nomen suum, et nomen Comitatus in quo natus fuerit, ante electionis diem Præposito aut (eo absente) Vice-Præposito tradendum non curaverit, aut qui dictis quatuor diebus, horis præscriptis Electorum questiones examinationesque non sustinuerit, in eligendorum numero pro eo tempore non habeatur, neque in ea electione in coetum Sociorum cooptetur. Sumantur autem potissimum et eligantur ex numero eorum (si modo idonei habeantur, et cæteris pares) qui nati sunt in Regno Hiberniæ : alioqui ex aliis locis coronæ Magnæ Britanniæ subjectis, ad numerum supplendum, qui maxime idonei videbuntur semper sumantur. Postridie ejus diei, vel intra triduum quo Electio facta est, omnes electi admittantur in plenum jus juniorum Sociorum, et percipiant ea commoda et fructus, qui hujusmodi Sociis ex statutis præscribuntur. Et si quispiam eorum die admissionis vel ægrotaverit, vel justa de causa abfuerit, nihilominus tamen senioritatem suam habeat, pro ratione inferius præscripta. Senioritas Sociorum constituatur, si teneatur, juxta ordinem et prioritatem admissionis in Sociorum numerum, nisi disparitas gradus aut anni impediat. Jus Sociorum retineant Socii, quamdiu per Chartam fundationis, aut aliam a Regia Majestate impetrandam permissum erit. Quod si quem Sociorum aut Scholarium uxorem duxisse compertum sit, eum Societatis omni jure privari volumus.

NOTE.—This is Cap. VII. in Laud. He, however, abolishes the condition of seven terms standing, which Bedell had taken from Christ's College, Cambridge. He fixes Trinity Monday as the only day of election, and it has so remained till to-day. The admission was made more formal, and in the Chapel. The submission of juniors to seniors is made more explicit, and the Fellowships made for life instead of a vague or seven years' tenure, the existing Fellows being specially excluded from the new privilege of life tenure. It is clear from the wording that a new Charter was already in prospect when this chapter was written.

JURAMENTUM ELECTI SOCII, VEL DISCIPULI.

Cap. 7.

Ego A.B. electus in numerum Sociorum (Discipulorum) hujus Collegii, sancte coram Deo profiteor, me sacræ Scripturæ authoritatem in Religione summam agnoscere, et quæcunque in sancto Dei verbo continentur vere ex animo credere, et pro facultate mea omnibus opinionibus quas vel pontificii vel alii contra sacræ Scripturæ veritatem tuentur, constanter repugnaturum. Quod ad Regiam Auctoritatem attinet, Serenissimi Regis CAROLI eam secundum Deum summam in regnis Angliæ, Scotiæ et Hiberniæ esse agnosco, et nullius externi Principis aut Pontificis potestati obnoxiam. Profiteor insuper me nullum Ecclesiasticum Beneficium jam possidere, nec quamdiu in hoc Collegio versabor, ejusdem sumptibus aliqua ex parte sustentatus, deinceps accepturum; nisi in Urbe Dubliniensi, vel in loco ita vicino ut et discipuli (Socii) et fidelis Ministri officio defungi possim. Distantiam Loci intelligo, trium milliarium ab urbe Dubliniensi.

Quinetiam Statutis Collegii, quæ legitima authoritate sancita fuerint, et in quorum approbationem Præpositus et major pars Sociorum Seniorum consensuri sint, libenter obtemperabo, et ea observanda curabo : scholastica exercitia singula, quæ præstari a me oportet, diligenter præstabo ; et si mihi cura prælegendi aliis, aut officii alicujus ad bonum Collegii regimen obeundi commissa fuerit, ea studiose perfungar. Collegii et singulorum in eo studentium, præsertim Præpositi et eorum qui præsunt salutem et dignitatem, pacem, et commodum, pro virili mea tuebor, et procurabo : consilia, coitiones, conjurationes, et insidias quæ contra quemcunque in Collegio degentem fiunt, si de iisdem cognovero, omni honesta ratione quantum potero impediam ; et iis quorum intererit renunciabo. Præposito in omnibus licitis et honestis promptissima voluntate et studio parebo, quamdiu in Collegio versabor ; ac proinde factiones contra Præpositum et partium studia nunquam inibo, nec iniri procurabo, sed quantum in me est vitabo, et ne ab aliis ineantur impediam. Studiorum finis erit mihi Theologiæ Professio, ut Ecclesiæ Dei prodesse possim, obeundo ministerio Verbi, si aliter Deus mentem meam deinceps non disposuerit. In negotiis Collegii administrandis quæ curanda suscepero

APPENDIX

fidelem operam præstabo. Hæc omnia supra memorata in me recipio, Deoque teste me sedulo facturum promitto, ac spondeo.

NOTE.—Laud extends the right of holding a living to fifteen miles distance, and if there be no cure to thirty miles, but in neither case to exceed £10 sterling in value. Provision is made for a Jurist and a Medicus among the Fellows, and the oath is made by touching the Gospels. There are variations also here as elsewhere in the wording, which do not affect the sense.

DE TUTORUM AC PUPILLORUM OFFICIO.

Cap. 8.

Ea fere est Academicarum societatum consuetudo, ut præter membra cujusque propria, quosdam Sociorum Commensales Pensionarios, et Sizatores, quos appellant, in Collegia admittant. Quoniam vero juvenilis ætatis imbecillitas provectiorum consilio et prudentia sustentanda est ac moderanda, Statuimus et ordinamus, ut nemo vel ex Discipulis, vel in Sociorum convictum admissis, vel Pensionariis, aut omnino studii causa in Collegio commorantibus, Tutore careat. Qui autem caruerit, nisi intra quindecim dies aliquem sibi paraverit, Collegio ejiciatur. Quod si quis in Collegium admissus vel admittendus, ad persequenda doctrinæ studia, id gratiæ per se obtinere nequeat, ut in alicujus tutelam recipiatur, volumus ut Præpositus et major pars Seniorum illi de Tutore provideant. Quo casu si quis designatus ad id munus forte renuerit, volumus ut pænam contemptus adversus Collegii regimen incurrat, nisi justam recusationis causam afferre possit, eaque a Præposito et majore parte Seniorum approbetur. Ac cum Tutoris officium sit multi laboris et curæ, quo alacrius et fidelius munere suo defungatur, placet ut quivis Pupillus (nisi de ipsius inopia plane et liquido constiterit) Tutori suo annuum salarium gestæ tutelæ nomine persolvat. Pensionarii nempe et Scholares Collegii sumptibus sustentati quadraginta solidos : commensales vero

Sociorum quatuor libellas. Placet insuper ut nemo pro pupillo re et actu admittatur, priusquam Tutori partem dimidiam et annui salarii pro tutela, et expensarum pro communiis faciendarum in manu tradiderit. Neque admissus retineatur diutius, nisi Tutori caveat, tum de certa et expedita solutione debitorum et Collegio debendorum; tum si Sociorum Commensalis fuerit, de calice argenteo ad usum Collegii conferendo. Pupilli Tutoribus pareant honoremque paternum ac reverentiam deferant, quorum studium, labor, et diligentia in illis ad Pietatem et Scientias informandis ponuntur. Tutores (quos non alios quam Præpositum et Socios esse volumus) sedulo quæ discenda sunt pupillos suos per singulos dies doceant, quæque etiam agenda sunt moneant. Omnia Pupillorum cujusque generis et ordinis expensa Tutores Collegio præstent, et intra decem dies cujusque mensis finiti æs debitum pro se et suis omnibus pupillis officiario solvant : quod ni fecerint, tantisper commeatu priventur, dum Pecunia ab ipsis et Pupillis ipsorum debita solvatur. Cautumque esto, ne pupillus quispiam stipendium suum ab officiario recipiat, vel rationem per se cum eo ineat; sed utrumque per Tutorem proprium, sub pœna commeatus menstrui a dicto Tutore Collegio solvendi, fieri volumus. Quod si Tutor quispiam aut Pupillis ad pietatem et bonas artes quotidie erudiendis, aut eorum dissolutis moribus reformandis non attenderit; si pupillos vel Urbem Dubliniensem frequentare, vel in Sodaliciis aut Exercitiis minime necessariis obeundis tempus Studiis aptum et destinatum ponere patiatur; ordinamus ut si post binas admonitiones majorem in re pupillari curam non adhibuerit quinque Solidis multetur. Quod si nihilominus se in pupillis erudiendis et reformandis negligentius gesserit, ordinario cujusque Septimanæ Commeatu eo usque privetur, dum Tutoris Officio eum diligenter perfunctum esse constiterit. Pupilli omnes quocunque vocentur nomine, volumus et quoad Gradum Bacclaureatus susceperint, iisdem Legibus ac Statutis teneantur et pareant, quibus Discipuli et Scholares Collegii expensis sustentati, et eodem modo si deliquerint puniantur : Exceptis Nobilibus, et filiis hæredibus alicujus Consiliarii Regii.

NOTE.—Laud, Cap. X., gives the Provost the right of assigning pupils to a Fellow ; the alleged misuse of this privilege by Provost Hely Hutchinson caused a celebrated visitation in 1791. The Tutor's fees are left to the discretion of the Tutor, the maximum being still £4 per annum for Fellow Commoners, 40s. for Pensioners, 20s. for Scholars. The ordinance that Fellow Commoners should present argent to the College was dropped, though the practice continued as before.

DE MODESTIA ET MORUM HONESTATE COLENDA ; ITEMQUE DE TUENDA COLLEGII EXISTIMATIONE PUBLICA.

Cap. 9.

Nihil est quod literatis plus adferat ornamentum, quam modestia et morum Integritas. Tum ad publicam Collegii existimationem permagni interest, eam opinionem vulgo concipi, vigere in eo curam boni regiminis, ac morum disciplinam, Academicosque dignos esse, qui nomine diligentiæ in Literarum studiis commendentur. Idcirco ut quilibet Academicus ad tuendam hanc Collegii existimationem incumbat, tam vitando ea quæ illam quovis modo violare posse videbuntur, quam iis in communi vita persequendis, quæ ipsi conservandæ et augendæ inservire queant, vehementer hortamur, et rogamus, denunciantes interim, pro eo quo Collegium et Collegii bonum nomen complectimur amore singulari, non impune laturum esse, qui in hoc genere deliquerit. Statuimus igitur et ordinamus, ut inferiores omnes submisse erga seniores et reverenter se gerant, Discipuli juniores erga Baccalaureos, hi erga Magistros artium, Socii Juniores erga Seniores tanquam Patres, omnes denique erga Præpositum tanquam summum Moderatorem. Nemo nondum graduatus in Urbem exeat nisi Tutoris permissu, significato per Chirographum ipsius : qui secus fecerit, primo tempore commeatu unius hebdomadæ, secundo duarum, tertio mensis mulctetur, quarto ex consensu

Præpositi et majoris partis seniorum Sociorum Collegio amoveatur. Seditionis domesticæ, detractionis, dissentionis, rixæ authores, itemque aliorum percussores, primo tempore commeatu menstruo, secundo trimestri multentur, tertio Collegio expellantur. Omnes lites domesticæ intra Collegium et cognoscantur, et dijudicentur. Qui foras aliquem in jus vocaverit, sine Præpositi et Sociorum consensu, Collegio amoveatur. Dissentiones inter Socios et Discipulos ortas, si fieri potest, intra biduum a Præposito et Sociis sedentur ; sin id fieri nequit, quatuor Socii Seniores per dissentientes eligendi, cum Præposito, aut eo absente Vice-Præposito, litem disceptent, eamque cum æquitate dirimant ; et quam illi sententiam tulerint, in ea quiescant dissentientes : qui secus fecerit, Collegio amoveatur. Statuimus quoque, mandamus, et hortamur, ut Præpositus, Socii, Discipuli, et cæteri in Collegio vitam degentes, concordiam, unitatem, pacem, et mutuam inter se charitatem pro virili alant, foveant, et observent : scurrilitatem et obscæna verba, scommata, probra et scandala verbo et facto omnino vitent ; præsertim adversus eos qui in Regimine Collegii funguntur officio suo. Quod si quispiam in his deliquerit, arbitrio Præpositi et majoris partis Sociorum Seniorum puniatur. Quod si ter pro illis castigatus non abstinuerit, Collegio expellatur.

Quinetiam statuimus, ne quis Collegii, vel alterius muros aut sepimenta transcendat, aut fores fenestrasve diffringat : qui semel fecerit, si ætate adultus fuerit, commeatu trimestri privetur ; si ætate puer, virgis castigetur : qui autem bis, Collegio amoveatur. Eadem pœna multetur, qui furtum admiserit, aut aliorum pomaria expilaverit. Porro aleæ aut chartarum ludo nemo in Collegio omnino utatur : qui in hoc deliquerit, primo a Præposito admoneatur ; secundo commeatu menstruo careat ; tertio admonitus Collegio amoveatur. Nemo canes venaticos, accipitres, aut aves vocales in Collegio nutriat teneatve : neque aucupio, neque venationi sit deditus : qui contra fecerit, puniatur, ut supra dictum est. Nulli lusus discipulis in Area vel hortis Collegii permittantur, nec Discipulorum ulla fiant in area conventicula, nec ibi colloquendi causa moram faciant, neque in aula, nisi tempore merendæ dum simul bibunt. Post prandium vero et cœnam ex aula sine mora discedant. Neque quisquam prædictorum in urbe aut in alieno cubiculo, nisi petita a Præposito aut Tutore facultate, aliquando pernoctet. Qui in his deliquerit, primo a Præposito menstruo commeatu privetur, secundo trimestri, tertio per Præpositum et majorem partem Sociorum seniorum Collegio privetur. Quod si ejusmodi causa inciderit, ut nullo modo ad veniam petendam possit venire, tum si postea ad Præpositum intra viginti duas horas accesserit, suamque Causam illi probaverit, eum tum neutiquam multari volumus. Statuimus porro, ut nemo sociorum aut discipulorum extra aulam prandeat cænetve, nisi petita a Præposito venia : Qui secus fecerit, pro toto prandio aut cœna solvat. Atque ut nunquam supra quatuor e Sociis in Cubiculis prandeant aut cænent ; excepto semper cubiculo Præpositi, nisi forte vel Socius ægrotaverit, vel peregrinum invitaverit. Quinetiam si cujusvis vel insolentiori consuetudine vitæ, intra domesticos Collegii parietes, aut alibi, vel frequentiori in urbem Dubliniensem profectione, vel sodalitiorum aut ædium suspectarum frequentatione evenerit, ut Collegium publice male audiat, nomine neglecti regiminis, aut incuriæ in studiis doctrinarum, volumus et ordinamus, ut is coram Præposito et senioribus citatus, a Præposito pro prima vice admoneatur tantummodo et increpetur (nisi crimen ejusmodi fuerit, de quo cautum est Statuto de pœna majorum Criminum) : si admonitus non abstinuerit ab eo, quo aliqua Collegio Labes aspergitur, per quatuor Septimanas Commeatu suo privetur. Quod si idem crimen tertio incurrisse constiterit, pro delicti gravitate graviori censura puniatur, ea scilicet quæ Præposito et majori parti Seniorum par tanto scandalo videbitur. Statuimus etiam atque ordinamus, ut Socii et Discipuli singuli habeant Togam, eaque semper utantur in Collegio et si commode pro temporis ratione fieri possit, euntes in Oppidum :

exceptis Doctoribus et Baccalaureis Theologiæ. Permittimus vero ut singuli studentes cujuscunque gradus et conditionis extra Academiam et Urbem Dubliniensem pro arbitratu vestiantur ; dummodo decenter et vestimentis obscuri cujuspiam Coloris induti incedant. Quod si quis hanc legem violet, primo sex denariis multetur, secundo duodecim, tertio duobus Solidis, quarto si admonitus a Præposito non se emendaverit, pro qualitate Contumaciæ puniatur. Porro statuimus et ordinamus ut nullus prædictorum armis aut Telis, veluti Gladiis, Sicis, aut Pugionibus in Collegio aut in Urbe utatur, nisi gravi de causa ei a Præpositio permissum sit. Quod si quis hoc Statutum violaverit, primo Commeatu duarum hebdomadarum, secundo menstruo, tertio Collegio privetur.

NOTE.—Laud, Cap. XI., adds a permission to appeal to the Visitors from the decision of the Provost and Board, also a permission to play at dice and cards at Christmas time, publicly, in the Hall. Fellows having benefices outside the city are allowed to keep a horse. There is also less provision for hospitality, and for Fellows dining in their rooms, in Laud's chapter.

DE VICE-PRÆPOSITI OFFICIO.

Cap. 10.

Cæterum ne solis Studentium Conscientiis hanc morum curam relinquamus, necessarium existimamus, præter Præpositum cui maxime incumbit, eam aliis quibusdam Curatoribus demandare. Quoniam igitur Præpositus neque semper adesse, neque solus tantæ Regiminis moli par esse potest, volumus ut e Senioribus Sociis quotannis eligatur aliquis ad Officium Vice-præpositi, qui Præposito in Collegii regimine Loco et honore proximus, ei in omnibus suppetias ferat. Quoties vero aut deest Præpositus, aut abest a Collegio, semper præsideat, et primas teneat, ejusque in cultus divini, ordinis, modestiæque conservatione vicem gerat. Provideat itaque Vice-præpositus solicite, ne qua vel intermissio fiat frequentandi preces, audiendi conciones, præstandi in Collegio cujuscunque generis scholastica exercitia ; vel obrepat incuria inquirendi de iis, qui Urbem Dubliniensem frequentant, qui in eadem pernoctant, qui dissoluto Vitæ genere scandalum et dedecus regimini et disciplinæ Collegii creant. Ordinis etiam prandii cœnæque tempore conservationi sollicite prospiciat, et ne quisquam alio sermone quam Latino utatur, aut vocem nimis intendat, aut immodeste omnino se gerat, aut exeat ante gratiarum actionem. Quod si istiusmodi delicta committi intellexerit, vel alterius generis alia Statuis vetita, curabit sedulo ut delinquentes puniantur secundum Statuta. Cætera quæ ad officium Vice-præpositi pertinent, variis supra infraque Statutis exponuntur.

NOTE.—Laud, Cap. XII., transcribing this chapter, adds that the Vice-Provost shall be elected at the time of the annual accounts (November 20), and gives the Provost an absolute veto on the appointment. He is here assumed to be the senior at Commons.

DE DECANI OFFICIO.

Cap. II.

Quo melius vero et Pietas erga Deum et morum probitas honestasque conservetur, statuimus et ordinamus, ut unus e Sociis Senioribus quotannis Decanus sit, qui Dei inprimis cultum pie ac religiose et decenter exequendum curet, videatque ut omnes socii, Discipuli, Pensionarii, Sizatores (quos vocant) ac subsizatores diebus Dominicis Precibus, Sacræ Communioni, et concionibus, diebus autem profestis, precibus matutinis et vespertinis ad horam constitutam intersint, Socios, si qui a sacro Dei Cultu abfuerint, observet ; quod si quis Sociorum qui Doctor aut Baccalaureus Theologiæ non est, sæpius quam bis in Septimana abfuerit a publicis precibus, volumus ut octo denariis multetur ; nisi constiterit eum justa de causa abfuisse. Omnes autem Discipuli, Pensionarii item, Sizatores, et Subsizatores, si absint a Precibus, aut ante eas finitas exierint, si fuerint adulti (hoc est, si decimum octavum annum compleverint) singuli denario, tarde autem venientes obolo multentur. Si autem eum ætatis annum quem diximus non confecerint, in aula die Veneris, pro arbitrio Decani virgis, vel alio modo corrigantur. Praeterea statuimus et ordinamus, ut Baccalaurei correctionibus die Veneris numquam interesse cogantur, sed Decanus eorum nomina scripta in schedula habeat ut tam in festis diebus quam in profestis, diligenter per se et per monitorem animadvertat, quis a re divina absit, quisve tardus venerit, et absentes denario, tarde autem venientes multet obolo. Tardos venire eos dicimus, qui aut post primam nominum recitationem tempore precum vespertinarum sacellum introeunt[1] out qui mane post primum Psalmum finitum veniunt. Quod si qui in inferiori parte Sacelli maneant, et chorum non ingrediantur, perinde puniantur ac si absentes fuissent.[2] Si quis dum nomina ullo tempore vel loco recitantur, pro absente respondeat, aut nomen alicujus in recitando omiserit, virgis corrigatur, si ætate minore fuerit, si adultus, pro arbitrio Decani sic puniatur ut omnibus appareat grave ab eo delictum commissum fuisse. Die autem Veneris statim a peracta cœna, semper vesperi, correctiones per eundem Decanum instituantur, quibus omnes discipuli intersint : qui autem dum eædem peraguntur nomini interrogatus non responderit, et ad finem non permanserit, si adultus denario multetur ; si puer fuerit, arbitrio Decani castigetur. Deinde eodem tempore monitor constituatur, qui discipulorum qui his rebus peccaverint nomina sedulo notet, et quoties deliquerint. Aliqui etiam e Scholaribus observatores occulti constituantur, qui dejerantes, otiosos, emansores in Urbe, rixantes, et in ganeis perpotantes, aut moribus quovis modo Collegium dehonestantes ad Decanum deferant. Quod si quispiam Sociorum aut Discipulorum ægrotaverit, aut gravi Causa per Decanum approbanda impeditus fuerit, eum neutiquam pro

---

[1] From this it appears that night roll and evening Chapel were held together, and the roll read both before and after prayers.

[2] The present Chapel has no ante-Chapel, but this clause presupposes one in the original building.

rebus supradictis multari volumus. Decanus a Collegio ne absit, nisi gravissima de Causa, eaque a Præposito, vel eo absente, Vice-Præposito cum majori parte Sociorum approbanda. Denique a Collegio ne discedat, nisi fido ac diligenti Vicario, qui Decani munere ipso absente sedulo fungatur, post se relicto; ejus nomine in Registro (uti in Statuto "de exitu e Collegio" præstitutum est) conscripto. Volumus insuper et ordinamus ut Decanus una cum duobus aut tribus e Sociis, quos sibi adjungendos putabit, singulis Septimanis ter ad minimum Discipulorum Cameras vesperi post Cænam ante Somni capiendi tempus invisat, ut quomodo se gerant discipuli intelligat. Si quos vel abesse a cameris suis, vel immodestius et contra bonos mores se in iisdem aut alibi gerere, aut negligentius in Studiis versari deprehenderit, licebit ei pro arbitrio delinquentes punire, nisi de pœnæ qualitate et genere aliter in Statutis provisum fuerit.

NOTE.—The main differences in Laud's Chapter XIII. are that he has two Deans; he makes the work of Senior Dean mostly theological; he appoints corrections during the hour of supper on Fridays when the students are to fast; and he does not follow Bedell in making some of the scholars spies upon the rest. It is very curious that the inspection of rooms by the Dean and Fellows is to be carried on without reference to the Tutors of each student so visited, but Laud follows this regulation.

DE PRIMARIO LECTORE, ET SUBLECTORIBUS.
Cap. 12.

Quoniam ad juventutem non modo in pietate et virtute excolendam, sed etiam in bonis artibus erudiendam hoc Collegium institutum est; Lectores quosdam in his constituendos, et pro ætate captuque, et profectu ingeniorum, certas classes variaque exercitia scholastica duximus ordinanda. Atque imprimis, Lectorem quendam primarium e senioribus Sociis quotannis eligi volumus, cujus munus esto, solicite videre, ut prælectores inferiores singuli locum tempusque prælegendi quotidie et diligenter obeant, et si quando aliqua prælectio intermittatur, de intermissionis causa cognoscere, eamque si minus justam esse comperuerit, ad Præpositum rem deferre, aut eo absente ad Vice-Præpositum, ut in deliquentem secundum statuta animadvertatur.

Discipulos cujuscunque generis quos abesse deprehenderit a prælectionibus, disputationibus, declamationibus, et aliis scholasticiis exercitiis, quibus interesse tenentur, pro arbitrio puniat ; nisi de certa pæna aliquo Statuto cautum fuerit. Disputationes, et declamationes Scholarium et Baccalaureorum, curabit suis temporibus et locis præstandas; et earum ipse moderator esto. Ac proinde volumus, Theses disputandas et declamandas præscribi ab eo, et quo quisquam ordine et vice exercitium præstare debeat. Quod si quis vicem suam in disputando et declamando omiserit, vel in eo se negligentius gesserit, curabit ut in hoc genere delinquens pænam sustineat quam Statuta præscribunt. Prælector cujusvis classis inferior (quem a Præposito quotannis eligi volumus) horæ ad prælegendam constitutæ partem alteram prælectioni, alteram Examinationi discipulorum tribuat. In Examinatione, volumus ut interrogationibus et responsionibus rem eandem clarius explicet, repetat, et sæpius inculcat, nec sibi ipsi ante satisfaciat, quam discipulus rem propositam aliquatenus animo et intelligentia comprehenderit. Usum præceptorum ostendet, et urgebit. Quod ad humanitatis et vitæ communis usum transferri nequit, id allato argumento refutatum abjucabit, et rejiciet. Ordinamus insuper et volumus, ut Prælector quivis inferior solicite observet, et attendat, quemadmodum discipuli suæ Classis se gerant ipsius Lectionis tempore ; et in negligentes animadvertat. Porro si observet ipse, aut ab aliis audiverit, discipulum aliquem vel Urbem Dubliniensem frequentare, vel horas studiis destinatas in otio et lusu in Collegio campisve consumere, adeo ut officio scholastico non satisfaciat, volumus ut Prælectori primario delictum deferat, qui delinquentem puniat, non modo si prælectioni cui interesse oportebat non interfuerit, aut ad eandem tardius accesserit, sed etiam si negligentius attenderit; vel multæ impositione, vel compositione exercitii extraordinarii, vel publica agnitione delicti, vel adhibita virga, si ita ferat necessitas, et ætate puer fuerit.

NOTE.—This chapter is wholly adopted by Laud (Cap. XIV).

DE CLASSIUM SCHOLASTICIS EXERCITIIS.
Cap. 13.

Classes sunto quatuor, in quas ii qui nondum sunt graduati distribuantur. Communia omnium Classium exercitia sunto hujusmodi. Commentarius in præcepta disciplinæ prælectæ sermone latino per singulas septimanas conficiendus, et prælectori ostendendus. Thema aut versio ex Anglico in Latinum, per singulas item Septimanas. Thema aut versionem .Prælector et quidem expresse præscribat, et quovis die Sabbathi exercitium factum repetat a discipulis suis.

Declamatio. Bini singulis septimanis declament per vices, idque memoriter, in aula, die Sabbathi aut Veneris, post peractas preces matutinas. Thesis tractanda esto e communi vita, aut e morali aut politica disciplina. Omnes Classium discipuli, si commode fieri potest, in Græcis et Hebraicis erudiantur, a prælectore ad id munus constituto.

Classis Prima.

In hac Classe Dialectica prælegatur : quam bis ad minimum quotannis integram prælegi volumus. Discipulus hujus Classis aliquam quavis hebdomada Analysin Inventionis et Elocutionis Rhetoricæ præstato, eamque Prælectoris Examini et Censuræ subjicito.

Classis Secunda.

Prælector secundæ Classis controversa Logicæ disciplinæ capita explicato, et disceptato. Quæ veritati consentanea reperientur, ea Auditoribus suis commendabit : Quæ vero falsa fuerint, ea argumentorum viribus convicta repudiabit. Hujus Classis Discipuli aliquam Inventionis et Judicii Analysin per singulas Septimanas instituant.

Classis Tertia.

Prælector tertiæ Classis præcepta physiologiæ de Elementis, de Corporibus mixtis sive imperfectis, qualia sunt meteora ; sive perfectis, qualia sunt metalla, Plantæ, Animalia, Auditoribus suis interpretetur.

Classis Quarta.

In Classe quarta Psychologiæ doctrina diligenter exponatur, sed interdum per Vices quasdam Ethicæ disciplinæ præcepta doceantur. Discipuli tertiæ quartæque Classis per singulas termini hebdomadas, prima excepta, disputationes præstent, de Thesi duplici : Illi de Thesi Logica, hi de binis quæstionibus e Physiologia. Thesis a respondente tractetur, oratione perpetua, adhibito vario Argumentorum genere et Elocutionis Rhetoricæ ornamentis. Sed cum ad congressum deventum est, opponentes quos ad minimum duos esse volumus, quodcunque argumentum opponunt, id ad Syllogismi Legis breviter conclusum proponant, de eo Respondens et Moderator videto. Disputatio intra horam et horæ quartam concludatur. Dies præstandis Disputationibus assignati sunto dies Lunæ, Martis, Mercurii, hora secunda pomeridiana.

NOTE.—Laud adds details regarding the appointment of a special Lecturer in Greek and, whenever the post can be endowed, in Hebrew also.

There are many variations of detail in his description of the work of each class, especially a long addition concerning the work of the fourth class. The general scheme has lasted till the present time with the exception of the excellent practice of public disputation, which has disappeared from modern education.

APPENDIX

De Baccalaureorum et Magistrorum Exercitiis.

Cap. 14.

Baccalaurei in Mathematicis et Politicis a Prælectore instituantur accuratius. Disputationem quolibet die Veneris hora secunda pomeridiana quovis Termino præstent e Mathematicis aut Physicis, et declament mane in Aula quolibet die Sabbathi durante Termino. Statuimus etiam et ordinamus, ut quilibet in Artibus Magister, per vices, quolibet die Lunæ et Martis aliquem e Scriptura textum ad morem Theologicæ Concionis tractet, eundem accurate interpretando, et doctrinæ capita inde deducta ad auditorum varios usus pro varia capitum natura accommodando. In hac tam gravi et utili exercitatione, omnibus et singulis Artium Magistris præcipimus, eosque vehementius hortamur et obtestamur, ut in id unum omni animi contentione incumbant, quo auditores suos in fide et fidei praxi ædificare possint; volumus etiam ut quilibet in artibus Magister, si Theologiæ aut Baccalaureus aut Doctor non sit, statim a finita suscepti textus tractatione, se et textus suscepti translationem Præpositi et Sociorum seniorum censuræ submittat; ac si quid ab ipsis improbetur, eo deinceps abstineat; sequatur autem in posterum et in praxin deducat quicquid ædificationi, aut commodo audientium expedire, ab ipsis judicabitur. Ac proinde volumus, ut Præpositus ac Socii seniores in Sacello aut alibi congregati, libere inter se exponant quid de habita concione opinentur, ut si qua in re contra leges hoc Statuto præscriptas a concionante peccatum fuerit, de eo per Præpositum amice et benevole admoneatur. Statuimus insuper, ut artium Magistri, etiam ii qui in Theologia Doctoratum aut Baccalaureatum adepti sunt, per vices præstent disputationem aliquam, de binis Quæstionibus Theologicis, quovis die Jovis, hora secunda pomeridiana, nisi dies festus sit. Quod ad Theologicam disputationem attinet, ordinamus et volumus, ut quæstio disputanda sit quæstio plerumque inter Protestantes et Pontificios controversa. Hujus Disputationis Professor Theologicarum Controversiarum Moderator esto. Volumus etiam et statuimus, ut singuli in artibus Magistri, tam Commensales quam Socii (exceptis Jurisprudentiæ et Medicinæ Professoribus) semper ante elapsum a Magisterii gradu triennum, in Ecclesia aliqua Urbis Dubliniensis Parochiali, bis concionentur; ante exactum vero quadriennium unam in Christi Ecclesia Cathedrali concionem habeant idque per se, non autem per alium; et post annos quatuor expletos concionem aliquam in prædicta Cathedrali semel quotannis præstent, quandiu locum aut Cameram in Collegio obtinent: Quod si quis contra hanc legem deliquerit, nisi morbo graviore impeditus, aut ab Archiepiscopo Dubliniensi, aliisve quorum interest, prohibitus, aut alia inductus causa quæ Præposito et Sociis merito possit satisfacere, volumus et ordinamus, ut pro singularum Concionum ab ipso requisitarum omissione, quadraginta solidis multetur, ac præterea ordinario Communarum demenso per tres menses privetur.

NOTE.—Laud adds some details regarding the conducting of the controversial disputes between Protestants and Papists. He also imposes punishments upon any teaching opposed to the Established Church of England and Ireland, a provision quite foreign to the semi-Puritan Bedell. It is further to be noticed that Bedell requires lay masters of art to preach in Dublin, and even at the Cathedral, and that this was upheld by Laud. Up to 1850 Resident masters, whether lay or clerical, were required to deliver "Commonplaces" or read Homilies in the Chapel.

DE VITANDA ALIENI EXERCITII USURPATIONE, ET VICE SUA A QUOVIS DILIGENTER OBEUNDA.

Cap. 15.

Si quis Exercitium ab alio compositum pro suo aut privatim obtendat, aut in publicum deducat, volumus si de admissa hujus generis fraude constiterit, ut tam Author exercitii, quam is qui alienæ industriæ fructum pro suo exhibet gravius puniatur. Uterque ergo istius delicti convictus, tempore prandii in Aulæ medio consistens culpam suam omnibus audientibus confiteatur, pænamque deprecetur. Quod si alteruter in hoc genere secundo deliquerit, non modo prædictam pænam sustineat, sed commeatu suo per septimanam privetur, et ad declamandum in Aula tempore prandii intra octiduum cogatur. Ac quia fraudem hanc dignam gravi animadversione censemus, statuimus insuper et volumus, ut qui illam detulerit, notamque fecerit, illi loco mercedis ab utriusque delinquentis Tutore sex denarii tribuantur et persolvantur. Si quis delatorem isto nomine verbis factisve violaverit, is pro delinquente in hoc fraudis genere habeatur, et eandem pœnam subito. Statuimus etiam et volumus, ut Exercitia Scholastica, sive ea Theologica sint, sive generis alterius, a quolibet in propria persona præstentur. Quod si quis morbo aliave justa causa per Præpositum et Decanum approbanda impeditus, vicem suam præstare nequeat, proximo denunciet, eumque opportune admoneat de præstando exercitio, et cessante causa intermissi exercitii, omissum exercitium præstet ipse. At si contigerit ut exercitium ordinarium cujusque generis omittatur, cum nulla gravis causa afferri queat, quamobrem omitti necesse fuerit, omittens a Præposito et Decano unius septimanæ commeatu privetur, aut multetur, et tamen ad præstationem exercitii teneatur. Qua in re si secundo deliquerit, eum mensis unius commeatu privari, aut multari volumus; et in exercitii omissione ulterius persistentem, pro arbitrio Præpositi et Sociorum Seniorum puniri gravius. Ac si quis munus disputandi aut declamandi negligenter obierit, denuo disputare ac declamare cogatur.

NOTE.—This chapter is wholly omitted by Laud, as being already covered by other Statutes by a clause introduced into the previous chapter, or the general control of the Provost.

De Terminis Observandis et de Examinando Scholarium in Disciplinis Progressu.

Cap. 16.

Termini in quibus publice a Studentibus Exercitia præstari volumus, pro quatuor anni partibus quatuor sunto. Terminus Nativitatis Christi initium capiat Januarii decimo quinto, exitum vero Martii decimo. Terminus Paschæ inchoetur Aprilis decimo sexto, desinat Junii octavo. Terminus Johannis Baptistæ esto a nono Julii inclusive, ad octavum Septembris. Denique Terminus Michaelis incipito Octobris decimo quinto, et finiatur Decembris octavo.

Quoniam vero frequenti Examinatione efficitur, ut discentium Studia et Progressiones in bonarum Artium disciplinis majorem in modum promoveantur, volumus ut quater quotannis, nempe in cujusvis termini principio singularum Classium Discipuli publice in Aula congregati examinentur, quomodo profecerint in earum Artium cognitione, quibus studuerint, aut studere debuerint. Examinatores sunto singuli Artium Magistri, sive Socii fuerint, sive Pensionarii et Commensales; Doctores etiam et Professores cujuscunque facultatis, si modo ipsis videbitur: sed illi præsertim qui eligentur per Præpositum et majorem partem Seniorum Sociorum. Examinationi huic Biduum tribuatur; mane horæ duæ, ab octava scilicet ad decimam, et a prandio item horæ duæ, a secunda nempe ad quartam. Si facta Examinatione Discipulus quispiam se in Studiis negligentius gessisse comperiatur, re cum Præposito communicata, volumus ut eam pænam sustineat, quæ Præposito et Examinatoribus videbitur digna, qua tantæ negligentiæ crimen notetur, et corrigatur. Quod si de pæna expulsionis sive amotionis agatur, volumus rem dijudicari et transigi per Præpositum et majorem partem Seniorum. Et si non tantum profecisse videbitur, quantum a mediocri ingenio et industria expectari poterat, eum principio hac ignominia notari placet, ut Senioritatis suæ Gradum amittat, et in Classem inferiorem dejiciatur; et deinceps etiam, si graduatus non fuerit, careat adultorum privilegio. Quod si quis post alterius termini experimentum prorsus incorrigibilis videatur, eum sine ulteriori monitione e Collegio amovendum decernimus.

NOTE.—Instead of this admirable arrangement of the four terms defined by fixed dates, one of them a short summer term, such as has recently been reintroduced at Oxford and Cambridge, Laud marks the terms by Feasts of the Church, in some cases variable, and establishes a summer vacation, at least for the senior two classes. In the rest of the chapter regarding the Term Examinations and the degrading of students who failed in them, he follows Bedell, and this ordinance has prevailed to the present day.

DE ADMITTENDIS IN COLLEGIUM PROFESSORIBUS JURISPRUDENTIAE ET MEDICINÆ.

Cap. 17.

Quoniam professio Jurisprudentiæ et Medicinæ et Chartæ fundationis istius Collegii, et collegiorum apud Anglos receptis legibus consentanea est, quippe quæ non solum mirifice ornet Societatem Studentium in quam admittatur, sed etiam singularem Utilitatem secum afferat Ecclesiæ et Reipublicæ: Hinc est quod licitum esse volumus et statuimus, ut pro Arbitrio Præpositi et majoris partis Sociorum Seniorum e Sociis unus ad Professionem Jurisprudentiæ, alter ad studium Medicinæ, idque statim ab Electione, vel intra sex menses a suscepto gradu Magisterii divertatur. Quod si ante admissionem fieri contigerit, volumus ut Clausula illa Juramenti (de fine Studiorum) omittatur ab electo: vel in eam loco Theologiæ, "Jurisprudentiæ," vel "Medicinæ" respective interponatur. Quod vero ad Exercitia attinet requisita a Theologis durante quovis termino, nolumus ea Professori Jurisprudentiæ aut Medicinæ remitti, sed ab utroque præstari, sive communes Loci fuerint, sive Theologiæ Disputationes. Volumus insuper, ut Juris et Medicinæ Professores singuli, post primum initæ Professionis semel quovis termino in sua facultate prælegant.

> NOTE.—Laud adds that he wishes no one to be forced to abandon Theology for these studies, but that upon a vacancy a man with a taste for Law or Medicine should be chosen. If such cannot be found, he adds most inconsistently, that the junior M.A. among the Fellows must take the post, under pain of dismissal. So popular was theology then among the learned! The provision that both Lawyers and Doctors should make some theological studies is also very commendable, and tended to produce such broad men as John Stearne.

DE BURSARII OFFICIO.

Cap. 18.

De pietate, probitate, et doctrina hactenus statutum est. Quoniam vero sine rei familiaris provida administratione, nedum Collegium, sed ne privata quidem domus consistere potest; statuimus et ordinamus, ut e Sociis Senioribus quispiam frugi, integer, nec impar rebus gerendis, a Præposito et majori parte Seniorum pro Bursario eligatur. Cujus officium sit redditus et quæcunque in universum debentur Collegio recipere, et quæ opus erunt in usus Collegii expendere. Is Officium suum exerceto quotannis statim a festo D. Johannis Baptistæ, neque computum præcedentis anni cum suo permisceri patiatur. Quoties igitur Bursarius a Collegii Tenentibus, vel ab aliis nummos Collegio debitos receperit, apocham testem solutæ pecuniæ conficito; sed nunquam solus, verum subscribente etiam Præposito aut ejus vice gerente, vel Decano. Quicquid vero receperit, eodem die in communi Cista reponatur. Sitque in eadem cista Codex rationum, in quem adscripto receptionis die, referatur summa recepta, et a quo soluta sit, et quo nomine, et utrum sit integer redditus anni, an pars aliqua, aut si quid forte antea debebatur. Quum pecuniæ aliqua summa e communi Collegii cista expromitur, sive ad ordinarias diætæ expensas, sive ad persolvenda salaria, sive ad reparationes ædificiorum aut utensilium, aut quacunque demum de causa, volumus ut eam Bursarius in codicem prædictum referat acceptam, et id subscripta manu testetur, nec ea ad alios usus abutatur. Codicem præterea privatum expensorum et receptorum penes se habeto, et in eum omnia a se accepta et expensa fideliter per singulas septimanas referto. Ad Bursarii curam pertineto, ut sociis, scholaribus, et reliquis Collegii studentibus, de alimentis ordinariis in aula sumendis recte provideatur, atque ut ea in aula prandii cænæque tempore ordine dispensentur. Ac proinde volumus observari ab eo inferiorum officiariorum actiones, ut si quando officio defuerint, eos admoneat, increpetque ; ac nisi gravius delictum fuerit, possit solus pro suo jure in eos animadvertere. Aliquot etiam e studentibus pauperioribus (quos Sub-Sizatores appellant) constituat, qui Scholarium mensis ministrent. At vero qui Sociorum mensæ attendant et inserviant Præpositus et e quatuor Senioribus Sociis singuli unum aliquem sibi e Studentium numero eligant et constituant ; ita tamen ut ex iis neminem removeant, qui ad mensæ ministerium designatus jam est. Si quando aliquis vacaverit, volumus ut prædicti Socii cum Præposito pro ea qua sunt senioritate, procedant ad locum supplendum, suo quisque ordine ac vice. Nemini extra aulam prandenti cænantive Bursarius Communias concedito, nisi constiterit ei veniam prandendi aut cænandi extra Aulam a Præposito vel ejus locum tenente concessam. Quod si ratione absentium ex aula communiarum aliqua fercula supererunt, de iis in usum mensis ministrantium, aut aliorum pauperum pro arbitratu suo Bursarius disponito. Praeterea Bursarii esse volumus, prospicere ne quid incommodi ad Collegium redundet, e neglecta observatione eorum, quibus abesse a Collegio ad tempus concessum est, aut quibus ratione delicti ordinaria diæta judicialiter ad tempus substracta est. Ac proinde præcipimus, ut quam primum provideat, ne absenti, aut hujusmodi censuram sustinenti quicquam ex ordinariis diætæ expensis allocetur. Ac ne quid Bursarium lateat hac in re, volumus, ut tam ii qui impetrata venia peregre proficiscuntur, quam qui Communiarum beneficio quenquam privarint, de eo Bursarium admoneant, sub pœna quam Præpositus et Bursarius in hoc genere delinquenti infligendam esse censebunt. Quicquid argenteum est, quod prandii cænæve tempore quotidianis usibus inservit, ejus custodiam Bursarius suscipito. Si quæ labes in aliqua ædificii et structuræ parte, eam curato. Si quid Utensilibus sacelli, Bibliothecæ, Culinæ, et Promptuarii, aut in quacunque Collegii parte reficiendum est, de eo Bursarius inquirito, et reficiendum provideat. Ligna denique, lapides, carbones, et cætera usui necessaria tempestive comparato. Denique Bursario injunctum esto, ut solicite caveat, nequid detrimenti Collegium capiat, ex dilata solutione pecuniæ, quæ vel a Collegio vel a pupillis cujuscunque generis et ordinis, pro ordinario commeatu debetur, sive pistori, sive potifici, sive aliis. Volumus ergo, ut et apocham ab iis quibus soluta pecunia fuerit accipiat, et ad finem cujusque mensis, vel intra decem dies a finito mense, advocato promo, et aliis quorum interest, diligenter inquirat de pecuniis commeatus nomine debitis. Quod si intellexerit aliquem esse qui requisitus non solverit, Volumus ut adversus delinquentem sic procedat, quemadmodum in Statuto de Tutoribus præscribitur. Ut vero opportune constare queat, quam recte et utiliter officio suo Bursarius satisfaciat, Volumus ut ad cujusque quartæ exitum, aut intra Septimanam, Præposito, Vice-Præposito et Decano (vel absente Præposito, Vice-Præposito et Decano) in Aula congregatis, rationem accurate reddat omnium receptorum et expensorum. Quod si inutilis et officio ineptus deprehendatur, amoveatur illico aliusque in ejus locum sufficiatur. Finito anno Bursarius coram Præposito et omnibus Senioribus Sociis computum reddat integrum totius anni præteriti, quo status Collegii innotescat : qui et in Codice quem supra memoravimus clare describatur, una cum renovato nominum nondum expunctorum breviculo. Id vero quo melius et accuratius præstetur, Statuimus et ordinamus ut sit Auditor quispiam, Collegii stipendiis conductus, qui computo faciendo semper die præscripta intersit, et rationes totius anni acceptorum et expensorum accurate consideret, et consideratas fideliter subducendas et examinandas, easdemque intra tres menses in membranas transcribendas, et ad Collegium deferendas curet. De pecunia collegii nemini quidquam unquam commodetur.

NOTE.—The differences in Laud's version are characteristic. In the first place, the great independence of action which Bedell grants the Bursar is shackled by requiring constant sanction from the Provost. Then the sub-sizars (here appointed by the Bursar) are ignored, and the appointment of one Sizar granted to each Fellow, "eight or more" to the Provost, and the whole number limited to thirty. The Provost's Chambers are to be kept in repair by the Bursar. The date of election is fixed, as of all the other officers, for the 20th November.

DE TUTA RERUM CUSTODIA, ET BIBLIOTHECARIO.

Cap. 19.

Nihil est quod ad Collegii in re familiari commodum plus referat, quam evidentiarum et monumentorum diligens Custodia. Idcirco statuimus et ordinamus, ut Literæ Patentes fundationis, cæteraque omnia monumenta evidentiæ, rentalia et terraria in cistulis et capsulis diligenter reponantur, quarum claves Præpositus, aut in ejus abentia Vice-præpositus, Bursarius et Decanus, servent. Nihil horum nisi gravissima de causa, a Præposito et majore parte Sociorum Seniorum approbanda, inde depromatur, aut cuipiam ostendatur. Si quid forte efferendum e cistula et alicui necessario committendum sit, in Registro res extracta, et dies quo extrahitur scribatur, et nomen etiam illius cui committitur. Bona Collegii sive ad sacellum, sive ad Bibliothecam, sive ad Culinam spectent, omnia particulatim in tria registra referri statuimus : Quorum unum apud Vice-præpositum vel Socium Seniorem, alterum apud Bursarium servetur, tertium apud Bibliothecæ Custodem : et quotannis per eosdem hæc registra renoventur, ut quid superioris anni et quomodo amissum sit videatur. Si quid tale accidit, in registro notetur, ut is cujus negligentia amissum sit sine tergiversatione præstet. Sin intra mensem non fecerit, duplum reddat Collegio, et usque eo Commeatu careat, quoad id præstiterit. Vasa aurea et argentea, et quicquid præterea pretiosum est, quod quotidianis usibus non subserviat, in communi cista conserventur ; nec unquam ex eo depromantur, nisi singulis rebus in registro aliquo apud Præpositum reservato eorum manu qui depromunt descriptis.

Quoniam vero inter Collegii supellectilem Librorum est vel pretiosissima, volumus ut quispiam e junioribus Sociis, aut Discipulis Baccalaureis, vir frugi, quique domi se fere continere solitus sit, studiis deditus, et librorum studiosus, huic custodiæ præficiatur : ita tamen ut confecto registro librorum eos recognoscat, de iis præstandis caveat, juretque se munus suum fideliter executurum. Bibliothecarius quotidie ab hora nona ante meridiem ad undecimam, et a tertia rursus pomeridiana ad quintam, operam suam et Bibliothecæ copiam poscentibus dabit. Volumus insuper ut non aliis quam Præposito et Sociis, ac Theologiæ saltem Baccalaureis aditus ad Bibliothecam interiorem ad librorum usum concedatur. Cæteri si qui sunt qui Bibliothecæ opportunitate et commodo uti velint, in exteriori Bibliotheca consistant, et libros quibus legendis operam dare cupiunt a Bibliothecæ Custode mutuentur, sub conditione restituendi priusquam discesserint. E Sociis Senioribus cuique clavem habere fas esto, sed ea lege, ut nemini clavem suam commodet ; fidemque det post admissionem ad jus Senioris, coram Deo, Præposito, et senioribus, se nunquam librum e Bibliotheca asportaturum, nisi descripto prius in Registro Bibliothecæ et suo ipsius et libri nomine, et die mensis quo mutuatus sit ; et rediturum, cum eo ad duas hebdomadas usus fuerit. Quod si quis contra hanc præscriptam statuti normam librum quemcunque asportaverit, volumus ut Bibliothecæ ingressu et usu in perpetuum privetur, nisi publice agnita culpa veniam impetraverit. Si quis liber ablatus aut amissus fuerit, volumus ut e Sociis vel Artium Magistris duo a Præposito et majori parte seniorum designati, una cum Custode Bibliothecæ, cameras in Collegio studentium singulas et privata musæa adeant, et accuratissime perscrutentur. Si quis e Studentibus in hoc recuperandi libri negotio obstiterit inquirentibus, quominus cameram et musæum ingrediantur eo consilio, is ablati libri reus judicabitur, pænamque sustinebit libri asportatoribus supra constitutam. Denique id Bibliothecarius provideat, ne aut ipse aut quispiam alius commentarios cujuscunque generis qui in frequentiori studiosorum usu sunt, e Bibliotheca ad privatum musæum auferat, aut libros tribus plures e Bibliotheca acceptos habeat penes se ; sub pœna delinquenti pro arbitrio Præpositi et majoris partis seniorum infligenda.

NOTE.—Laud only allows a second key to the Provost, and appoints that the Librarian, like the Bursar, must deposit caution money on taking up his duties. Otherwise the chapter follows Bedell with few variations. *Musæa* is a term known at Oxford for studies, which were then the only private rooms of students, who occupied their *cameræ* or sleeping-rooms in groups of three or four.

DE SOCIORUM ET SCHOLARIUM NUMERO, COMMEATU, SALARIIS, ET CUBICULIS.

Cap. 20.

Cum ex Serenissimi Regis JACOBI Munificentia erga Collegium istud singulari, magna non ita pridem accessio facta sit ad annuos Collegii redditus, placet proportionaliter tum numerum Sociorum et Scholarium augere, tum in ordinario victu et salariis ipsorum conditionem auctiorem melioremque reddere. Volumus igitur et statuimus, ut Socii sint numero sedecim, septem nempe proprii nominis, Seniores, et reliqui

Juniores. Discipuli Collegii sumptibus sustentandi sint septuaginta, e quibus triginta Hibernicis pauperibus ad eorum in studiis invitandam diligentiam liberalior allocatio fieri poterit, sed ea lege, ut linguam Hibernicam excolant, vel addiscant, et exercitia quædam religionis in ea præstent prout Præposito et majori parti Seniorum videbitur expedire. Atque hunc numerum Sociorum et Discipulorum quotannis expleri volumus, temporibus Electionibus præstitutis : nisi Collegii insigne aliquod detrimentum cogat numerum Scholarium ad tempus imminuere. Pro Commeatu Præposito et Sociorum cuivis e culina allocentur sedecim denarii et obolus hebdomadatim. E promptuario per singulos dies ad panem et potum duo denarii, unus ad prandium, alter ad cænam : et extra ordinem per hebdomadam, octo denarii et obolus. E promptuario cuivis pro pane prandii tempore obolus, et tantundem ad cænam ; pro cervisia quotidie obolus, et extra ordinem per hebdomadam quatuor denarii. Pro salario allocentur per annum :

	li.	s.	d.
Præposito...	100	0	0
Sociis septem Senioribus cuilibet	9	13	4
Juniorum cuilibet	3	0	0
Discipulo cuique...	0	10	0
Hibernicis pauperibus cuique...	3	0	0
Catechistæ	13	6	8
Decano	4	0	0
Primario Lectori...	6	0	0
Sociis [lectoribus] inferioribus, singulis per annum...	4	0	0
Bursario...	10	0	0
Auditori...	6	13	4
Bibliothecario	3	0	0

In cubiculis distribuendis, etsi doctrinæ, et virtutis ratio habenda est, tamen ne ex illa ulla controversia aut invidia oriatur, secundum suum gradum seniorem juniori tam inter Socios quam inter discipulos semper præferendum statuimus. Distribuendorum cubiculorum potestas sit penes Præpositum, aut eo absente Vice-Præpositum. Nemo Cubiculum ut proprium et suum teneat, nisi ante a Præposito, aut eo absente Vice-Præposito ad id admissus fuerit. Quum autem quispiam cubiculum suum relinquit, Clavem ad Præpositum, aut eo absente ad Vice-Præpositum deferat. Quodsi quispiam in cubiculo vel extruat quid, vel reficiat, suo sumptu faciat; nisi Præpositum, aut absente Præposito Vice-Præpositum et Socios consuluerit. Ac si Collegio discedens compensationem expensi postulet, tum una tertia facti sumptus deducatur ; aut si res ita exigat, a Præposito et majori parte Seniorum quæstio compensationis decidatur.

NOTE.—In Laud's corresponding chapter (XXI.) the allowance for Commons is doubled (3s. 4½d. per week) in the case of Fellows, increased by one-half (1s. 4½d. per week) for scholars, the allowance for bread and beer remaining unaltered. There is special provision for a feast on Trinity Sunday. The fellows and scholars are to be elected on Trinity Monday (as they now are). The salaries of all the offices remain unchanged, but a special clause is added by the King ordering that in all leases from the Crown in Ireland, a moiety (medietas) of the rent is reserved for the College, and to be paid by the tenant to the Bursar for the purpose of increasing the salaries. The distribution of rooms is reserved to the Provost alone, so that up to the present day, on the death of the Provost all the chambers in the College become formally vacant, and the first act of the new Provost is to regrant them.

DE ABSENTIA SOCIORUM ET SCHOLARIUM.
Cap. 21.

Quoniam multæ hujusmodi causæ non raro incidunt, ut Socii et Discipuli necessario ex Academia egredi cogantur, idcirco statuimus et ordinamus, ut singuli Sociorum et Discipulorum cum causam exeundi necessariam habent, a Præposito, aut eo absente, Vice-Præposito, facultatem egrediendi petant, causaque approbata nomen suum et diem quo egrediuntur in registro ad eam rem comparato scribant ; et vel ipso die quo ad Collegium redeunt, vel ad summum postridie ejus diei in registro reditus scribant diem. Quod si quispiam ex Sociis vel discipulis hoc præ negligentia vel consulto omiserit, primo Commeatu unius hebdomadæ, secundo duarum, tertio trium, quarto pro arbitrio Præpositi et majoris partis Seniorum puniatur. Sociorum singulis dies absentiæ sexaginta tres, discipulorum autem singulis quadraginta duos, vel continuos, vel interpolatos in annos singulos, incipiendo a festo Sancti Archangeli Michaelis concedimus, modo suis prælectionibus non desint, per se vel per alium Prælectorem. Quam tamen licentiam ita Præpositum moderari volumus, ut nunquam supra tertiam partem Sociorum vel Discipulorum simul a Collegio abesse patiatur. Quod si quis prædictorum Sociorum vel discipulorum ad Collegium intra præstitutos dies non redierit, is nisi plures dies a Præposito aut in ejus absentia a Vice-Præposito et majori parte Seniorum propter gravem aliquam causam ab iisdem approbandam obtinuerit, Collegio expellatur. Quinetiam si quispiam exeat ex Academia non petita, ut supra dictum est, venia, et intra quindecim dies per literas aut per amicum absentiæ veniam non petiverit, et nomen suum et diem ut præscipsimus in registro scribendum non curaverit, Collegio omnino privetur. Si quis porro intra integrum triduum redierit, is nomen suum scribere non teneatur, sed solum exeundi facultatem a Præposito aut ejus Vicario postulet. Si quis dum abfuerit in morbum forte inciderit, et per literas Præpositum aut Socios certiores fecerit, idque certis testimoniis postea ita habere compertum fuerit, dies quibus ægrotaverit inter præscriptos absentiæ dies numerari nolumus. Statuimus item ut nemini Sociorum vel Discipulorum, præter dies hisce Statutis præscriptos, ultra unam in singulis annis quartam a Præposito, vel eo absente Vice-Præposito, et majori parte Seniorum, nisi gravissima urgentissimaque de causa unquam concedatur. Atque toto illo tempore quo absunt, volumus ut actus suos scholasticos observandos curent, et pro commeatu nullam compensationem habeant, nisi vel ægrotaverint, vel forte in Collegii negotiis exsequendis occupentur.

Æquum est enim ut qui ad alicujus commodum laborem capit, ei sumptus necessarius ab eodem suppeditetur. Statuimus igitur ut Præpositus aut alius quicunque ad Collegii negotia obeunda emissus, de sententia Præpositi, aut eo absente Vice-Præpositi et majoris partis seniorum, qui et negotium ipsum, loci distantiam, dierum numerum et alias circumstantias diligenter considerent, sumptus allocatos habeat. Ipse intra breve tempus postquam ad Collegium redierit, expensa in schedula quadam particulatim scripta ad Præpositum, aut eo absente Vice-Præpositum deferat, sub pœna amissionis eorundem. Quod si quispiam ultra viginti dies in dictis negotiis abfuerit, commeatum ad vestes reficiendas pro toto absentiæ tempore recipiat. Statuimus etiam et ordinamus, ut cum pestis aut alterius contagiosi ac lethalis morbi vis ingruit, Præpositus, aut eo absente Vice-Præpositus, convocatis Sociis, de majoris partis eorum sententia, potestatem Sociis ac Discipulis faciat, se rus ad aliquem opportunum locum conferendi. Quod si repentinus pestis aut alicujus lethalis morbi metus acciderit, sic ut in unum coacti de vita propter morbi contagionem periclitentur, tum permittimus, ut de prædictorum consensu, Sociorum et Discipulorum cœtus ad trium vel quatuor hebdomadarum spatium dissolvantur, et singuli ad diversa loca pro arbitratu suo secedant, proque illis hebdomadis commeatum sibi debitum habeant. Post quod quidem spatium in unum denuo congregari (si id commode et absque periculo fieri poterit) Discipulos universos volumus : ac illo temporis spatio quo rure manserint simul, omnes actus scholasticos quos præstare in Collegio tenentur, observare, et cætera obire volumus, quæ Statuta Collegii exigunt. Quibus toto illo tempore quo simul rusticantur Lectorem primarium et Decanum præesse volumus. Lector autem omnium acceptorum et expensorum rationem accipiat, Decanus vero morum honestati provideat. Nulli Sociorum aut Discipulorum eo tempore quo simul rure manent Commeatum concedimus, nisi vel in Collegio, vel cum Discipulis versetur. Socii autem si sint simul plures, eo tempore actus scholasticos observent. Baccalaureos autem declamare et unum problema singulis hebdomadis (si terminus sit) die Lunæ in Philosophia, incipiendo inter se a senioribus, observare volumus, et nihilominus cum ad Collegium redierint, singuli in suo manipulo vices suas ubi desitum est expleant. Statuimus porro et volumus, ut dum rusticantur discipuli, Præpositus, et eo absente Vice-Præpositus in Collegio ad ejus conservationem maneat, aut Socios idoneos per Præpositum et Vice-Præpositum et majorem partem Sociorum Seniorum approbandos in suo loco substituant.

NOTE.—Laud made hardly any changes in this chapter, in which the provisions for carrying on education in a healthy retreat in days of pestilence remind us of the famous transference of Uppingham School under Thring to Borthwick, in Wales. On the whole Bedell seems somewhat stricter regarding absences than his successor.

DE PŒNIS MAJORUM CRIMINUM, MULCTISQUE AUT EXIGENDIS AUT COMMUTANDIS.

Cap. 22.

Nihil est quod magis homines ad delinquendum incitet, quam Impunitas. Propterea statuimus et ordinamus, ut si quis Sociorum aut Discipulorum, aut aliorum intra Collegium vita degentium Hærescos, aut Simoniæ, aut impiæ et perversæ opinionis aut dogmatis, aut læsæ Majestatis, aut contumaciæ et contemptus adversus Statuta Collegii, aut perjurii, furti notabilis, homicidii voluntarii, stupri, adulterii, incestus, raptionis injuriosæ, aut violentæ percussionis Socii aut Discipuli cujusquam convictus sit, qua vulnus grave cuiquam ex prædictis inflixerit, aut si Præpositum, Vice-Præpositum, Decanum, Doctorem aut Baccalaureum Theologiæ vel leviter percusserit, vel portarum seras dedita opera corruperit, læseritve; quin etiam si portas Collegii furtim reseraverit, aut conjurationes aut insidias contra Collegium comparaverit, vel seditiones in Collegio aliquando excitaverit, vel damnum grave ei intulerit, aut per alios hoc fieri aliquando procuraverit, aut dedecus infamiamve prædicto Collegio inusserit, et id confessus fuerit, aut idoneis testibus convictus fuerit, Præpositi et majoris partis Sociorum Seniorum consensu sine ulla monitione Collegio privetur. Aliorum autem Criminum pæna de qua in Statutis nulla est mentio, judicio Præpositi, aut ejus Vicarii, et majoris partis Sociorum Seniorum semper relinquatur. Mulctæ vero impositor eandem per se vel adhibito promo exigat a delinquente, aut a Bursario Collegii subducendam et persolvendam ex annuo delinquentis stipendio, aut si id nullum fuerit, ex ordinario ipsius commeatu, nisi de ea aliter solvenda statim providere possit. Statuimus igitur et volumus, ut Bursarius multam impositam quam primum exigitur exigenti persolvat, sub pœna contumaciæ adversus Statuta Collegii. Idem Tutori delinquentis Pupilli quod Bursario injungimus, et sub eadem pæna, si mulctam Pupilli impositam persolvere renuerit, cum a mulctæ impositore exigitur, et a Bursario justa de causa non solvitur. Multa persoluta a Bursario reservetur, et ex consensu Præpositi et majoris partis Seniorum erogetur ad usus necessarios pauperum Scholarium, et in fine cujusque quartæ disponatur. Quoniam vero usu deprehensum est, pœnam illam qua studentibus ordinaria diæta ad tempus subtrahitur, ad correctionem et disciplinam quorundam studentium parum proficere, placet igitur, ubi dè subtractione ordinarii commeatus, nomine impositæ pœnæ, Statuta loquuntur, ut liceat iis quibus Statuti pœnam hujusmodi injungentis executio committitur, eandem vel imponere delinquenti, vel in aliam pro arbitrio commutare, quæ ipsis ad præventionem delictorum et reformationem videbitur esse commodior.

NOTE.—Laud's great change in this chapter is that he gives the power of expulsion for grave offences to the Provost, *accitis duobus Decanis*, apparently for the sake of greater solemnity, for they are allowed no independent voice in the matter.

De Inferioribus Collegii Ministris.

Cap. 23.

Adhuc deesse quædam membra videntur huic corpori, non illa quidem venustissima, sed tamen omnino necessaria, cujusmodi sunt Coquus, Manceps, Cellarius, Janitor. Quorum officia tametsi usu notissima sunt, tamen ne quid his Statutis desit, placet et hoc supremum pertexere. Ejusmodi igitur ministros eligi volumus, deinceps si quidem idonei reperiantur cælibes, religiosos certe, probos, sobrios, et honestos, ne aut malo exemplo corrumpant juventutem, aut infamia sua Collegio ipsi sint dedecori. Manceps sive obsonator accepta a Bursario pecunia ad macellum quotidie cum Coquo proficiscatur; operam suam uterque diligenter det, ut edulia salubria et recte emantur, coquus præterea, ut recte apparentur, et in Aulam distribuantur. Idem vasa coquinaria habeat in numerato, ineunte anno, quæ expleto rursus anno novo Bursario representet. Promus præter curam panis et cervisiæ (quæ ut justo pondere, mensura, et bonitate respondeant, Bursarius potissimum videto) mappas et linteamina lavanda curabit a lotrice, Collegii sumptibus. Idem quolibet die Sabbathi, prandio finito, coram Præposito, aut Vice-præposito et Sociis, librum promptuarii ostendat, et seorsim in libello nomina eorum qui aut per totam aut dimidiam septimanam abfuerint, eorum insuper, quibus aut communiæ subtractæ, aut multa imposita, quantaque et a quo; ut et Collegii indemnitati, et pauperum prospiciatur. Janitor portas Collegii, tum quæ Urbem spectant, tum quæ campos orientales, mane aperiet,[1] paulo ante inceptas preces matutinas, aut maturius etiam, si Præposito videbitur. Vesperi easdem statim a vespertinis precibus inceptis, obserabit, clavesque finitis precibus ad Præpositum deferet. Eadem tempore prandii et cænæ, et concionum publicarum, semper obseratæ sunto. Januæ majores numquam nisi vecturæ causa aperiantur, statimque

---

[1] Hence there was clearly no west entrance at this time, though there was a back door for tradesmen, as appears from appendix to Chapter V. Possibly the *Januæ majores* refers to this cart-way, but I think not.

claudantur. Idem Janitor sacellum, aulam, vestibulum, aream utramque, a sordibus expurgabit, et munda custodiet, Quod si quenquam in vestibulo mingentem, aut Aream projecta urina sive quisquiliis conspurcantem deprehenderit, licebit ei sex denarios capiti ejus in promptuario inscriptos multæ nomine deposcere, a Cellario, vel Bursario solvendos sine mora. Idem canes a Collegio, et præcipue a Sacello tempore precum exigat ; videatque ne qui calones puerive in Collegio pernoctent, aut omnino ministeria peragant, nisi quos Præpositus, aut ejus vicem gerens probaverit. Et ne illius curæ tantum rem tanti momenti relinquamns, Volumus et Statuimus ut præter Præ-positum et Vice-Præpositum Decanus videat ne quis Servulum aut puerum sibi ministrantem habeat, nisi scholarem, aut qui literis saltem operam det : nec id sine licentia Præpositi fiat ; quo casu Decanus ejus herique nomen in Libellum peculiarem conscribat ; et cujusque Seniorum Sociorum fas esto eum quoties placuerit examinare, quomodo in literis proficiat. Hoc Statutum qui violarit, tanquam Collegii splendorem offuscans, eam censuram subeat, quam Præpositus et major pars Seniorum irrogabit.

NOTE.—Laud fixes the hours of opening and closing the gates without reference to prayers, but agrees that they shall always be shut during prayers. Assuming that all within the College attended, this was a measure of safety.

Otherwise Laud adopts the whole chapter, with slight verbal alterations.

The clause that even the servants shall pursue their education in the College is probably due to a clause in the Grant of the site by the City of Dublin, which Grant is revoked if the Society shall ever consist of members not devoted to the pursuit of Letters. In Oxford Colleges, however, the servitors were also generally poor students.

Epilogus.

Cap. 24.

Atque haec fere sunt quæ Prædecessores nostri aut ab aliis sapienter inventa, aut usu ipso comperta, ac prudenter constituta tradiderunt. Quæ nos in unum Statutorum corpus compacta et ordinata posteris tradenda duximus, rogantes, et in Domino obsecrantes eos qui præsunt, ut ex iis hoc Collegium regant, et administrent, nec temere quicquam sibi innovandum putent. Nam et mali moris est Leges semel fixas mutare, et recens inventa plerumque experimento fallunt, licet novitate blandiantur. Ac ne quis eorum quibus parendi officium incumbit, ignoratione peccet, Volumus ut hæc Statuta, initio cujusque Termini, publice in sacello per Decanum promulgentur.

Soli autem sapienti, DEO TRIN-UNI, PATRI, FILIO, ET SPIRITUI SANCTO, sit Laus, honor et Gloria, in Secula Seculorum, AMEN.

        Guilielmus Bedell Præpos.
        Josephus Travers, Bursar.
        David Thomas.   Gulielmus Fitz-Gerald.
Randulphus Ince.

NOTE.—The chapter under this title in Laud's book (xxvii) begins indeed with these phrases, but then goes on to declare the law in case of doubts and difficulties, and especially the duties and powers of the two Visitors, substituted for the seven in Bedell's time. The reading out of the statutes on the first day of term lasted till about 1840.

DE ELECTIONUM FORMA.

Cap. 25.

Quoniam ad pacem et Tranquillitatem Collegii permultum retulerit, legitimam in Electionibus formam observari, placuit hac de re aliquid Statutis prioribus tametsi jam perfectis attexere. Quoties igitur Præpositi locum vacare contigerit, Electio ad hanc formam instituetur. Vice-Præpositus, aut si nullus Vice-præpositus tum domi fuerit, Socius Senior, convocato quamprimum Collegii Senatu, de die Electionis ad eum referet : quod si quem ex Electoribus tum a Collegio abesse contigerit, ejus reditum haud ultra octiduum expectari volumus, atque interea diem Electioni præfinitum valvis sacelli affigi. Qui cum advenerit, post precum solennia Sacra Synaxis celebretur a Decano, si Minister fuerit ; alioqui ab alio ex Sociis, cui id munus a majori parte impositum fuerit, una cum Sermone, in quo Electores cohortabitur, ut Deum et Collegii bonum præ oculis habentes, talem Præpositum eligant, qualem Statuta designant. Præmissa concione, Electores soli in Sacello remanebunt ; lectisque Statutis de officio et juramento Præpositi, et hoc capite de Electionum forma, cuique suo ordine permissum esto quem velit nominare, et de ejusdem pietate, doctrina, prudentia, et integritate verba facere. Quo peracto, quisque juxta ordinem Senioritatis hoc jusjurandum dabit : Ego, N. Deum testor in conscientia mea, me Statuta nuper lecta fideliter et integre observaturum, et illum in Præpositum electurum, quem Statuta nuper lecta significare et apertius describere mea conscientia judicabit, omni illegitima affectione, odio, amore, et similibus sepositis. Considebunt inde Vice-Præpositus vel senior socius, cumque eo alii duo præsentium maxime Seniores, et suffragia sua primi omnium descripta deponent ; quod idem exemplum reliqui sequentur ; et in quem major pars totius numeri Sociorum Seniorum consenserit, is pro electo habeatur. Quod si primo et secundo scrutinio suffragia partis majoris in aliquem unum non consenserint, præsentes omnes Suffragia sua in Vice-præpositum sive Socium Seniorem et proximos duos seniores compromittere volumus, eorumque saltem duos electionem absolvere ; eamque ab omnibus ratam habendam decernimus. Electio mox publicabitur nomine majoris partis Sociorum, et electus, præstito juramento Collegii, Præposituram gerat.

Quoties vero Socii probationarii vel Discipuli eligendi sunt, peracta examinatione ex Statutis requisita, Senatus Collegii postridie convocabitur, et perlectis Statutis de eorum qualitate et electione, una cum hoc Capite de forma electionum, nomina candidatorum publice recitabuntur, et cuique ex Electoribus permissum esto, de eorum doctrina, ingenio, probitate, vel inopia breviter verba facere. Quo peracto, quisque Elector hoc juramentum dabit. Ego N. Deum testor in conscientia mea, me Statuta nuper lecta fideliter et integre observaturum et illum (vel illos) in Socium (vel Socios) (aut Scholarem Discipulum, sive scholares Discipulos) electurum quem (vel quos) Statuta nuper Lecta significare, et apertius describere mea conscientia judicabit; omni illegitima affectione, odio, amore, et similibus sepositis. Considebunt inde in scrutinio secreto Præpositus, vel eo absente Vice-præpositus, cum duobus Sociis præsentium maxime senioribus, et Suffragia sua primi omnium descripta deponent. Post omnes reliqui Socii juxta ordinem senioritatis suæ ibidem suffragia pro numero locorum supplendorum simul et semel in acervum conferent. Ea Scrutatores discriminabunt, et in quem vel quos major pars Sociorum una cum Præposito consensisse deprehendetur, is iique pro electis habeantur, et mox Electi pronunciabuntur. Quod si primo vel secundo scrutinio numerus suppleri non possit, tertio palam omnes suffragabuntur, incipientes a junioribus, atque ita ascendendo, donec ad Præpositum ventum sit. Quod si ne sic quidem altera et tertia Suffragatione convenerint Præpositus et major pars, Electio pro ea vice terminata judicabitur.

In Seniorum vero sociorum numerum quoties quispiam cooptandus est, omissa Examinatione et juramento, utpote jam antea factis, Præpositus vel Vice-Præpositus de prælectis probationariis maxime seniorem nominabit, et de ipso suffragia rogabit, an dignus videatur qui in decedentis locum succedat. Quod si a Præposito et majari parte propter gravem aliquam causam approbatus non fuerit, de proximo verba fient; quoad in aliquem consenserint: quem deinceps secundum fundationis Chartam plene Socium constitui, et admitti placet; et parem cum cæteris proprie dictis potestatem, authoritatem, et stipendia obtinere.

> Guilielmus Bedell : Præp :
> Joseph Travers.
> David Thomas.
> Guilielmus FitzGerald.
> Ric. Jordan.
> Tho. Price.
> Randulphus Ince.

NOTE.—This chapter was deeply modified in substance, though not in form, by Laud. The election of the Provost disappears, being henceforth reserved to the Crown. With regard to the cases where a majority do not agree with the Provost, Laud solves the difficulty by giving the decision to the Provost in the third scrutiny. Both one and the other clearly intended the Provost to have not only a casting vote, but an absolute veto in all elections, Laud specially ordaining that while the Provostship is vacant no elections can be held, though an existing Provost may delegate his power to his Vice-Provost. This veto, and the power of electing in spite of a majority against him, was exercised by several Provosts till 1791, when Lord Clare, as Vice-Chancellor, decided that the Provost had no absolute negative, and that the phrase "Quem major pars, &c., una cum Præposito" only meant that the Provost must be present and voting. The whole matter is acutely argued by Matthew Young—*The Provost's Negative*, Dublin, 1792, and the written opinions of several distinguished lawyers, all in harmony with Lord Clare's decision, are added in an appendix to that book.

INDEX

A

Abbot, Archbishop of Canterbury, nominated Chancellor of Trinity College (16.2), 166; rebukes disuse of surplice and neglect of Book of Common Prayer in Trinity College, 166
Abercorn, Earl of, Scottish nobleman, yet Papist, 210
"Accompt of the Yearely Charge of the Colledge," &c., 312, 313
Adultage, or Adultship, privilege of exemption from the rod, 191, 212 *n*.
Agher, estate in Westmeath, acquired by Winter, still owned by his descendants, 301 and *n*.
Allemand, his *Histoire Monastique d'Irlande*, 1690, 6
Allen, John, borrows books from College Library, 250
All Hallowes, religious house near Dublin, 10; site granted by City for the building of Trinity College, 61
All Saints' (or All Hallowes) Monastery, value of, 49
Alvey, Henry, Second Provost, 112; also Vice-Chancellor, 115 *n*.; a leading Puritan, 134; leaves for England in 1600-1601, 115; his return, 116; leaves a second time on account of plague (1605), 129; his rule lax, 133; his chief bequests to St. John's College, Cambridge, 133; reasons of his resignation discussed, 138; disappears without comment, 139; growth of prosperity under him, 140; his enlightened policy of bringing learned men from Cambridge, 140; list of College plate under his rule, 140; growth of College library, 142, 143; his accounts, 74 *n*.; his College pott, 133

Alvey, John, related to above; Travers' old master, 113
Anabaptists, Winter's opposition to, 300, 301
Anglo-Irish, converted by Jesuits, 45 *sqq*.
Anglo-Irish intellect, superior to pure English; its many-sidedness, 323
Animi Medela (J. Stearne) contains interesting autobiographical note, 319
Anon. Neat manuscript history of College; cites Dr. Barrett; probable author, Introd. x.; referred to on pages 76, 77. 79, 93, 116, 157, 175, 178, 241 *notes*; suggests that Alvey's absence was connected with buying books, 116
Antagonism between English and Irish: Is it of race or of creed? 53-55
Andrew's (Saint) Church used as stable by Lord Deputy, 72
Anglican substituted for Irish Church in Laud's Statutes, 256
Aphorisms of J. Stearne: Its dedication to Ormond, 322
Appendix I. to Chap. II.: (*a*) Scheme for Endowment of University by G. Browne (1547), 99; (*b*) Letter from A. Loftus to Cecil, 104
Appendix II.: A. Ussher's tutorial account, 105
Appendix III.: Specimens of Travers' style, 107
Appendix IV.: Letter of Holmes to Challoner, 109
Appendix V.: Petition of Provost and Fellows to Burghley for £100 in lands, 110
Appendix VI.: Circular sent to Munster to give Patrick Crosbie facilities, 110, 111
Appendices to Chap. v.: I. Latin letter of R. Ussher, 220; II. Petition of the College to City against building close to their gate, 222-224; III. Examination of William Smith, 225
Appendix, General: Bedell's Statutes; Latin; Laud's alterations discussed in notes, 327-375
Aqua vitæ "sets the Irishman a-madding." 15
Arbour of Plunkett's house in Bridge Street, 208, 226
Ardmachanus, Ja., Primate's signature, 216, 224
Archer, Jesuit leader, 32, 33
Aristotle, 51, 317
Armagh, a barbarous place; Cathedral burnt by Shan O'Neill, 34
Armada, Failure of, 28
Arrears, Alarm of Bedell concerning, 205
Ars Concionandi, Chappell's book, 234
Arthur, Alderman, gets lease from Corporation of strip of land along west wall of College; College objects to his building on it; their petition to Corporation, 201; students carry off boards of enclosure, 202; censured by Provost, 225
Arthure, Doctor, borrowed books from College Library, 250
Ashwood, Robert, "indebted to the College," 19, 250
Atherton, Captain, 96
Atkinson, Professor, 121 *n*.
Attainted lands, 90, 110
Augustinian chapel, 49 *n*.
Augustine, S., Mountjoy confutes Jesuits from, 52
Auld, Robert, appointed by mistake to two rectories 300

B

Back Lane, Mass house in, granted to College named Kildare Hall; its site, 214, 215

377

INDEX

Baggotrath, College gets lease of, 94
Bagwell, *Ireland under the Tudors*, 20 n.
Baker, George, bequeaths £500 to College, 238
Baker, native scholar, 203
Balfour, 223
Bath, Father (de Bathe? a well-known Jesuit), 226
Barnewall, Patrick, accepts sequestrated estate of Grace Dieu, near Swords, 55 n.
Barnewell, Mr. John, false name, 274
Barnewell, Capucin, 226
Barry, Librarian of Kildare Hall, 250
Basil, William, his letter to Lord Deputy and Council, referring to Kerdiff's statements of College property in Tralee and Limerick, printed as Appendix to Chap. viii., 324-326
Bastardy, no bar to inheritance among the Irish, 15 n.
Bedell, William, third Provost, recommended by Abbot, 193; educated at Emanuel College, Cambridge, 194; his Venetian experiences, 194; sworn as Provost in 1627, 195; disorder of College, wrangling of Fellows, 196, 198; he returns to England and stays away till ordered by the king to go back to Dublin, 197; his influence, 197, 198; he writes out the College statutes, 198; following Temple and not copying those of Emanuel College, 199; becomes Bishop of Kilmore, 198; encourages law and medicine, 206; often at variance with Ussher, 233; respected by natives during the Great Rebellion, 275; disliked by Wentworth, 233; Laud expunges his clause encouraging the study of Irish in College, 258; his manuscript code published in this volume for the first time, 255 n.
Bedell's staff (mace), large sum subscribed for under Alvey, 140
Bedell's Statutes, define College terms, 113 n.
Benefactions, Book of, ignores Adam Loftus; list of first donors, 63, 67
Berkeley, George, 157
Bernard, Dr., funeral sermon on Ussher; his inaccuracy, 70; statement about Cromwell's soldiers and College library, 316; misconduct as to livings, and Bedell's opposition, 210
Billeting soldiers in College forbidden, 286
Bingham, Sir R., keeps down Connaught, 3; his cruelties, 38, 39 n.; he complains of growing old, 51; contributes to Trinity College, 67; defeats and massacres Scots at Ardnaree, 126
Binnes, J., borrowed books from College Library, 250
Birmingham, Friar, 208
Bishop, Raymond, Senior Fellow, 289
Blayney, E., 223
Blount, Sir Charles, v. Mountjoy
Bodkin, merchant, in whose house Friars proselytise students, 208
Booth, student, condemned to be whipped in Hall for taking and roasting a pig found in the street, 205, 206
Book of Benefactions, 70
Borlase, Lord Justice, 279
Boswell, rector of Kildare Hall (and a Fellow), 217, 240, 250
Bourk, Richard, owes the College £7, 250
Bourke, David, educated at Oxford, 12
Boyle, Richard (Earl of Cork), 41; adventurer, 91; his opinion on Ireland in 1630, 210, 211; erects a monument to his wife in S. Patrick's, 235. *See* Cork
Brabazon, Sir H., ancestor of Earl of Meath, 49 n.
Brady, Hugh, Bishop of Meath, his letter about Loftus and the Deanery, 57 n.
Brass, in Library, records Baker's gift, 239; Henry Jones' gift, 297
Breddam, George, tenant of Bridewell, 189
Brereton, Sir, "allowed 12 artists" (bachelors in arts?), "appointed Master in Bridge Street," 217
Brereton, Sir W., compares Dublin favourably with Edinburgh; travels through mountainous parts near Newry and Wicklow without danger in 1637; dines with Ussher, 253, 254; admires his sermons, dines with Bishop Richardson, 254; describes Ussher's private chapel at Drogheda, 236 n.
Brewer's Introduction to the *Carew Papers*, 7 n.
Bridewell built in Hoggen Green to restrain beggars, who carried infection of plague, 1603, 130; Chichester acquired it from Corporation of Dublin, 188, 189; residence for students under name of Trinity Hall till 1641, 189
Bridge Street, Mass houses in, granted to College; named S. Stephen's Hall, 214, 215
Brodeley, Mr., borrows books from the College Library, 250
Brook, his *History of the Puritans*, 83 n., 85 n., 86
Brooking's map of Dublin, 1728, 202
Brouncker, Sir H., President of Munster, orders all Roman ecclesiastics to leave the country, and offers rewards for their apprehension, 33
Browne, Mary, love-letter to Thomas Clansie (Clanchy), 252
Browne, Archbishop of Dublin, his important letter about transforming Collegiate Church of S. Patrick into an University, 57 and Appendix, 99
Bryen, Denis, Munster agent, Temple's letter to him, 178 n.
Bull and bear-baiting, students forbidden to witness, 190
Burgh, Lord (Lord Deputy), 40; died in harness, 51
Burgh, Tho., bishop of Kilmacduagh, 12
Burke, Lord, of Castleconnell, educated in the College, 184
Burkes of Mayo, children barbarously executed, 39
Burghley, Lord (Chancellor), his Protestantism; his appointment of Travers, 82; his letters to Napper and Bingham, 89 n.
Bursar, first appointed in 1612, 174; they husband the little resources of College during years of disaster, 289; list of, 289
Burton, native scholar, 203
But, Mr., "for writing out the statutes," 160
Byse (or Bysshe), John Robert, 272

C

Cambridge, its Puritan influence on the founders of Trinity College, 58
Cambridge Statutes, copied by Dublin University, 166
Cambridge Chancellor adopted by Dublin University 166

INDEX

Cantwell, William, complains of seizure of his property, 14
Capuchins, College of, 208
Caput of the Congregation, 163
Carroll, Sir James, helps to manage financial affairs of the College, 129; his money transactions, 142; vice-treasurer, 70, 71
Carew, writes that mayors refuse to come to the church, 35
Caroline Constitution, 1637, 198; minute differences show the mind of Laud; its fatuous prohibition of games, 205; the work of Laud, but founded on Bedell's Statutes, 255
Carson, Dr., xiii.
Carte, his life of Ormond, 131
Carter, borrowed from Kildare Hall, 250
Cartwright, translates Travers' Latin work, 84
Cary, Sir G., acquires piece of ground between College and Hoggen Green, 188
Case, author of *Speculum Moralium Quæstionum*, 58 n.
Catalogue of Library of 1604, inaccurately termed the first, 143
Caulfield, Sir Toby (and Lord), builds a house between Hoggen Green and Suffolk Street, 188; his son in Exeter College, 200; his house bought by Ussher, 254
Celibacy clause in Fellowship oath, abolished under Victoria, 156 n.
Caulfield, W., signs petition, 223
Challoner, Luke, earnest reformer, 58; the real founder of Trinity College, 60; his letter about cashing bills of captains, 70; lends his books freely, 78; educated at Trinity College, Cambridge, 118; "painful preacher" and lover of books, 119; shrewd man of business, 119; his monument neglected and defaced, 120; obtains site for Bridewell, 130; his scheme for enlarging the usefulness of College, 170; his death in 1613, a loss, 171
Challoner, Phœbe, daughter of above, married James Ussher, 118
Chancellor of Trinity College, his importance to mediate between the College and the Crown, 259
Clanchy (or Clancy), Thomas, agent for College in Limerick; two interesting letters among his business papers, 251
Chantry lands, Challoner's catalogue of, about Dublin, 169
Chappell, W., seventh Provost, sent to Trinity College as a High Churchman by Laud, 231; his autobiography, gap of twenty-five years in, 231, 232; invited by Temple as a Ramist and Low Churchman in 1612, 231; the King compliments him on his disputation at Cambridge; tutor at Christ's College, Cambridge, where he flogged young Milton, 232; he becomes a High Churchman, which gains him the favour of Laud and the hostility of Ussher, 232; changes introduced by; Irish lecture abandoned, surplice imposed on students, 237; made bishop of Cork and Ross, he retains the provostship, contrary to statute, 248; resigns the provostship, 249, 266; charges against him in Irish Parliament of 1641, 271
Charges in College, not lower than in Oxford or Cambridge; 2d. a liberal price for a meal, 134
Charles II. gains the credit of Cromwell's ideas, 316
Charter of Queen Elizabeth, 63; Abbot as Chancellor demands its surrender; refused by Fellows; their argument quoted by Hely Hutchinson, *Anon.*, and Stubbs, 167
Chambers, College, rent of, 217
Chatham, Lord, trains his son in *viva voce* translation, 187
Chatterton, his failure to settle in Ulster, 158
Chichester, Lord Deputy, 1604-1616, brought up in school of Mountjoy, 179, 180; puzzled by James's vacillating treatment of Jesuits, 183 and *note;* applies for lease of Sir G. Carey's house, 189
Chieftain's household, barbarism of, 13
Christ Church Cathedral, Dublin, Friday lecture in, 176, 177
"Christ's College," title proposed for Dublin College, 57
Cimbri, compared to savage Scots, 126
Clandeboye, Lord, *see* Hamilton, James
Clanrickard, strong ruler, 3
Clare, Lord, his decision at visitation of 1791, 262
Clark, Edward, aspires to provostship, 192
Clearke, John, admitted M.D., 304
Clelow, James, 305
Clergy, slothful, selfish, 25
Coburne, Chris, 250
Collections, Winter's MS. notebook in Library, 300 n.
College Library, earliest catalogue, 1600; second catalogue, doubtless begun by Ambrose Ussher, 143; did not contain a single specimen of fine early printing; theological commentaries in coarse binding (that of John Francton in 1604 the earliest), 143
College plate, pledged during great Rebellion; £50 received on it from Jacob Kirwan, 283, 287; only pieces remaining from before the Rebellion, 285 n.
College seal, the original, 124 n.; that of 1612, 169
Collins, John, vintner, his bequest, 293
Commissary of Prerogatives, a lay post, 192
Commonwealth Records, 295 n.
Communion table, none in College Chapel at Bedell's election, 196; position of, 236; in Ussher's chapel at his palace, 236; in S. Peter's, Drogheda, 236
"Concealed lands," 40, 41, 111
College Halls in city, Wentworth allows these to be recovered by lawsuit and re-occupied by Papists, 238
Collectanea, Leland's, 231
Commencements (conferring of degrees), 114, 115; the principal at end of Trinity Term, 186
Concordatum Fund, surrendered by College under Victoria, 156 n.
Commissioners of Ulster plantation, 127
Cohonnogh Dowin, entry concerning in P.B., 137
Conosius Dovinus, not O'Cahan's heir, but probably an O'Doyne; his tutor A. Ussher, 137. See Cohonnogh Dowin
Conway, Robert, Senior Fellow, signs act to abrogate the *nempe quatuor*, 242; deprived of Fellowship by Privy Council, 243; restored to Fellowship by Wentworth, 244; summoned before Irish Parliament, 269; charges against, 271

INDEX

Conway, native scholar, not Irish name, 203; (Sir), 206
Conway, Lord, his letter to Lord Dorchester, 211
Cotterel, James, his bequest, 124
Conall, a monastery, also spelt Connall, suppressed religious house, 8; part of its lands in grant to College, 154
Conway, Lord, invites Jeremy Taylor to Portmore, near Lisburn, 322
Cook Street Carmelite house seized; Mayor and Primate stoned by mob; house razed by Lords Justices, 214 and *note*
Coote, Sir Charles, subscribes £50 to College or £95? (see *note*), 239
Cork House, the Restoration prevents Ussher's library being deposited there, 316
Cork, Richard, Earl of, describes improved state of country in 1630, letter to Lord Dorchester, 210, 211; Lord Justice of Ireland, 211; his remarkable letter to Dorchester, describing magnificent house of Jesuits, 218; monument to his wife, set up in east end of chancel in S. Patrick's, 236; his seizure of Friar's house declared illegal, 238
Cork, Lady, dies in Sir T. Caulfield's house, 254; her great tomb in S. Patrick's Cathedral, 234
Cork and Ross, Chappell Bishop of, 249, 252
Corporation of Dublin, grant site of College, 67; still hold formal document, 65, 66
Cottingham, admitted to Fellowship by Falkland, but displaced, 197
Coughlan, Richard, turbulent Fellow, 290
Cowley, Joshua, leave of absence, 305
Coyne, a College student, 184
Coyne, old Irish exaction, 44
C.P., or Carew Papers, referred to, pp. 4, 5, 13, 14, 15, 16, 29, 37, 38, 39, 44, 47, 58, 79, 86, xvi
Creagh, Dr., Pope's Legate, 23
Crompton, Thomas, from Brazenose College, 304
Cromwell, Henry, 299; elected Chancellor by Winter, 302; his benefaction to College, 302; his reception on landing near Kingstown, 302 *n.*; not much of a Puritan, 321 and *note*

Cromwell, Oliver, 288, 289, 296, 297; less cruel than he has been painted; his enlightened treatment of Irish industries, 306, 307; his proposals (1) to found a new college near Trinity, (2) to endow Dublin with a public library, 309
Cromwellian settlement, its harshness exaggerated, 309
Crosbie, Patrick, appointed agent to seek out attainted lands, 41, 111; his friendly intercourse with tenants, 91, 92 and *note*
Crown, dictation of in election of Provost, 212
Cudworth, Ralph, Trustee of College, 295
Cuellar, Captain, wrecked from Armada on Sligo coast, 24
Cullen, 239 *sq.*
Cultu divino, de, first chapter of Bedell's Statutes, 199; degraded to ninth place by Laud, 256
Cusack, mentioned as English name, 4; Adam, 272, 297
Custodium, of temporalities of archbishopric of Tuam, 88

D

Dale, John, 300
Dame's Gate, in Castle wall, nearest point of city to monastery of All Hallowes, 72
Daniell, William (also O'Donnell), one of the original scholars, Fellow in 1593, 77; burns a sacred image in Galway, 45; writes of "traitorous seminaries," 35; his Irish version of the New Testament, 121
Davis, Sir John, his tract on why Ireland was not subdued, 5 *n.*, 7 *n.*; thinks all Irish difficulties are overcome, 1616, 21, 23, 34, 53; acute observer, 144
Davis, native scholar, 203
Decadence of College felt by James Ussher, 200
Declamation, required weekly from students, 185
Decrements (detriments), College fee for wear and tear of house, 80 and *note*
Degree examination, proficiency required for, 185
Denationalisation of Trinity College effected by Laud and Wentworth; Englishmen imported; no O or Mac among scholars elected, 247

Denization, right of pleading like English subjects, 5
Denny, Sir Henry, his "outrageousnes toward the Irish, 39
Deputation of Fellows goes to London in 1629 to obtain freedom of election, 211
Desmond, Earl of, vast estates, 30
Detriments, Fellow Commoners' and Pensioners' weekly payment, 4d. ob. and 2d., 131, 153. See Decrements
Devenish, Ed., mayor of Dublin, 1591, 62
Dialectic, first year's course, 187
Diet, cost of in College, 153, 154, *n.*
Dillon, Garret, College offers to pay him for recovering chantry lands, 156
Dillon, James, relative of James Ussher, 200
Dillon, Lord, mention in petition of College, 223, 224
Dio Chrysostom, 43
Directory ordered to be used instead of Prayer Book by Puritan Government, 289
Discipline of students: all games forbidden; park reserved for Fellows divided by walls, and let for orchards, &c.; young offenders birched by junior Dean; confession on their knees during dinner time, 190, 191
Disqualification of marriage, 200
Dissension of Fellows under Chappell; question of seniority; conflict between High and Low Church; the four candidates—Hoyle, Pheasant, Cullen, Ware; appeal to the visitors, 239-244
Dissertation on Death (J. Stearne): its dedication; its attack on ignorant Calvinists; letter of commendation from Jeremy Taylor, 321, 322
Dix, Mr., author of "Earliest Dublin Printing," 97; his catalogue shows dearth of Dublin printing in Temple's time, 150
Dixon, Prof. MacNeile, writes first of "College Histories," xiii.
Docwra, Lord, mention in petition of College, 223, 224
Dodwell, Henry, enters College in 1655, 290
Donegal, monastery of, possessed library where Four Masters wrote, 9

INDEX

Donellan, Edmund, entries concerning in P.B., 164
Donnellan, Nehemiah, translates Bible into Irish, 1594, 12
Dopping, Anthony, enters College in 1655, 290
Dowdall, Sir J., letter to Burghley, 36 n.
Drury, Sir W., Lord Deputy, his cruelty, 39
Dublin Castle, heads exposed on ; hostages ill-treated in, 37, 38
Duke, Sir Henry, speaks Irish and English, 12
Dun (Dunn), Dr. Charles, Vice-Chancellor, 162 ; Fellow in 1608, 115 n.
Dungan, John, 272

E

"Ecclesiastical Benefice" defined, 199
Edward VI., Irish replica of his act seizing chantry lands, 156, 157
Elizabeth, Queen, why does she found Trinity College ? 1 ; her letter authorising it, 62 ; hostility to Scots in Ulster, 125
Elrington, Charles, Professor of Divinity, 1829, Introd. x.
English rule, cruelty of, 37 sqq.
English settlers in Ireland, sell their land through distrust of James's gifts, 182
Esmonde, Laur, 223
Essex, Robert, Earl of, his expedition to Munster, 113 ; Chancellor of Cambridge and Trinity College, Dublin, 112 ; his execution, 114
Essex, Lord, the elder, his failure to settle in Ulster, 158
Ethic and rhetoric, fourth year's course, 187
Eustace, Rowland, 250
Evangelical spirit of Church of Ireland, 230 ; due to Travers and his school, 87
Examination of William Smith, Appendix iii. to Chap. v., 225
Exeter College, Ussher sends young Dillon there, 200
Extern students, Bedell's suggestion, 206
Eyre, William, comes to Dublin, 140 ; correspondent of Ussher ; recommends Martin for Fellowship, 179, 180

F

Falkland, Lord Deputy, complains of being thwarted, 183; petitioned to admit candidates to Fellowship, 197 and note ; orders their admission, retracts order, 197 ; his proclamation against religious houses disregarded ; himself recalled, 213 ; he protests against the weakness of the Government in dealing with the "contagion of Popery," 209, 223
Falkland, Captain, son of Lord Deputy, educated in Trinity College, Dublin, 184
Feasant, see Pheasant
Fen, Humphrey, controversial Puritan, 86 n.
Fenton, Sir Geoffrey, Lord Cork's father-in-law, 235 ; complains of his old age, 51 n.
Field, his letter to General of Order of Jesuits, 48
Finances of College, improving in 1606, 137
Financial distress of College during Rebellion, 285–288
Fitzgerald, Will., Fellow, 216
Fitzgeralds, two, their building in the College, 238
Fitzmaurice, Lord Lixnaw's son, educated in the College, 184
FitzSimon, leading Jesuit, 33
Fitzwilliam, Lord Deputy, his coat-of-arms falsely said to be set over the gate, 66 ; issues circular letter ; contributes £200 to College, 67 ; smallness of his force against Spaniards, 24
Fleetwood, Lord Deputy, 299 and note
"Flight of the Earls," a relief to the country, 136
Floyd, J., Welsh Vice-provost, 196
Floyd, William, cousin of Vice-Provost, admitted to Fellowship by Falkland, 196, 197
Folliott, Sir H., Vice-Provost's bond to, 175
Four Masters, The, on the year 1595, 2
Foxes and Firebrands, J. Nalson's, 214 n.
Franciscans, keep alive some respect for sacraments, 24
Friday, Laud makes it a fast-day in College, 257
Froude, makes the Irish difficulty one of religion, 54
Fuller, records in his *Church Hist.* that it never rained a day during the building of Trinity College, 66 and note
Fullerton, James, one of the original Fellows, a Scotch schoolmaster, 77, 78 ; probably political agent of King James, 123 ; works in Munster with Crosbie, 125 ; invaluable as bursar, 127; Commissioner of Ulster plantation, 127 ; obtains grants of lands in Munster, 128 ; epitaph in Westminster Abbey, 128 ; his influence on King James, 155 ; last mention of, 212
Furniture, no accounts for, very little used by students, 135

G

Galloway, Galway, "From which there went shipping daily to Spain" (Walworth), 226 ; Bodkin offers to convey students to, 208, 226
Galway, compared to the Arcadia of to-day in regard of glass windows, 16 ; founded by English families, yet becomes very Irish, 17
Games of cards, &c., permitted by Laud's Statutes "at the time of Christmas," 257
Gardiner, contributes to Trinity College, 67 ; enemy of Boyle, 87, 88 n.
Garstin, J. R., author of "Irish State and Civic Maces," 140 n.
Gearnan, name superscribed in A. Ussher's account, 82
General Convention of Ireland, petition addressed to, contrary to statutes, 305, 306
Gerald, Earl of Kildare, founder of Maynooth, 9
Gilbert, Sir John, author of "History of the City of Dublin," 73, 201, 254 n.
Glyn, Knight of, his infant son, a pledge in Carew's hands, 39
Goodwin, Thos., 295
Gore, Sir A., Vice-Provost's bond to, 175
Gorges, Dr., 313, 315
Gowns, debate between Provost and Chancellor as to whether students should wear them in the street, 206
Grace before meat, Bedell's still used in College ; Laud changes one word, 257
Gracedieu, nunnery at Swords, 8
Grammar schools in Dublin, Waterford, Cork, Kilkenny, Limerick, 10
Gray of Wilton, Lord, bloody deputyship, 37
Greek, required from all College students, 185
Greene, Mr., London goldsmith, makes College seal of 1612, 169 n.

INDEX

Guñ, Sir, appointed Master in Bridge Street Hall, 217
Gylippus, mission to Syracuse, compared to the Jesuit Archer, 32
Gunpowder explosion in 1596, killed many students, 140

H

Hamilton, Archibald, 272
Hamilton, James, collects temporalities in Tuam, 2, 3; one of the earliest Fellows, 77; sent to Tuam and York, 78; tries to collect rents for College, 89; obtains large grants in Co. Down, 128; becomes Lord Clandeboye, 123, 129; is granted lease of northern College estates, afterwards broken, 169
Harding, John, M.A., of Cambridge, imposed on Trinity College, Dublin, as Senior Fellow by Wentworth, and tutor to Wentworth's son, 247; accepts a living which voids his Fellowship, reappointed Senior Fellow by letters patent, 247; his official perjury, 249; Vice-Provost; he disappears; his reappearance, 276 *n.*; his degradation, Appendix ot Chap. vii., 291, 292
Harrison, Sir, lecturer in Bridge Street Hall, 217
Hawking, an offence punished in Trinity College. 79
Hawks, Irish, presented to Burghley and Cecil, 79
Hebrew (first two Psalms) required for degree, 185; made compulsory for M.A. degree by Winter, 299
Healing of the Soul, The (J. Stearne). Fulsome dedication to H. Cromwell; complimentary letters from three bishops, 320, 321
Hegel, undisturbed by Napoleon's capture of Jena, 28
Hely Hutchinson, Provost, composes history of Trinity College, 1790-1792; notes that Loftus did not draw up Statutes, 71; had seen an earlier portion of Temple's Statutes than was come down to us, 161; quarrel with his Senior Fellows, 262 *n.*; his MS. exposes injustice of attack on Chappell, 272
H. H. = Hely Hutchinson MS.; frequently cited in notes, xvi.
Henry VIII. no Protestant, 55
Herbert, Sir Wm., humane, 39; his house (in Kerry) seized by rebels, 48; not in list of subscribers to Trinity College, 69; his correspondence quoted, 158
Hermathena, xxviii; article on College Library, 98 *n.*
Herrings, four barrels of, granted to College, 287
Hist. MSS. Commission, 313 *n.*
Hogan, Father, author of *Ibernia Ignatiana*, 48, 273
Holmes, Matthew (Fellow), 69 and Appendix
Hoggen Green, opposite Trinity College. From Hogges, ancient mounds, 72, 73; encroachments on, 188; begins to be called College Green about 1629, 201
Hoile (Hoyle), rector of Kildare Hall, 250
Holmpatrick, Priory, value of, 49
Holy Sacrament, none in College Chapel for eleven years, 196
Houling, Father, S.J., founds Irish College in Lisbon, 32; his grief over Dublin University, 60
Hoyle, Nathaniel, refuses to wear surplice, 240, 241; preaches at S. Werburgh's, 254; Senior Fellow, 290; returns from Oxford as Vice-Provost, 297
Howth, Lord, his affray in Thomas Street, 190

I

Ibernia Ignatiana (Father Hogan's), 48
Ignatius suggests Irish mission, 25
Ince, Randal, elected Fellow, 196, 240
In commendam, Provost directed to hold his place, 247
Indian Mutiny, compared to Irish Rebellion, 275
Ingram, Dr. Thomas, criticises Mr. Lecky's views on Irish affairs, 54
Isham (George), his grant in Munster from Queen Elizabeth bought by the College, 125
Irish lecture and prayers in College, instituted by Bedell, 203
Irish names, adoption of by English in sixteenth century, 4
Irish Parliament of 1641, its charges against the Bishop of Cork for his government of the College, 269
"Irish Question" now one of religion, 56
Irish race, taken under royal protection of King James; beneficent effect of this act, 160
Irish studies, encouraged by English, not by Anglo-Irish Provosts, 204
Irish teaching in the College suppressed by Laud and Wentworth, 258
Irish tongue, University required by James I. to train natives to preach in, 177 *n.*
Italic hand, elegantly written by Temple and Ussher, 152

J

James I., his change of religion, 32; seeks to influence Ireland, 125; secretly encourages Scotch immigration during Elizabeth's lifetime, 126; grants lands in Connaught and Donegal to Fullerton, 127; his munificence to College; first grant to J. Ware of attainted lands in Tipperary, Waterford, &c.; second grant confirms by letters patent the gift of Elizabeth in 1599; third grant gives estates in Armagh, Fermanagh, Donegal; fourth grant, chantry lands in Dublin; fifth grant (small), attainted lands in Limerick and Kerry; sixth and seventh grants make perpetual yearly subsidy from Crown of £388 15s., procured by Temple; eighth grant, patent for election of burgesses to Parliament; ninth grant empowers College to plant Ulster estates; tenth and eleventh, modifications of tenure, 154-156; his vacillation between the Reformed Church and Spain, 183
Jans, Edward, receipt for rent, 238
Jerpoint, a monastery in Co. Kilkenny, 8
Jesuits, their crusade against Protestant England, 16; they convert Irish schools, 26, 28; influence chieftains, 28; reward for their apprehension, 33; they translate the quarrel of race into one of creed, 56; James orders their expulsion, and retracts it, 183; they increase under Charles I., 207

INDEX 383

John Baptist, S., value of monastery, 49
Jordan, Rich., Fellow, 216
Jones, Henry, £10 debt to College, 250
Johnson, Charles, 250
Jones, Colonel Michael, Governor of Dublin, patron of College; Cromwellian general, 288
Jones, Henry, Vice-Chancellor and Bishop of Meath; his gifts to Library, 297
Jones, Sir Roger, his affray in Thomas Street, 190
Junior Fellows, deprived by Temple of right of legislating for the College, 163; unsoundness of this statute; its result that governing body consists of very old men, 164
Jus quinque sanguinum, 5

K

Kearney, W., carries off printing press, benches, &c.,from College, 135
Kenlis, a nunnery in Co. Kilkenny, 8
Kerdiffe (Kerdiff), John, "native scholar," 203; Sir, one of the city, 225; John, Fellow, 240; entrusted with re-letting of College lands by Cromwell; resigned to avoid accepting Laud's Statutes, 289; made Senior Fellow by special act of Chancellor, 289; saves College estates from confiscation, 302
Kerdiff, Senior Fellow, 240
Kildare, Dowager Countess of, owns splendid house of Jesuits, 218; plaintiff against the College, 238
Kildare Hall, books borrowed from, 249; Lord Cork endows theological lecture at, 218
Kilkenny Castle, contains deed of appointment of Ormond as Chancellor of Trinity College, 287
Kilmainham, plundered, 46; residence of Lord Deputy at, 19; grant of chantry lands at, 156
Kilmallock, More Dom, 223
King's letter granting privileges, payment of fee for, 136
Kinsale, siege of, 70
Kilmacrenan, Abbey of, passes to the College (from Fullerton and O'Donnell), 127 *n.*; part of King James's grant to the College; small rents paid by Irish tenants, 155;

during Protectorate the natives were not extirpated by Cromwell, 307
Kyffin, 43

L

Lacy, Brother Jacob, 274 *n.*
Lally, Wm., Archbishop of Tuam, time-serving prelate, 23; silent about the College, 59; his death; his widow in possession, 88, 89
Land, Irish love of, 31 and *note*
Lane, Sir R., complains of old age, 51
Latin, Irish chiefs converse in, 13l; spoken at Commons by Bedell's order, 203
Latwar (Latewar), Richard, D.D., brought over as chaplain by Mountjoy; killed by bullet near Benburb, 141; memorial slab in St. John's College, Oxford, 141 *n.*; donor of silver pott and books to Trinity College, Dublin, 141
Laud, William, Archbishop of Canterbury, Chancellor of Trinity College; his English primacy of import to Ireland, 228; creates mischievous division between the Protestant communions of the North, 230; his anti-Puritan policy; he and Wentworth endeavour to make Trinity College ecclesiastical, 256; his Code of Statutes *not* entirely new, 230; his imprisonment, 275; general intention of his Statutes to make the College English in tone and Anglican in creed, in opposition to the Anglo-Irish sympathies of Bedell and the evangelical principles of Ussher, 256; removes the chapter *De Cultu Divino* from first to ninth place, 199; insists on removing Earl of Cork's monument to his wife in S. Patrick's, 236; has in hands University Charter, 247 *n.*
Lawyers, Anglo-Irish, help to emancipate the people, 5; their *rôle* on the Roman Catholic side, 46
Lawyers, English, place-hunters, 46; their dislike to Ireland, 47
Lazar Hill (now Townsend Street) in Dublin, 73
Lazy (Lazar) Hill in Dublin, 202
Lecale, Barony of (in Co. Down), 67

Lecky, Mr. W. H., differs from Froude in his estimate of Irish affairs, 54
Lee, Captain Thomas, his barbarity, 39
Leicester, Earl of, petitioned by Fellows to relieve the distress of College caused by great Rebellion, 282, 283
Letters Patent, empowering College to send representatives to Parliament in 1613; mentions possible founding of other colleges, 162, 165, 166
Letters, scarcity of private, in this epoch, 2
Liber Munerum Hiberniæ, 148
Library of Primate Ussher, offered for sale by his daughter, 314; Cromwell's scheme to present it to City of Dublin altered by his death; presented by Charles II. to Trinity College, 316
Library, College, books borrowed from 249; Brereton speaks sneeringly of, 255; earliest catalogue of, 98; use of, confined to graduates, 126
Linen industry in the north, older than Strafford, 159
Lissagh, John, 273
Lishag(t) Thad, Fellow, 216
Lismore Papers, 178 *n.*
Loftus, Dudley, translates from the Armenian; edits posthumous works of Stearne, 322, 323
Loftus, Adam, Archbishop of Dublin, his speech urging the establishment of an university, 9; secures appointments in S. Patrick's, 29; delays foundation of Trinity College, 30; complains of increase of recusancy, 33; his dishonesty, 57, 58 *n.*; first Provost of Trinity College, 61; speech to the Corporation, 61; contributes £100, 67; his palace at S. Sepulchre's, 71; did no work for the College, 71, 72; resigns the provostship, 72
Loftus, A., Chancellor, signs petition, 223
Logic, second year's course, 187
Lords Justices (Cork and Loftus) order seizure of Mass houses, 213, 214
Lord's Prayer, in Irish, 203
Ludlow, his country house at Moncktown, 322
Lydiat, Thomas, brought over to Trinity College, Dublin, by A. Ussher, 122

INDEX

Lynch, mentioned as an English name, 4
Lyon, William, Bishop of Cork, describes rapid growth of Roman Catholic religion in Cork and Waterford, 34, 35; commits schoolmasters to prison, 36

M

MacDonnells of Antrim, Scottish immigrants, 126
Mace, earliest college, disappeared; larger one of Queen Anne's time, 140 n.
Magister, applied to butler, 253
Magrath, Miler, time-serving bishop, 23; makes no allusion to Trinity College, 30
Malbie, Sir N., valuable notes on Ireland (1582), 36 n.
Marchers, the Lords, in Wales, parallel to the Lords of the Pale in Ireland, 54
Margetson, Dean, 247
Marriages, of English with Irish frequent, 4
Marsdens, English Puritans, 297, 298
Marshall, Thomas, M.A., of Cambridge, imposed as Senior Fellow, to help in passing new Charter, 247
Martin, Anthony, Bishop of Meath, Dean and Catechist in 1613, 174; gives account of College money, 174; close friend of Ussher, 233; comes to Dublin from Emanuel College, Cambridge, 140; invited to take charge of College, 278; appointed lecturer, 280; his salary not completely paid, 281; his numerous benefices, 281; his property looted, imprisoned by justices, 282; delays in his formal appointment as Provost, 283, 284; his see non-existent during Rebellion, 284; he preaches against Puritan heresy, 289; dies of plague, buried beside College Chapel, 289; exact date of his death unknown, 293
Mary, Queen, built Maryborough and Philipstown, 30
Mary's Abbey, S. (in Dublin), 8, 74
Mathers, from New England, 298; Mather, Samuel, nonconformist, yet declines to displace episcopal ministers, 300
Matriculation Book, earliest, lost by Alvey, 131; shows increase of students in 1639, 1640, 264; very scanty entrances from 1641-1657 when prosperity returns, 290; entries wrongly placed in, 304
Maxwell, Dr. Robert, lease of lands in Armagh, 304
Mayor of Dublin, one of the Board of Visitors, removed by Laud's Statutes, 259; Irish Parliament censures this ungrateful act, 272
Maynooth, ancient College of, not founded to teach, 9; Royal College of, neglected Irish studies for a hundred years, 98 n.
McCarthy More, admission to title, 20
McDonnell, Sorley Boy, speaks Irish, 12
McGeoghan, Brian, petitions Elizabeth, 11
McGeoghegan, Richard, letter from, 48
McGuinnis, Sir Hugh, contributes to Trinity College, 67
McMahon's children know English, 11
McWilliam, Eughter, chief in Mayo, 12; advises Elizabeth to recognise Irish chiefs, 20
Mead, Garrett, owes the College £18 13s. 6d., 250
Meade, Joseph, Evangelical Divine, 147; elected Provost by Senior Fellows, 193
Melvill, Andrew, teacher of Fullerton and Hamilton, 148
Mendoza, Bernardino de, Spanish ambassador, 32
Merchants, lean towards Spain, 45
Michan's, Saint, Church, 74
Midensis (Bishop of Meath), Arth., signature to petition, 223
Mixture of blood, English or Scotch with Irish, admirable results of, 157
Monasticon Hibernicum, 72 n.
Money, or Monie, Launcelot, letter about cashing bills, 70; one of the original Fellows of Trinity College, Dublin, 77
Morality, lack of, among native Irish, 15
Morum, magister, abolished in 1821, 263 n.
Moryson, Fynes, private see of Mountjoy, 71
" Mother of an University," meaning of this phrase in the Charter of the College, 63
Mountjoy, a master mind; changes the course of events in Ireland, 51; a lover of books, 71; his campaign to Waterford and his controversy with a Jesuit, 126
Mullinex, Mr., 81
Muniment Room (M.R.), loose papers in, catalogued by author, xiv; contains the old statutes signed by Temple, beginning with chap. v; Bedell's Statutes founded on these, 255-264; referred to, pp. 76, 81, 94, 110, 124, 125, 130, 172, 173, 192, 195, 202, 208, 222, 251, 252, 274, 287, 303, 304, xvi (A ii.), document about repayment of loans in copper, 142; (G. 2) Cook's account, gives number of Fellows and "schollers," 132; (F. 77) curious petition to recover books borrowed from Kildare Hall, 249
Munster plantation, 1588, 36

N

Napper, Sir R., friend of Richard Boyle, 87; chief Baron, 89 n.
Native scholars, their names do not appear to be Irish; better paid than others, 203
Nevell, Sir Patrick, ecclesiastic, signs with his mark X, 1619, 7
New College, scheme for, under Commonwealth quoted from Urwick, 309-314; proposed site, between Trinity College and Stephen's Green, 309, 310; its intention to imitate the type of Oxford and Cambridge, 314
New England, sends a lad to Trinity College in 1657, 291
Newman, William, his election as Fellow disputed, he obtains mandate from Lords Justices, countersigned by Primate; the king commands him to be elected, 219; he signs act to abrogate *nempe quatuor*, 242; deprived of Fellowship by Privy Council, 243; restored to Fellowship by Wentworth, 244; summoned before Irish Parliament, 269; charges against him and Conway, 271; indebted to College, £12, 250
New Testament, Irish version of, by William Daniell, 121 and *note*
Neylan, Bursar, 293
Nicholson, John, 157

INDEX

"Noblemen's Sonnes" need not salute Provost, 218
Non-errability of the Church, discussed by proselytising Friars, 226
Norbury (a Puritan), 297
Norreys, Sir J., describes the Irish as "Spanish in heart," 35 ; dies in harness, 51 ; contributes to Trinity College, 67
Nugent, Capuchin, seduces students to Spain, 208

O

Oath for Fellows and scholars, Laud's changes in, 257-258
O'Brien, son of Sir Turlough, educated in College ; his favoured treatment, 184
Observatore :occulti, scholars appointed to report students' misconduct to Dean, 262
O'Cahan, Sir Donald, his son kept as ward in Trinity College, 131 ; disappears from notice, 136
O'Conor, recognised by Henry VIII. as a king in west of Ireland, 5
O'Connor, Brian, his property escheated, 41
O'Connor, Sligo, speaks to Elizabeth through an interpreter, 13
O'Dogherty, Sir Cahir, cultivated young chief, his outbreak, 136
O'Donnell, Bern, a priest, 12
O'Donnell, Sir Neale, son kept as ward in Trinity College, 131 ; "bred in the College," 184
O'Flahertys, wild chieftains in Iar Connaught, 17 ; Sir Morogh ne Doe, signs with his mark, 11
Oge, Rory (O'More), his children pledges, 39
O'Heyne, Teig, native scholar, 203
Omey, Davies, secretary to Sir T. O'Neill, 11
O'Neale, Brian, 272
O'Neill, Shan, burns monasteries, 8 ; poses as a devout Catholic in London, 28, 29
O'Neill, Sir Turlough, has a secretary to write for him, 11 ; contributes to Trinity College, 67 ; claims to be *the O'Neill,* 68
Ormond, Lord Lieutenant (1643), allows College £3 10s. a weekly "dead pay," 285 ; appointed Chancellor, his generosity, 287,

288 ; vigorous and soldierly, 274 ; returns as Chancellor at Restoration, 64, 317.
O'Rorke, sent to school in Limerick, and afterwards to Oxford, 11
O'Sheneshon = O'Shaughnessy, 14
O'Sullivan, Bere, 20
O'Toole, Art, a pardoned rebel, brutally treated by Captain Lee, 39
O'Tooles in Dublin mountains, 322
Owen, John, leading member of Trustees for College (under Protectorate), 295
Oxmantown, 74

P

Pale, the, oppressed by England, 43
Parliament House, architectural glory of Dublin, 202
Parliamentarian sympathies of Fellows, due to their evangelical doctrine, 297
Parliament in Ireland, summoned by Wentworth in 1639, to vote subsidies for Charles, 264 ; their extraordinary contentment with Strafford's government, 265
Parry, a Fellow, removed from benefice, 199, 200
Parsons, Lord Justice, 279
Particular Book, the, xiv ; account for "mending of locks," 74 *n.* ; stray notices in, 96 ; receipts for *Detriments* ; no Christian names, 131 ; entry for "Sir James Carroll's scholar," 132
Patent of chantry lands, loss of, 205
Patent Rolls of James I., 131
Patrick's Cathedral, S., old collegiate church, 29 ; proposal to convert into University, 60
Patrick Street, rebels steal cows in, 96
Patrick's Well, S., 73
P.B. = Particular Book, *passim*
Pearson, 140
Pedantry of Chappell, his entry of appointment of College butler, 252
Pemberton, Master John, College butler, 253
Pensionarius, John Stearne the first student so styled in the Matric. Book [pensioners are mentioned in College accounts of 1595], 296
Pepper, Gilbert, Bursar, his accounts, 283 *n.,* 285
Perrot, Lord Deputy, quarrels

with Loftus, 29; declares for liberty of conscience, 34
Peter de Rabio, S., suppressed religious house, part of grant to College, 155
Petition of the Provost and Fellows to the Mayor and Aldermen, against building near the College gate, Chap. v., App. ii., 222 ; for Bridewell, 130; to Wentworth, to have Crown pensions commuted for lands in Connaught, 251
Pheasant (Feasant), Thomas, narrative of his expulsion from Fellowship, 240 *sqq.* ; presents petition to the House against Chappell, 268, 290
Philip II. criticises Papal bull, 26, 27 ; his cautious character, 27, 28
Physiology, *i.e.,* natural philosophy, third year's course, 187
Physic, school of, its charter formally due to Charles II. ; its basis previously laid by John Stearne, 316, 317
Pierce, John Oge, receipt for rent paid to College, 94 *n.*
Pius IV. authorises endowment of Universities from ecclesiastical property in Ireland, 26
Plague, College practically dissolved by, in 1603, 129 ; in 1649, 295
Plantation of Ulster, attempted by Elizabeth, 29
Plautine iambics, Chappell's, 239
Plunckett, William, 272
Pole, Cardinal, 25
Policy, twofold, subjection or conciliation, 3-5
Pompeii, 274
Prendergast, J. (author of *Cromwellian Settlement of Ireland*), ignores influence of Popery, 53, 54 ; calls Ormond an Englishman, 56 *n.* ; his account of Cromwellian settlement often taken from harsh orders not really executed, 308
Prescott, Mrs., inherited H. Cromwell's letters as heirlooms (Urwick), 310, 313 *n.*
Price, Mr., claims Senior Fellowship on the ground that Mr. Thomas was married, 200 ; as Dean, forbids game of bowls, as contrary to statute, 205
Priest's orders, Laud requires Fellows to take, except they be jurist or medicus, 258
Prince Charles, his Spanish escapade, 183

INDEX

Privy Council censures Provost Chappell; his punishment referred to King, who refers it to Laud, 243
Proctors, given power of visitation of houses, 245
Proposal to separate University and College favoured by Temple and Abbot; their motives, 167
Proselytising, Archbishop Walsh on, 208 *n.*
Proselytisers, seduce young men to Spain, 208
Prosperity of Ireland, dates from James' plantation of Ulster, 157
Protectorate, public safety in Ireland under, 322
Providence, East Indies, 291
Provost and Fellows, inhibited from electing by Parliament of 1641, 273
Provost's Negative, The, by Mathew Young, 262 *n.*
Provost's oath, Winter presumably had not taken it, 306
Provost, position of, altered by Laud, 261
Provost's salary £100, 160 and *note*
Prynne, Mr., makes a charge against Strafford, 269 *n.*
Ptolemies, their wise policy in Egypt, 18, 19
Public Library, Cork House transferred to Henry Cromwell for, 310
Purdon, M., his interesting private letter, 251
Puritanism, its harshness, 44; of College, inquiry into, Easter, 1615. 173
Puritan tendencies of College, its ministers acceptable to Scots in Ulster, 160
Puttock, Mr., 250

Q

Quadrangle, drying of clothes forbidden in, 304
Quinque sanguines, five privileged tribes, 21
Quorum of electors in the College (nempe quatuor) established by Bedell, 335; abrogated by Chappell, 242

R

Races in Ireland, mixture of in sixteenth century, 4
Radcliffe, Sir Geo., subscribes £20 to the College, 239
Ramus, spiritual forerunner of Bacon and Descartes; a partial reformer in logic;

studied by Protestant divines; his dialectics edited by Temple in 1584; first book published by Cambridge Press attacked by Aristotelians, 145
Ranelagh, R., 223
Records of the Corporation; gift of All Hallowes to the College, 62; grant to Alderman Arthur of land on College Green, 201; permission to any man to kill any pig seen in the streets, 206 *n.*
Record Office in London, copy of James I.'s patent obtained from, by author, 155, *n.*
Red Indians, 180
"Redshanks," Scotch savages, 125
Reformed clergy, new pack of wolves, 25
Register, College, interesting items quoted, 212 *n.*; scanty under Chappell, 249; blanks in, 293
Religious houses, abolished by Henry VIII., 7; hospitality of, causes petition against their destruction, 8, 9
Revival of Roman Catholic Creed, 25, 26
Reynolds, Paul, 272
Rich, Barnabe, decries Dublin, 2; attributes Irish difficulty to Popery, 53; censures reformed clergy who did not contribute to University, 68
Richard II., planted settlers in Wexford, 30
Richardson, Bishop of Ardagh, presents chalice and flagon to College Chapel, 254
Riche, Sir N., Bedell's letter to, 196
Rollo, Mr., 206
Roman Catholic Church, its neglect of education, 6-9
Roman Dictator, 237
Roman Catholics, Laud's Statute admits to scholarship, 258
Roque's map, 188; also spelt Rocques, 239
Roscommon, held by O'Rourke, 181
Route, The, territory near the Bann, secured by Scotch, 126
Royal prerogative, 230
Rupert, Prince, employed Irish kerne, 22
Russell. Deputy, complains of the number of heads rotting on battlements, 38
Ryves, Sir W., Commissary of Prerogatives, 192

S

Salary, of Senior Fellows, £9 13s. 4d.; of Junior Fellows, £3, 312
Salisbury, Earl of, Chancellor of the College, ob. 1612, 166
Saints' days, as limits of terms, introduced by Laud, 257
Sarpi, Fra Paolo, Venetian Reformer, his connection with Bedell, 194
Saunders, Francis, Senior Fellow, 306
Saviour, S., Dominican Friary of, school of theology, 9
Saxey, Chief Justice, complains of age, 51
Scholarium commensalis, this class of student disappears after 1662, 296 *n.*
Schoolmaster, the College, teaches unmatriculated students in chapel, 185
Schools, lay, hot-beds of opposition to English interests, 11
Scots in Ulster, hail King James, spread industry, build towns, 159
Scott, Sir George, subscribes £20, 239
Scout (Schout), Theodore, coins some of the College plate, 286 and *note*
Script, old German, used by Travers, Alvey, Ware, 152
Seal of Trinity College, old seal of 1612, impression of, discovered in Kilkenny Castle, xiii; specimens of the original 124 *n,* 168; affixed to all University documents, 162; of University, granted 1851, a mere curiosity, 163
Seele, Thomas, Fellow, resigns living, returns to College, afterwards Provost, 253; first Senior Fellow elected under new charter, 253 *n.*; solitary Anglo-Irish Fellow in 1641, 276; Bursar, Provost under Restoration, 289
Sejanus, his fall compared to Strafford's, 265
Senior Fellows, first separated from Junior, by Temple, 163
Senior Master Non-Regent, place in Caput of Senate, 163
Seminarists, seminaries, priests educated abroad, reward for, 33
Shakspere signs in old script, 152
Shane, Sir Francis, contributes to Trinity College, 68
Shuckburgh, ed. of *Lives of Bedell,* quoted, 234 *n.*
Shurley, signs petition, 223

INDEX

Sibbes, Richard, evangelical divine, 147; refuses invitation to come to Trinity College as Provost, 193
Sidney (also spelt Sydney), Sir H., tour through west of Ireland in 1575, 4; thwarted by Loftus, 57
"Silver pott" or "boll," early presentations to the College, 140
Sizarius, sizar, student who gets commons free, 134; sizings, derivation of term, 134
Sizator, 296 n.
Skull, found under Old College Chapel, 191 n.
Slutmulrooney, manor of, in Fermanagh, part of James's grant to College, 155
Smith, Sir Samuel, his pig, 206
Smith, Sir Thomas, his failure to settle in Ulster, 158
Smith, William, student, Friars attempt to convert; his depositions, Appendix, p. 225, 208
Sociorum commensalis, 296 n.
Soria, Joanes de, Provincial of Castile, 274 n.
S.P. = State Papers (Ireland), Record Office, London. Referred to, pp. 11, 12, 16, 17, 20, 21, 25, 27, 28, 33, 34, 35, 37, 38, 39, 41, 43, 46, 51, 54, 59, 68, 70, 78, 86, 87, 96, 114, 126, 127, 148, 169, 176, 177, 180, 182, 183, 193, 206, 209, 210, 211, 214, 215, 234, 241, 267, 284, xvi
Spanish conquest, hoped for by Jesuits, 28
Speed's map, 1610, 72, n.
Spenser, Edmund, describes lack of religion in Ireland, 24 n.; not in list of subscribers to Trinity College, 69
Spes, Don Guerau de, Spanish ambassador, 27
Sport, absence of, 79
Stafford, private secretary of Sir G. Carew, author of *Hibernia Pacta*, 71
Stafford, Captain, afraid to sally out of Dublin, 96
Stanihurst, James, favourably describes Dublin, 2; grandfather of Primate Ussher, 10
Statutes, Bedell's, three manuscript copies extant, 198; clause expunged by Laud, 249 n. *See also* notes to Latin Appendix
Statuta, Bedell's—
  1. De Cultu Divino, 329–332
  2. De Qualitate et Officio Præpositi, 332, 333
  3. De Juramento Præpositi, 333
  4. De Senatu Collegii, constante ex Præposito et Sociis Senioribus, 335
  5. De Scholaribus, 336
  6. De Sociorum Electione, 337
  7. Juramentum Electi Socii, vel Discipuli, 339
  8. De Tutorum ac Pupillorum Officio, 341
  9. De Modestia, et Morum Honestate Colenda; Itemque de tuenda Collegii existimatione Publica, 343
  10 De Vice-Præpositi Officio, 346
  11. De Decani Officio, 347
  12. De Primario Lectore et Sublectoribus, 349
  13. De Classium Scholasticis Exercitiis, 351
  14. De Baccalaureorum et Magistrorum Exercitiis, 353
  15. De Vitanda Alieni Exercitii Usurpatione et vice sua a Quovis Diligenter Obeunda, 354
  16. De Terminis Observandis et de Examinando Scholarium in Disciplinis Progressum, 356
  17. De Admittendis in Collegium Professoribus Jurisprudentiæ et Medicinæ, 357
  18. De Bursarii Officio, 358
  19. De Tuta Rerum Custodia, et Bibliothecario, 361
  20. De Sociorum et Scholarium Numero, Commeatu, Salariis et Cubiculis, 363
  21. De Absentia Sociorum et Scholarium, 365
  22. De Pœnis Majorum Criminum, Multiscique aut Exigendis aut Exigendis et Commutandis, 368
  23. De Inferioribus Collegii Ministris, 370
  24. Epilogus, 371
  25. De Electionum Forma, 372
Statutes, Book of, published by College, places Caroline Statutes after Elizabethan Charter, 255 n.
Statutes sent from London, Ussher warns Challoner against, 168
Stearne, John, his philosophy, 291; Senior Fellow, Professor of Civil Law, Hebrew, Physic, 305; his birth and education, grand-nephew of James Ussher, 319; first president of College of Physicians, 320; his Stoic philosophy, his books and their dedications, 320–322; type of versatile Anglo-Irish intellect, 323, 324
Stearne, John, junior, Vice-Chancellor, son of preceding, 323 n.
Stearne, Robert, empowered to dispose of College lands in Limerick, 305
St. John, Deputy, knights Temple, summons Provost and Fellows to maintain lecture at Christ Church, 173; his discreditable report on the College, 176
St. Leger, Sir Anth., Deputy, 21 n.; orders all rhymers, &c., in Munster to be executed, 38; contributes to Trinity College, 67
Strafford, Earl of, hated for enlisting Irish savages, 21. *See* Wentworth
Stubbs, Dr., author of History of Dublin University, x, xi, xii; says list of original subscribers to Trinity College is incomplete, 69; quoted on cost of living in College (extract from Challoner's note-book), 154; mentions some blunders of Winter and his Fellows, 300. Also frequently referred to in the notes.
Studies, rent for, in Bridge Street house, 217
Summer term—July and August, kept in Temple's time, 186; and in Bedell's, 356
Sunday, Saint, image of, burned in Cork, 44 n.
Surplice, objected to by Provost Temple; its use insisted on by Abbot, 166
Symner, Major Miles, appointed Professor of Mathematics, to teach surveying, 296; Bursar, 293

T

Taaffe, says gentry are too poor to contribute to Trinity College, 69
Tables in College (four), Fellows', Bachelors', Scholars', Pensioners', 151
Tailor, John, admitted M.D., 304
Taylor, Bishop Jeremy, Vice-Chancellor, his gloomy account of the College

INDEX

only Restoration rubbish; he persecutes Presbyterians, 318

Taylor, publishes History of Trinity College, 1845, rhetorical, partial, x, xi

Teate, Faithful, *Temporarius Subrector*, 277; a failure, summoned before Council, 278; his degradation, 279

Temple, Fourth Provost, 145; birth and education, 145; edits Ramus' Dialectics, 145; dedicates it to Sir Philip Sidney and becomes his private secretary, 146; Sidney dies in his arms, 146; secretary to Essex in 1594, 146; Parliamentary seat for Tamworth, *ib.*; saved on Essex' fall by favour of Cecil, *ib.* 146; publishes a logical analysis of twenty select Psalms, dedicated to Prince Henry, 146; becomes Provost in 1609, probably by influence of Fullerton and Hamilton, 147, 148; no evidence to show that he was selected by Ussher; as a layman objects to wearing surplice, 147; Master in Chancery, 148; leading Ramist in England, logician and scholar, 148; brings over his wife and children, who may have been allowed to live in Provost's lodgings, 149; publishes Latin Exposition of Psalms i–xxx, and dedicates it to Robert Cecil, printed in London, 149; no copy of his Ramus in Trinity College, 150; shrewd man of business, 150; his note of cost of diet in P.B., 153; his work on College Statutes, 160-165; first four chapters, loose sheets sewed together, existed till recently, 161; statute on use of surplice, as reported by Hely Hutchinson, shows unwilling submission to the King, 161: statute against use of tobacco, 162; his plan for increasing number of Fellows compared with Challoner's, 170; his honesty suspected by Junior Fellows, 172, 173; his ill-composed defence, 173; his hands not clean, *ib.*; knighted by Lord Deputy St. John, *ib.*; no theologian ready to lecture in Christ Church, 177, 178; his neglect of Irish Church, 178; College declines under his rule, 179; his failure to educate an Irish Church clergy, 181; death in January, 1626, 191; buried under old College Chapel, skull exhumed, probably his, low type, 191 *n.*; died discreditably in debt to College, 192

Termonfechan, Primate's Palace of, 195

Thirty Years' War, promoted by Jesuits, 25

Thomas à Becket, S., religious house near Dublin, 10; value of, 49; granted by Henry VIII. to Sir H. Brabazon, now the Earl of Meath's Liberty, in Dublin, 49 *n.*

Thomas, David, Fellow, 216

Thomond, Earl of, writes from Limerick of the obstinacy of the people, 35; signs return of the revenues of public institutions in Ireland, 313

Thompson, John, admitted M.A., 304

Thucydides, 275

Thurloe Papers referred to, contain Langley's letter about decay of Irish towns, 308; on H. Cromwell going to church in state, 321

Toaghy, in Armagh, part of King James's grant, 155

Tobacco, statute against use of, lost, 162

Todd, Dr., *Introduction to first College Calendar* (1833), x

Trafford, student, Friar's attempt to convert, 208

Travers, Joseph, Professor of Civil Law, 216, 297

Travers, Walter, Second (First acting) Provost, 59; his letter to Burgley describing the "poore and harde beginnings of Trinity College," 75, 76; his early life, Christ's College, Cambridge, 82; tutor to Lord Burgley's son, 82; visits Geneva, 83; writes against Anglicanism, 84, 85; silenced by Whitgift, 86; his evangelical zeal, 86; elected Provost of Trinity in 1594, 86; influences Ussher towards Puritanism; permanent Low Church character of Irish Church, due in part to his influence, 86, 87; retires to England, and dies long after, leaving his Oriental books and plate to Sion College, London, 95; specimen of his style, 107

Trevor, Sir E., brother-in-law of Robert Ussher, 76 *n.*

Trinity College, Book of, xii, xiii

Trinity College, came too late, 57; regarded as Protestant, 58; escapes plunder by its poverty, 97

Trinity Hall, no mention of students living in, 207

Trinity Monday, election of Fellows and scholars since Laud's Day, 257

Trinity Sunday, increased allowance for Commons, Laud, 257

Trustees appointed for College by Parliament, 1649, 294; their interesting letter, 295; list of for 1649, 313

Tudor, Hugh, describes the exactions of soldiery, 43

"Turbulent scholars" save the open space opposite west front of College, 202

Tyrone, Earl of, imports English refinements, 14; demands a Roman Catholic University at suggestion of Jesuits, 29; addresses Elizabeth on equal terms, 48; his rebellion, 30; drives out planters of Munster in 1598, 42

Tyrrell, Lady, impoverished daughter of Primate Ussher, 314

Tyrrell's Park, 72 *n.*

U

Undertakers, planted by Elizabeth in Munster, swept away by Tyrone, 157

University of Dublin: is it distinct from Trinity College? 63, 64; as such, has no charter, 161; University only a particular aspect of Trinity College, 162

Urwick, Nonconformist, writes early history of Trinity College, 1591-1660, xii; throws light on the chasm in history of the College following the Rebellion, plague, and Protectorate, 293; gathered facts about Teat, 277

Ussher, Ambrose, brother of James, the first librarian, 121; his learning, 122; his tutorial account, 81, 82

Ussher, Henry, Archdeacon, one of the real founders of the College, spends £300 on buildings there; made Primate of Armagh, 1595; very perfect in Irish, 20 *n.*

Ussher, James, elected scholar, 78; Fellow, 97; Professor of Theological Controversies, 122; European man of letters, 122; evangelical, yet episcopalian, 166; proposes Laud as Chancellor

INDEX 389

on account of bad discipline among the Fellows, 229; censures the Provost in Privy Council, 243; Wentworth's hostility to, part of his policy of crushing all independence in Ireland, 244; his letter on Chappell s eluding of oaths, 248; chairman of Board of Visitors, as Vice-Chancellor; Laud's changes in Board an insult to him; he loses interest in College, 259, 260; his house destroyed during his absence in England in 1641; never returns to Ireland; evangelical, commanded the respect of Cromwell, 297; his library acquired for the State by Cromwell, 314, 315; Bernard's funeral sermon on, 70; buried with pomp in Westminster Abbey, 128

Ussher, Robert, cousin of Primate, Vice-Chancellor, 171; heads Junior Fellows in objecting to leasing College lands for more than 21 years, 171, 172; opposes Bedell's provostship, 195; elected on Bedell's resignation, 200; easy-going man, 212; Puritanical, 213; disapproves of extern students, 213; his letter to Bishop of London, with scheme for settling scholars' house of Back Lane, 215, 216; quarrel with Fellows about auditor, 218–219; favours election of Laud as Chancellor, 219; promoted to see of Kildare; his influence effaced even before his resignation in 1634; his bombastic Latin letter and verses to James Ussher, Appendix i. to Chap. v., 220, 221

Ussher, William, Castle official, writes to his "Cossen Dr. Ussher," about payment of £30 for Bridewell house, 189

V

Valentia, Lord, 223
Veale, or Veele, Fellow, "natus in hoc Collegio," 298
Vesey, admitted to Fellowship by Falkland, 197
Visitation, of Easter, 1615, 173; of May, 1635, Provost worsted, 241, 242; of 1791, changes interpretation of Laud's Statute, and limits power of Provost, 262
Visitors, Board of, the original, 64; Laud reduces their number from seven to two, and makes himself the primary visitor, 168, 259
Viva voce, for Fellowship examination, only recently abandoned; its value as training, 187

W

Wales, subjection of, 54; sends students to Trinity College, 229
Wallop, Sir H., complains of age, 51; persuades Lord Deputy to seize Boyle's trunk, 87
Walworth, student, Friar's attempt to convert, 208; his evidence varies slightly from Smith's 226 n.
War with Tyrone, compared to Boer War, 129
Ward, Michael, enters College in 1656, 291
Ward, Samuel, of Ipswich, invited to the College by Alvey, 140; correspondent of Ussher, 139; appointed Professor of Theological Controversies, 177
Ward, Seth, Savilian, Professor of Geometry at Oxford, 319
Warden of the beggars, 14
Wardships, granted to College, 131
Ware, Arthur, claims seniority, 240
Ware's Bishops, 237
Ware, Sir James, helps to manage financial affairs of College, 129; signs petition to city for Bridewell, 130; writes Alvey's accounts in 1609, 138; receives grant from the King of lands in Tipperary, Waterford, &c., as trustee for College, 154; unsatisfactory auditor, Fellows refuse to appoint his son, 218
Wassington, B.D. of Oxford, appointed Provost of Trinity College by Charles I., silence concerning him, 267; his flight to England, 275, 276
Watson, John, 250
Weld, Daniel, student, found harboured in suspicious alehouse; sentenced by Privy Council with astounding severity, 245; pedantic sentence by Provost, 245, 246

Wellesley, Arthur, 157
Wentworth, Lord Deputy, makes Bramhall, High Churchman, Bishop of Derry, 230; gets rid of R. Ussher with an archdeaconry, and forces College to elect Chappell Provost, 232; his policy, to discredit the Protestant party in Ireland, and import Englishmen who would submit to the divine right of Charles, 235; humours Roman Catholic gentry, 235; encourages private subscription for enlarging College, 238; his donation of £100, 238; petitioned by College about books borrowed from Library, 250; also about commuting Crown pensions for land in Connaught, 251; his fall, 265
Weston, Chancellor, grandfather of Countess of Cork, 235
White, Richard, 238
White, S. J., founds Irish College at Salamanca, 32
White, Sir Nich., speaks Irish, 12
Whyte, Nich., eminent native lawyer, his interesting letter to Burghley, 34
Widow Jones, severe sentence on, for harbouring student (Weld), 245
Whitgift, Master of Trinity, Cambridge (and Archbishop), censures Travers, 83
Wiggett, John, 250
Wilkinson, borrowed books from Kildare Hall, 250
Williamson, Cæsar, Senior Fellow, promoter of petition to general Convention aimed at Winter, 306
Winter, Samuel, Provost, appointed by Oliver Cromwell, 296; his Collections, 300 n.; his piety and learning, 298, 299; his love of horses, some of them stolen by "the Irish army," 301, 307; he disappears quietly at the close of the Protectorate, 306
Woulfe, David, Jesuit, 25, 26

Z

Zize (sizing), Fellow's allowance for, weekly 8d, ob.; "scholler's," 4d, 153

CALDWELL COLLEGE LIBRARY
CALDWELL, NEW JERSEY